A CONCISE
ENCYCLOPEDIA
of

CHRISTIANITY

A CONCISE
ENCYCLOPEDIA
of
CHRISTIANITY

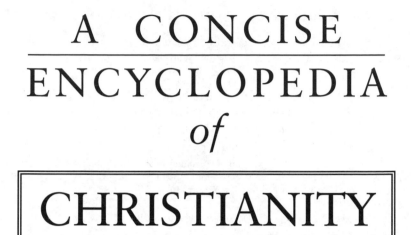

GEOFFREY PARRINDER

ONEWORLD

OXFORD

A CONCISE ENCYCLOPEDIA OF CHRISTIANITY

Oneworld Publications
(Sales and Editorial)
185 Banbury Road
Oxford OX2 7AR
England
http://www.oneworld-publications.com

Oneworld Publications
(US Marketing Office)
160 N. Washington St.
4th Floor, Boston
MA 02114

ISBN 1–85168–174–4

Cover design by Design Deluxe
Typeset by Saxon Graphics Ltd, Derby
Printed in England by Clays Ltd, St Ives plc

Contents

Acknowledgements

The author and publishers wish to thank the following for permission to reproduce material in this volume:

Ancient Civilizations and Historical Persons (pp. 82, 96); Brazilian Tourist Board (pp. 35, 55); British Israel Public Affairs Centre and the Zionist Federation of Great Britain and Ireland (p. 190); British Library Board (pp. 70, 241); Evangelistic Association (p. 113); Guardian News Service Limited (p. 252); Israeli Government Tourist Office (pp. 166, 247); Italian Cultural Institute (pp. 15, 24, 76, 100, 128, 156, 228 and cover); Moojan Momen (pp. 89, 123, 160, 171); Oxford University Press (p. 60); PA News (p. 233 and cover); Penguin Books (pp. 27–8); The Salvation Army (pp. 47, 212); Sonia Halliday Photographs (pp. 41, 44, 208, 225); Turkish Ministry of Tourism (pp. 136, 183 and cover); West Maryland College Slide Collection (p. 198).

Every effort has been made to trace and acknowledge ownership of copyright. If any credits have been omitted or any rights overlooked, it is completely unintentional.

Introduction

Christianity takes its name from belief in Jesus of Nazareth as the Christ or Messiah, both terms meaning the 'Anointed One' of God. The religion began as a movement within Judaism; Jesus himself was a Jew, as were all his first followers and the writers of the Christian scriptures, with the probable exception of Luke. The disciples or adherents of Jesus were called Christians first in Antioch in Syria (Acts 11:26) when gentiles began to enter the Church.

Christianity is the largest of the world's religions, with an estimated 2,020 million members by the year 2000, the next in size being Islam with 1,200 million, then Hinduism with 860 million and Buddhism with 360 million (all estimates for 2000; see Table 2 on p. 9). The three principal branches of Christianity, in terms of the numbers of their adherents, are the Roman Catholic, Protestant and Eastern Orthodox (in that order), though the latter two contain various denominations and subdivisions.

Table 1   Adherents of churches, 1900–2000 CE (millions)

	1900	1975	2000
ROMAN CATHOLIC	272	734	1,170
EASTERN ORTHODOX	121	118	153
ANGLICAN	33	62	82
PROTESTANT	120	280	357
NON-WHITE AND MARGINAL	12	122	258
TOTALS	558	1,316	2,020

Source: Extracted from D.B. Barrett, ed., *World Christian Encyclopedia* (1982), global table 4.

History

It is said that Jesus was born in the reign of Herod the Great, who died in 4 BCE – a fact which caused some confusion after the sixth century, when the Christian calendar aimed at beginning in the Year of our Lord Christ (Anno Domini = AD). Jesus lived for most of his life, and exercised a ministry of from one to three years, in the region of Galilee in northern Palestine. He was a charismatic prophet, preaching to people in the open air about the imminent kingdom of God, healing the sick, talking to and eating with ordinary people and social outcasts whom he regarded as the lost sheep of the House of Israel.

Eventually Jesus went to Jerusalem, the religious and political centre of the Jewish people, and was shocked to find buying and selling in the courts of the Temple itself. He cast out money-changers and merchants, against the authority of the leading priestly Sadducees who decided that he must be silenced. With the connivance of the Roman governor, Pontius Pilate, Jesus was arrested and crucified and his followers scattered. It was a devastating blow, but within a short time his disciples, men and women, declared that Jesus had risen from the dead and that they had seen him; and they began in turn to announce the coming kingdom of God and the rule of Jesus as the Christ.

Though limited at first in scope and impact, the Christian movement received a great impetus with the entry into its ranks of Paul (formerly called Saul) from Tarsus in Asia Minor: a Jew who was also a Roman citizen, he converted non-Jews to the Christian faith and became the apostle of the gentiles. The commensalism – eating together – which Jesus had practised with 'publicans and sinners' was extended to gentiles by Paul, and with baptism and renunciation of idolatry by converts the way was set for the expansion of Christianity as an international religion. The early Christian groups were probably small; the Acts of the Apostles and Paul's letters give some idea of their establishment and spread in Syria, Asia Minor, Greece and, finally, Rome itself, capital of the Empire, where Paul arrived as a prisoner in 59 CE to find a sizeable Christian community already in existence.

The Christian societies had three advantages in their development and diffusion: the Jewish monotheistic religion; the Greek international language; and the general peace and open communications of the Roman Empire. It has been queried how a religion which honoured a crucified man, from a marginal country and faith, could have become so popular that by the end of the fourth century it was the official religion of the Roman Empire. But it must be recognized that for the faithful

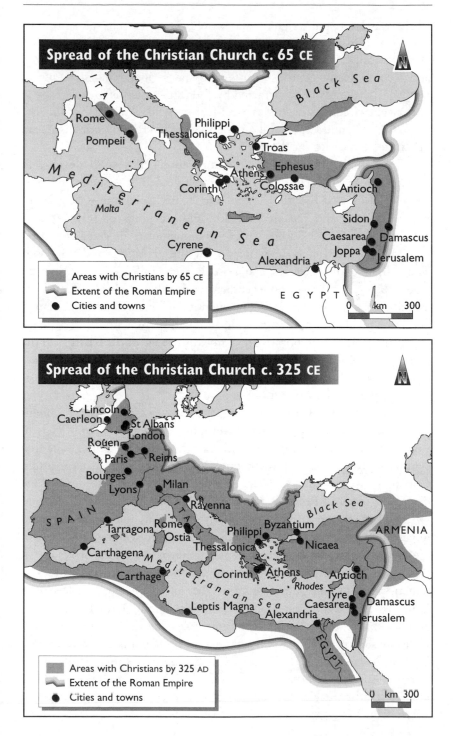

Spread of the Christian Church c. 65 CE

Black Sea

ITALY

Rome

Pompeii

Philippi
Thessalonica

Troas

Mediterranean Sea

Athens

Ephesus

Corinth

Colossae

Antioch

Malta

Sidon

Caesarea

Damascus

Cyrene

Joppa

Jerusalem

Alexandria

EGYPT

Areas with Christians by 65 CE

Extent of the Roman Empire

Cities and towns

0   km   300

Spread of the Christian Church c. 325 CE

Lincoln

Caerleon

St Albans

London

Rouen

Reims

Paris

Bourges

Lyons

Milan

Ravenna

SPAIN

Tarragona

Rome

Ostia

ITALY

Philippi

Byzantium

Black Sea

ARMENIA

Thessalonica

Nicaea

Carthagena

Corinth

Athens

Antioch

Carthage

Mediterranean Sea

Rhodes

Tyre

Damascus

Leptis Magna

Caesarea

Alexandria

Jerusalem

EGYPT

Areas with Christians by 325 AD

Extent of the Roman Empire

Cities and towns

0   km   300

Christ was living and reigning and would return to rule the earth. His story was told in four official gospels, all in Greek, and in countless lesser writings. The monotheistic theology and high moral teachings appealed to many gentile enquirers. Some serious-minded men and women had already been attracted by Judaism, either as proselytes who underwent circumcision, or as God-fearers who admired but did not enter Judaism, and Christianity made the entry into a monotheistic and moral religion easier for them.

Considerable Christian writings and apologetics soon developed. The letters of Paul to churches that he had founded or wished to encourage were followed by other letters and in particular the four gospels, which outlined and repeated the life and teachings of Jesus as they appeared to different authors, presenting memories of Peter and other early disciples as well as the writers' own interpretations and emphases. These first-century epistles and gospels were followed by masses of 'apocrypha', speculative and legendary works; then there were defensive and doctrinal theses, increasing in quantity as time passed. Christianity became a highly literary religion, and though there is no clear evidence that Paul or his contemporaries had any knowledge of the writings of the great Greek philosophers and dramatists, many of their ideas were nevertheless in the air, and words such as 'wisdom,' 'mystery' and 'fullness' were adopted in the context of the new faith.

The extension of Christianity into the gentile world caused problems and aroused suspicions. Its Jewish monotheism entailed conflict with Roman cults of divine emperors and ancient and plural deities. The first centuries saw not only growth but also opposition and persecution. Christians were blamed by the Emperor Nero for the fire which destroyed much of Rome in 64 CE which he had probably started himself; Paul, Peter and his wife, and many other Christians were executed in various ways: beheaded, crucified, or thrown to wild beasts as part of the entertainment on Roman holidays. Other persecutions broke out at later times and in different regions, though there was no general and systematic persecution of Christians until the time of the emperor Decius in 250. This period saw many lapses from the Church by the half-hearted, and also brave and self-sacrificing martyrs. Then in 313 the Emperors Constantine (of the West) and Licinius (of the East) issued the tolerant Edict of Milan, giving to Christians (and indeed all others) freedom of religion. Finally, in 380 the Emperor Theodosius declared the establishment of Christianity as the religion of the empire, and the exclusion of heretics.

The religious practices of the early Christians both resembled and also differed from those of their converts. The Jewish background was prominent, with the Hebrew scriptures accepted as inspired and authoritative alongside the distinctively Christian gospels and epistles. No other great religion has accepted and used the scriptures of its parent religion in such a way. Entry into the community by an initiation rite, baptism, was comparable both with Jewish purifications and also with Greek agricultural rituals in emphasizing the 'mysteries' of dying and rising again to new life. This theme was also celebrated in the symbolic meal, the Lord's Supper, which re-enacted the dying and rising of Christ and has remained down the ages as the Eucharist, the Liturgy or the Mass.

From small groups the churches grew in the cities of the Roman Empire and beyond. When they received the patronage of the state they extended over wide areas, organized in parishes and dioceses; complex systems of workers, priests and bishops, deacons and deaconesses were developed, with distinctions increasing between clergy and laity. The Empire was already in decline and Rome fell to the Visigoths in 410. In the West, Augustine of Hippo wrote of the Church as the true empire and City of God, but his work was unknown in the East, where the Greek city of Byzantium had been rebuilt as Constantinople and the seat of the emperor. In theology and liturgy the Eastern Orthodox Church evolved differently from the Church in the West, preparing for the schism between Orthodox and Catholic which was formalized in the eleventh century and has lasted to this day.

As the Church increased in both popularity and official status, it was also seen by many as increasingly impure, even corrupt, and from the third century ardent spirits began to found monastic movements, in deserts and wild places, where monks and nuns followed strict rules of life and prayer. During the dark ages and middle ages the monasteries became centres of religious life, learning, agriculture, architecture and hospitality.

Christianity was diffused throughout Roman Europe, Egypt and North Africa, and eastwards from Syria to Persia, India, and even to China where Nestorian Christians laboured to spread the gospel from the seventh to the fourteenth centuries. But a radical challenge to Christian dominance of the Middle East came with the rise of Islam in the seventh century. This new monotheistic faith, akin to but different from Judaism and Christianity, with its own prophet and scripture, burst out of Arabia and flooded over the Middle East with the conquering Arab armies. Syria and Persia fell to Islam in 635 and 637; Jerusalem surrendered in 638 and Alexandria in 642. The Christian patriarchs of both these cities had fallen out with their Byzantine Christian overlords and welcomed the Arabs, not realizing they would stay so long.

The Coptic (Egyptian) Church was strong, with its own priests and language, and it has persevered as an educated and active minority, its members today forming about one-fifth of the population of Egypt. But in the rest of North Africa, where many of the priests were foreign and the Latin language of the liturgy was also alien, the churches were overcome and eventually disappeared. The Arab armies advanced speedily along all of North Africa, and in 711 one of their soldiers, Tariq, led his battalion into Spain and left his name at Gibraltar, the Jabal (mount) of Tariq. The Muslim forces crossed Spain, almost, it has been said, 'like a promenade', with only a few towns resisting. Spain was to remain under Muslim rule for nearly eight centuries, till King Ferdinand in 1492 expelled the last of the Moors from Granada.

Soon after arriving in Spain the Arabs had invaded France, storming Bordeaux and pushing on to Tours. There in 732 they met the fierce armies of the Frankish Charles Martel, the 'Hammer', and after seven days the Arabs folded their tents and silently slipped away. It was just a hundred years after the death of Muhammad, and his successors had already seen his Arab chiefdom become a world empire. For the Christians, Tours was a decisive battle, though the later Turkish invasions of Eastern Europe provided another threat. Some have speculated that if the Arab advance of the eighth century had continued, there might be mosques instead of cathedrals in Paris and London (there are, of course, mosques now), and the Qur'an instead of the Bible might have been expounded at Oxford and Cambridge.

By the early middle ages Christianity was propagated throughout northern Europe, with missionaries like Patrick, Columba, Augustine of Canterbury and Boniface, and Russia was evangelized from Constantinople. The ill-named Crusades from the late eleventh century were attempts to wrest the Christian holy places from the 'infidel' Turks, with varying success. Jerusalem was taken only once, for a short time, and the Fourth Crusade turned against the Christian city of Constantinople, its desecration adding to the alienation of East and West. Then, in 1453, Constantinople fell to the Turks; it was renamed Istanbul, and its great cathedral of Hagia Sophia, 'Holy Wisdom', became a mosque with minarets erected round it. Now it is a museum and tourist attraction, its splendid mosaics again revealed showing Christ and his mother.

Greek scholars fled from the Turks to the West, where they contributed to the revival of humanist learning in the Renaissance. Greek philosophy, medicine and astronomy, which had been lost to Europe during the dark ages, returned via Arabic translations of Greek into the Latin of Western scholarship. Rome had recovered its power through the Church, but then faced a challenge from the north. In the sixteenth century the Protestant Reformation detached much of northern Europe, and eventually much wider areas, from Roman Catholic rule. As well as the radical re-interpreters of Christianity, like Luther and Calvin, there were many other teachers who sought return to what they understood as the purity of primitive Christianity. The development of West European languages and literatures was accompanied by translations of the Bible from the original Hebrew and Greek into modern languages, and these versions were used instead of the official Latin Vulgate. Notes on the text often led to diverse interpretations, fostering breakaway movements, such as Lutheran, Reformed and Baptist, among many others.

Fresh horizons opened up with the discovery of the Americas, Africa and Asia. Christianity had always been essentially a missionary and international religion. Movements of population were followed by religious colonization. Now, in the Roman Catholic world, new religious orders, Franciscans, Dominicans and Jesuits, sought not only to combat Protestantism but also to evangelize the rest of the world – the Americas, Africa, India, China and Japan. Similarly, Protestant evangelical revival movements from the eighteenth century realized that their faith implied universal salvation and sought to implement it, sending envoys to nearly every country.

Christian missions in recent centuries were highly successful in America and tropical Africa, where great Christian growth has offset decline in Europe. They have had less influence in Asia, where they encountered ancient and literate religions, such as Hinduism and Buddhism. The earlier confrontation with Islam, resulting in defeat or resistance for Christianity, did not lead to understanding or dialogue, and only in recent times has there been impartial Christian examination of the faith and history of Islam and attempts to come to terms with it. The same applies to an even greater degree to the literate and historical religions of Asia. The belief of missionary Christianity in its superiority and inevitable eventual triumph over all others has been severely questioned, and again study and dialogue have been found essential – at least in the older churches and missions; new fundamentalism and televangelism tend to condemn or ignore other faiths, leading to conflict or disillusion.

Modern times have posed the challenge of science, as well as of social and political revolutions, to the claims of all religion, and have brought both reform within the churches and a lessening of their public roles. In the Soviet Union, persecution and destruction of people and churches were far more thorough than was admitted until recently, and while since the collapse of Russian Communism the Orthodox and other churches have shown some revival, they need reform and inspiration, and are far from having regained their previous state.

Faith and Worship

In some ways Christianity is the most complex of religions, with major divisions and many subdivisions. From the earliest days there were differences of conviction and interpretation. Against the background of Jewish belief in one God and his purpose for humanity, there arose constant debates about the place and person of Jesus as Christ and Son of God. It is clear from the gospels that Jesus was seen as a man from Galilee, and stories about him are based on his historicity. But Paul, who had not seen the human Jesus, was more concerned with Christ as divine, and his interpretations doubtless affected the gospels which were written down after Paul's death.

The early Church was soon involved in controversy, such as that arising from the difference between Jewish Christian Ebionites who saw Jesus as the human Messiah, and gentile Gnostics who taught a Christology which involved an appearance, not a human life 'in flesh'. Then the second-century apologists developed the doctrine of the Logos, the eternal Word of God in Christ. In the fourth century the Arian controversy split the Church between those who denied that the Son was fully divine and others who held that there were two natures in Christ, divine and human. Athanasius 'against the world' championed what became the orthodox doctrine, while later Nestorians almost separated Christ into two persons, and Monophysites held to one, wholly divine, nature. The medieval schoolmen and the principal reformers of the sixteenth century emphasized the unity of Christ's person, while nineteenth-century Kenotic theories explained that the Son of God was divine but laid aside his attributes to become limited in a full humanity.

The controversies that raged, especially in the first five centuries of the Church, led to the calling of councils, largely of bishops. Some were convened by the emperor, as when Constantine called them to Nicaea in 325, deploring a divided Church and seeking to impose uniformity. Ecumenical (universal) councils are still held to have had special authority for both Eastern and Western churches. From these councils the

Table 2   Adherents of all religions, 1900–2000 CE (millions)

	1900	1975	2000
CHRISTIANS	558	1,316	2,020
MUSLIMS	200	628	1,200
HINDUS	203	518	860
BUDDHISTS	127	252	360
JEWS	12	16	20
SIKHS	3	12	24
SHINTO*	60	84	95
BAHA'IS	0.009	3	8
JAINS	1	3	4
PARSIS	0.108	0.137	0.219
TRIBAL RELIGIONS	106	89	100
NEW RELIGIONS	6	86	138
TOTAL WORLD POPULATION	1,620	3,967	6,260

* Figures adjusted from official census.
Source: Extracted from D.B. Barrett, ed., *World Christian Encyclopedia* (1982), global table 4.

orthodox faith emerged: of the Trinity of three persons in one God (Father, Son and Holy Spirit), of divine and human natures in Christ, of authentic or canonical scriptures in the Old Testament and recognized books of the New Testament, and of the bishops as church authorities in faith and morals.

The worship of the first Church was fairly simple, growing out of synagogue services of psalms, prayers, scripture readings and exhortations. To these the Christians added the Lord's Supper, the bread and wine symbolizing the body and blood of the divine Redeemer. Those who died for their convictions in the early persecutions were venerated as martyrs (witnesses), and shrines erected over their remains became places of pilgrimage. As the theologian Tertullian said, 'As often as we are mown down, the more we grow in numbers; the blood of Christians is the seed.' Churches were built at the tombs of martyrs, and anniversaries of their deaths helped to form the Christian calendar.

Table 3 Numbers of Christians on eight continents, 1900–2000
CE (millions)

	1900	1975	2000
AFRICA	10	171	393
EAST ASIA	2	16	32
EUROPE	278	410	432
LATIN AMERICA	62	305	571
NORTH AMERICA	79	212	254
OCEANIA	5	19	28
SOUTH ASIA	17	92	192
CIS (USSR)	105	91	118
TOTALS	558	1,316	2,020

Source: Extracted from D.B. Barrett, ed., *World Christian Encyclopedia* (1982), global
table 2.

When Christianity became tolerated, and then the state Church, new
and official converts took interest in building large structures. The first
meeting places had been like 'house churches', but after Constantine the
dominant type was a basilica, with columned aisles and a central nave
along which clergy processed towards the altar at the eastern end. In
time decorative screens, icons or images, tablets and stained-glass windows made the church both a shrine and a place of assembly, combining
devotions at special shrines in side chapels with congregational worship
in the principal building.

In the late middle ages great structures were built, cathedrals and
countless parish churches, which showed the wealth and confidence of
the Church, with mass congregations swollen by the work of the preaching friars. The Eucharist or Mass was central, but in later Protestant
churches the sacrament was less frequent, and the preached word
became dominant in the large gatherings of evangelical and Victorian
revivals. These may now often be replaced by radio and television in the
home, with churches struggling to keep going.

Table 4   Membership of Protestant churches, 1970 and 1985 CE
(millions)

	1970	1985
LUTHERAN (AND SOME REFORMED)	62	109
REFORMED (PRESBYTERIAN)	19	39
BAPTIST (INC. NON-WHITE)	29	50
METHODIST	16	32
PENTECOSTAL	18	58
HOLINESS	7	14
ADVENTIST	2	6
CONGREGATIONAL	1	2
SALVATIONIST	1	4
BRETHREN	0.5	2
MENNONITE	0.5	1
MORAVIAN	0.25	0.75
FRIENDS (QUAKERS)	0.25	0.50
JEHOVAH'S WITNESSES	2	6
MORMONS (LATTER-DAY)	4	7
MARGINALS	30	50

Source: Extracted from D.B. Barrett, ed., *World Christian Encyclopedia* (1982), global table 9.

Using the Encyclopedia

This *Concise Encyclopedia* aims at providing information about people, churches, movements, beliefs, doctrines, rituals, devotions and practices from the earliest days to the present. It seeks to answer enquiries on a vast number of subjects in brief but informative terms. The many cross-references (indicated by text in small capitals, e.g. CHALICE) are intended to provide fuller information by directing the reader to similar or related matters. For readers wishing to explore Christianity from a thematic viewpoint, the Thematic Index on pp. 268–75 will refer them to the appropriate entries. The Chronology on pp. 261–4 gives a full picture of the major events through the life of the faith.

There are other encyclopedias and dictionaries of Christianity, some arranged country by country, others reflecting particular doctrinal or social interests of the authors or editors. The present book aims at comprehensiveness, impartiality and modernism, including people and movements from many countries. The information presented has been gathered from a large number of sources, including original texts. Every effort has been made to establish accuracy of names, dates and other details.

Christianity has an immense literature, and there is unlimited related matter, so that it would be impossible for anyone to read all the available material. Selection has to be made, and in this book the names of church leaders, teachers and writers are given, but not those of other historical or literary characters, in so far as they may be found elsewhere. Thus there is a brief note on Dante, but Chaucer appears only in references. Similarly with historical persons of influence, such as Henry VIII or Oliver Cromwell: there are references, but readers must have recourse to other historical works for their details.

In common with other volumes in this series, dates are given as BCE (Before the Common Era) and CE (the Common Era) for the period starting after the approximate date of the birth of Christ, formerly called AD.

A

Abba

Aramaic for 'father', recorded once used by Jesus (Mark 14:36) and twice by Paul (Rom. 8:15; Gal. 4:6). Some modern translators render 'Abba' as 'Daddy', a child's address to God as father, but there is no linguistic support for this and Abba was used in prayer and other solemn situations where such informality would not have been appropriate.

abbey

A large religious house of a monastic order. Monks are governed by an abbot, and nuns by an abbess. The French term *abbé*, originally used of the abbot of a monastery, is now applied to priests in general. After the DISSOLUTION OF THE MONASTERIES in England in the 16th century the word abbey was retained for centres such as WESTMINSTER ABBEY, known to Londoners as 'the Abbey'. Many isolated abbey buildings, like Fountains and Rievaulx, lie in ruins; others, such as Tewkesbury, survive as parish churches.

Abelard/Abailard, Peter
(1079–1142)

French scholar and lover of HÉLOÏSE. Born near Brittany he early went to Paris

Fountains Abbey, Yorkshire: A splendid 12th-century Cistercian abbey dissolved by Henry VIII in 1539, now a 'perfection of ruin'.

and by brilliant lectures attracted many students. He fell in love with a teenage beauty, Héloïse, niece of Canon Fulbert, and their son was born in Brittany. Abelard offered to marry Héloïse as long as it was not made public; Fulbert agreed, and there was a secret wedding. Abelard then put Héloïse in a convent but Fulbert sent his servants by night to castrate Abelard. Only after ten years did he meet Héloïse again; when he died she buried him.

Abelard wrote *The Story of my Misfortunes* about his life and love. His major theological work, *Sic et Non* ('Yes and No'), put apparently contradictory statements from Scripture and traditions side by side. He rejected a common theory of the ATONEMENT as satisfaction, seeing the death of Christ as an example to evoke love from sinners. He made enemies and his views were condemned by a church council.

ablution

Ritual washing, usually with water, to remove impurity. The term is used of washing fingers, CHALICE and PATEN after the celebration of HOLY COMMUNION.

Aboriginal Church

See NICHOLLS.

abortion

The Bible does not mention abortion, but by the second century the practice was condemned, along with infanticide. Later Roman Catholic teaching forbade abortion at any time after conception and a papal encyclical *Evangelium vitae* ('The Gospel of Life') in 1995 ranked abortion and contraception alongside homicide and prostitution. Many Protestants support a woman's right to choose whether to have a child or not, though they would resist being called pro-abortion. (*See also* BIRTH CONTROL; CHILDREN.)

Abraham (?20th century BCE)

Great Hebrew patriarch, regarded as the common spiritual father of the Abrahamic monotheistic religions: Judaism, Christianity and Islam. Paul wrote of all those who have faith being children of Abraham (Gal. 3:7), and the example and faith of Abraham are cited by many Christian writers. Jesus spoke of Abraham's bosom as a symbol of Paradise (Luke 16:22).

absolution

Freeing or loosing from sin and its penalties, as when Jesus said to the paralytic, 'Your sins are forgiven' (Mark 2:5). The early Church believed that the power to remit sins was given to the apostles (Matt. 16:19; John 20:23), and the promise of the keys of the kingdom in the former passage provided an association of keys with Peter widely used symbolically in later art. (*See also* CONFESSION; KINGDOM OF GOD.)

abstinence

Abstaining from different foods or drinks has been practised by various groups. The first gentile Christian converts were forbidden sacrificial and blood foods (Acts 15:29). Later, flesh meat was renounced at certain periods, such as LENT, and some abstainers also gave up fish, eggs and cheese. Friday FASTING was imposed in the West, though it is less strictly observed nowadays. Some monastic orders were VEGETARIANS: these included the Trappists, and Orthodox monks on Mount ATHOS. Among Protestants, 'total abstinence' may be regarded as meaning not drinking alcohol. Mormons abstain from hot drinks, and Mennonites from worldly ornament or dress. (*See also* ASCETICISM; CELIBACY; TEMPERANCE.)

Abuna

See ETHIOPIAN CHURCH.

Abyssinia

See ETHIOPIAN CHURCH.

accidie

From a Greek word for 'indifference', a state of sadness, heaviness or sloth, to which monks might be particularly prone owing to the monotony of their life. (*See also* SEVEN DEADLY SINS.)

acolyte

A follower or member of a MINOR ORDER in the Western Church, whose duties are to carry candles and assist at MASS.

Acts of the Apostles

New Testament book. Written by the evangelist LUKE, the book of Acts provides the only existing consecutive account of the earliest Church, though much may be gleaned from the epistles. The first 12 chapters are chiefly about PETER and his fellows; chapters 13–28 sketch PAUL's travels and teachings. From 16:10 onwards come the 'we-passages', apparently from Luke's own diary when he travelled with Paul, up to his arrival and imprisonment in Rome. Acts is invaluable for what it presents, and tantalizing for what it omits. What happened to the other apostles? JAMES, the brother of Jesus, appears as head of the Church in Jerusalem, but without introduction (Acts 12:17; Gal. 1:19). The emphasis and detail on Paul clearly indicate the interest of this book for the growing gentile Church after the fall of Jerusalem in 70 CE. If Luke's Gospel is dated about 80–85 then Acts would have been written shortly thereafter. (*See also* GLOSSOLALIA.)

AD

See CALENDAR.

Adam

The first human being, from whom both man and woman were derived, according to the Genesis story. Adam became the prototype of humanity under the Old Covenant, and in Church teachings Christ was called the Second Adam. Christian writers could not think of Adam remaining in perdition, so in legend he was delivered by Christ. (*See also* DESCENT INTO HELL.)

Adam, from Michelangelo's Creation of Adam, Sistine Chapel: Michelangelo painted the Sistine Chapel single-handed from 1508 to 1512.

Adamites

An early Christian sect of this name practised nudity in an attempt to regain primitive innocence, and some later Protestant groups among the WALDENSES and Dutch ANABAPTISTS did the same.

Adonai

Hebrew term for 'Lord', still used in Jewish congregations for the unutterable name of God, represented by the Tetragrammaton, the four consonants YHWH. The vowels of Adonai were adapted by Christian writers into the German form of YHWH, 'Jehovah', now usually rendered in English as 'Yahweh'. In English Bibles YHWH was translated as 'the LORD', though under feminist influence some now render it as 'the Eternal'.

adoptionism

The theory, held by EBIONITES and others, that Jesus was the natural son of Joseph and Mary but adopted as Son of God at his baptism. The words given on that occasion, 'You are my beloved Son' (Mark 1:11), were linked with Psalm 2:7: 'You are my Son, today I have begotten you.' (*See also* NESTORIUS; VIRGIN BIRTH.)

adultery

Sexual intercourse of married persons with others than their spouses. It is forbidden in the seventh commandment (Exod. 20:14), and even the lustful desire is reprimanded in the Sermon on the Mount (Matt. 5:28). The Church allowed divorce on the grounds of adultery on the basis of this same passage (v. 32). In modern times, charges of adultery have been complicated by the availability of contraception and the practice of artificial insemination. (*See also* DIVORCE.)

Advent

The season before Christmas. From Latin for the 'coming' of Christ, the term is applied to the four Sundays preceding Christmas Day, beginning the Church's CALENDAR year. Advent was linked to expectation of a Second Advent, the appearance or return of Christ for judgement on the Last Day. (*See also* PAROUSIA.)

Adventism

Anticipation of the visible return of Christ in a Second Advent. Such hopes have been prevalent among Christians since early times, and will doubtless flourish again at the end of the second millennium. IRVINGITES and MORMONS, SEVENTH-DAY ADVENTISTS and JEHOVAH'S WITNESSES all expressed this hope. William Miller (1782–1849) interpreted the prophecy of Daniel and the Book of REVELATION to predict the return of Christ on 21 March 1843. When this failed it was adjusted to 1844, and disappointment led to disillusion and persecution. Miller's followers regrouped in the Seventh-Day Adventists, and further predictions have been made. (*See*

also BRANCH DAVIDIANS; CHILIASM; MILLENNIUM; SHAKERS.)

Aetherius Society

One of many 20th-century movements drawing on different religious traditions. Its founder, George King (b. 1919), is known as its Metropolitan Archbishop; he practises yoga, quotes Christian, Eastern and New Age philosophies, and claims to receive messages from a Cosmic Master in Venus, and from 'Master Jesus'. (*See also* NEW AGE; THEOSOPHY.)

affinity table

See KINDRED AND AFFINITY.

affusion

See BAPTISM.

Africa

It is estimated that at the beginning of the 20th century there were about 10 million Christians in Africa, and that by the year 2000 there will be nearly 400 million. The major churches have countless places of worship on the continent, but in addition to those of missionary origin many churches of African inspiration and leadership have developed independently in Africa and the Americas, with an emphasis on indigenous expressions of Christianity. In America an African Methodist Episcopal Church appeared in Philadelphia in 1787, and another group in New York in 1796 added Zion to the title. In South Africa in 1948 130 church groups had 'African' as the first element in their titles, and another 40 were listed as Ethiopian though not directly connected with Ethiopia; there are many more now. There have been innumerable African Christian prophets, and over 8,000 African Christian independent movements. Most of these hold to the Bible and the main orthodox doctrines, and relatively few make overt use of

African village church, Kilibo, Benin: This was built c. 1940 by railway workers and lay preachers as they travelled to the interior.

pre-Christian practices. (*See also* AGGREY; ALADURA; BLYDEN; CHERUBIM AND SERAPHIM; HARRIS; KIMBANGU; SHEMBE; SPARTAS; ZIONIST AFRICAN CHURCHES.)

afterlife

See HEAVEN; HELL; PURGATORY; RESURRECTION.

Agabus

An early Christian prophet who foretold a famine and PAUL's imprisonment (Acts 11:28, 21:10).

agapé

A Greek word for 'love'. It is sometimes distinguished from *eros* which is deemed to mean sexual love, but the Greek SEPTUAGINT version of the SONG OF SONGS used *agapé* for erotic expressions. In the New Testament, *agapé* is employed most frequently in the writings of JOHN and PAUL. In the great hymn to *agapé* in 1 Corinthians 13 the word was rightly translated as 'love' by William TYNDALE, but it was changed to 'charity' in the Authorized Version to conform to the Latin *caritas*. Later translators have reverted to 'love'.

In the early Church, an *agapé* was a fellowship meal related to the Lord's Supper (1 Cor. 11:17ff), at which food was shared and hymns sung. Similar 'love-feasts' developed in the eighteenth-century evangelical revival.

aggiornamento

See VATICAN.

Aggrey, James Emman Kwegyir (1875–1927)

Born in the Gold Coast (Ghana) he went to the United States, became a minister in the American Methodist Episcopal Zion Church and married an American woman. He preached the collaboration of whites and blacks, 'the black and white keys of the piano' for harmony, and became Vice-Principal of Achimota School which prepared the way for higher education in Ghana.

Agnes

A virgin martyr at Rome about 350. Legends are confused, but her popularity is shown by the appearance of her name in the Roman CANON of the Mass. Since Agnes resembled the Latin word for 'lamb' (*agnus*), she was represented with a lamb in art. Feast day 21 January.

agnostic

The term was invented in 1869 by biologist Thomas Henry Huxley for those who rejected atheism but believed in an 'unknown and unknowable God', on the pattern of the inscription on the altar mentioned in Acts 17:23 'To an unknown God' (*agnōstō theō*).

Agnus Dei

'O Lamb of God', a formula recited three times in the Latin liturgy, and derived from John 1:29, in which JOHN THE BAPTIST says of Jesus, 'Behold the Lamb of God.'

Aidan (d. 651 CE)

A monk of IONA who was sent to Northumbria at the request of King OSWALD to revive Christian work. IN 635 CE he settled on the island of LINDISFARNE, from where he travelled to the mainland, founding churches and monasteries. BEDE wrote eloquently of Aidan, for his devotion, humility and care of the sick and poor. Aidan died at Bamburgh and was buried at Lindisfarne, but some of his bones were removed to Ireland. The church at Bamburgh is the principal one dedicated to him. Saint's day 31 August. (*See also* CHAD; OSWALD.)

aisle

From a French word *aile* meaning 'wing': a side passage in a church parallel to the main nave, choir or transept.

Akinyele

See ALADURA.

Aladura

'Prayer people' in the Yoruba language of Nigeria. The term is used of prophetic-healing churches which have spread in Nigeria and to Britain. From 1930 there was a mass movement of healing, led by Joseph Babalola and supported by Isaac Akinyele of the Christ Apostolic Church. The Church of the Lord (Aladura) and many smaller groups are often included under the general term Aladura. (*See also* AFRICA; CHERUBIM AND SERAPHIM.)

alb

See VESTMENTS.

Alban

The first British martyr. Legends of Alban, followed by BEDE in his *Ecclesiastical History*, say that he was a third-century pagan soldier at Verulamium (St Albans) who sheltered a Christian priest during persecution, was converted by him, dressed in the priest's cloak to enable him to escape, and was condemned to death after refusing to perform a pagan sacrifice. Alban's shrine still stands in St Albans Abbey, and his cult spread all over England and parts of France.

Albertus Magnus/Albert the Great (1200–80)

Dominican friar and bishop, a vastly learned medieval theologian and prolific writer. He was influenced by Jewish and Arabic writers, as well as by ARISTOTLE and AUGUSTINE OF HIPPO, and he prepared the way for the synthesis of theology and philosophy created by THOMAS AQUINAS. Albertus was commonly called the Universal Doctor and was placed by Dante among the lovers of wisdom.

Albigenses

Followers of a dualistic movement which flourished from the 11th to the 14th century. They were named after the city of Albi in southern France. (*See also* CATHARI; DOMINIC.)

Alcoran

Former English spelling of the Islamic 'the QUR'ĀN'. Chaucer wrote of 'the holy laws of our Alkaron.' (*Man of Law's Tale*, l.332).

Alcuin (735–804 CE)

English scholar and monk. Born and educated in York, he was appointed by the Emperor Charlemagne to head the monastery of St Martin in Tours, where he began a revival of classical and biblical learning which was called the Carolingian Renaissance. Alcuin wrote poetry, letters, lives of saints, and works on ethics, theology and liturgy.

Alexandrian Fathers

See CLEMENT OF ALEXANDRIA; ORIGEN.

Alfred (849–99 CE)

British king, scholar and devout Christian; the only British monarch to be entitled 'the Great'. With others from England and the continent, Alfred translated popular Latin works, founded monasteries and promoted the education of clergy and nobles. (*See also* BEDE; BOETHIUS.)

All Saints

The commemoration, originally of martyrs, was established by the seventh century in the dedication of the Pantheon in Rome to St Mary and Martyrs, but the observance of All Saints' Day in the West on 1 November dates from the following century. It was known in England also as All Hallows, and the day before, or 'eve', was Hallowe'en. (*See also* HALLOWE'EN; SAINTS.)

All Souls

Commemoration of all the faithful departed on 2 November, following All Saints' Day. Also called the Day of the Dead. Prayers are made for the departed, graves visited and flowers presented.

allegory

Description of a subject under the guise of another. In interpreting Scripture, new meanings were read into old texts. PAUL said 'these things are an allegory' (Gal. 4:24) of the two sons of ABRAHAM, by a slave and a free woman, foreshadowing the old and new COVENANTS. The use of allegory sometimes went to strange lengths, and the Reformers declared that Scripture should speak for itself. Nevertheless, the sensual descriptions of the Song of Songs were still interpreted allegorically as applying to

Christ and the Church, as may be seen in page headings of the Authorized Version. (*See also* ORIGEN; SONG OF SOLOMON.)

alleluia

See HALLELUJAH.

Alms

Charitable gifts. Ultimately derived from Greek *eleemosune*, mercy or compassion, alms became part of eucharistic worship, with offerings 'for the poor, and the needs of the Church'. The modern tendency is to speak of the 'collection' or 'offertory' in public worship, but the correct phrase would be 'the collection of alms'. An almoner is an official who dispenses alms, in England on Maundy Thursday if the monarch is absent. In France an *aumônier* is commonly a 'chaplain'. *See also* FOOT-WASHING.

Alpha and Omega

First and last letters of the Greek alphabet, applied to Christ in the APOCALYPSE (Rev. 1:8, 21:6, 22:13) as the beginning and the end, 'which is, and which was, and which is to come'.

Alphonsus Liguori (1696–1787)

Italian moral theologian, founder of the Redemptorist Congregation in 1732 to work among the poor. He opposed JESUIT and JANSENIST rigorism, and wrote devotional works which were popular though criticized for sentimentality.

altar

Table or stone on which the EUCHARIST or MASS is celebrated. The Latin *altare* meant a place where sacrifice was offered. Early Christian altars were of wood, and called the Lord's Table, but stone altars became prevalent from the practice of celebrating on the tombs of martyrs, and RELICS enclosed in stone altars became the rule throughout the Roman Catholic Church. At the

REFORMATION the BOOK OF COMMON PRAYER never used the word altar, though it appears in the work of some Protestant writers, notably the WESLEYS. Altars were placed at the end of the SANCTUARY, before the REREDOS, but modern liturgical reforms have taken altars down among the people, and they are often of wood. The placing of CANDLES (altar lights), two or seven, was a late innovation in the West, as was also putting a cross or even flowers on the altar. Altar rails were unknown till the reign of Elizabeth I, abolished under the Commonwealth and replaced at the Restoration. Liturgical reforms favour standing to receive Communion, dispensing with rails, as has always been the custom in Eastern ORTHODOXY.

Alternative Service Book

See BOOK OF COMMON PRAYER.

Altizer, Thomas

See DEATH OF GOD.

Ama Nazaretha

See NAZIRITE; SHEMBE.

Amana

A Christian commune, founded in Germany in 1714 and registered in the USA in 1859. Known as the Community of True Inspiration, it became involved in manufacturing, especially electrical goods.

Ambrose (339–97 CE)

Scholar and cleric. Born in Trier, now in Germany, Ambrose was a lawyer and administrator of part of northern Italy, with residence in Milan. He was a popular governor and when the Arian bishop died the crowd cried, 'Ambrose bishop'. Only a catechumen and unbaptized, Ambrose hesitated; but eventually he was baptized, ordained and appointed bishop. He studied theology, became a popular preacher and opposed Arian teachings. He excommunicated the

Emperor Theodosius who had massacred rebellious Thessalonians, and restored him only after severe penance. Ambrose was reckoned one of the four great doctors or teachers of the Latin Church, along with JEROME, AUGUSTINE and Gregory the Great. Feast day 7 December. (*See also* ARIUS; THEODOSIUS.)

Amen

A Hebrew word meaning 'verily' or 'certainly', used in synagogue worship for community response. Amen is common in the words of Jesus, as given by Matthew and more frequently by John. It was taken into the Christian liturgy, people saying Amen at 'the giving of thanks' (1 Cor. 14:16), and this has continued with 'Amen' used in responding to and affirming prayers.

Amish

General name for ANABAPTIST groups from 1590, led by a Swiss MENNONITE preacher, Jacob Amman or Ammon. The Amish migrated to America, settling first in Pennsylvania and then Ohio, Indiana, mid-western states and Ontario, Canada. There are still several Amish groups, the best known being the Old Order who dress in black, old-fashioned clothes and refuse modern technology and education, demanding freedom of religion. There are around 150,000 Amish in 225 settlements in the USA, Canada and Europe. (*See also* HUTTERITES.)

Anabaptists

The common name, meaning 'rebaptizers', given to a group of sixteenth-century reformers. It was not appropriate, since such groups denied the validity of infant baptism and regarded adult or 'believers' baptism' as the only true act. At the Reformation Anabaptists were persecuted, but spread their doctrines through Germany and the Netherlands. Eventually many fled to America. (*See also* BAPTISTS; MENNONITES.)

Analogy

See BUTLER, JOSEPH.

Ananias

Name of New Testament figures. One Ananias, along with his wife Sapphira, pretended that they had given all their goods to the early Church community, when they had kept part for themselves. Being challenged by Peter, they both fell down dead (Acts 5). Another Ananias bravely went to the erstwhile persecutor Saul (PAUL) to restore his sight (Acts 9:10ff), and a further Ananias was high priest at Jerusalem when Paul was tried (Acts 23:2).

anaphora

A Greek word for 'offering', used from early times in the central eucharistic prayer, or prayer of consecration, beginning with the *Sursum corda*, 'lift up your hearts'.

anathema

A Greek word meaning 'suspended' and thus excommunicated. PAUL said that if anyone does not love the Lord 'let him be anathema' (1 Cor. 16:22), implying exclusion from the community. In the growing Church heretics were cast out, and in 431 CE CYRIL of Alexandria issued 12 anathemas against NESTORIUS. Excommunication meant exclusion from the sacraments, but anathema involved complete separation from the Church, later formalized in sentences from a bishop. (*See also* HERESY.)

anchorite

A person leaving the world for a life of prayer and silence. (The term is derived from a Greek word meaning 'to withdraw'.) In distinction from a desert HERMIT, the anchorite or anchoress lived in a cell or confined quarters; some parish churches had such a cell attached to them. (*See also* JULIAN OF NORWICH.)

Ancren Riwle

An English 'rule' or set of regulations for anchoresses, written about 1200, showing the strength of women's movements of spirituality, and ascribed to various authors. It gives guidance for the solitary life, and warns against both excessive austerity in flagellation and idle chatter or 'cackling'. The SEVEN DEADLY SINS are compared to animals and their offspring, ACCIDIE having eight children which include idleness and grumbling.

Andrew

APOSTLE and brother of PETER. In MARK's Gospel (1:16) he is called with Peter from their fishing, though in JOHN (1:41) he brought Peter to Jesus. Because of this Andrew has been taken as the patron of missions. The St Andrew's Cross, like a capital X, can only be traced back to the fourteenth century, but legend related the martyrdom of Andrew by crucifixion in 60 CE, which would be before the better-attested martyrdom of Peter in Rome. Andrew was adopted as patron saint of Scotland in about 750 CE. His feast day is 30 November.

Andrewes, Lancelot (1555–1626)

Scholar and linguist, eventually Bishop of Winchester and one of the translators of the Authorized Version of the Bible. Born in Barking, Essex, he was at first a Puritan; later he became strongly anti-Calvinist and accompanied James I to Scotland trying to recommend episcopacy. His *Ninety-Six Sermons* became a classic work, praised in modern times by T.S. Eliot in an essay 'For Lancelot Andrewes'. Andrewes' famous 'Private Prayers', *Preces Privatae*, written in Greek and Latin, were found in manuscript blotted with tears and not published till after his death.

angel

Heavenly being. The name derives from the Greek for 'messenger'. Angels appear in the Bible as messengers and agents of God; later they became intermediaries, perhaps under ZOROASTRIAN influence. There were superior figures, known as ARCHANGELS, and some were named, notably Gabriel and Michael (Dan. 8:16, 10:13). In the New Testament angels appeared at important periods in the life of Christ: his birth, temptation, agony and resurrection. MATTHEW mentions angels in dreams, and LUKE names Gabriel in the temple (Luke 1:19). Church writers speculated about the nature and number of angels, and DIONYSIUS the Areopagite in the sixth century wrote of celestial hierarchies, arranging angels in categories. The schoolmen of the middle ages agreed that angels are intelligences without bodies, so different from human souls. Since they occupied no space, myriads of them could dance on the point of a pin. The Reformers did not bother about angels, but in the 17th century Milton's *Paradise Lost* described them in detail (see esp. Book III). (*See also* GUARDIAN ANGEL.)

Angelic Doctor

A title applied to THOMAS AQUINAS.

Angelus

A devotion of the Western Church, recalling the INCARNATION. It was so called from its opening words, 'Angelus Domini', 'the angel of the Lord', based on Luke 1:26. Bells are rung at repetitions of the angelic salutation, 'AVE MARIA', and for the COLLECT. A famous painting by Millet (1859) shows workers in the field with bowed heads at the Angelus bell.

Anglicanism

The expression of Christianity in the Church of England, composed of those who in doctrine and practice accept the leadership of the see of Canterbury.

English, as distinct from Celtic, Christianity may be dated from 597 CE when Pope Gregory the Great sent AUGUSTINE to CANTERBURY. After a SYNOD at Whitby in 664 CE Roman practice was accepted, and native leaders emerged such as ALCUIN, BEDE and BONIFACE. In the later middle ages came building of great churches and cathedrals, the re-emergence of the English language in mystical writings, and the Wycliffite and Tyndale Bible translations. In the REFORMATION which convulsed Europe in the 16th century, England tried to have it both ways, remaining Catholic but becoming Reformed. Henry VIII declared independence from Rome but persecuted Protestants; Thomas CRANMER prepared a revised Prayer Book but was executed by Catholic MARY TUDOR. Reactions one way and another ended with the Elizabethan Settlement, a national church with traditional but Reformed worship. The Anglican VIA MEDIA (middle way) sought to contain both Catholic and evangelical elements, but the divisions separating Nonconformists, Protestants and Catholics, persisted. The Toleration Act of 1689 allowed Dissenting worship, and Catholic emancipation came in 1829. The state church in England has the monarch as its head, though the increasing variety of religions in the country has made that position increasingly problematic. Meanwhile the Anglican Communion spread to many countries, notably as the Protestant Episcopal Church in the USA. Numbers of Anglicans are estimated to reach 82 million by the year 2000. (*See also* ARTICLES; AUTHORIZED VERSION; BOOK OF COMMON PRAYER; CELTIC CHURCH; DEFENDER OF THE FAITH; SUPREMACY.)

Anglo-Catholicism

Catholicism of an Anglican 'High Church' type, repudiating the name

'Protestant'. The title Anglo-Catholic dates from 1838. It began with the Oxford or Tractarian Movement, sparked by John KEBLE's sermon in Oxford on 'National Apostasy' in 1833, followed by *Tracts for the Times* begun by J. H. NEWMAN in the same year. Newman's move to Rome in 1845 checked but did not halt the Anglo-Catholic cause. Recently the ordination of women in the Church of England has prompted some Anglo-Catholics, even married priests, to move over to Rome, while others prefer to wait for a move towards female ordination by the universal Church. (*See also* PUSEY; TRACTS.)

Anima Christi

Latin for 'Soul of Christ', the invocation has been used since the 14th century, and stands at the beginning of the *Spiritual Exercises* of IGNATIUS LOYOLA: 'Soul of Christ, sanctify me; Body of Christ, save me.'

animals

The general biblical view is that human beings and animals form one community. God made a COVENANT with 'every living creature' though humanity had been given domination (Gen. 1:28, 9:10). Jesus said that God cares for the sparrows, even the odd one out of five (Luke 12:6). Some of the saints, notably FRANCIS OF ASSISI, lived with or cared for animals, but the animal welfare movement is a modern concern.

annates

The first-fruits of revenue of one year (*annus*) paid to the Pope in the medieval Church by bishops on their appointment. This irritated monarchs and in 1534 Henry VIII decreed that the payment of annates should be transferred to the crown. In 1704 Queen Anne converted them into the augmentation of poor livings, called Queen Anne's Bounty. (*See also* PRAEMUNIRE.)

Anne

The mother of Mary, mother of Jesus, is not named in the gospels, but she appears as Anne in the apocryphal Protevangelium or PSEUDO-JAMES in the second century. The name may have been taken from the prophetess Anna (Luke 2:36), or from Hannah the mother of Samuel (1 Sam. 1–2), whose story the legend of Anne resembles. Churches and feasts were dedicated to Anne on 26 July, and she often appears in paintings of the infancy of Jesus. (*See also* JOACHIM.)

anniversary

A church or chapel anniversary in the British Free Churches corresponds to a DEDICATION feast elsewhere, celebrating years of worship. Other popular anniversaries are for choir or SUNDAY SCHOOL. The latter were for a long time the great occasions of the year, with special platforms, dresses and processions.

Anno Domini

See CALENDAR.

Annunciation

The announcement by the ANGEL Gabriel to Mary that she would bear a son Jesus (Luke 1:26ff). The date was calculated when Christmas had been fixed for 25 December. Nine months earlier gave 25 March, known in England as Lady Day. The feast became universal in the West and was a RED LETTER DAY.

anointing

See UNCTION.

Anselm (1033–1109)

Italian theologian who became Archbishop of Canterbury under William Rufus and Henry I. He was a reformer, holding regular SYNODS, insisting on clerical CELIBACY and opposing the king over

The Annunciation, Leonardo da Vinci: An early painting, said to combine languor and intensity, now in the Uffizi Gallery, Florence.

the rights of the Church, for which he was twice sent into exile. He died at Canterbury and was canonized and declared a doctor of the Church. Anselm was famous for his writings, setting out a form of the Ontological Argument for the 'being' or existence of God which stated that if we mean by God 'that than which nothing greater can be conceived', then God must exist. In *Cur Deus Homo?* ('Why did God become Man?') Anselm argued against a theory of ransom for the atonement of Christ, which he saw as a SATISFACTION to God for the injury of human sin. This was contradicted by ABELARD, who explained Christ's death as an example. Feast day 21 April.

Ante-Communion

The first part of the Communion service in the BOOK OF COMMON PRAYER, including the Prayer for the Church, comparable to the Dry Mass of the middle ages for the first part of the liturgy.

anthem

Probably the English form of ANTIPHON. Traditionally, an anthem was a musical setting of words from the Psalms, sung by a choir. Anthems may be accompanied or not, with or without soloists.

anthroposophy

20th-century religious movement. Taking its title from the Greek for 'wisdom of humanity', the Anthroposophical Society was founded in Berlin in 1913 by Rudolf STEINER, a former Roman Catholic. Breaking with the Theosophical Society, Steiner's system gave a central place to Christ, the great solar being who saves the world from ruin. The Society organized into Christian Fellowships, in which the celebration of the SACRAMENT is the central act. It was condemned by the Roman Catholic Church in 1919. (*See also* THEOSOPHY.)

Anti-Christ

New Testament figure opposed to Christ. He appears in late writings by John, where he tells of an Anti-Christ, or 'many anti-christs' who deny that Jesus is Christ or fail to confess him come in the flesh (1 John 2:18ff, 4:3; 2 John 7). Some linked him with the 'man of sin' and 'son of perdition' to be revealed (2 Thess. 2:3), or with the great beast of Revelation whose number is 666 (Rev. 13:18), which has been interpreted as Nero Caesar in Hebrew notation. Later writers refer to popular fears of Nero reborn as the Anti-Christ, and the Beast was identified variously with Muhammad, Napoleon, Hitler or the Pope. In Islam orthodox creeds reflect popular belief in the appearance of Anti-Christ with GOG AND MAGOG. Jesus will descend from heaven to kill the Anti-Christ and enter Jerusalem at the time of morning prayer. (*See also* WYCLIFFE.)

anti-clericalism

Opposition to the dominance of the clergy has appeared in many times, whether in the mockery of Voltaire or the refusal of Quakers to have an ordained ministry. Struggles of church and state for dominance were calmed in CONCORDATS. (*See also* COMMUNISM.)

anti-cult movement

Backlash against NEW RELIGIOUS MOVEMENTS or 'CULTS'. Its members are often relatives of converts, or former members, who accuse the 'cults' of brain-washing, breaking up families and/or bizarre sexual practices. In America there has arisen also an anti-anti-cult movement.

antinomianism

Rejection of the moral law, an accusation made against those who hold that believers are set free from morality. PAUL rejected the charge that he had said 'Let us do evil that good may come' (Rom. 3:8), yet his disparagement of the external Mosaic Law in favour of the new law in the heart could suggest neglect of morality. Various GNOSTICS and later ANABAPTISTS were accused of antinomianism because of their opposition of flesh and spirit, or insistence on faith before works. (*See also* RANTERS.)

Antipope

See CONSTANCE, COUNCIL OF; SCHISM; WYCLIFFE.

antiphon

A verse or sentence, often from the Psalms, sung by one choir in response to another, or by a soloist in response to a choir. (*See also* ANTHEM; O SAPIENTIA.)

anti-semitism

A term first used in 1880 to distinguish hostility to Jews as a people from opposition to their religion, it came to indicate attacks on both Jews and Judaism. Its roots go back to the early Church, though since all the first Christians were Jews it was family quarrelling. The Crucifixion was blamed on Jews, in Matthew's report of the words 'his blood be on us and on our children' (27:25). In John's later gospel 'the Jews' are accused many times of plotting to kill Jesus (deicide). The CRUSADES unleashed persecution of Jews, and LUTHER made virulent attacks on them and their synagogues, helping to create the atmosphere that allowed the HOLOCAUST of the mid-20th century to take place. (*See also* BRITISH ISRAELITES; HOLOCAUST; HUGH; JEWS FOR JESUS; JUDAISM; WANDERING JEW; WILLIAM OF NORWICH.)

Antony (251–356 CE)

An Egyptian, of the COPTIC Church, regarded as the founder of Christian MONASTICISM. Taking literally the words of Jesus to the rich young ruler (Mark 10:21), Antony gave up his possessions to live alone in the desert. He is said to have fought demons in the form of wild beasts, which modern readers may interpret as sexual temptations. He attracted followers who were repelled by the worldliness of the Church after it had become the state religion. Some lived alone, and others in groups like later monastics. Feast day 17 January. (*See also* ASCETICISM; PACHOMIUS.)

apartheid

'Apartness' in Afrikaans: official separation of the races, practised in South Africa before the introduction of democracy in 1994. The policy divided the churches, most Dutch Reformed Churches claiming biblical and theological support for apartheid, and then arguing for its practical necessity. Other churches affirmed that Christians could not be excluded by race and that the state must not block a universal Gospel. Some Dutch Reformed spokesmen against apartheid were charged with HERESY or removed from pastoral or professorial posts. (*See also* RACE RELATIONS.)

Apocalypse

Greek for 'uncovering' or revelation. Prediction of the fall of Jerusalem to the Romans (Mark 13 and parallels) is sometimes called the 'little apocalypse'. The book of REVELATION (the Apocalypse of John) treats of Neronic and later persecution of the early Church. Other apocalypses were ascribed to PETER, PAUL and THOMAS. Apocalypticism emphasizes the evil of the present age and predicts a new age of righteousness. (*See also* ESCHATOLOGY.)

Apocrypha

Greek, 'hidden' things. The Old Testament Apocrypha are Jewish Greek books not included in the Hebrew Bible: 12 or 15 of them are printed in Roman Catholic but not usually in Protestant editions of the Bible and other collections of Scripture. The New Testament or Christian Apocrypha are so-called gospels, acts, epistles and apocalypses outside and later than the recognized CANON of Scripture. These books may contain some oral traditions, of Jesus and the APOSTLES, but for the most part they are pale and speculative. (*See also* PSEUDO-JAMES.)

Apollinarianism

Doctrines named after a fourth-century teacher Apollinarius, most of whose beliefs were traceable only in fragments. In debates about the nature of Christ he seems to have held that in Christ there was a human body, but the spirit was replaced by the divine LOGOS. While this supported orthodox views of the divinity of Christ, it denied his humanity and failed to show him as an exemplar of the moral life.

Apollos

A learned Jew from Alexandria who joined the Christians at Ephesus (Acts 18:24ff). Later at Corinth some saw him as a rival to PAUL (1 Cor. 1:12).

apologetics

From a Greek word for 'defence': the presentation of the faith by reasoned argument. Second-century Apologists like JUSTIN MARTYR and TERTULLIAN sought to expound Christianity in face of Jewish and Greek objections. In the middle ages apologetics developed positively in proving belief in God. J.H. NEWMAN's *Apologia pro vita sua* (1864) described his passage from the Church of England to Roman Catholicism.

apostasy

From Greek for 'withdrawal', indicating abandonment of religious faith or leaving one religious community for another. (*See also* KEBLE; SCHISM.)

apostles

From Greek 'sent out': the men sent out by Jesus to spread the new faith. The apostleship began when Jesus despatched his disciples two by two (Mark 6:7). Lists of 12 apostles given in the Gospels and Acts vary slightly; the number 12 was probably taken from the 12 tribes of Israel. PAUL later defended his right to be called an apostle because of his vision of Christ (1 Cor. 9:1). 'Apostolic Father' is a title given to some early Christian writers, such as CLEMENT OF ROME, IGNATIUS and PAPIAS.

Apostles' Creed

Used only in the Western Church, this brief summary of faith was believed to go back to the APOSTLES at Jerusalem, though the title first appeared in 390 and the contents compare with baptismal confessions used about that time. While the birth and death of Jesus are affirmed, neither here nor in the longer Nicene CREED is there any reference to his life and teaching. Protestant Nonconformist churches generally accept the Apostles' Creed but do not use it in regular worship.

apostolic succession

The claimed continuity of church ministry from the first APOSTLES to the present, regarded as guaranteed by bishops as heirs of the apostles. This doctrine is held by Roman Catholicism, Eastern Orthodoxy and Anglicanism, though the validity of succession in the last is denied by the Vatican. Protestants generally regard succession to be embodied in the faith and practice of the apostles, rather than in historical descent.

Aquarius

Latin, 'water-carrier'; the eleventh sign of the Zodiac. In modern esoteric thought the Age of Aquarius is a coming time of peace and spiritual advancement ruled by this sign. An *Aquarian Gospel of Jesus Christ*, published in 1911 by the American Levi Dowling, is claimed to tell of the travels and teaching of Jesus in India. (*See also* NEW AGE.)

Aquila

See PRISCA/PRISCILLA.

Aquinas

See THOMAS AQUINAS.

archangel

In the one-chapter Epistle of Jude (v. 9), Michael the archangel appears; 'the voice of the archangel' is heard in 1 Thess. 4:16. Gabriel and Raphael were also reckoned as archangels. (*See also* ANGEL; MICHAEL.)

archbishop

An honorific title for a bishop of a distinguished see, applied also to PATRIARCHS and METROPOLITANS. (*See also* PRIMATE.)

archdeacon

Originally a chief of deacons, now a priest entrusted with the supervision of clergy and property, presenting candidates for ordination and inducting priests to new parishes.

arches

See DEAN.

archimandrite

In Eastern churches, head of a monastery, or several monasteries such as those on Mount ATHOS, corresponding to an ABBOT in the West.

architecture

The first apostles met in an upper room (Acts 1:13). As their numbers grew, Christians came together in buildings, like synagogues; these were of no fixed design but provided for a congregation and for reading scriptures, prayer, singing and exhortation.

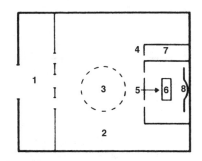

A. EASTERN
1. Narthex – porch for preparation
2. Nave – no seating; congregation stands, walks
3. Dome above, painted with Christ as ruler
4. Iconostasis – screen covered with icons
5. Central door – opened during service
6. Altar
7. Chapel for preparation of bread and wine
8. Bishop's seat in semi-circular 'apse'

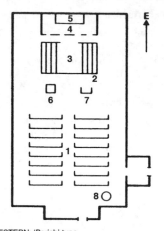

B. WESTERN: 'Parish' type
1. Nave – seated congregation
2. Screen (in older churches) – open door
3. Choir (where service is led)
4. Sanctuary (railed)
5. Altar table
6. Pulpit (for preaching)
7. Lectern (for reading Scriptures)
8. Font (for baptism)

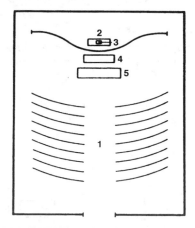

C. NORTHERN: 'Meeting-house' type
1. Congregation seated
2. Pulpit (where service is led)
3. Bible (open for service)
4. Communion table
5. Baptistery (covered when not in use)

Types of church building demonstrating the uses of the religious space: The Eastern style allows congregational movement; the Western style seats the congregation looking towards a distant sanctuary; the Northern, Protestant, style has a dominant pulpit with the congregation in front or in a gallery. From J. Hinnells, A Handbook of Living Religions, *Penguin.*

During persecution they met in catacombs, but once allowed to worship freely could meet openly, and the Roman BASILICA became the dominant building type. Development of the liturgy and the dominance of clergy required space for processions, and decoration in ICONS and inscribed tablets evolved. Movements of religious fervour produced great buildings, including the CATHEDRALS and churches of the middle ages, and the chapels and churches of the Evangelical Revival and Anglo-Catholicism. (*See also* ABBEY; HAGIA SOPHIA; WESTMINSTER ABBEY.)

Areopagus

Greek, 'hill of Ares', god of war, similar to the Roman Mars; thus the Areopagus where PAUL preached in Athens was translated Mars' Hill (Acts 17:22, Authorized Version). A man named DIONYSIUS the Areopagite was converted here (v. 34), but a mystical writer Dionysius of the fifth century was wrongly identified with him.

Arianism

A form of early Christological teaching. Arius was a priest of Alexandria (250–336 CE) whose strict monotheism made him unable to accept the equality of the LOGOS with the Father, and he seems to have taught the subordination of Christ, who was not eternal but a creature. Only fragments of his writing survive. Agitation for and against his teaching caused the Emperor Constantine to call the Council of NICAEA in 325. ATHANASIUS championed the orthodox view of Christ's co-eternity and co-equality, insisting that Christ was HOMOOUSION (of one substance) with God the Father. Arianism was defeated, for a time, but it returned with political links, being embraced by Constantine's successor. Further councils accepted Semi-Arianism, a doctrinally vague version but orthodoxy recovered and triumphed at Constantinople in 381. Many of the barbarian tribes which overran the Roman Empire were converted by Arian preachers but were gradually brought to orthodoxy. (*See also* SEMI-ARIANS.)

Aristotle

The great Greek philosopher became the inspirer of medieval Thomistic Christian philosophy. His works were not known in Europe during the dark ages, coming to light only through Arabic translations from Greek made by Muslims and Jews and then put into Latin. (*See also* PLATONISM; THOMAS AQUINAS.)

Armageddon

Hebrew, 'hill of Megiddo', in northern Israel. A great international highway from Mesopotamia to Egypt passed by here and it is mentioned as a place of battle (2 Chr. 35:22). In the book of Revelation (16:16) it is the site for 'the battle of that great day'. Christian ADVENTIST prophecy has often foretold a world combat at Armageddon.

Armenia

Claimed as the first nation to adopt Christianity as the state religion. Armenians were converted by Gregory the Illuminator at the beginning of the fourth century, and will celebrate their 1,700th anniversary as Christians in 2001. This helps to explain struggles for independence from Turkish and Soviet control, and conflicts with Muslim Azerbaijan. Old Christological disputes are now ending and Armenian orthodoxy was recognized by Rome in an agreement signed in 1996.

Arminianism

Jakob Arminius (1560–1609), a Dutch Reformer, rejected CALVIN's doctrine of PREDESTINATION, and emphasized FREE WILL and the love of God for all people. His teachings were set forth in a Remonstrance after his early death, provoking opposition and persecution, though eventually there was tolerance. Arminian thought spread to England and America, being agreeable to the anti-Calvinist wing of the Church of England, and inspiring John WESLEY in differences from the Calvinist George WHITEFIELD. Wesley published an *Arminian Magazine* to propound his news and views.

Armstrong, Herbert

See WORLDWIDE CHURCH OF GOD.

art

Christian art is not 'for art's sake' but, like other religious art, it is the handmaid of faith. There were decorations in synagogues and paintings in catacombs. Debate over the prohibition of Exodus 20:4, 'you shall not make any graven image', soon gave rise to iconoclastic controversies over the display of two-dimensional ICONS in the East and rounded images in the West. At the REFORMATION countless sculptures and paintings were destroyed, some no doubt poor art, some irreplaceable. Protestant churches contain two-dimensional stained-glass windows, though Quakers and some others tend to renounce all representative art in their buildings. Literature, however, is one of the major art forms, and the written and spoken word has often received almost idolatrous reverence. (*See also* ARCHITECTURE; DRAMA; IMAGE.)

Artemis

Greek goddess of the earth and of cities, giver of fertility but also a virgin. She is identified with the Italian Diana in Acts 19:28 (Authorized Version).

Arthur

See GRAIL.

Articles

Various lists of Articles were compiled in the Church of England to define and impose the faith. First published in 1563 under Elizabeth I, the THIRTY-NINE ARTICLES proceeded from faith in the Trinity to a Christian man's oath. Articles were drawn up with controversies in mind and sought the mean between extremes of Calvinism and Catholicism with what *The Oxford Dictionary of the Christian Church* called 'masterly ambiguity'. They were imposed on all clergy and public teachers; any who disagreed were threatened with Church censure and royal displeasure.

artificial insemination

AIH, artificial insemination from the husband, may be carried out using semen produced from masturbation and is generally acceptable to Protestants, but is condemned by Roman Catholics as 'against nature'. AID, by donor, known or not, has aroused more criticism and adoption is often recommended in preference for childless women. The disposal of unused embryos after a certain period also causes misgivings, and the implications of the sacredness of life continue to be discussed.

ASB

See BOOK OF COMMON PRAYER.

Asbury, Francis (1745–1816)

Methodist minister. Born at Handsworth in Staffordshire, Asbury was sent by John WESLEY to America as a missionary in 1771, and soon had supervision of all METHODIST work. Wesley set aside Thomas COKE as 'superintendent' and ordained Asbury to the same office in 1784; Asbury took the title of 'bishop' against Wesley's advice. A Baltimore conference agreed to constitute the 'Methodist Episcopal Church of the United States of America', and Asbury spent the rest of his life organizing and extending it. He was a man of simple character and deep piety, and died unmarried.

Ascension

The last appearance of the risen Christ to the APOSTLES before he was 'taken from them'. Luke's Gospel (24:50ff) seems to suggest that it took place at Bethany on the day of the RESURRECTION, but Acts (1:3ff), also by Luke, speaks of Jesus appearing during 40 days at Jerusalem, after which 'he was taken up.' Perhaps this enlargement came to Luke from other traditions. Matthew (28:16ff) describes a last appearance in Galilee, and Mark (16:12ff) is from later manuscripts. Following Acts, Ascension Day is celebrated on a Thursday, the 40th day after EASTER Sunday.

asceticism

From a Greek word for 'exercise' or 'training': bodily self-denial to aid spiritual development. PAUL compared Christian life to running a race (1 Cor. 9:24ff), and later writers took over from the Stoics notions of ascetic discipline. The sufferings of MARTYRS and development of MONASTICISM led to emphasis on denial of the flesh and the 'world', to the detriment of understanding sex and social living. (*See also* ABSTINENCE; CELIBACY; MORTIFICATION.)

Ash Wednesday

The first day of LENT, 40 days before EASTER, fixed at Rome in the fifth century. Ashes were sprinkled on the heads of clergy and people as a symbol of penitence, a rite directed in the Roman missal and also practised by some modern African independent churches. (*See also* COMMINATION.)

ashram

Sanskrit for a hermitage. Such retreat-houses have been adapted by some

Christians in India, to develop local ways of faith and practice (See GRIFFITHS.)

Aske, Robert

See PILGRIMAGE OF GRACE.

asperges

Sprinkling holy water over altar and people before MASS. The word comes from Psalm 51:7: 'Asperge me with hyssop.' People may sprinkle themselves with holy water when entering church and reciting this verse.

Assemblies of God

A PENTECOSTAL denomination originating in Hot Springs, Arkansas in 1914, moving its headquarters to Springfield, Missouri in 1918. Against a trend towards 'Oneness', the Trinitarian faith was affirmed in a Statement of Fundamental Truths in 1916. The Assemblies emphasize gifts of the Spirit, with HEALINGS and speaking in tongues. By the 1980s there were 10,000 churches and 2 million members. (See also GLOSSOLALIA.)

Assumption

Parallel to belief in the Ascension of Christ came belief in the Assumption of his mother, body and soul, into heaven. Not mentioned in the Bible or early Church, the concept was formulated from the sixth century but promulgated as a dogma only by Pope Pius XII in 1950. The feast became popular in East and West and is celebrated on 15 August. (See also IMMACULATE CONCEPTION; MARY.)

Assyrian churches

See NESTORIUS.

Athanasius (296–373 CE)

Only a DEACON in the first stages of the ARIAN controversy, Athanasius became bishop of Alexandria in 328 CE, and though deposed and exiled several times his resolution brought final doctrinal victory. In a short treatise on the INCARNATION, Athanasius insisted that salvation depended on the full humanity and divinity of Christ: 'He was made man that we might be made divine.' It was a hard struggle, with 'Athanasius against the world', but his orthodoxy triumphed at the Council of Constantinople in 381 CE. Feast day 2 May.

A so-called Athanasian Creed was composed later, in Latin and not Greek, containing matter which arose centuries after Athanasius; it is not recognized in Eastern Orthodoxy. This creed, also known as 'Quicunque vult' ('Whosoever would be saved') from its opening Latin words, has been used in the West but criticized because of its assertion that unbelievers in its doctrines would 'perish everlastingly'. Traditionally restricted to certain festivals, this CREED has been widely abandoned in modern times.

Athos, Mount

A collection of some 20 Eastern ORTHODOX MONASTERIES on a peninsula in Macedonia, known as the 'holy mountain'. They are remarkable for their rigorous discipline, and no female persons or animals are allowed on the

The Great Lavra, Mount Athos: Founded in the 11th century on a terrace above the sea and like a small fortified town, the Lavra, or Laura, is a collection of hermits' cells.

peninsula. The Turkish overlords respected this rule but the Greek colonels in the 1960s ignored it.

atonement

The old English word, at-one-ment, indicates the reconciliation of man with God through Christ. Tyndale translated 'to preach the atonement' (2 Cor. 5:18). Many theories of the working of atonement were put forth: of Christ paying a ransom, to God or the devil; of his SATISFACTION of divine justice; of his substitution in place of sinners; of his example and love. There has been no credal or imposed doctrine of the atonement, and modern explanations have varied between legalistic and exemplary theories. (*See also* ABELARD; ANSELM; REDEEMER.)

Augsburg, Confession of

A statement of faith of LUTHERAN churches. Mostly compiled by MELANCHTHON, it was presented to the Emperor Charles V at the Diet of Augsburg in 1530. Its 21 articles summarized Lutheran doctrines, and listed abuses in Church practice that needed correction. A revised text is accepted by many Reformed or Calvinist churches in Germany.

Augustine of Canterbury
(d. 604 CE)

Roman monk sent by Pope Gregory the Great to evangelize England after Gregory saw, according to BEDE, fair Anglo-Saxon slaves whom he called 'Not Angles but angels'. Augustine landed at Thanet in Kent in 597 CE and was kindly received by King Ethelbert, whose French wife BERTHA was a Christian. Ethelbert was converted and mass baptisms of his subjects took place. Augustine was consecrated Archbishop of Canterbury and himself appointed bishops of Rochester and London. His early death hindered attempts to reach agreement with leaders of the surviving CELTIC CHURCH. Feast day 28 May. (*See also* ANGLICANISM; HILDA.)

Augustine of Hippo (354–430 CE)

Doctor of the Church. He was born of a pagan father and a Christian mother, MONICA. He became a MANICHAEAN, holding that matter is evil, and this affected both his personal life and his later moral teaching. He took a mistress but abandoned her after 15 years, was betrothed and then took another concubine, and finally renounced all on hearing a child recite, 'Take up and read.' He did this, and found the words 'not in wantonness' (Rom. 13:13). Augustine renounced Manichaeism and was baptized and ordained, and in 396 CE became bishop of Hippo in North Africa. He was a powerful writer; his *Confessions* describe his personal struggles, and later prayers with his mother. His large work *City of God* followed the fall of Rome to the Visigoths in 410 CE, and portrayed the visible Church as the kingdom of God. Feast day 28 August. (*See also* ORIGINAL SIN; PELAGIUS.)

Augustinian Canons

Also known as Austin or Black Canons, these were members of a religious order from the eleventh century. They lived a common life of CELIBACY, obedience and POVERTY, following a Rule of St Augustine of Hippo, but formulated much later than his time.

aumbry, ambry

From Latin: a cupboard or recess in the wall of a church, containing vessels or books and sometimes the reserved sacrament.

aureole

From Latin for 'golden': in art, a golden background to a sacred figure, different from the HALO which surrounded the head.

Austin

See AUGUSTINIAN CANONS; FRIAR.

Authorized Version

Known in America as the King James Version, this translation of the Bible was ordered by James I and published in 1611. It was the work of some 50 scholars, working on Hebrew and Greek original texts, who revised rather than made new translations and mediated between Protestant and Roman Catholic versions. The major influence was William TYNDALE, some 80 per cent of whose Bible translation was incorporated, thus explaining how a committee produced a masterpiece. Though never strictly authorized, it was appointed to be read in churches, and was the standard version for nearly 300 years and a great influence on English prose. Among the many translations the Authorized is now cherished by curiously different groups, including conservative Protestants and liberal lovers of classical English. (See also AGAPÉ; BOOK OF COMMON PRAYER; REVISED VERSION.)

autocephalous

Greek, 'having a head of its own': a term used of churches and bishops which are independent of ARCHBISHOPS or PATRIARCHS. See also ORTHODOX.

auto da fé

Portuguese, 'act of Faith': a sentence of the INQUISITION and its execution in burning a heretic. The last instance occurred at Seville in 1781.

avatar

The Sanskrit word *avatara* means a 'down-coming', comparable with the Christian INCARNATION. There are many Hindu avatars, but in Christian belief there is only one incarnation, though Christ may be called an avatar by Indian apologists.

Ave Maria

'Hail Mary', Latin version of the angelic salutation to Mary (Luke 1:28). Repeated many times in devotion, the 'Ave Maria' in its full form goes back to the eleventh century. The text is as follows: 'Hail Mary, full of grace, the Lord is with thee, blessed art thou among women, and blessed is the fruit of thy womb, Jesus. Holy Mary, Mother of God, pray for us sinners now and at the hour of our death.' (See also ROSARY.)

Averroes

Medieval Latin form of the name of Islamic scholar Ibn Rushd (1126–98), whose writings influenced Christian theologians. DANTE placed him in LIMBO and said that he wrote 'the Great Commentary'. He was born in Cordova and defended the use of reason against conservatives. (See also AVICENNA.)

Avicenna

Medieval Latin form of the name of Arab Islamic scholar Ibn Sina (980–1037), who influenced Christian writers and was recognized by DANTE. Neoplatonist in philosophy, his work *The Canon of Medicine* was a standard medical text in Europe till the 17th century. (See also AVERROES.)

Avignon

An ancient town in southern France, residence of Popes in exile in the 14th century. (See also BABYLONIAN CAPTIVITY.)

Awakening, Great

See BAPTISTS; CONGREGATIONALISM; EDWARDS, JONATHAN; GREAT AWAKENING.

B

Babalola, Joseph

See ALADURA.

Babylonian Captivity

Originally the deportation of groups of Jews from Jerusalem to Babylon in 597 and 586 BCE. The term was applied to the exile of the Popes from Rome to Avignon in France from 1309 to 1377. Later still, Martin LUTHER's treatise on the *Babylonish Captivity of the Church* (1520) complained of bondage through Roman abuses.

Baker, Augustine (1575–1641)

Benedictine writer on theology and history.

baldachin

A canopy over an altar. The name is derived from the Italian *baldacco*, meaning Baghdad, whence came woven materials for the canopy. A canopy may be of cloth, wood, metal or stone; one of the most famous is Bernini's altar cover on twisted pillars at St Peter's in Rome.

Ball, John (d. 1381)

A priest of egalitarian and Wycliffite sympathies, he took part in the Peasants' Revolt of 1381, led by Wat Tyler, and preached at Blackheath on a popular rhyme: 'When Adam delved and Eve span, Who was then a gentleman?' When Tyler was betrayed and executed Ball fled to the Midlands, but was captured and hanged as a traitor at St Albans. (*See also* WYCLIFFE.)

Balokole

'Saved ones' in the Luganda language. Name for the East African revival which spread powerfully from 1927. Large numbers left mission churches for a more emotional religious experience. (*See also* LUWUM.)

Balthasar

See MAGI.

banns

Proclamation in Anglican churches of intended marriage, so that if there was any impediment objection might be made. The custom of reading banns dates from the 13th century, but in 1996 the General Synod agreed to abolish the practice. For Nonconformist and civil marriages, notice is given at registry offices.

baptism

From a Greek word meaning 'to dip in water'. Baptism by full immersion was the rite of admission to the early Christian community. It is not clear whether the practice began with Jesus himself or his disciples, and how much was due to Jewish custom and John the Baptist. John 4:2 says that Jesus himself did not baptize, and the command to baptize in the name of the Trinity (Matt. 28:19) reflects Church faith and practice. Whether children were at first included in baptisms with their parents is disputed, but by the fourth century high infant mortality, and teaching on ORIGINAL SIN, led to pressure for babies to be baptized to ensure their salvation. Later Anglican and most Protestant churches retained infant baptism, but usually with affusion (pouring or sprinkling) taking the place of immersion. Some now prefer dedication to baptism, and emphasize the reception of the child into the community.

baptistery

Place where BAPTISM is carried out. Baptism does not require a separate building, and for infant baptism a FONT may be placed in a small baptistery near the entrance of the church, symbolizing admission to the society. For baptismal full immersion a tank is needed; this is usually placed in front of the main body of the church, enabling the congregation to see and share in the ceremony.

Baptists

At the REFORMATION, some Christians thought that Church reform did not go far enough and insisted on return to believers' baptism by immersion. Known first as ANABAPTISTS, then as Baptists, their numbers grew rapidly in the 17th century, despite opposition. General Baptists argued for religious liberty and held ARMINIAN views on universal salvation, while Particular Baptists accepted the strict PREDESTINARIAN theology of Calvinism. Baptist groups migrated to America and multiplied in the GREAT AWAKENING of 1725–60. In the 19th century there were more divisions over slavery, resulting in the formation of Northern and Southern Baptist Conventions, and in modern times there are disagreements between fundamentalists and liberals. Today there are some 50 million Baptists, 90 per cent of whom are American or British.

Adult baptism taking place in a river in Brazil: Full immersion, in rivers or tanks, expresses the cleaning of body and soul.

Barabbas

All the gospels mention this robber, whose name means 'son of a father'. He was released by Pilate instead of Jesus (Mark 15:7 etc.). Some manuscripts also call him Jesus Barabbas, perhaps to compare and contrast him with Christ.

Barclay, John (1734–98)

Scottish minister who founded the Barclayites or Bereans, ardent Scripture searchers named after similar people in Berea in Acts (17:10ff). He founded a new church, the Berean Assembly, which spread to London, but after his death most of his followers joined the CONGREGATIONALISTS.

Barclay, Robert (1648–90)

Scottish Quaker whose *Apology for the True Christian Divinity* was a defence of the FRIENDS. He travelled with George FOX and William PENN and was later favoured by King James II of England. Barclay became nominal governor of East New Jersey in 1683 and helped to establish Quakerism in America.

Barlaam and Josaphat

Figures of medieval legend by which the Buddha entered the Christian calendar; he was never officially canonized but was given a feast on 27 November. In a popular medieval legend an Indian prince, Josaphat (Bodhisattva, a Buddha-to-be), was converted by a hermit, Barlaam. As in the Buddhist story he saw four signs, renounced the world and taught in parables; his relics were buried in a gold urn.

Barmen Declaration

See CONFESSING CHURCH.

Barnabas

In Acts 4:36ff a Jewish Levite from Cyprus named Joseph brings money from the sale of his land to the APOSTLES and is called Barnabas, 'son of consolation'. He was a partner of PAUL on the first missionary journey and was hailed by pagans at Lystra as the god Zeus (Acts 14:12), Barnabas parted from Paul in a sharp contention over John Mark, whom he took to Cyprus. Legend says he founded the Church in Cyprus and was martyred at Salamis.

A so-called Gospel of Barnabas was written in Italian in the 16th century. It has no authenticity as a gospel, but it repeats the DOCETIC legend that Judas was crucified in place of Jesus who ascended to heaven; this story has been used in Muslim polemic but it is virtually unknown in the West.

Barth, Karl (1886–1968)

Swiss Reformed theologian, one of the most influential modern thinkers. Rejecting liberalism and humanistic religion, he insisted on the mysterious Word of God and the deity as 'wholly other'. His thought is expressed in a commentary

Karl Barth (1886–1968): His neo-orthodoxy or dialectical theology insisted on the 'wholly other' nature of God.

on *Romans* (1919) and in a huge, unfinished *Church Dogmatics*. A professor in Germany, after some hesitation Barth attacked Nazism, joined in the Barmen Declaration on the primacy of the Gospel against the state, and refused to swear allegiance to Hitler. Deprived of his chair at Bonn, he returned to Switzerland and remained there till his death. Barthian theology affected many people, even where some of its particular viewpoints were not shared. (*See also* BRUNNER; BULTMANN; CONFESSING CHURCH; DIALECTIC.)

Bartholomew

An APOSTLE mentioned only by name in the SYNOPTIC GOSPELS and Acts, sometimes identified with NATHANAEL (Mark 3:18; John 1:45). Feast day 24 August. (*See also* COLIGNY; HUGUENOTS.)

Bartimaeus

A blind beggar healed by Jesus near Jericho (Mark 10:46ff).

Base Communities

In 1975 at Vitoria in Brazil 70 people met to form what became known as Basic Ecclesial Communities to work out the faith and action of ordinary Catholic people. In 1997 there gathered over 2,000 delegates, including 57 bishops, black Brazilians and also Indians and Protestants. Leadership is exercised by the laity, often women, and this, with the inclusion of non-Catholics, worries some bishops. The Base Communities involve 2 million people, though CHARISMATIC renewal claims to reach four million. (*See also* BOFF; CAMARA; CHARISMATIC.)

Basil (330–79 CE)

Called 'the Great', one of three CAPPADOCIAN FATHERS of the Eastern Church. After education in Greek and Christian culture he became a HERMIT, but was called back to combat the ARIAN HERESY and became bishop of Caesarea.

Basil wrote books, a liturgy and a rule for monastics which became a foundation for ORTHODOXY.

basilica

From a Greek word for 'royal', this early form of church developed from secular law courts and commercial exchanges. Christian basilicas were characterized by wide naves with two aisles, high window openings and an altar in the apse which was decorated with mosaics. Today some privileged Roman Catholic churches are called basilicas; there are 11 minor ones in Rome. (*See also* ARCHITECTURE.)

Basilides

A second-century GNOSTIC at Alexandria who claimed to have secret traditions coming from PETER. He seems to have taught that the supreme God can only be described by negatives and that under him there are 365 CE intermediate worlds, with the God of the Jews in the lowest rank. (*See also* DEMIURGE.)

Baxter, Richard (1615–91)

Puritan theologian. Self-educated, he acquired immense knowledge and wrote 200 books, of which *The Saint's Everlasting Rest* is a devotional classic. Ordained in the Church of England, Baxter studied Nonconformity, championed moderation and declined the bishopric of Hereford. He joined the Parliamentary Army, but helped in the recall of Charles II. Baxter's views excluded him from the established Church in 1662, and he was persecuted by Judge Jeffreys, who called him a dog who should be whipped through the city. Baxter's tolerant spirit was expressed in his motto: 'In necessary things, unity; in doubtful things, liberty; in all things, charity.'

beadle

An official in the Church of Scotland responsible for the place of worship

St Mark's Basilica, Venice: Modelled on an Orthodox basilica in Constantinople on the plan of a Greek cross, St Mark's was completed in 883 CE, and burnt down and was rebuilt in 1071.

under the direction of the minister, and called 'the minister's man'.

beads

See PRAYER; ROSARY.

Beast

See ANTI-CHRIST.

beatific vision

The vision of God which is the final goal of SAINTS. In the middle ages it was debated whether God could be seen face to face by intuition, or whether this was impossible except through divine grace.

beatification

See VENERABLE.

beating bounds

See ROGATION DAYS.

Beatitudes

The blessings listed in the SERMON ON THE MOUNT in Matthew 5:3–11, with eight or nine blessings, and in the Sermon on the Plain in Luke 6:20–2, with four blessings followed by four woes. A Church of the Beatitudes near Capernaum marks the supposed site where Jesus uttered them, though an open-air setting is implied.

Becket, Thomas (1118–70)

English cleric. Born in London of Norman settlers, Thomas was early in public circles, fighting in France and being made Chancellor by Henry II. Created Archbishop of Canterbury in 1162, he defended the Church against royal encroachments. Henry tried to keep the clergy under his control, but Becket refused to accept this. Fleeing to France, from there he threatened disobedient bishops with excommunication and England with an interdict. He returned to England after apparently reaching agreement with Henry, but when he refused to absolve the dissenting bishops the king cried: 'Who will rid me of this turbulent priest?' Four knights went to Canterbury and slew Becket in his cathedral. There was an outcry throughout Europe; Becket was canonized in 1173, Henry did penance at his tomb and it became a place of pilgrimage to what Chaucer called 'the holy blissful martyr' (*Canterbury Tales*, Prologue). T. S. Eliot's play *Murder in the Cathedral* (1938) explores some of the issues of church–state conflict raised by this episode. Feast day 29 December.

Bede, Baeda (673–735 CE)

Regarded as the 'Father of English History'. Born near Monkwearmouth in Durham, he studied at a Benedictine monastery and then at Jarrow, where he spent most of his life. Bede was a great biblical scholar, and even while dying managed to complete a translation of John's Gospel from Latin into Anglo-Saxon. His most important writing was the *Ecclesiastical History of the English People*, based on written works and oral tradition. It was in Latin; King ALFRED translated it into Anglo-Saxon. Bede died in Jarrow and his bones were later taken to Durham Cathedral. He was soon popularly called the VENERABLE. Feast day 27 May.

Beelzebub

Name of a Philistine god in the Old Testament (2 Kgs. 1:16), where it means 'Lord of the Flies' (from which the title of William Golding's 1954 novel was taken). The word appears several times in the gospels (e.g. Mark 3:22), where Beelzebub is identified with SATAN, prince of the DEMONS. Beelzebub is 'next in crime' to Satan in Milton's *Paradise Lost* (Book 1).

Béguines

Charitable sisterhoods in the Netherlands from the 12th century. Their name was said to come from a revivalist preacher called Le Bègue, 'the stammerer' (d. 1177). They had male counterparts, the Béghards. They prayed and served the sick, but were free to marry. Some communities still exist in Belgium, at Louvain and Bruges. (*See also* ECKHART.)

Behmenists

See BOEHME.

Belial

An Old Testament name which appears only once in the New Testament, as Belial or Beliar, where it is identical with SATAN (2 Cor. 6:15). Milton wrote of Belial in *Paradise Lost* (1. 490) as the most lewd of spirits.

Bellarmine, Robert (1542–1621)

Italian theologian and JESUIT. He became a leading opponent of Protestantism during the COUNTER-REFORMATION, preferring reasoned argument to the dogmatism and abuse that had become common. He argued against James I of England, but was sympathetic to Galileo. Feast day 13 May.

bells

First mentioned in Christian worship in the sixth century, bells became popular all over Europe. They were blessed by bishops with holy water and oils, and given names and inscriptions. Bell-towers were erected, sometimes separate from the main church, and bell-ringers worked out complicated patterns of ringing. A 'passing bell' was rung at a death, and small bells are used at the altar in both Western and Eastern liturgies.

Benedict (480–547 CE)

Italian monk. Regarded as the 'Father of Western Monasticism'. He lived as a HERMIT in a cave for three years but was persuaded to become ABBOT of a community of monks and founded 12 other monasteries in Italy. The most famous was at Monte Cassino, where he spent the rest of his life. This monastery was virtually destroyed in fierce fighting between allied and German troops in the Second World War, but has been rebuilt. Benedict wrote the Rule which is followed by Benedictines and Cistercians, ordering a monk's life into three parts: prayer, study and work. The Benedictine Order, known as the Black Monks, is still widely spread. Feast day 21 March.

benediction

A word meaning 'BLESSING' generally, and applied also to an afternoon or evening service at which people are blessed with the RESERVED sacrament.

Benedictus

The canticle 'Blessed [Benedictus] be the Lord God of Israel', attributed to Zachariah at the naming of his son John the Baptist (Luke 1: 68ff). It is also a word used in GRACE before meals.

benefice

A church office or property held by an ecclesiastic, notably a RECTOR or VICAR. The duties of the benefice include the spiritual and moral welfare of the parishioners.

Bennett, John

See NEW AGE.

Berdyaev, Nikolas (1874–1948)

Russian philosopher, born in Kiev. At first he studied Marx and welcomed the 1917 revolution, but he came to reject atheistic COMMUNISM and returned to the ORTHODOX Church. He taught a 'spiritual Christianity', independent of doctrine and worship, which some saw as PANTHEISTIC. Berdyaev taught in Berlin and then in Paris, where he died. Among his works translated into English are *Freedom and the Spirit* and *The Destiny of Man*. (*See also* BULGAKOV.)

Bereans

See BARCLAY, JOHN.

Berg, David (b. 1919)

American religious leader. Born into a family of travelling evangelists in the USA, Berg worked for a time as pastor in the Christian Missionary Alliance and then with the ASSEMBLIES OF GOD. He led his own movement called variously the Children of God, the Family of Love and Heaven's Magic. His fundamentalism was part of a JESUS PEOPLE revival, millenarian in character and opposed to Church authority and American values. He introduced 'Hookers for Jesus', said to offer sexual favours to new members. Berg is called Moses David, or MO, or Dad, and spreads his Endtime teaching through MO letters.

Berkeley, George (1685–1753)

Anglican bishop and idealist philosopher. Born in Ireland, in 1728 he tried to found a college in Bermuda which failed for lack of funds; after holding a bishopric at Cloyne he retired to Oxford. Berkeley was the complete idealist, holding that only spirits truly exist; material objects 'exist' simply because they are perceived. To the question whether the 'tree in the quad' exists when no one perceives it, the Berkleian answer is that it is an object of the thought of God.

Bernadette, Marie Bernarde Soubirous (1844–79)

French nun and visionary. Daughter of a miller at Lourdes in southern France, from 1858 she had 18 visions of the Virgin Mary, showing her a miraculous spring of water and commanding the building of a church. After much publicity she became a nun at Nevers, and was canonized in 1933. Lourdes is one of the greatest European places of pilgrimage, where many healings are claimed. Feast day in France 18 February.

Bernard (1090–1153)

Born near Dijon in France, he became the first ABBOT of a newly founded monastery at Clairvaux, one of the chief Cistercian centres, and later founded over 70 monasteries. He drew up the statutes of the Knights TEMPLAR and preached in favour of the Second CRUSADE. Bernard was severely orthodox, attacking ABELARD and practising austerities. He wrote mystical works, expounding the Song of Songs in a spiritual sense. Feast day 20 August. (*See also* SONG OF SOLOMON.)

Bertha

See AUGUSTINE OF CANTERBURY.

Bérulle

See ORATORIANS.

Besant, Annie (1847–1933)

Leader of THEOSOPHY. Born in London, she was married at 20 to the Revd Frank Besant, from whom she separated by the age of 26. She became a socialist and atheist but was converted to theosophy and was president of its Society by 1907. Meanwhile she went to India and settled at Adyar, Madras. She searched for a 'new Christ' and discovered Krishnamurti, who eventually left the Theosophical Society. Her book *Esoteric Christianity* argued for a hidden core without which the RESURRECTION could not be understood.

Bethlehem

A small town five miles south of Jerusalem, from where came King David. The name means 'house of bread'. In Matthew's Gospel, Joseph

Bethlehem: Aerial view from the east, showing the Church of the Holy Nativity and Manger Square.

and Mary were there when the MAGI arrived, directed by a prophecy that a ruler of Israel would come from Bethlehem. John's Gospel (7:42) reflects debates over Bethlehem, which the evangelist sees as irrelevant since the Christ comes from God. The Church of the Holy Nativity in Bethlehem was built by CONSTANTINE in 330 CE and is one of the oldest in the world.

betting

See GAMBLING.

Beza, Theodore (1519–1605)

French Calvinist theologian. After studying law he went to Geneva, where he became professor of Greek and Reformed leader after the death of CALVIN in 1564. He had previously defended the burning of the Unitarian SERVETUS. Beza is renowned for producing the first critical text of the Greek New Testament, and for discovering a Greek–Latin manuscript which he presented to Cambridge University and which bears his name (CODEX BEZAE).

Bible

Christian holy scriptures. The title derives from a Greek word for 'books'. The Christian Church is the only major religion to include the scriptures of its parent religion (Judaism) within its own holy book: the Old Testament with the New, the respective titles implying an Old Covenant completed or replaced by a Messianic covenant. The Hebrew scriptures were divided into three sections: Law, Prophets and Writings, known to early Christians in the Greek (SEPTUAGINT) into which they had been translated for Greek-speaking Jews. The New Testament was written entirely in Greek, although Jesus and the first Christians were Jews and Jesus taught in Aramaic. Greek was replaced as the international language of Scripture by Latin versions in the Western Church, beginning with JEROME's production of the VULGATE at the end of the fourth century. Translation of the Bible into West European languages, directly from Hebrew and Greek, began with ERASMUS, LUTHER and TYNDALE in the 16th century.

The Bible was accepted as authoritative for faith with the fixing of the CANON in the fourth century, but it was not always taken literally (*see* ALLEGORY), and in modern times critical study of the text has brought new understanding, for example, in respect of the varied authorship of the PENTATEUCH or the priority of Mark among the gospel writers. FUNDAMENTALISTS, however, continue to treat the Bible as by one hand, divine, literally true and infallible even where self-contradictory. (*See also* APOCRYPHA; AUTHORIZED VERSION; CRITICISM.)

Bible Christians

A group resulting from a revival and division within early British METHODISM, when a Wesleyan 'LOCAL' PREACHER called William O'Bryan (1778–1868) became a 'travelling' preacher in Devon and Cornwall. In 1816 he formed a society of ARMINIAN Bible Christians at Shebbear in Devon. O'Bryan went to America where he preached but did not found a church; he died in Brooklyn. In 1907 the Bible Christians helped to form the United Methodist Church and in 1932 joined the Methodist Church in Great Britain.

bidding

In early times this meant simply praying, as in 'bidding the beads'. It later became used of direction to pray for certain things or people. In modern times, bidding prayers may begin, 'I bid you pray for . . . .'.

bigamy

See POLYGAMY.

birth control

Largely a modern problem; in earlier times high infant mortality kept down population numbers. The medieval Church taught, following Augustine, of the 'evil appliance' of contraception and the 'sin' of concupiscence, sexual desire. Modern statements by the Roman Catholic Church range from an encyclical by Pope Pius XI in 1930 condemning 'any use whatsoever' for the frustration of generation to the even stronger statement by John Paul II, ranking contraception with 'intrinsically evil acts'. However, Anglican and Protestant churches have issued statements on 'responsible parenthood', holding that the 'one-flesh' union of man and wife allows them freedom to use the gifts of science to promote or defer conception. (*See also* ABORTION.)

bishop

The English word comes indirectly from Greek *episkopos*, an overseer; the Old English word was *biscop*. In 1 Timothy 3, old translations gave 'bishop', but modern translations give 'leader' or 'overseer', since the hierarchy of bishop, priest and deacon was not established in the earliest Church. Later, bishops were elected by the DEAN and chapter of a CATHEDRAL, or by public acclamation (*see* AMBROSE). Pope John Paul II has directly appointed many bishops, conservative like himself, causing controversy.

Anglican and Lutheran churches generally retained the title of bishop, but it was abolished in Scotland and Calvinistic communities. American Methodists appointed bishops (*see* COKE), as have some modern AFRICAN churches. Bishops have a 'throne' in cathedrals, ordain priests and confirm laity. *Episcopi vagantes*, 'wandering bishops', were those who had been consecrated in an irregular manner. 'Flying bishops' is a modern term for 'provincial visitors', appointed in 1994 to encourage clergy opposed to women priests to 'remain with dignity' in the churches of England and Wales. (*See also* APOSTOLIC SUCCESSION; PRESBYTER; SUPERINTENDENT.)

Bishops' Bible

See PARKER.

Black Friars

Popular name for DOMINICAN monks, derived from the black mantles worn over white robes.

black letter days

In prayer books, lesser saints' days were printed in black to distinguish them from the RED LETTER DAYS of major festivals.

black mass

Popular name for a Mass for the Dead, from the black vestments that are worn. In the witchcraft fever of the middle ages it was supposed that witches performed an anti-Christian black mass, reversing traditional words or inserting immoral phrases and actions, but there is no clear evidence that such black masses were ever held. In Calvinistic Scotland it was claimed that long sermons or the Lord's Prayer were recited backwards by witches, again without evidence. (*See also* SATANISM; WITCHCRAFT.)

black rubric

A statement at the end of the Communion service in the Anglican Prayer Book of 1662 that 'the communicants should receive the same kneeling . . . but no adoration is intended' to the sacramental elements or to any 'corporal presence'. This was meant to exclude medieval ideas of the physical presence of Christ. Not strictly a rubric, this was a liturgical direction and was only called such after printers in the 19th century distinguished red and black letters. (*See also* BLACK LETTER DAYS; RUBRIC; TRANSUBSTANTIATION.)

black theology

In 1969 the National Committee of Black Churchmen in the United States declared that 'Black theology is a theology of "blackness". It emancipates black people from white racism.' The development of theology in positive ways, indigenous to black cultures, awaits teaching from African churches, especially in South Africa. (*See also* AFRICA, BLYDEN; CONE; FATHER DIVINE; LIBERATION THEOLOGY.)

Black Virgin

In 1531 a Mexican Indian, Juan Diego, claimed to have had a vision of the Virgin Mary, whose dark-coloured face was printed on his body cloth. A church was built near an old shrine of an Aztec earth goddess at Guadalupe near Mexico City, and it became an international centre for the Black Virgin which was untouched even during the religious persecutions in Mexico in the 1920s. In 1976 a huge new BASILICA was opened at Guadalupe, attracting 2 million pilgrims a year, many coming distances on their

Statue of the Black Virgin in Tarragona Cathedral, Spain.

knees. There are dark images of the Madonna in other countries, a notable one at Czestochowa in Poland receiving official visits from Pope John Paul II from 1979, and others at Tarragona and Montserrat in Spain.

blasphemy

From Greek words meaning to 'blame' or 'damage the reputation', blasphemy has the particular meaning of speech against God. The Bible said, 'you shall not take the name of the LORD your God in vain' (Exod. 20:7), and 'he that blasphemes the name of the LORD shall surely be put to death' (Lev. 24:16). In medieval times THOMAS AQUINAS noted that blasphemy cannot hurt God, and later thinkers said that an atheist cannot blaspheme a being in whom he does not believe; only a believer can do that. Blasphemy laws in the West have protected the established religion, rather than either all faiths or none. It is notable that people seem more offended by blasphemous words on television than by violent or immoral pictures. (*See also* SACRILEGE.)

Blavatsky, Helena Petrovna
(1831–91)

Born in the Ukraine, she went to New York and founded the Theosophical Society in 1875 with Colonel OLCOTT. In *Isis Unveiled* (1877), Blavatsky produced an amalgam of Western and Eastern ideas, which she claimed to have received from sages in Tibet. She taught of God as one's Higher Self, of karma, reincarnation and nirvana. (*See also* BESANT; TARA CENTRES; THEOSOPHY.)

Blessed Virgin

See MARY.

blessing

A declaration of divine favour, used during a liturgy, especially at the end. The right hand may be raised, with or without the sign of the cross. Blessings may be made of objects, water or oil, and at the anointing of the sick. 'Ask a blessing' is a popular phrase for saying grace. (*See also* BENEDICTION; GRACE; SIGN OF THE CROSS.)

blood

A powerful ritual and religious symbol that can have healthful or dangerous, cleansing or polluting connotations. The blood represented the life or soul (Lev. 17:14), forbidden in food; thus Jews and Muslims prepare flesh for consumption by draining blood away. Gentile Christians were told to abstain from blood (Acts 15:29), though this prohibition was probably soon neglected. 'The blood of Christ' is a phrase used in the Holy Communion service.

blood libel

See WILLIAM OF NORWICH.

Blyden, Edward Wilmot (1832–1912)

Born in the Danish West Indies, Blyden went to Liberia at the age of 17, taught in a mission school and was ordained a Presbyterian minister in 1858. Later he became Professor at Liberia College, Secretary of State and Ambassador in London. Blyden preached the dignity of African peoples and inspired a United Native African Church. He saw the major place of Islam in Africa, though he never left Christianity. His essays are collected in *Christianity, Islam and the Negro Race* (1887). (*See also* AFRICA; BLACK THEOLOGY; GARVEY.)

body

In the Bible the body is good, created by God, and its functions and appetites – sex, eating, drinking, and so on – are natural and legitimate. In Christian times there arose world- and body-renouncing teaching, GNOSTIC, MANICHAEAN and monastic, which encouraged ASCETIC attitudes and practices. On the other hand, the Church is

the Body of Christ, and the consecrated bread is also spoken of as 'the body of Christ' in the Holy Communion Service. (*See also* BLOOD; CORPUS CHRISTI.)

Boehme, Jakob (1575–1624)

LUTHERAN mystic, born in Saxony, known as the 'Teutonic philosopher'. His book *Aurora*, on God and evil, was condemned as heretical and he moved to Dresden. He published works on the INCARNATION, the divine essence, the matter of the universe, and ALLEGORY in Genesis and the EUCHARIST. Boehme was a difficult writer, using terms from theo-logy and also from astrology and alchemy; but his influence was considerable in German- and English-speaking countries, affecting Quakers and Romantics. His disciples, called Behmenists, joined up with the Quakers.

Boethius (480–524 CE)

Roman statesman and philosopher. His *Consolation of Philosophy* showed how the soul attains the vision of God. Probably Christian, he emphasized the place of reason. His work was popular in the middle ages, being translated by King ALFRED into Anglo-Saxon and by Chaucer into Middle English.

Boff, Leonardo (b. 1938)

Born in Brazil, after studying in Europe he became a Franciscan priest. He wrote widely in Portuguese and was one of the major LIBERATION THEOLOGIANS, which brought him into conflict with the Vatican. He described the relationships of the Church hierarchy and the laity in terms of Marxist class struggle, and was forbidden to speak openly. In 1992 Boff resigned from the priesthood and the Franciscan order 'to be free to work without impediment', signing himself 'brother, minor theologian and sinner'. He has written *Jesus Christ Liberator* and *The Base Communities Reinvent the Church*. (*See also* BASE COMMUNITIES; CAMARA; CARDENAL; GUTIÉRREZ.)

Bogomiles

A Bulgarian movement of the 10th century, probably called after the name of the founder Theophilus, Bogomile in Bulgarian. He and his followers taught a dualism, like the CATHARI, and flourished in the Balkans until absorbed by conquering Islam, when some of them became the Bosnian Muslims.

Bohemian Brethren

A movement of 15th-century Czech reformers who adopted poverty and renunciation to practise the teachings of the SERMON ON THE MOUNT. They stressed education and translated the whole Bible. In the 17th century they joined the MORAVIANS, and influenced early METHODISM. (*See also* HUSS; UNITAS FRATRUM.)

Bonhoeffer, Dietrich (1906–45)

German Protestant theologian and martyr. He studied in Berlin and New York and was pastor at a German church in London. He early opposed the Nazis, and chose to return to Germany to train pastors for the CONFESSING CHURCH. He was arrested in 1943, knew of the plot to assassinate Hitler in 1944, and was executed after its failure. Bonhoeffer's most famous publication, *Letters and Papers from Prison* (1951), challenged current views of religion and SECULARISM and influenced theological debate.

Boniface (680–754 CE)

An English monk from Crediton in Devon who became the Apostle of Germany. Originally called Wynfrith, he won success by cutting down a sacred oak of the god Thor (depicted in stained glass in Truro Cathedral), and he was able to organize the Church in Germany with the patronage of King Charles Martel and his sons. Boniface became Archbishop of Mainz but gave it up for missionary work in Frisia, where he and his companions were killed. He was buried in the abbey of Fulda which he had founded.

Book of Common Prayer

Monument of Archbishop Thomas CRANMER, comparable in influence to the AUTHORIZED VERSION of the Bible. Beginning with the First Prayer Book of Edward VI in 1549, Cranmer reformed and simplified medieval Latin services, putting them into common English. There were further revisions up to 1662, after which there were no more until 1928, when a further revision was rejected by Parliament. Roman Catholics and Nonconformists rejected this Prayer Book, though some used parts of it; Methodist forms came closest to the Anglican texts. Lovers of good English lament the decline in use of the Prayer Book, finding modern versions banal though they may cater for a wider range of needs. An Alternative Service Book, authorized for use in the Church of England, with variant rites, was published in 1980.

Book of Kells

A finely decorated manuscript of the gospels in an Irish hand, now at Trinity College, Dublin. Tradition ascribed it to the sixth-century monk COLUMBA, but the book is probably from the eighth century. It was named after the monastery at Kells in Meath. (*See also* LINDISFARNE.)

Booth, William (1829–1912)

The founder of the SALVATION ARMY. Of partly Jewish origin, he became a Methodist minister. Appalled by conditions in the East End of London, Booth and his wife Catherine (*née* Mumford) left Methodism to hold open-air mission services outside the Blind Beggar public house in Whitechapel from 2 July 1865. At first called the Christian Revival Association, their movement was renamed the Salvation Army, with Booth as its first General, in 1878. The Army developed evangelical and social work and Booth spent his life organizing it. His major published work was *In Darkest England and the Way Out* (1890). On his death his son William Bramwell Booth became General.

General William Booth: Booth organized the Salvation Army with discipline, orthodox evangelical doctrine and social service, aiming at conversion of individuals and care of the needy.

Borgia, Cesare (1475–1507)

Illegitimate son of Borgia Pope Alexander VI, Cesare was made a cardinal before he was 20. Given a dispensation to marry, he became a competent soldier and recovered many papal provinces. Machiavelli's *The Prince* is said to have been based on Cesare. His sister was the equally notorious Lucrezia Borgia, also a papal child.

born again

According to John (3·3), Jesus told Nicodemus that 'unless one is born again [or 'from above'] he cannot see the kingdom of God.' In theory all Christians are born again, at baptism by water and the Spirit, and at confirmation. 'Born-again Christians' is a modern title claimed especially by those who emphasize emotion and experience, knowing Jesus, putting off the old self, and displaying spiritual gifts. (*See also* CHARISMATIC.)

Bosanquet, Mary

See FLETCHER, JOHN WILLIAM.

Bosnia

See BOGOMILES.

Bossuet, Jacques Bénigne (1627–1704)

Noted French preacher, popular at the court of Louis XIV, and bishop of Meaux. He disputed with Protestants, approved the revocation of the tolerant Edict of NANTES (1685), and attacked biblical criticism and mysticism. (*See also* FÉNELON.)

Bourne, Hugh

See PRIMITIVE METHODISTS.

boy bishop

It was a medieval custom, especially prevalent in England, to elect a boy to fulfil the functions of a bishop from St Nicholas' Day, 6 December, until the Feast of the Holy Innocents on 28 December. The purpose was to show the reverence given to childhood in the gospels at Christmas time. (*See also* MISRULE.)

Bradlaugh, Charles (1833–91)

Brought up an Anglican, he became an atheist and struggled for freedom of thought. When elected member of Parliament for Northampton he refused to take the oath; he was several times excluded and re elected until he was allowed to make an affirmation, as Quakers had done. Bradlaugh wrote with Annie BESANT in the *National Reformer*, working for freedom of the press, but left her when she became a THEOSOPHIST.

Brahmo Samaj

See RAM MOHUN ROY.

Braide, Garrick (1880–1918)

Nigerian Christian prophet, from the Niger delta region, known as the Second Elijah for preaching and healing. Braide revived the Anglican Niger Delta Pastorate, preached against animistic cults and worked for an indigenous church liturgy. After early Anglican support, Braide's movement broke away to form the Christ Army Church, the major branch of which survives with some 40,000 members. (*See also* AFRICA.)

Branch Davidians

American ADVENTIST group, originally the Davidian Seventh-Day Adventist Association, led by Mrs Houteff who predicted that God would restore the Davidic monarchy on 22 April 1959. When this failed the Davidian Association was dissolved, but a splinter group, the Branch Davidians, continued. Leadership came to Vernon Howell (1958–93); he took the name of David Koresh or Cyrus, who in Isaiah 45:1 is called Messiah. The Branch Davidians settled on 'Mount Carmel' in Waco, Texas, and stockpiled arms for the final world conflict. This attracted government attention and led to a siege in 1993 when the settlement was destroyed, Koresh and others killed, and many members arrested. The movement continues but with no clear leadership.

Bray, Billy (1794–1868)

Popular Cornish Methodist preacher, converted from a miner's life and hard drinking. Billy had homely ways of referring to God as 'Feyther' and the devil as 'Old Smutty Face', and there were many tales of his supernatural encounters. Several chapels in Cornwall were named after him.

Bray, Vicar of

The parson, celebrated in the ballad that bears his name, who held his living through different reigns and regimes has not been clearly identified. One candidate was Simon Aleyn, who lasted through the times of Henry VIII, Edward VI, Mary and Elizabeth. But the vicar of the popular song lives under Charles II, James II, William III, Anne and George I, and the ballad seems to date from 1720.

bread and wine

Eastern ORTHODOX churches use leavened bread in the EUCHARIST, but Catholics in the West adopted unleavened. The Anglican Prayer Book of 1552 permitted either, and variety continues, with FREE CHURCHES using ordinary bread. Fermented grape juice has traditionally been used for the wine, though some say it should be non-alcoholic; some Free Churches insist it should be unfermented. *See also* BLOOD; BODY.

Breastplate of St Patrick

A strongly Trinitarian Irish hymn, attributed to PATRICK (389–461) though traceable only to the ninth century. Translated into English by Mrs C. F. Alexander in 1889, its traditional Irish melody was arranged by C. V. Stanford.

Breeches Bible

See GENEVA BIBLE.

Brethren

See DARBY.

Brethren of the Common Life

A devotional movement of the 14th century, first led by Geert de Groote, a canon of Utrecht, who preached against clerical abuses. He and his followers founded schools all over the Netherlands. Among the Brethren were Thomas à KEMPIS and NICHOLAS OF CUSA.

Brethren of the Free Spirit

A name given to mystical movements in the middle ages, which rejected church authority to live in the freedom of the Spirit.

Brethren of the Lord

See BROTHERS AND SISTERS OF JESUS.

breviary

Roman Catholic prayer book, from Latin *breviarium*, a summary, bringing together prayers, psalms, hymns and readings for different hours of the day. A *Breviarium Romanum* was issued in 1568 and a modern version in 1911, from which all priests, monks and nuns should recite.

Bridget (1303–73)

Mystic, patron saint of Sweden and founder of the Brigittine Order. Her *Revelations* (published in 1492) gave accounts of mystical experiences and were very popular. Feast day 8 October.

British and Foreign Bible Society (BFBS)

Founded in London in 1804 and strictly interdenominational, it has aimed at distributing the Bible throughout the world, without commentary. The whole Bible is published in all major and many minor languages, and portions of the New Testament in others.

British Israelites

Ten tribes from northern Israel were deported to Assyria in 722 BCE (2 Kgs. 17). They disappeared from history. In the 19th century some Christian fundamentalists thought that the British were these lost tribes citing as evidence the spread of the British Empire and later British expansion in the Holy Land and Middle East after World War I. The British Israel theory was taken up and enlarged for the USA and Canada at a convention in Detroit in 1930. It became Identity Christianity, finding texts in the infallible Bible to trace the lost tribes to America; the USA was proclaimed the New Jerusalem and the Jews denigrated as the 'synagogue of Satan'. British Israel has declined but Identity Christianity has spread and divided and anticipates the millennium. (*See also* WORLDWIDE CHURCH OF GOD.)

Brother Lawrence (1605–91)

A French soldier who became a lay brother in a Carmelite monastery in Paris, where he worked in the kitchen. His meditations, *The Practice of the Presence of God*, were simple devotions and became popular.

brothers and sisters of Jesus

James, Joseph, Jude and Simon are named as brothers in Mark 6:3 and in Matthew 13:55; sisters of Jesus are also mentioned. TERTULLIAN in the second century and HELVIDIUS in the fourth gave the natural interpretation that these were blood brothers and sisters of Christ, further children of Joseph and Mary. Some writers suggested, without biblical evidence, that they were children of Joseph by a previous marriage or even cousins of Jesus. But a firm modern interpretation accepts that they were other children in the Holy Family, which with Jesus as the first-born and the parents would have had nine or more members. (*See also* HOLY FAMILY; JAMES; JUDE; VIRGIN BIRTH.)

Browne, Robert (1550–1633)

PURITAN minister who established independent congregations, which were called Separatists, in Norwich and elsewhere. He took some of them to Holland, returned to Scotland and finally entered the Church of England. He became a master at St Olave's school in Southwark and rector at Achurch. He died in gaol, where he had been sent for having assaulted a constable. Browne had a lively temper but considerable influence on the growth of CONGREGATIONALISM, whose early members were called Brownists.

Brunner, Emil (1889–1966)

Swiss Protestant theologian who reacted against liberal theology, while retaining some of its views, for example questioning the VIRGIN BIRTH. He was repudiated by BARTH in *No: Answer to Emil Brunner.* Brunner wrote an important study of the work of Christ in *The Mediator.*

Bruno

See CARTHUSIANS.

Bucer, Martin (1491–1551)

A Dominican monk, he came under the influence of ERASMUS and LUTHER, obtained dispensation from monastic vows and married in 1522. He instituted changes in worship in Alsace and became leader of Reformed Churches in Switzerland after the death of ZWINGLI in 1531. He went to England where he was made professor at Cambridge. Bucer helped CRANMER with the BOOK OF COMMON PRAYER, especially the Ordinal (service of clerical ordination). He was buried in Great St Mary's at Cambridge, but under MARY TUDOR his body was exhumed and burned.

Buchman, Frank (1878–1961)

American Lutheran minister of Swiss descent. He visited Europe and Asia and found a larger ministry among students. At Oxford in 1929 he developed the Oxford Group, which spread with visits to America, Europe and South Africa. In 1938 in London Buchman inaugurated a Moral Rearmament movement, stressing four absolute moral principles: honesty, selflessness, purity and love.

Buddhism

See BARLAAM.

Bulgakov, Sergius (1870–1944)

Son of a Russian priest, he became attracted to Communism but returned to the ORTHODOX Church, first as a layman and then as a priest. He escaped from Russia after the revolution of 1917 and became Dean of the Orthodox Theological Academy in Paris. Bulgakov wrote of Sophiology, reviving Eastern teachings on the relation of God and the world through the Divine Sophia or Wisdom. Condemned in his own country for political reasons, he was welcomed in the Western ecumenical movement. (*See also* BERDYAEV.)

Bultmann, Rudolf (1884–1976)

German New Testament scholar who sympathized with some of the views of Karl BARTH but developed historical scepticism in biblical studies. Bultmann's 'demythologization' was applied not only to narratives, such as the VIRGIN BIRTH, but to the mythical conception of the universe, the three-storeyed structure of heaven, earth and hell, which affected the outlook of the Bible. Bultmann was critical of tradition but tried to apply the Gospel message to modern society. (*See also* SECULARISM.)

Bunting, Jabez (1779–1858)

Wesleyan Methodist minister, called the second founder of Methodism (after John WESLEY). He began with a society and made it into a church, completing its detachment from the Church of England. Bunting was president of the Wesleyan Conference four times (the usual term being one year), and though he taught church self-government he ruled with a firm hand. Despite secessions he did not waver, controlling the spiritual interests of half a million people like the head of a religious order.

Bunyan, John (1628–88)

Called by the poet Rudyard Kipling in 1917 'A tinker out of Bedford', he was largely self-educated from study of the Bible. He fought on the Parliamentary side in the Civil War and became preacher to an independent congregation in Bedford, so popular that he was imprisoned for most of the years 1660–72, though he was occasionally let out to preach. In gaol he wrote part of his classics PILGRIM'S PROGRESS and *Grace Abounding*, the latter one of the most moving Christian autobiographies. Bunyan died in London and was buried in Bunhill Fields, alongside other Nonconformists. The following year came the TOLERATION ACT which gave some freedom to Dissenting chapels.

burial

Ritual interment of the dead has been practised in the Church since earliest days. At first attendants wore white robes and burial was an occasion of joy, but later the service became 'black' and prayers were for deliverance from hell. Joy returned in evangelical movements, and Charles WESLEY wrote: 'Rejoice for a brother deceased, our loss is his infinite gain.' Prayers for the DEAD were offered, with REQUIEM MASSES and cemetery visits at the feast of ALL SOULS in Catholic churches. Cremation has become common in modern times; it is allowed in the Anglican revised Prayer Book, and remains more prevalent in Britain than in Catholic countries of Europe. *See also* DEAD, PRAYERS FOR; REQUIEM.

burning heretics

See DE HAERETICO COMBURENDO.

Bushnell, Horace (1802–76)

American CONGREGATIONAL minister who pioneered liberal theology in New England and also influenced Britain. He restated doctrines of the Trinity and atonement without recourse to legalistic theories, and explained MIRACLES as part of the laws of nature.

Butler, Joseph (1692–1752)

A Presbyterian who became an Anglican minister and bishop of Durham. His *Analogy of Religion* (1736) sought to expound both natural and revealed religion, against the DEISTS who held that the deity had no interest in human affairs. (*See also* REVELATION.)

Butler, Josephine (1828–1906)

Social reformer who crusaded against the 'white slave trade', the treatment of prostitutes in seaports and military towns. She was married to a canon of Winchester and led a life of frequent prayer based on that of CATHARINE OF SIENA.

Buxton, Thomas Fowell (1786–1845)

A trader and Member of Parliament, of Anglican and Quaker sympathies. He worked to modify the criminal law and succeeded Wilberforce at the head of the anti-slavery movement, piloting the freedom of slaves in British possessions in 1833. His book *The African Slave Trade and its Remedy* (1839) proposed agricultural development, though the Niger expedition to Lokoja was a disaster.

BVM

See MARY.

Byrd, William (1543–1623)

Born in Lincoln, he became organist at Lincoln Cathedral and later co-organist at the Chapel Royal with Thomas TALLIS. Of Catholic sympathies, Byrd wrote MASSES which were used in the Church of England. He also composed ANTHEMS and secular choral music.

Byzantium

See CONSTANTINE; CRUSADES; HAGIA SOPHIA; ORTHODOX CHURCH.

C

cabbala

See KABBALA.

Caedmon (d. 680 CE)

A layman who composed verse in praise of God; after an angelic vision in middle life he was admitted to Whitby Abbey to develop his skills. He was the first Anglo-Saxon Christian poet, singing hymns on biblical stories; only one has survived, in a manuscript by BEDE.

Caiaphas

High priest in Jerusalem at the trial of Jesus (Matt. 26:3ff). According to the Jewish historian JOSEPHUS, Caiaphas was a protégé of the Roman governor Pontius PILATE and held office for ten years, longer than any other high priest. The comment in John 11:50 is apt, that Caiaphas sacrificed Jesus to save the whole nation from perishing. (*See also* SADDUCEES.)

calendar

The Julian Calendar was introduced by Julius Caesar in 46 BCE, a year of 365 days fitted to the sun's cycle, with an extra day every fourth year. In the sixth century a monk, Dionysius Exiguus, adapted this calendar to Christian usage by starting it 'in the year of our Lord', Anno Domini, the year after the birth of Christ. But the Julian Calendar was not accurate, being ten days out from the sun's year; consequently, in 1582 Pope Gregory XIII proclaimed his New Style or Gregorian Calendar which is still in use. At first only Roman Catholic states accepted the new dating, but others gradually fell into line, Britain accepting it in 1752 and Russia in 1917.

The Christian calendar fitted uneasily into the Julian system. EASTER and PENTECOST had been observed from the beginning as they were both Jewish and Christian feasts, though geared to a lunar cycle. In the Gregorian calendar the new year was 1 January, though the Christian year began four weeks earlier at ADVENT. Thus there were both fixed feasts, like CHRISTMAS, and movable feasts, like Easter. Saints' and martyrs' celebrations were also fitted into the church's year, along with other commemorations. A reform of the Roman Calendar of Saints in 1969 omitted a number of legendary saints, or relegated them to local use. A proposal for a World Calendar has not yet been adopted. But the inter-religious situation has brought the adoption of CE for the Common Era, in place of AD, and BCE for Before the Common Era, in place of BC, Before Christ. (*See also* HAGIOGRAPHY; OLD CALENDARISTS; SABBATH.)

Calvary

From Latin *calvaria*, 'skull': the place of the crucifixion of Jesus, called *kranion* in Greek (Luke 23:33), and Golgotha in

Hebrew (Mark 15:22). Ths site is not certainly known, though there is a place marked in the Church of the Holy Sepulchre in Jerusalem. A Calvary is a shrine with a crucifix, found in many places on the European continent. (*See also* GARDEN TOMB.)

Calvin, John (1509–64)

A leader of the REFORMATION. Born in France, he studied for the Catholic priesthood but came to see the need for Church reform. Threatened with persecution, he went to Switzerland and organized the Reformation in Geneva. Calvin and his party imposed a theocratic rule, with a consistory ruling the lives of citizens and banning games and dancing. Calvin's *Institutes of the Christian Religion*, published in Latin and French, was a massive, logical and severe exposition of Reformed theology. Calvinism became a reforming movement distinct from LUTHERAN or ANGLICAN reforms. Accepted in Scotland through John KNOX, its hold on English Nonconformity was weakened by the rise of ARMINIAN Methodism, but it spread to many American communities. In Wales it was strengthened by revivalism, producing a constitutional deed of Welsh Calvinistic Methodism in 1826. (*See also* INSTITUTES; SERVETUS.)

Camara, (Dom) Helder Pessoa (b. 1909)

Brazilian cleric and theologian. Born in Brazil, he was ordained and became involved in a movement to provide basic education for the poor. At first rightwing, Camara decided to devote his life to justice for the masses, and as a consequence was called a 'Communist', 'subversive' and a non-person who must not be named. From 1965 he was archbishop in the poverty-stricken north-east; he retired in 1984, though remaining involved with the Base Ecclesial Communities. His writings have been translated into many languages, and

include *Church and Colonialism* and *Hoping against all Hope*. (*See also* BASE COMMUNITIES; BOFF.)

Cambridge Platonists

Not a party nor all at Cambridge, they were a group of 17th-century philosophical theologians who believed that reason could bring the soul to a vision of God, quoting 'The spirit of man is the candle of the Lord' (Prov. 20:27). They included Cudworth, More, Smith and Whichcote. (*See also* THEISM.)

Cambridge Seven

See STUDD.

Camisards

French Protestant groups. After the revocation of the tolerant Edict of NANTES by Louis XIV in 1685, harsh attempts were made to suppress French Protestantism. In the south revolt was led by inspired prophets called Camisards, perhaps from the 'shirt' (*camise*) which they wore as disguise in night attacks on government troops. There was violence on both sides; many Camisards and other HUGUENOTS were killed or tortured. They are remembered to this day by tablets in Protestant churches in the Cévennes mountains and in towns like Montpellier and Nîmes.

camp meeting

In the 19th century the American frontier was the scene of revivalist meetings which preached of God or the devil, heaven or hell. There were emotional gatherings and some gave birth to HOLINESS denominations producing 'holy laughter', 'barking' and 'jerks', like the TORONTO BLESSING of the late 20th century. Camp meetings continue in PENTECOSTALIST movements; participants are accommodated in country houses or tents around camp fires, far from the temptations of cities.

Campbell, Alexander
(1788–1866)

Irish-American church leader. Born in Northern Ireland, he went to America, after a shipwreck, and joined his father's Christian Association, based on the Bible alone. He led a Restoration Movement and Disciples of Christ, popularly known as Campbellites. Differences over scripture, and the North–South conflict, gave rise to three main groups: the Disciples of Christ (now the Christian Church), independent Christian churches, and Churches of Christ.

Campion, Edmund (1540–81)

Missionary and martyr. A Londoner, he went to Oxford and was chosen to welcome Queen Elizabeth there. Although an Anglican deacon, Campion had Catholic leanings, went to Dublin and then to Douai, and was ordained into the Jesuit order in 1578. He returned to England as a Jesuit missionary and preached in London and Lancashire. He was charged with conspiracy against the crown, tortured and executed at Tyburn. He was canonized in 1970. Feast day 1 December. (*See also* DOUAI; SOUTHWELL.)

Campus Crusade for Christ

Founded by Bill Bright in 1951 at the University of California, this is one of the largest evangelical college fellowships, with home and campus ministries, as well as athletic and military activities.

Candle

Lights were used in early church processions, and candles replaced them on or beside the altar. Votive ('vowed') candles are lit before statues or for special devotions. Some churches give a candle to parents at infant baptism, as a sign that Christ is the light of the world. A candle wrapped in barbed wire is a reminder of prisoners of conscience. (*See also* ALTAR.)

Candlemas

A feast on 2 February for the Presentation of Christ in the Temple, 40 days after his birth (Luke 2:22ff); also called the Purification of Saint Mary the Virgin. Candles were blessed and carried in procession. (*See also* CHURCHING; NUNC DIMITTIS.)

Candomblé

The meaning of the term is not clear but is said to combine 'custom' and 'black'. Candomblé preserves names and cults of some West African deities, chiefly Yoruba and Dahomean, in groups known under both African and Catholic saints' names at sacred sites in Northern Brazil. There is belief in a supreme God, beneath whom are spirits that 'mount' their followers during rituals of possession. (*See also* SANTERIA.)

canon

From the Greek for 'rod' or 'rule'. 'Canon' is used to denote the list of books of Scripture accepted as authentic and authoritative. The New Testament canon was primarily the four gospels and the thirteen epistles ascribed to Paul, arranged roughly in order of length from Romans to Philemon. There were doubts about Hebrews, Revelation and some smaller books, but by 382 a council at Rome listed the books that we now have, along with those accepted as canonical in Judaism, the Old Testament.

Canon is also a term for a member of clergy belonging to a cathedral and responsible for its services.

Canon law was so called to distinguish the law of the Church from civil law.

The Canon of the Mass is a term for the prayer of consecration which contains the Words of Institution of the Lord's Supper.

Canonization is the process in the Roman Catholic Church whereby a departed person is declared by the Pope

A woman in a trance state on the floor during a ritual of Candomblé, Brazil: Under the direction of priests and priestesses, mediums are held to be possessed by spirits of African and Christian origin.

to be a SAINT. The new saint's name is put in the list of saints, he or she is invoked in prayers, and churches may be dedicated in his or her memory.

Canossa

In 1077 an investiture controversy, wherein the German emperor Henry IV invested new bishops with a ring, led to his excommunication by Pope Gregory VII (Hildebrand). Henry had to spend three days barefoot in the snow at the Pope's lodging at Canossa in northern Italy before the ban was lifted. In 1872 a 'cultural conflict' (*Kulturkampf*) between the Prussian state and the Vatican prompted Chancellor Bismarck to declare: 'We will not go to Canossa.' The conflict subsided under a new Pope.

cantata

Originally an elaborate vocal solo, this developed into a series of recitals ending with a chorale. The cantata grew into the oratorio, famous examples of which were composed by Bach and Handel. Bach's popular Christmas Oratorio comprises six separate cantatas.

Canterbury

City in Kent, home to the mother church of the ANGLICAN Communion and see of the Archbishop of the southern province of England, styled since the 14th century the PRIMATE of All England. The see was founded by AUGUSTINE in 597, an existing British church being reconsecrated and a monastery established; the great present CATHEDRAL was built from the 13th century. The archbishop and his office are often called simply Canterbury, and take precedence in the worldwide Anglican Communion.

canticles

Songs used in church liturgy, apart from the Psalms and HYMNS, such as BENEDICTUS, MAGNIFICAT, NUNC DIMITTIS and TE DEUM.

The term Canticles is also applied to the Song of Songs (SONG OF SOLOMON).

A Canticle of the Sun was attributed to FRANCIS OF ASSISI, popularly translated as 'All creatures of our God and King'.

Canudos

A fortified town near Bahia in Brazil, scene of a messianic uprising in 1893–7 led by Antonio Maciel who healed the sick, repaired churches and predicted the end of the world. Military expeditions were sent against the Canudos devotees in which Antonio died of starvation and 20,000 followers perished in a fourth siege.

Cao Dai

A Vietnamese new religion mingling Buddhism, Confucianism and some Western philosophy and religion. Cao Dai means 'high tower', the name of the creator God who rules with a mother goddess, representing male and female principles, giving harmony to the universe. Founded in 1919, the movement claims more than 2 million adherents. Reverence is paid to Buddha, Confucius, Jesus, Muhammad, and even figures of French culture like Joan of Arc and Victor Hugo.

capital punishment

The Church accepted the use of the death sentence from legal systems and the Bible: 'Whoso sheddeth man's blood, by man shall his blood be shed' (Gen. 9:6). Article 37 in the BOOK OF COMMON PRAYER stated that 'the Laws of the Realm may punish Christian men with death'. However, the Lollards declared that manslaughter 'by pretended law of justice for a temporal cause' was contrary to the New Testament, and Quakers confirmed that. In modern times the deterrent effect of capital punishment has been denied, while retribution seems contrary to Christian teaching. Most European states have now abolished capital punishment, but many American states retain it. In 1994 a new CATECHISM of the Roman Catholic Church allowed capital punishment, but commentators considered it was rarely if ever justifiable.

Cappadocian Fathers

Three Eastern theologians who helped in the defeat of ARIANISM at the Council of Constantinople in 381. They were BASIL of Caesarea, Gregory Nazianzus and Gregory of Nyssa.

Capuchins

Members of a Franciscan order who wear cowls (Italian: *capuche*), sandals and beards. Wishing to return to the simplicity and austerity of the original Franciscans, the Capuchins followed a more severe Rule than the rest of the Order. At first they met opposition, but they were powerful preachers and missionaries, and effective against the Reformation. Now less severe, they remain strict and active workers. (*See also* FRANCIS OF ASSISI.)

Cardenal, Ernesto (b. 1925)

Born in Nicaragua, he went to a Trappist monastery in the USA and became a priest. Back home he taught the social and political implications of the Bible and after the 1979 revolution became Minister of Culture in the Sandinista government. For this he was rebuked by the Pope, wagging his finger at the kneeling priest in 1983, since priests should not engage in politics. He refused to resign or repent, and was suspended from the priesthood. His brother Fernando, also a priest and government minister for a time, rejoined the Jesuits but as a novice. Ernesto Cardenal eventually resigned from the government over its autocracy and corruption. He remains critical of 'excess of conservatism' in the Church, among other places in OPUS DEI and Ulster, and he writes poetry for the people. (*See also* LIBERATION THEOLOGY; TORRES.)

Cardinal

Derived from Latin for a 'hinge': a priest attached to a church, and then chiefly a cleric in Rome. The cardinals form a college, whose duty is to elect a new Pope. They meet privately in a conclave, and announce the election by a sign of smoke. Originally 70 in number, in 1998 there were 166 cardinals, but only 123 could vote as those over the age of 80 were excluded. Pope John Paul II has increased the number of cardinals more than any other Pope, apparently to try to ensure a conservative successor.

The title 'cardinal' was retained for two minor canons at St Paul's Cathedral in London.

cardinal virtues

Also known as natural virtues. In Christian tradition they were taken over from the Greek philosophers who named them as prudence, justice, temperance and courage. To these are added the theological virtues of faith, hope and charity or love. (*See also* AGAPÉ.)

Carey, William (1761–1834)

Born at Paulerspury near Towcester in Northamptonshire, he was a shoemaker but taught himself Latin, Greek, Hebrew, French and Dutch. He joined the BAPTISTS in 1783 and became a minister. A founder of the Baptist Missionary Society, Carey went to India and settled at Serampore in Bengal. He translated the New Testament into Bengali and eventually the whole or parts of the Bible into 24 other Indian languages. He became Professor of Sanskrit, Bengali and Marathi at Fort William College in Calcutta and held the position for 30 years. He edited the Hindu religious classic *Ramayana* ('The Story of Rama') and helped to bring about the abolition in 1829 of *sati* (suttee), widow-burning.

cargo cults

Religious movements in the Pacific Islands of Melanesia which awaited the arrival of trade goods or cargoes, like those enjoyed by Westerners. Some 200 cults were reported in the 19th and 20th centuries which either rejected the religion of the missionaries or combined it with indigenous traditions. Some cargo cults were short-lived; others survive in Christian congregations in independent states. (*See also* HALLELUJAH MOVEMENT.)

Carmelites

The Order of Our Lady of Mount Carmel was founded there, near Haifa in Israel, in 1154, though it claims to be descended from Elijah and his activities on the mountain (1 Kgs. 18:19ff) Carmelites practised POVERTY and VEGETARIANISM, but after the CRUSADES they migrated to Europe and became MENDICANT FRIARS. TERESA and JOHN OF THE CROSS formed the Discalced (barefoot) Carmelites, in contrast to the Calced of the Ancient Observance. There are men and women in both branches, popularly called White Friars from their white and brown habits.

carnival

From Latin meaning 'put away flesh', this is the name of three days of revelry in Europe before LENT and the renunciation of flesh. It ends with Mardi Gras, 'Fat Tuesday'. (*See also* SHROVE TUESDAY.)

carol

A simple rhythmic song, the origin of the term is obscure. Carols appeared in England from the 14th century, including but not only at Christmas. Declining in popularity after the REFORMATION, carols were revived in the 19th century and there has been a flood in recent times, some trite but others with meaning and vigour.

Carthusians

A contemplative monastic order founded in 1084 by Bruno at the Grande Chartreuse or Charterhouse in the

French Alps (Latin: *Cartusiani montes*). He built a monastery there, which was many times destroyed and rebuilt, and other houses were established in different countries. From 1901 the famous Chartreuse liqueur was made by monks at Tarragona in Spain, until 1931.

Cassino

See BENEDICT.

cassock

A long gown worn under liturgical vestments. The name is of uncertain origin. Called *soutane* in French, it is usually black for clergy; bishops wear violet cassocks, cardinals red and the Pope white. But nowadays ministers of many churches wear cassocks of various colours.

casuistry

From Latin for a 'case': the application of moral principles to specific cases, considering whether particular judgements are in accordance with general rules. In a negative sense the term is used to denote quibbling or petty reasoning. (*See also* PASCAL; PROBABILISM.)

catacombs

Underground Christian burial-places, especially in Rome where they extend for several hundred miles with galleries and niches for bodies. It was once thought that Christians hid or worshipped there regularly, but the chief services were the anniversaries of MARTYRS. Wall paintings in the catacombs are early examples of Christian art and inscriptions give a guide to historical events.

catechism

From the Greek word meaning 'to instruct': a term applied to oral and then written teachings of the faith. Important were LUTHER's German Catechism (1529), the Heidelberg Catechism (1563), the Westminster Catechism (1647), the Roman Catechism (1566) and the latest Catechism of the Catholic Church (English version 1994).

A catechist in the early Church was a teacher of new converts and children. In modern times it is a title given to LAY PREACHERS and pastors in mission or independent churches in Africa and elsewhere.

A catechumen is one undergoing instruction before BAPTISM.

Cathari

From the Greek word meaning 'pure': a name applied especially to those in the middle ages who held, like the ancient Manichees, that matter was evil, including human reproduction, and salvation was attained by self- and world-denial. The 'perfect' renounced marriage, war, oaths and eating flesh, though the majority of 'believers' could hold property, marry and enjoy material things. The Cathari reacted against the corruption of society and Church, and were fought by CRUSADERS and the INQUISITION. (*See also* ALBIGENSES; BOGOMILES; MANICHAEISM.)

Catharine of Alexandria
(fourth century)

Saint and martyr. She was killed by being bound to a wheel and beheaded. She gave her name to the Catharine Wheel. Feast day 25 November.

Catharine of Genoa
(1447–1510)

Italian mystic who remained in the world and, with her husband, cared for the sick in a hospital in Genoa. Feast day 15 September. (*See also* HÜGEL.)

Catharine of Siena (1347–80)

Italian nun who served the sick and poor. She joined the Dominican third order, and tried to persuade the Pope to return from Avignon to Rome. Her life was an inspiration to the Englishwoman Josephine Butler. Feast day 30 April.

catharsis

From the Greek word for 'cleansing': freeing from impediments which hinder union with God. Spiritual progress has traditionally been described in three stages: catharsis or purgation, illumination, and contemplation. (*See also* JOHN OF THE CROSS.)

cathedral

The principal church of a DIOCESE, containing the 'chair' (Greek: *cathedra*) of a BISHOP. Originally the cathedral was the care of the bishop himself, but with his increasing duties the administration went to a DEAN and chapter, with the bishop visiting on special occasions when he sat in his throne. At the DISSO-LUTION OF THE MONASTERIES some monastic foundations were added to the traditional cathedrals, and new cathe-

Chartres cathedral, west front: The most famous French Gothic building, dedicated in 1260. Particularly notable are the fine stained-glass windows and the rich sculpture.

drals have been built. The largest cathedral in the world, at Yamoussoukro in Côte d'Ivoire, West Africa, was consecrated by Pope John Paul II in 1990, dedicated to Our Lady of Peace. (*See also* SEE.)

Catholic

From the Greek word meaning 'general' or 'universal', the term Catholic has been used to indicate the whole Church and its faith, believed 'everywhere, always, and by all'. Since the separation of the Western and Eastern churches in 1054 (see chart on following page), the two branches have been known respectively as Catholic and ORTHODOX, though both would claim the two titles. After the REFORMATION the name Catholic was loosely used of ROMAN CATHOLICISM, though Anglicans claim to be Catholic, and so do Free Churches who may use or accept the CREED which affirms faith in 'the holy catholic church'. (*See also* ANGLO-CATHOLICISM; HERESY; ORTHODOXY.)

Catholic Apostolic Church

A movement which prepared for the Second Coming of Christ by return to some of the offices and practices of the early Church. Apostles, prophets, evangelists, pastors and teachers were appointed by Henry Drummond in 1832, with Edward IRVING, and members were also known as Irvingites. They built a large church in Gordon Square, London, now the Anglican University Church. At its height the Catholic Apostolic Church had congregations across northern Europe from Denmark to Latvia, and its central church in Berlin had 1,000 communicants. (*See also* ADVENTISM.)

Catholic Emancipation

From 1778 in Britain Roman Catholics were given more freedom, such as the right to own landed property, and in

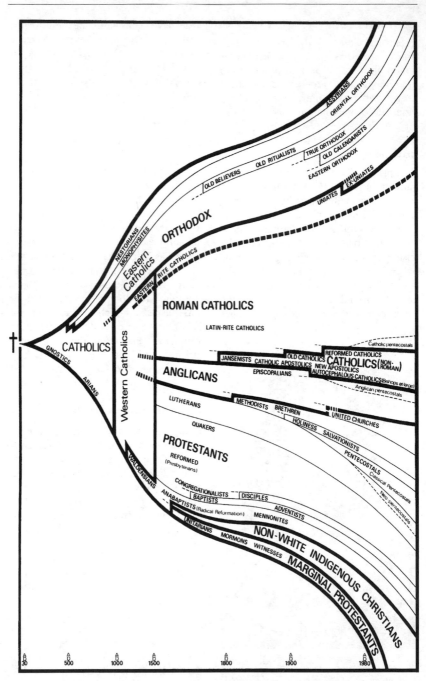

The expansion of the churches: From a single beginning, the churches developed in three main branches – Roman Catholic, Eastern Orthodox and varieties of Protestant. From D. B. Barrett, ed., World Christian Encyclopedia *(1982).*

1829 the Roman Catholic Relief Act removed most remaining disabilities. But the monarch in Britain still may not be a Roman Catholic.

Catholic epistles

Those general letters of the New Testament attributed to JAMES, PETER, JOHN and JUDE.

Cecilia

A popular martyr of the second or third century about whom little is known. As she was depicted playing the organ, she became patron of church music. Feast day 22 November.

Celebrant

In early times Christian worship was probably conducted by a president who directed or celebrated the ritual. Then presbyters and bishops became the normal celebrants at the EUCHARIST. The liturgical movement of recent times has revived 'concelebration', with several ministers taking part. Normally the celebrant is ordained, but some Free Churches allow laymen to preside, if authorized.

Celestius

See PELAGIUS.

celibacy

Abstention from marriage and sexual relations. Christianity arose from Judaism, where marriage was normal and God-given, for priests and rabbis as well as others. The first APOSTLES were married and took their wives with them on their travels, as did PETER and JAMES, head of the Church in Jerusalem (1 Cor. 9:5). Early Church councils gave clergy the right to marry, and this has persisted in Eastern ORTHODOXY where probably 90 per cent of priests marry; bishops, however, must be celibate, which means they are chiefly chosen from monastic orders. In the West there was pressure for clerical celibacy from the 11th century, though this gave rise to widespread concubinage. At the REFORMATION, LUTHER married a former nun and CRANMER married twice before it was officially allowed. Roman Catholicism has considered celibacy a matter of Church rather than divine law, but recent Popes continue to insist on it for clergy. It is estimated that in modern times 100,000 Roman Catholic priests, about a quarter of the total number, have resigned in order to enable them to marry. (See also CHASTITY; MARRIAGE.)

Celtic Church

Christianity first came to the British Isles in the second or third century, and there are remains from a little later at Lullingstone in Kent and Hinton St Mary in Dorset. After the collapse of the Roman occupation of England and the invasion of the Saxons, the Church was stronger in Ireland, where PATRICK went in 431, and in Scotland, where COLUMBA arrived in 563. When AUGUSTINE brought the Roman mission to Kent in 597 there was a small British Church surviving. At the Synod of Whitby in 664 Celtic customs were changed to Roman. There has been a modern revival of interest in Celtic spirituality. (See also ALBAN; HILDA.)

censer

A metal pan which holds heated charcoal on which grains of incense are sprinkled. It is suspended on chains and swung to cense the altar, ministers and congregation. Censing was abolished at the REFORMATION, but revived in ANGLO-CATHOLIC churches. The censer is also known as a thurible, from the Latin *thus*, incense.

Cephas

See PETER.

ceremonial

See RITES, RITUAL.

Chad (d. 672 CE)

From Northumbria, he became a pupil of AIDAN at LINDISFARNE and then abbot of Lastingham in Yorkshire, and finally bishop of Lichfield.

Chalcedon

A city in Asia Minor where the fourth ecumenical council was held in 451CE, drawing up a statement of doctrine called the Chalcedonian Definition. This was done in opposition to MONOPHYSITES and NESTORIANS, and affirmed that the nature of Christ was both divine and human, and the Virgin Mary was Theotokos, 'God-bearer'. (*See also* JACOBITES.)

Chaldeans

Small groups of former NESTORIAN churches in Turkey, Iran and India, now in communion with Rome.

chalice

From the Latin, *calix*, 'cup', this word is used for the cup containing the wine in the EUCHARIST.

Chalmers, James (1841–1901)

Scottish CONGREGATIONALIST missionary to New Guinea. He helped in the annexation of the country to Britain to protect the people from exploitation, and opposed westernization of their dress and customs. In further work off the coast of Papua Chalmers was killed, along with a colleague and ten teachers.

Chalmers, Thomas (1780–1847)

Scottish theologian and professor. He led the movement for the choice of ministers by the people and in 1843 left the established Church to found the United Free Church of Scotland, which lasted till a reunion with the Church of Scotland in 1929.

chancel

The eastern part of a church around the altar, also called the sanctuary. The word 'chancel' comes ultimately from the Latin, *cancelli*, meaning 'lattice-bars', referring to the screen which often separated chancel and nave in medieval churches.

Channing, William Ellery (1780–1842)

One of the best-known American theologians, pastor of a Congregational Church in Boston. In divisions between conservatives and liberals he preached against the doctrine of TOTAL DEPRAVITY and gave new interpretations of the ATONEMENT and TRINITY. He was considered to be a UNITARIAN, but claimed to belong not to any particular Church but to the 'community of free minds'. (*See also* BUSHNELL.)

Chantal, Madame

See FRANCIS OF SALES.

chantry

A chapel, altar or priest endowed to provide sung (chanted) masses for the soul of the founder. It was hoped that the endowment would ensure prayers were offered for ever, but at the REFORMATION the king was not slow to suppress the chantries and pocket their money. However, since the priests had often been schoolmasters, some of the chantries developed into grammar schools. (*See also* DISSOLUTION OF THE MONASTERIES.)

chapel

Named apparently from late Latin *cappella*, a shrine for the cloak or 'cape' of St Martin kept as a relic. The term came to be applied to other shrines and subordinate churches, including chapels in colleges and hospitals. Roman Catholic and Free Church buildings have been called chapels to distinguish them from the established Church; hence the contrast, opposition or co-operation, between 'Church and Chapel'. A Chapel of Ease was a subordinate church provided if the parish church was far distant. A chaplain is a minister of a chapel in a school, in the armed forces, or in other services. (*See also* ALMS; MARTIN.)

charismatic

Charismata, the 'gifts of grace' in Greek, are listed by PAUL in 1 Corinthians 12 as wisdom, knowledge, faith, healing, miracles, prophecy, discerning spirits, tongues, interpretation of tongues. From the 1960s a Charismatic Renewal movement developed in America and spread worldwide, with television stations helping diffusion. It emphasized emotion, miracles, healing and tongues. Roman Catholics joined the movement from 1967, bringing more formal theology and organization. Other churches postponed recognizing the movement and, impatient of delay, some charismatics set up their own house churches and other communities. (*See also* BASE COMMUNITIES; EVANGELICALS; GLOSSOLALIA; HOUSE CHURCHES; PENTECOSTALS.)

charity

See AGAPÉ; ALMS.

Charterhouse

See CARTHUSIANS.

chastity

Often regarded negatively as preference for virginity against marriage, ABSTINENCE against physical love. PAUL spoke of the body as the temple of the Holy Spirit (1 Cor. 6:19) and saw fornication as violating the body of Christ. The ideal of chastity is continence before marriage, and loyalty to one partner for life. (*See also* ADULTERY; AGAPÉ; CELIBACY; MARRIAGE.)

chasuble

A sleeveless vestment worn by priests at the EUCHARIST. The name derives from late Latin for a hooded cloak. Abolished by the Anglican Prayer Book of 1552, it was reintroduced in the 19th-century liturgical revival. (*See also* VESTMENTS.)

Cherubim and Seraphim

African independent revival movement founded in Nigeria in the 1920s by Moses Orimolade and Christianah Abiodun. The former was an itinerant preacher, known as 'praying Father' (Baba Aladura) from his emphasis on prayer and healing. Christianah was an Anglican, but after spiritual experiences she led prayer meetings which developed into the Seraphim Society and eventually the Eternal Order of the Cherubim and Seraphim. Forms of worship draw on various traditions: removing shoes in church, crossing, burning incense, African music and clapping, close reading and exposition of the Bible, emphasis on prayer and healing. The movement has spread to other lands in Africa and to Europe and America. (*See also* ALADURA.)

Childermas

An old name for Holy Innocents' Day, 28 December, 'Mass of the Children'.

children

Jesus said, 'Let the children come to me . . . for of such is the kingdom of God' (Mark 10:14). From the first century the Church opposed abortion and exposing unwanted children to death. In the industrial revolution there arose protest against child labour and laws to restrict it were slowly enacted. Modern concerns with paedophiles (an unhappy term, since it actually means child-love, whereas it should indicate lust) and exploitation of child labour stress the need for parental nurture and social legislation. (*See also* ABORTION; RAIKES; SHAFTESBURY.)

Children of God

See BERG, DAVID.

Children's Crusade

See CRUSADES.

Chilembwe, John (1860–1915)

An African prophet from Nyasaland (Malawi) who led an uprising against colonial rule and is regarded as a national martyr. Trained in the USA, he was ordained by the National Baptist Convention and returned home to found a Providence Industrial Mission in 1901. He was killed by government troops but his movement persists.

chiliasm

From the Greek word for 'thousand': the belief that the devil will be bound and Christ reign for a thousand years, based on Revelation 20: 1–6.

China

There have been three main Christian missions to China. In the seventh century NESTORIANS built monasteries and schools; they were dispersed in the ninth century and returned, briefly, in the thirteenth. JESUITS arrived in the 1570s, but declined after a 'rites controversy' over the retention of some traditional customs. Protestants and Catholics had more success in the 19th century and Chinese leadership developed when missionaries were expelled in the 20th. In 1997 Chinese government statistics recognized 10 million Protestants with 12,000 churches, and 4 million Catholics with 4,000 churches. But an 'underground' Roman Catholic Church, loyal to the Pope, is said to be considerably more numerous. (*See also* RICCI; STUDD.)

choir

From the fourth century singers are recorded as assisting in church worship, and by the middle ages MONASTERIES and CATHEDRALS were notable for music, especially PLAINCHANT. The choir sat in the chancel or railed-off spaces in the nave, augmented by laypersons who after the REFORMATION became the chief members. English cathedral choirs have maintained traditional singing; other church choirs include women.

Ch'ondogyo

The 'Religion of the Heavenly Way', a 19th-century development in Korea combining Neo-Confucian moral discipline with Roman Catholic beliefs in God or the Lord on High. The movement survives despite persecution and schism and maintains daily and Sunday services.

chosen people

See ELECTION.

chrism

See UNCTION.

Christ

Greek for 'Anointed One', translating the Hebrew 'MESSIAH'. A title rather than a name, Christ was used to express faith in JESUS as the promised Messiah, but soon was used as a proper name and followers of Jesus Christ were known as CHRISTIANS. (*See also* CHRISTOLOGY.)

Christ Apostolic Church

A Nigerian revival movement, associated first with an American Faith Tabernacle and establishing its own church in 1939. A prophet, Joseph Babalola, became its General Evangelist, and a traditional civil ruler, Isaac Akinyele, became chairman, head and father of this church in 1957. (*See also* ALADURA.)

Christ Army Church

Nigerian organization founded by Garrick BRAIDE.

Christadelphians

Originally known as Thomasites, from John Thomas (1805–71) who was the

founder in America in 1848.
Christadelphians means 'Christ's
Brothers' and was preferred to the name
Christian which seemed to suggest
developed doctrines. Thomas claimed to
return to beliefs of the first disciples,
accepting the Bible as infallible, practising BAPTISM by full immersion, rejecting
the doctrine of the TRINITY and expect-
ing the Second Coming of Christ. In
Britain their number is about 20,000,
with the main centre in Birmingham.
(*See also* ADVENTISM.)

Christening

An old English term for being made a
Christian, or used as popular equivalent
of BAPTISM. TYNDALE translated 1
Corinthians 1:14: 'I thank God that I
cristened none of you.' Christen was
also used for naming at baptism, for
standing sponsor, and for naming ships
and bells.

Christian

Name given to a believer in Jesus Christ.
According to Acts (11:26), 'the disciples
were called Christians first in Antioch'
but the name occurs in only two other
places in the New Testament (Acts
26:28; 1 Peter 4:16). They were also
known as followers of 'the Way' (Acts
9:2), and as Nazarenes (Acts 24:5). Paul
never used the word Christian, and the
name seems to have become attached to
gentile converts, while 'NAZARENES' was
applied to Jewish believers in the Way.

Christian Church

See CAMPBELL.

Christian Science

The Church of Christ, Scientist, was
founded in Boston, USA, in 1879, by
Mary Baker Eddy (1821–1910), and its
headquarters are still in Boston. Mrs
Eddy claimed healing from a serious fall
in 1866, and set out her teachings in
1875 in *Science and Health with Key to
the Scriptures*: prayer alone for healing,
knowledge of the Ultimate, an end to
disease, suffering and death. This church
insists on its Christian character; it bases
worship on readings from the Bible and
Science and Health, and testimonies
from believers. There are 3,000
branches in some 60 countries, with estimated membership of 475,000 in the
USA and about 75,000 in Britain. A
journal, *Christian Science Monitor*, has a
wide readership.

Christian Socialism

A social reform movement following the
collapse of the workers' Chartist
Movement of 1848, led by Christians
such as F.D. MAURICE and Charles
KINGSLEY. There were short-lived periodicals like *The Christian Socialist*
(1850–1), offering no precise economic
teaching but exposition of biblical references to justice. Christian Socialism
declined, but has revived recently in
Europe and found new life in Latin
America. (*See also* LIBERATION THEOLOGY.)

Christian Year

The Christian liturgical year begins in
ADVENT. The name was also given to a
book of hymns by John KEBLE in 1827.
(*See also* CALENDAR.)

Christianity

See Introduction.

Christmas

English name for the feast of the
Nativity, Christ's Mass, celebrated on
the eve and day of the festival. In France
it is the 'birth' day, Noël from Latin
Natalis, which in old English was a
'shout' or carol, as Chaucer wrote: 'And
nowel crieth every lusty man' (*The
Franklin's Tale*, l. 527). The date and
time of year of the birth of Jesus are
unknown and there is no evidence for its
having occurred 'in the bleak mid-
winter'. CLEMENT OF ALEXANDRIA

suggested the birth might have been in May, but 25 December was decided upon in Rome in 336, taken over from a pagan feast of the Invincible Sun. This was a new year festival, after the winter solstice, and Christ was regarded as the Sun of Righteousness. The date was soon accepted in West and East, though some ORTHODOX churches (not states), Russia, Georgia and Serbia, keep to the Old Style Julian CALENDAR which makes their Christmas fall on 6 January by Western dating. Christmas became a time of merry-making, banned by PURITANS but later very popular. Christmas trees were introduced to England from Germany by Prince Albert in the 19th century.

Christology

Study of Jesus as the Christ and his divine nature. The Gospels of Mark and Matthew, from their first verses, write of Jesus Christ, and John's Gospel speaks of the Word (LOGOS) made flesh. Paul wrote of Christ Jesus 'emptying himself', taking the form of a servant and dying on the cross (Phil. 2:7ff). From these and other passages early Christians debated what manner of person Christ was. Some Jewish Christians spoke of Jesus as a human MESSIAH, while GNOSTICS denied his real humanity. The greatest debate was with the ARIANS, who held Christ to be a creature of and subordinate to the Father, while ATHANASIUS insisted on two natures in Christ, full humanity and full divinity, and this was confirmed at the Council of CHALCEDON in 451. The Reformers generally kept the traditional doctrine, and modern writers emphasize the implications of humanity. (*See also* HOMOOUSION; KENOSIS.)

Christopher

From Greek for 'Christ-bearer': patron saint of travellers and now of motorists. His date and life are obscure; legend depicts him as a giant ferryman who bore the infant Jesus over a river but found him a great burden since the child carried the weight of the world. Christopher was often painted on medieval church walls, still to be seen in some places.

Chrysostom, John (347–407 CE)

Greek (his name means 'golden-mouthed') preacher and theologian at

Mural of Christopher at Shorwell, Isle of Wight: The giant crosses between two shores carrying the Christ child who says in Latin 'I am Alpha and Omega'.

Antioch in Syria, later Patriarch of Constantinople. He set about reforming the city but his ferocity, and anti-semitism, led to banishment as a heretic. Many of his sermons and letters survive. A collect in the BOOK OF COMMON PRAYER bears the name Chrysostom; CRANMER took it from an eastern litany, but the author is unknown. Feast day 27 January.

Church

The English word comes from the Greek *kuriakon*, 'belonging to the Lord', Scottish 'kirk' being closer. Strictly, the church is a place for the worship of Christ as Lord and it is incorrect to speak of a 'non-Christian church' or a 'secular church'. In the New Testament the word translated 'church' is ECCLESIA, congregation, and the words to Peter, 'on this rock I will build my church' (Matt. 16:18) refer to this body.

Church Army

An Anglican organization modelled on the SALVATION ARMY, founded in 1882 by Wilson Carlile.

Church Missionary Society

Popularly known as the CMS: an evangelical Anglican organization 'for Missions in Africa and the East', founded in 1799. (*See also* VENN.)

Church of Christ Scientist

See CHRISTIAN SCIENCE.

Church of England

See ANGLICANISM.

Church of Scotland

Early missionaries to Scotland were NINIAN and COLUMBA. The CELTIC CHURCH was gradually Romanized after the Synod of Whitby (664), but the Scottish Church resisted the claims of CANTERBURY and appointed its own archbishops at St Andrews and Glasgow. At the REFORMATION John KNOX led the Calvinist party to form a Presbyterian system. After struggles with episcopacy, the Church of Scotland was established, Presbyterian, national and free. Some schisms were healed in 1929, with the United Free Church joining the Church of Scotland. Episcopalians (Piskies) remain a small minority, in communion with the Church of England but with their own Prayer Book. (*See also* CHALMERS, THOMAS; IONA; WEE FREES.)

Church of South India

A union in 1947 of Indian churches, Congregational, Methodist and Presbyterian, unusually also incorporated Anglicans and accepted bishops. In 1970 the same denominations, along with Baptists, Brethren and Disciples of Christ, formed the Church of North India. In 1997 the CSI had 10,114 congregations and around 2.8 million members.

churching

A female ritual, based on the taboo of uncleanness of blood in childbirth, from Leviticus 12:2, 'She shall be unclean seven days.' The 1549 Prayer Book called this purification, but it was later changed to thanksgiving for a safe birth. The mother should go to church, accompanied by her husband 'if he so desire', and 'must offer accustomed offerings'. An unmarried woman could not be cleansed until she had done penance. (*See also* CANDLEMAS.)

circuit

A METHODIST term for a number of churches in a town or place under the care of itinerant ministers, 'travelling preachers', who go round in a circuit like judges, as distinct from LOCAL PREACHERS who live in the locality. The circuits are united in districts, corresponding to dioceses.

circumcision

Practised on all male Jews, who are 'circumcised the eighth day' (Phil. 3:5). It was the genius of Paul to recognize that this genital operation would deter European gentiles from joining the Church, and the so-called council of Jerusalem confirmed that they were exempt (Acts 15:24). Circumcision has been a Semitic and partly African practice, but it is remarkable that Egyptian and Ethiopian Christians have retained it, despite Paul, considering that an uncircumcised man is not a Christian. Female circumcision or excision is still widely practised in Africa, despite being condemned as unnecessary and dangerous by other churches, doctors and anthropologists.

Cistercians

A reformed order of Benedictine monks, founded in 1098 by Robert of Molesme at Cîteaux (Latin: *Cistercium*) in France. Cistercian houses were built in remote places and monks spent time in prayer, SILENCE and manual labour, developing farming. Cistercians spread rapidly, boosted by BERNARD of Clairvaux from 1112, and had foundations in England, notably at Rievaulx in Yorkshire. A reformed offshoot became the TRAPPISTS. (*See also* BENEDICT.)

Clapham Sect

A nickname given by clergyman and essayist Sydney Smith to 'the patent Christians at Clapham', a group of early 19th-century Anglican philanthropists who attended church at Clapham in London. (*See also* MACAULAY; MORE, HANNAH; VENN; WILBERFORCE.)

Clare (1194–1253)

An early follower of FRANCIS OF ASSISI, who established a separate community of which Clare became abbess. This 'Second Order' of Franciscans, called Poor Clares or Clarisses, spread rapidly

over Europe. It divided into a milder order of Urbanists, named after Pope Urban IV who sanctioned some relaxation, and a later strict order called Colettines after its leader.

Clarkson, Thomas (1760–1846)

Indefatigable worker against the slave trade, with WILBERFORCE and the Quakers, leading the Anti-slavery Society in 1823 and seeing West Indian SLAVERY abolished in 1833. He went to France and other countries to combat slavery and wrote a *History of the Abolition of the African Slave-trade.* In 1996, 150 years after his death, a memorial to Clarkson was unveiled in Westminster Abbey.

class meeting

METHODIST meeting, established by John WESLEY in 1742. Groups of Methodists met weekly under a class leader for instruction, Bible study and discipline, contributing one penny each to society funds. Class leaders, along with LOCAL PREACHERS, formed much of the lay leadership of Methodism. Declining in modern times, class meetings have been revived as house fellowships (to be distinguished from HOUSE CHURCHES), meeting monthly in homes of church members.

Clement of Alexandria
(150–215 CE)

Philosopher and theologian who sought to expound the faith in terms of Greek philosophy, which was 'a schoolmaster to the Greek world, as the law was to the Hebrews, to bring them to Christ'. Clement was head of the Catechetical School of Alexandria and was followed by his pupil ORIGEN. He wrote many works, including an enormous composition called *Stromateis* ('Miscellanies'). Feast day 4 December. *See also* PHILO.

Clement of Rome

A first-century slave who became free, said by some to have succeeded PETER at Rome and by others to have been the third or fourth after him. Clement wrote epistles (1 and perhaps 2 Clement) describing the Neronian persecution and the character of Christians.

Cleopas

One of two DISCIPLES who met the risen Christ on the road to Emmaus (Luke 24:18). He is not known otherwise, though a Clopas is mentioned as husband of another Mary (John 19:25).

clergy

Ordained priests and ministers, distinguished from the laity. They are clerks in holy orders, the word clerk or cleric coming from the 'lot' (Greek: *kleros*) by which Matthias was chosen (Acts 1:26).

Clifford, John (1836–1923)

Baptist minister in London from 1858, popular preacher and president of the Baptist Union in 1888. He led opposition to a government Education Act in 1902 which placed denominational schools on the rates. Clifford made 'passive resistance' by refusing to pay his rate and 'Clifford's teapot' became famous when it was seized in lieu of money. Clifford was more liberal than some leaders of his church, and welcomed HIGHER CRITICISM as bringing new light to bear on the Bible. (*See also* SPURGEON.)

Clitherow, Margaret (1556–86)

Daughter of the sheriff of York, she was converted to Roman Catholicism and sheltered fugitive priests. Charged with treason at York Assizes, she refused to plead in her defence and was crushed to death. Called the 'martyr of York', she was beatified in 1929.

cloister

From Latin for an 'enclosed' space: usually used of a covered walk, often round a quadrangle in a college, convent or cathedral. The word 'cloister' may also be used of a religious house or the religious life.

Cloud of Unknowing

A famous mystical treatise in English of the 14th century. The unknown author, sometimes identified with Walter Hilton, described it as 'A book of contemplation, the which is called the Cloud of Unknowing in the which the soul is oned with God.' Following DIONYSIUS, the writer finds a darkness, 'as it were a cloud of unknowing', between himself and God, which is pierced not by the intellect but by 'a sharp dart of love'. The book deals with doubts and defaults, meditation and contemplation, and ends with prayer for grace on all 'God's lovers'. (*See also* CONTEMPLATION.)

Clowes

See PRIMITIVE METHODISTS.

Cluny

A Benedictine monastery near Mâcon in France. Founded in 910, it became a centre for many other houses on the Cluniac model of strict observance, stress on worship and the CHOIR, and financial independence. (*See also* BENEDICT; TAIZÉ.)

codex

A manuscript of ancient texts. Some of the more famous Biblical codices are:

Codex Alexandrinus, an early fifth-century manuscript in Greek UNCIALS (capitals), perhaps written in Alexandria. Presented to James I by the Patriarch of Constantinople, it is now in the British Museum. Known by the letter A.

Codex Bezae, a fifth-century Greek and Latin manuscript of the Gospels and Acts, given to Cambridge University by BEZA. Known as D.

Codex Sinaiticus, a fourth-century Greek Bible, found by the German scholar Tischendorf at St Catharine's monastery on Mount Sinai in 1844. It was acquired by the Tsar of Russia, and bought by the British Museum in 1933. Known by the Hebrew letter Aleph.

Codex Vaticanus, a fourth-century Greek Bible, of unknown history, but in the Vatican library at least since the 15th century. Known as B.

The ancient codices, especially Sinaiticus and Vaticanus, have been used in modern translations of the Bible since the REVISED VERSION of 1881, giving late translators advantages over the scholars who produced the AUTHORIZED VERSION, who did not know of them.

Codex Sinaiticus: The famous fourth-century manuscript, written on vellum, four columns to a page, was probably compiled by several scribes in Egypt, like the Codex Vaticanus, with whose text it closely agrees. Additional MS 43725, f. 260. John 21: 1–25. From the British Library.

Coenobite

From Greek for 'common life': a monk or nun living in a community, as distinct from a solitary ANCHORITE or HERMIT. (*See also* PACHOMIUS.)

Coke, Thomas (1747–1814)

Born in Brecon in Wales, he became an Anglican clergyman and then a METHODIST in 1777. John WESLEY sent him to Ireland, and then to America, commissioned to pass ordination to others. This he did to ASBURY, but they were both called bishops, to the annoyance of Wesley. Coke went on to the West Indies and died on his way to a mission to India.

Colenso, John William (1814–83)

Born in Cornwall, he became the first bishop of Natal in 1853, mastered the Zulu language, championed dispossessed Africans and, against Church custom, did not insist on POLYGAMISTS dissolving their marriages on baptism. Colenso criticized the authorship and accuracy of the PENTATEUCH and the Book of Joshua and denied everlasting punishment, and was declared deposed by Metropolitan Gray of Capetown. Colenso refused to submit and appealed to the Privy Council which supported him. Gray appointed another bishop of Natal, but Colenso clung to his SEE, and there were rival bishops till 1911.

Colettine

See CLARE.

Coligny, Gaspard de (1519–72)

From a noble French family, he distinguished himself in war and became admiral of France. He was converted to the HUGUENOT cause and led its army until a peace was reached at St Germain in 1570. But Catharine de Medici, Queen Mother of France, alarmed at the growing Protestant power, ordered the Massacre of St Bartholomew on 24 August 1572, in which Coligny was one of the first victims.

collect

A short prayer, appropriate to days or seasons, derived from 'collecting' petitions of the congregation into a single prayer.

Colman (d. 676 CE)

Irish monk. He went to IONA and then became bishop of LINDISFARNE. At the Synod of Whitby in 664 CE he pleaded for the retention of Celtic customs, and when that failed he retired to Ireland. Feast day 18 February. (*See also* CELTIC CHURCH.)

Colossians, Epistle to the

A letter of PAUL to the Church at Colossae in Asia Minor. It begins with the 'mystery' of Christ, in whom all 'fullness' dwells, warns against vain 'philosophy' and fleshly circumcision, and goes on to extol Christian love and forbearance. Wives must submit to husbands, and husbands love their wives. The letter ends with greetings from others, including Mark and Luke. The date is uncertain; it may have been written at Ephesus or, more likely, at Rome.

colours

Colours for church VESTMENTS have varied but are generally prescribed for seasons of the year. Green is standard from EPIPHANY to LENT and TRINITY to ADVENT, purple in Lent and Advent, white at EASTER and Trinity, red at PENTECOST, and black on Good Friday and at offices for the dead. (*See also* CASSOCK.)

Columba (521–97 CE)

Trained in Irish monasteries, he went in 563 with 12 companions to the island of IONA in Scotland. From his base there, Columba travelled all over Scotland as far as the Orkneys for 30 years, founding monasteries. Although only a priest, he was the chief authority over the Columban houses in Scotland, and later those in the north of England and Ireland also came under Iona. Columba wrote many books and when he died he was translating the Psalter. Feast day 9 June.

Commandments

The Ten Commandments of Exodus 20: 2–17 are also called the Decalogue, from Greek for 'ten words'. Taken over by the Church, they were used in instructing catechumens (*see* CATECHISM). After the REFORMATION they were printed on boards in parish churches; some of them remain today. They were introduced into the Communion service of the Prayer Book, but are now omitted or replaced by the two great commandments of love to God and neighbour (Mark 12: 29–31).

commination

From Latin for 'threatening', a Prayer Book service 'denouncing of God's anger and judgements against sinners', dates from 1552 and was read on Ash Wednesday. Modern revisions omitted the curses with which the service began, and now it is generally abandoned, except in India and Africa where the old Commination may still be heard.

Common Life

See BRETHREN; DEVOTION.

Common Order

A Liturgy compiled by John KNOX for use in Geneva in 1556 and appointed for Scotland in 1562. A modern service book of this name was prepared by the General Assembly of the Church of Scotland in 1940, giving alternative orders for morning and evening, for the sacraments, and for the Christian year, drawing on old prayer books and new compositions.

communes

Groups of people living together and sharing common views. There are many modern communes, some utopian or millenarian, and others inspired by Christian, Hindu or Buddhist orders.

Communion

See EUCHARIST.

communion of saints

A phrase in the APOSTLES' CREED, following a statement on belief in the Church; it has been taken to mean the fellowship of all believers, the Church militant on earth, triumphant in heaven.

Communism

Communal living, or holding goods together, has been practised since ancient times. The first Church held 'all things common' (Acts 2:44), and this was the principle for monastic and later Protestant communities. Marxist, Soviet and Chinese Communism was based on class struggle and regarded religion as 'the opiate of the masses', a palliative which would pass away in a perfect society. Communism had its own ideology, almost religion: divinized leaders such as Lenin or Mao; sacred scripture in the Marxist *Das Kapital*; a strictly organized church in the Party; and faith in a coming ideal, a messianic eschatology. Like a medieval INQUISITION, modern Communism has been harshly persecuting and it is now admitted that in Russia from 1917 to 1989 over 200,000 priests, monks and nuns were shot or hanged, and half a million clergy and religious imprisoned or deported to Siberia. (*See also* HUMANISM; LEVELLERS; STATE AND RELIGION.)

Compline

Last service of the day before retiring, from Latin for 'completion'. Evening hymns, psalms or prayers are appropriate. (*See also* NUNC DIMITTIS.)

Compostela, Santiago de

Pilgrimage city in northern Spain. It became a centre for revolt against the Muslim rulers of Iberia when the cathedral was founded in 1078 above the supposed grave of Sant Iago el Mayor (Saint James the Elder), the Spanish national saint. (*See also* FATIMA; JAMES (1).)

concelebration

See CELEBRANT.

conciliarism

A theory that church councils have primacy in ecclesiastical affairs. It was developed in the 14th and 15th centuries. The Council of CONSTANCE in 1417 affirmed the supremacy of councils, decreeing that they should meet at regular intervals. (*See also* GENERAL COUNCILS.)

concordance

Strictly, this means 'agreement', but used of the Bible or other book it is an alphabetical arrangement of all the words and subjects which occur in it. Alexander Cruden compiled the best known Concordance of the English Bible in 1737, and it has been revised and enlarged since. More extensive is the Analytical Concordance first published by Robert Young in 1879, giving 311,000 references to English Bible verses, with Hebrew and Greek originals.

concordat

An agreement between church and STATE on mutual concerns such as taxation, education and appointment of clergy. By a concordat in 1801 between Napoleon and Pope Pius VII the Catholic Church was recognized as the religion of most French citizens, with rights to property. This concordat lasted till 1905. The Vatican concluded a concordat with the Italian ruler Mussolini in 1929.

concupiscence

A word used in moral theology for passion, 'eager desire' or lust. There was long a tendency to regard any sexual feeling as sinful, the ninth of the Articles of the 16th-century Prayer Book saying that 'concupiscence and lust hath of itself the nature of sin'. But not all agreed then, and now different views are held. (*See also* SEXUALITY; TAYLOR.)

Cone, James Hal (b. 1938)

African-American theologian, said to be the first to expound BLACK THEOLOGY as a separate theological discipline.

Confessing Church

German evangelicals opposed to the Nazi-sponsored German Christians led by the aryanizing Bishop Ludwig Müller. The Confessing Christians under Martin NIEMÖLLER held a synod at BARMEN in 1934 and issued a declaration denying that the Church was an organ of the state, but was based on Christ and preached the free grace of God. Niemöller and others were sent to concentration camps and the movement had to work largely underground. After the Second World War a Confessing Church Group continued, as a force within the Church for fidelity to the Gospel.

confession

'Confess your sins to one another' said James (5:16). General confession of sins is part of the public liturgy. Confession within church groups has been practised in many ways, in early Methodism, in the Oxford Group and in modern evangelical societies. Sacramental confession, especially in Roman Catholicism, provides for private confession to a priest and aims at repentance and assurance of ABSOLUTION. (*See also* PENANCE.)

Confirmation

Since the Reformation this word has been taken to apply to candidates confirming vows that were made for them by parents or sponsors in infant BAPTISM. But in earlier times 'confirming' meant 'strengthening', the laying on of hands or anointing by a bishop to ratify or complete what had been begun in baptism, giving a fuller grace or 'character' to the candidate. Free Churches have tended to adopt the convenient term Confirmation for reception into full membership of the Church. Catholics and Orthodox recognize Confirmation as one of seven SACRAMENTS.

Congregationalism

Belief in the independence and autonomy of each local church congregation, developed by the ANABAPTISTS. The first Congregational Church was established in London in 1567. Robert BROWNE has been called 'Father of the Congregationalists', who were first named Brownists. Persecuted by the established Church some Independents, as they were also called, fled to Holland and others to America with the *Mayflower* in 1620. The Toleration Act of 1689 allowed limited freedom of worship, but still excluded Nonconformists from the two English universities. Congregational Unions were established, and in 1972 they were united with English Presbyterians to form the United Reformed Church.

In the USA Congregationalism became the established Church of Connecticut and Massachusetts. There were mergers with other churches, forming eventually the United Church of Christ in 1957, with over 6,000 congregations.

conscience

From Latin for 'knowledge within oneself', defined by THOMAS AQUINAS as 'the mind of a human being making moral judgements'. There is a duty to obey conscience, checked by Scripture and church teaching. Conscientious objection to war is recognized by some

states, e.g. Britain, after a long struggle from the First World War to the Second, with alternative non-combatant service offered. Some other states punish refusal of military combat service with imprisonment or even death. (*See also* JUST WAR; NONCONFORMIST CONSCIENCE.)

consecration

Setting apart of persons, places or things for divine service. The term is used of the central prayer of the EUCHARIST, of the ordination of bishops, and of the blessing of churches, altars and vessels.

consistory

A term for certain ecclesiastical courts administering church law in a diocese. In the Roman Catholic Church it is an assembly of CARDINALS in the presence of the POPE. A consistory court in some Presbyterian churches in Europe and America corresponds to the Scottish kirk session.

Constance, Council of

A council held in Germany in 1414–18 to end the Great SCHISM of the papacy and reform the Church. Antipopes John XXIII and Benedict XIII were both deposed, Gregory XII resigned, and Martin V was elected Pope. The Bohemian reformer John HUSS was condemned for heresy and burnt at the stake in 1415. (*See also* CONCILIARISM.)

Constantine (d. 337 CE)

Proclaimed Roman emperor at York, it is said that he had a vision, adopted the Christian symbol LABARUM for his standard and defeated his rival Maxentius at Milvian Bridge. He brought persecution of Christians to an end and tried to unite the Church so as to strengthen the state, repressing the DONATISTS and summoning the Council of NICAEA to settle the ARIAN dispute. Constantine moved his capital from Rome to Byzantium, which was rebuilt and named Constantinople,

Constantine's City. He endowed church building and made Sunday a public holiday in 321 CE. Constantine was not baptized till just before his death, and whether his protection of the Church was a good thing has often been argued. (*See also* HELENA; IN HOC SIGNO VINCES; MILAN.)

Constantinople

See CRUSADES; HAGIA SOPHIA; ORTHODOX CHURCH.

consubstantiation

A LUTHERAN variant of the medieval doctrine of TRANSUBSTANTIATION. In this form it was held that after consecration in the EUCHARIST the substances of BREAD AND WINE continue to co-exist with those of the BODY and BLOOD of Christ.

contemplation

In Christian usage contemplation follows on from MEDITATION, on a doctrine, text or experience; it stays in simple attention and one-pointedness. The contemplative orders are especially CARTHUSIANS and CARMELITES. (*See also* CLOUD OF UNKNOWING.)

continence

'Containing': chastity, temperance. THOMAS AQUINAS took continence in two ways: virginal continence, as abstention from all sexual pleasure, and conjugal continence, as resisting evil desires. The Anglican Prayer Book saw matrimony as a remedy against sin, 'that such persons as have not the gift of continency might marry'. Nowadays a more positive evaluation of sex sees continence as self-understanding and self-control. (*See also* CELIBACY; CHASTITY; CONCUPISCENCE.)

contraception

See BIRTH CONTROL.

contrition

From Latin for 'bruising': the state of being penitent or broken in spirit by a sense of sin. It is expressed in Psalm 51:17: 'A broken and a contrite heart, O God, thou wilt not despise.'

convent

From Latin for a place of assembly, in Church usage it could refer either to a building or to a religious community. Although used of companies of either sex, today it indicates mainly houses of nuns. The word 'coven' for an assembly of witches was derived from 'convent' (*see* BLACK MASS).

conversion

From Latin 'to turn around': a change of heart and life, and sometimes a transfer from one religious system to another. The classic instance is the conversion of Saul (PAUL) on the road to Damascus (Acts 9). (*See also* TESTIMONY.)

convocation

A 'calling together', or an assembly: a term especially used for convocations of clergy and laity of the provinces of Canterbury and York in the Church of England, meeting two or three times a year.

Copernicus

See GALILEO.

Coptic

The term comes indirectly from a Greek word for Egyptian, the Coptic language being originally spoken by the Copts, indigenous inhabitants of Egypt. The language has long since been replaced in Egypt by Arabic, but it survives in the liturgy of the Coptic Church, the ancient tongue of the pyramid-builders mixed with Greek.

The Coptic Church claims foundation by the evangelist MARK, as first bishop of Alexandria. It separated from Greek (Byzantine) Christianity during doctrinal disputes and the Arab conquest which took over Egypt in 642. For centuries the Egyptian Church dominated that of ETHIOPIA. Although now a minority in Egypt among Muslims, Copts have long held important posts in government services. It is estimated that by 2000 there will be 10 million Copts in Egypt out of a total population of some 50 million. (*See also* Introduction; MONOPHYSITES.)

corban

Hebrew: a 'gift' offered to God. In Mark 7:11 Jesus criticized those who gave corban money for divine service but neglected their parents.

Corinthians, Epistles to the

Two letters written by PAUL to the Church at Corinth. 1 Corinthians deals with divisions in the Church, sexual and marital problems, the Lord's Supper, spiritual gifts and tongues, the great poem on love, the first written account of the Resurrection of Christ, and the general resurrection. (*See* AGAPÉ.)

2 Corinthians is less striking. There is reference to another letter (2:4) which has not survived in separate form, and another section (6:14–7:1) seems to be part of an earlier epistle. Chapters 10–13 may be part of a different letter. The epistle is mainly concerned with Paul's relationships with the Church, and tells of his sufferings and spiritual experiences.

Corpus Christi

'The body of Christ': a feast in the Roman Catholic Church on the Thursday after Trinity Sunday, to celebrate the EUCHARIST. In many countries there are processions with the sacrament in a MONSTRANCE, to be shown to the people.

Cosmas and Damian

Patron saints of doctors, but as their legends are held to be historically worthless they cannot be dated. A cult was established from the fifth century and spread across Europe. These twin brothers, physicians and surgeons, were popular partly because they were said to have practised their profession without asking for fees. Feast day 27 September (West), 27 October (East).

cosmogony, cosmology

Teachings about the origins and nature of the universe. The Cosmological Argument for the existence of God goes back to ARISTOTLE, and maintains that since there is a cause for everything there must be an original cause, an uncaused cause, which is God. (*See also* ANSELM.)

God creating the Sun, from the ceiling of the Sistine Chapel.

councils

See CONCILIARISM; GENERAL COUNCILS.

Counter-Reformation

Attempted reform and revival of the Roman Catholic Church in Europe, to combat the Protestant REFORMATION. It included the foundation of the JESUIT Order by IGNATIUS LOYOLA to strengthen the Church, the establishment of the INQUISITION, and the INDEX of

Prohibited Books aimed against heresy. The Council of TRENT in 1545–63: promulgated decrees against Protestant teachings.

coven

See CONVENT.

covenant

Belief in a pact or agreement between God and his people is found throughout the Old Testament; Jeremiah (31:31) spoke of a new covenant. This was taken up by Christian writers, especially the Epistle to the Hebrews, and the New Testament is in effect a New Covenant.

Covenanters in Scotland swore to maintain the Presbyterian cause, and a SOLEMN LEAGUE AND COVENANT was made by Scots and English Parliamentarians. Divisions in Scotland gave rise to more covenants, with minorities seceding.

An annual Covenant Service is distinctive of METHODISM; begun by John WESLEY in 1755, it is now usually held on the first Sunday in the new year. (See WATCH-NIGHT.)

Coverdale, Miles (1488–1568)

Born in Yorkshire, he became a priest and joined the Augustinian Friars but was involved in Protestant reform. He produced the first complete English Bible, partly based on TYNDALE, and although Tyndale had been burned at the stake for his translation, at the instigation of Henry VIII, Coverdale's Great Bible was presented to Henry by Thomas CROMWELL. The AUTHORIZED VERSION finally replaced this, but the BOOK OF COMMON PRAYER retained Coverdale's version of the Psalms which was known to many generations. Coverdale served as a Lutheran pastor in Europe, became Bishop of Exeter, and finally resigned a living in London from doubts about the Anglican liturgy. (See also TREACLE BIBLE.)

Cowper, William (1731–1800)

Poet and lawyer. He suffered from depression and religious mania and went for a time to an asylum. He was lay assistant to John NEWTON at Olney and wrote *Olney Hymns*, including 'God moves in a mysterious way'.

Cranmer, Thomas (1489–1556)

English Church Reformer. He married secretly, but his wife died and Cranmer was ordained in 1523. He married again and then was appointed Archbishop of Canterbury. In 1533 he annulled Henry VIII's marriage to Katharine, but three years later also declared the marriage to Anne Boleyn void. Cranmer promoted the Bible in English and guided the young Edward VI in Protestantism. In 1549 he produced the First Prayer Book of King Edward VI, a monument to Cranmer's reforming zeal and mastery of English. On the accession of the Catholic MARY TUDOR, Cranmer was deposed and sentenced for treason and heresy. He recanted several times, but finally withdrew his recantations and was burned at the stake in Oxford. (See also BOOK OF COMMON PRAYER.)

creation

See COSMOGONY.

creche

See CRIB.

creed

A confession of faith, originally made by candidates for BAPTISM, declaring 'I believe', Latin *credo*. In its simplest form it would be 'Jesus is Lord' (1 Cor. 12:3); this developed into longer statements. When Church councils defined doctrine then 'we believe' would express a conciliar creed. Two major creeds persisted and were incorporated into liturgies. See APOSTLES' CREED; NICAEA.

creeping to the Cross

See VENERATION.

cremation

See BURIAL.

Creme

See TARA CENTERS.

crib

FRANCIS OF ASSISI in 1223 is said to have made the first representation of the manger in which the infant Jesus was laid (Luke 2:7). The Gospel gives no indication of a stable or animals, but these and other details are added in models in churches from Christmas Eve to EPIPHANY.

Crispin, Crispinian

Legendary martyrs. They were said to have been shoemakers, and an unlikely tradition placed them at Faversham in Kent, where they have an altar in the parish church. Their popularity may explain their mention six times in Shakespeare's version of Henry V's speech before Agincourt: 'Crispin Crispian shall ne'er go by' (*Henry V,* IV. iii). Feast day 25 October.

criticism, higher/lower

The 'higher criticism' is a term used from the 19th century for literary and historical studies of the Bible, while the 'lower criticism' is study of the text. Both terms are disliked by FUNDAMEN-TALISTS, though the practices have been followed by many eminent scholars. (*See also* MODERNISM.)

Cromwell, Oliver

See DIVINE RIGHT; FIFTH MONARCHY; LEVELLERS; SOLEMN LEAGUE AND COVENANT; THEOCRACY.

Cromwell, Thomas (1485–1540)

Vicar-General under Henry VIII. He was responsible for the DISSOLUTION OF THE MONASTERIES, for installing a Bible in every Church, and for introducing registers of births, marriages and deaths in parishes. Cromwell worked hard to ensure the supremacy of the king in Church and state, but he lost the royal favour, was accused of treason and executed.

crosier, crozier

Perhaps from a shepherd's crook or hooked staff, but sometimes with the symbolism of a cross, the term is used of the pastoral staff of a bishop or abbot.

Cross

The original form of the Cross of Jesus is not known and early Christians were reluctant to depict the CRUCIFIXION. It does not appear in paintings in the CAT-ACOMBS or early mosaics. Processional crosses were used but altar crosses were rare in the middle ages. Franciscan emphasis on the passion from the 13th century developed realistic imagery, of CRUCIFIX rather than cross. Protestants disliked material imagery, but plenty of hymns were composed about the cross, for example 'When I survey the wondrous cross', and Bunyan's pilgrim lost his load of sin at a cross. The SIGN OF THE CROSS can be traced to the third century and was so prevalent in the medieval Church that the Reformers repudiated it; but it remained in Lutheranism and in restricted use in the BOOK OF COMMON PRAYER. (*See also* GESTURES.)

Crowther, Samuel Ajayi (1806–91)

African church leader. From a Yoruba home in Nigeria he was captured by slavers and taken to Sierra Leone, where he was freed and became a Christian and teacher for the CHURCH MISSIONARY SOCIETY. Ordained in 1843, he was sent back to his own people and translated the New Testament into

Yoruba. Appointed to lead a new mission on the Niger in 1857, with an all-African staff, Crowther was consecrated the first Anglican African bishop in Canterbury Cathedral in 1864 and made a Doctor of Divinity of Oxford University. His closing years were marked by controversy with young dogmatic European missionaries, but Crowther's honesty and sanctity were universally recognized. (*See also* VENN.)

crucifix

A cross bearing an image of the crucified Jesus. It was common in the West in the middle ages. In Eastern ORTHODOXY, with its preference for two-dimensional forms, it is a flat likeness similar to an ICON. Protestants, with the exception of Lutherans and High Church Anglicans, prefer a plain cross to the bodily crucifix. At God's Hill in the Isle of Wight a wall painting in the church shows the crucifix as a tree in which Christ hangs.

crucifixion

The Romans used this cruel punishment for rebels, slaves and non-Romans. The crucifixion of Jesus between two thieves or malefactors is recorded in all four gospels. Paul preached Christ crucified (1 Cor. 1:23), and saw redemptive power in the curse of hanging (Gal. 3:13). Many theories have been proposed as to why Jesus was crucified, and what his death meant, but the CROSS remains central to Christian thinking. (*See also* ATONEMENT.)

Cruden

See CONCORDANCE.

Crusades

PILGRIMAGES to the HOLY LAND were undertaken down the ages, permitted by Arab rulers after the seventh century. But the capture of Jerusalem by the Turks in 1071 led Pope Urban II in 1095 to declare a Crusade to regain the holy places. The ill-named 'Crusades', a use of war which earlier Christians had repudiated, expressed aggression and greed. Only the First Crusade reached Jerusalem, establishing a Latin kingdom in 1099 which lasted till the Muslim Saladin retook the city in 1187. The Fourth Crusade turned against the rich Eastern Christian city of Constantinople, breaching its walls on Good Friday and desecrating the Orthodox Cathedral of HAGIA SOPHIA on Easter Day. There was an ill-fated Children's Crusade in 1212, and the eighth and last, led by Louis of France, was in 1270; Louis died in Tunis. (*See also* HELENA, JUST WAR; TEMPLARS.)

Crutched Friars

'Cross-bearing' MENDICANTS, wearing a cross on their robes, who flourished from the 12th to the 17th centuries. There was a house of Crutched Friars in London in 1244, and there is still a street of that name.

crypt

From Greek 'hidden': an underground cell or vault, especially beneath a church. Often used as a chapel.

crypto-Christian

A modern term to designate some 5 per cent of all Christians who prefer not to make their allegiance known, or divulge it to the state, to avoid persecution. (*See also* HIDDEN CHRISTIANS.)

cult

From Latin, 'worship': in general, a term used to describe a faith or religious practice, but often employed, along with SECT, of a group that appears not to be ORTHODOX or socially sanctioned. (*See also* ANTI-CULT MOVEMENT; NEW RELIGIOUS MOVEMENTS.)

curate

One who had the 'cure' or charge of a parish. In England he or she may be assistant to a vicar, or a perpetual curate. In France a *curé* is a parish priest and a *vicaire* an assistant. (*See also* VICAR.)

curia

The offices and functionaries which provide administration for the papacy, or for a local bishop. (*See also* VATICAN.)

Cusa

See NICHOLAS OF CUSA.

Cuthbert (d. 687 CE)

Of Irish or Northumbrian origin, he had a vision as a shepherd boy and became a monk at Melrose, soon becoming prior. He moved to the monastery of LINDISFARNE and then to a solitary cell on the Farne islands. Under pressure he became bishop of Lindisfarne, and died two years later. In the Danish invasions the monks took Cuthbert's body to various places and finally to Durham, where it was believed to work miracles. Until the Reformation no woman was allowed to approach his shrine. Feast day 20 March.

Cyprian (d. 258 CE)

A pagan teacher of rhetoric in Carthage, he was converted to Christianity and made bishop two years later. The harsh persecution of Decius sent him into hiding and he ruled his church by letters. Many Christians lapsed from the faith, and Cyprian thought they were readmitted too easily afterwards. He demanded rebaptism and declared, like Augustine later, that 'outside the Church there is no salvation.' Another persecution breaking out under Valerian, Cyprian hid for a time but finally surrendered and was martyred in Carthage. Feast day 16 or 26 September. (*See also* DONATISM).

Cyril (d. 444 CE)

Patriarch of Alexandra, noted for his controversies. He or his followers were responsible for the murder of the Neoplatonist philosopher Hypatia. His chief conflict was with the Patriarch of of Constantinople, NESTORIUS, against whom Cyril launched 12 ANATHEMAS and whom he had condemned at a SYNOD before all the bishops had arrived. Feast day 18 March.

D

dalmatic

Perhaps named after Dalmatia in the Balkans, this wide-sleeved long VEST-MENT is worn by DEACONS at MASS, and sometimes by bishops, and in England by the monarch at the coronation.

Damascus

See CONVERSION.

Damian

See COSMAS.

Damien, Joseph Deveuster (1840–89)

Belgian missionary, known as Father Damien, who served in the Pacific islands. At his own request he went to a leprosy settlement at Molokai in 1873, where there was no medical care; here he ministered alone to 600 lepers, dressing their wounds and burying their dead. He caught the disease himself and died, but not before Sisters of Charity came to help. Damien was defended by R.L. Stevenson against criticism from other missionaries (*Letter to Dr Hyde*, 1890).

damnation

See HELL.

dance

An expression of religious devotion in the Bible, but the early Church was wary of dancing in view of lascivious spectacles in the Roman Empire. In the middle ages churches and cathedrals were often used for dance performances. Among Protestants the SHAKERS have given prominence to dancing. One of the most popular modern hymns, 'Lord of the Dance' (Sydney Carter, 1963), gives a new interpretation to the Gospel.

Daniel

A late Old Testament APOCALYPSE. It is quoted in the New Testament (Mark 13:14), where the 'abomination of desolation spoken of by Daniel the prophet' probably refers to the sack of Jerusalem and its temple by the Romans in 70 CE.

Dante Alighieri (1265–1321)

The great Florentine is noted for his *Divine Comedy*, a spiritual journey through Inferno, Purgatorio and Paradiso. Dante is highly critical of corruption in the Church, kind to godly non-Christians, and ends his epic poem with a vision of God.

Darby, John Nelson (1800–82)

Born in London, educated there and in Dublin, he was for a year curate at Wicklow, but resigned over doubts about church establishments. He joined a group led by A. N. Groves, called 'The Brethren', which rejected all church forms. Later, having moved to

Plymouth, they were named Plymouth Brethren. There were differences over the independence of each assembly and the Darbyites became 'exclusive brethren', separate from the Bethesda loose or 'open brethren'. Darby lectured on prophecy; his fundamentalist and millenarian approach was popular, and also controversial, in Europe and America.

dark night

See CATHARSIS; JOHN OF THE CROSS.

Darwinism

The theory of evolution promulgated by Charles Darwin (1809–82) had a great effect on interpretations of the Bible, creation, the nature of humanity, development, history and the goal of human endeavour. Darwin was first intended for a career in the Church, but his studies in zoology, travels and observations, writings and correspondence led him to

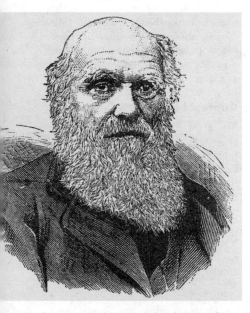

Charles Darwin, champion of evolution in his book The Origin of Species by Means of Natural Selection *(1859).*

doubt much of Victorian religion, though he felt impelled to postulate an intelligent First Cause. His house at Downe in Kent is a shrine for evolutionists. (*See also* AGNOSTIC; PALEY; WILBERFORCE, SAMUEL.)

David (1)

The great king of biblical Israel. Idealized though fallible, he served as a model for the expected Messiah. In the New Testament many links with David are made, Matthew's Gospel opening with a genealogy tracing the ancestry of Jesus back to David. The gospels record debates on Christ as 'son of David' (e.g. Mark 12:35ff), and Paul speaks of him as of 'the seed of David' (Rom. 1:3). David as a type of Christ is common in later Christian writings; he also appears in many books of hours and paintings with a crown and harp, and in Jesse windows, named after his father.

David (2) (d. 601 CE)

Patron saint of Wales. Little is known of him; a Life of Saint David from the 11th century is more propaganda against the primacy of CANTERBURY than biography. David is said to have been an extreme ASCETIC, founding 12 monasteries on Egyptian patterns. He settled at Menevia, now St David's, site of the present cathedral. Feast day 1 March.

Davidian

See BRANCH DAVIDIAN

De haeretico comburendo

Latin, 'Of burning heretics': an Act passed by the English Parliament in 1401, under Henry IV, to suppress the LOLLARDS. There was no INQUISITION in England, now heretics were to be tried by a bishop's court and handed over to secular authority which would 'cause them to be burnt, before the people, in a high place, that such punishment may strike fear in the minds of others'. The

Act was repealed under Henry VIII, revived under Mary, and finally repealed under Elizabeth. (*See also* HERESY.)

de Nobili, Robert (1577–1656)

Italian Jesuit missionary. He went to India and adopted priestly Brahmin dress and way of life. He learnt the Sanskrit and Tamil languages and held religious discussions with high-caste Hindus, some of whom were baptized. Criticized by other missionaries, his work was approved, on appeal, by Rome. De Nobili wrote many hymns and treatises, but spent his last years near Madras, poor and almost blind. (*See also* RICCI.)

De profundis

'Out of the depths': the first words of Psalm 130 in Latin. One of the penitential psalms, its combination of despair and hope seemed appropriate for funerals.

deacon

From Greek: 'servant' or 'minister'. Seven deacons were set apart to help the APOSTLES (Acts 6:1ff), though the word 'deacon' does not occur here. The work and behaviour of deacons are sketched in 1 Tim. (3:8ff). Deacons became a third order in the church hierarchy, below the presbyter and bishop. A deaconess was specially concerned with the poor and sick. In modern times women deacons prepare for the presbyterate, and deaconesses do pastoral and educational work. In Baptist and Reformed churches deacons have both administrative and pastoral functions. (*See also* SEVEN DEACONS.)

dead, prayers for the

Prayers for the departed are mentioned in the apocrypha (2 Macc. 12:44ff), and Paul wrote of those 'who are baptized for the dead' (1 Cor. 15:29). Since the earliest times there was firm belief in an afterlife, and Christians continued praying for their loved ones. The CATACOMBS have plenty of such inscriptions and early church fathers mention similar prayers. Abuses in the middle ages brought reaction against the practice at the Reformation, but there has been revival in modern times. General petitions may be offered, for example: 'Give to the dead, rest and light perpetual.' (*See also* BURIAL.)

Dead Sea Scrolls

Also named after Qumran, at the northern end of the Dead Sea, these are invaluable manuscripts discovered in caves from 1947, and dating from the third century BCE to the first century CE. They are in Hebrew and Aramaic, and are much older than any previously known texts. Out of a total of 520 texts, 157 are biblical. The scrolls have been connected with the ESSENES, though this is disputed, and some suggest that they were part of the Temple library, hidden away during Jewish wars. The scrolls give important background to life and teaching, but no clear reference to early Christianity. After long delays the full texts have now been published, but not all have been translated. (*See also* TEACHER OF RIGHTEOUSNESS.)

deadly sins

See SEVEN DEADLY SINS.

dean

From Latin for 'ten', this was a monk set over ten novices, and by extension was applied to administrators in different offices: a rural dean supervising clergy in a diocese, a dean of a cathedral responsible for services and buildings, and a college dean, usually a layman, head of a faculty. A Dean of Arches is a lay judge in a church court.

death of God

A slogan much used in debate in America in the 1960s. It derived from

Friedrich Nietzsche (1844–1900), who declared 'God is dead.' Much later, Karl BARTH insisted of the God of capitalism and war, 'he is dead.' In 1961 Gabriel Vahanian's *Death of God* predicted the end of American religiosity; Thomas Altizer and others wrote similarly, suggesting that the sacred must now be pursued through the profane. (*See also* BONHOEFFER; POST–MODERNISM; PROFANE.)

Decalogue

See COMMANDMENTS.

decretals

Papal decrees, collections of which helped to form canon law. A body of False Decretals, probably compiled in France in the ninth century, contained true and forged papal letters which upheld the rights of bishops and the supremacy of the Pope. They were long taken as genuine, but they have been rejected as false since the 15th century. (*See also* DONATION OF CONSTANTINE; NICHOLAS OF CUSA.)

dedication

A term used in various ways: as personal, offering one's life to God in private or public; as a blessing of a church, or naming after a saint, or consecrating it for worship. A dedication festival is an annual commemoration of the consecration of a church. Dedication is used to denote blessing of objects in the liturgy; in churches which do not practise infant baptism, it may be the blessing and naming of a child. (*See also* ANNIVERSARY.)

Defender of the Faith

A title (in Latin, *Fidei Defensor*) bestowed at his own request on Henry VIII of England by Pope Leo X in 1521, after the king had written against Luther's criticism of seven sacraments. The title has been used by British monarchs ever since and is still put on coins as F.D. Prince Charles has said it should now be 'defender of faiths', in view of the multi-religious character of modern British society.

deicide

See ANTI-SEMITISM; DEATH OF GOD, HOLOCAUST.

deism

Belief in God as creator, but not in providence; a natural religion as against revealed religion. Developed in England in the late 16th century, the doctrine was more popular in France where it was adopted by writers like Voltaire. In America, two of the founders of the USA, Jefferson and Franklin, were deists. Deism was counteracted by PIETISM, which emphasized religious feeling. (*See also* BUTLER; PANTHEISM; REVELATION; THEISM.)

demiurge

From Greek for a 'craftsman', this term was used by Plato for the creator of the world, and adopted by early Christian writers. It was employed by GNOSTICS in a derogatory manner for an inferior deity who made the universe, distinguished from the supreme God. (*See also* MARCION.)

demon

From Greek for 'power': a supernatural but inferior being, especially a malignant or evil spirit. In the inter-testamental period, demonology from Persian Zoroastrianism influenced Judaism and early Christianity. Demons are mentioned frequently in the gospels, less in the epistles, alongside the devil their father. (*See also* BEELZEBUB; DEVIL; ZOROASTER.)

demythologization

See BULTMANN.

Denis/Denys

Patron saint of France. Bishop of Paris, he was martyred in 250 CE. In legend he was confused with DIONYSIUS. The abbey of St Denis is on an island in the Seine and was the burial-place of French kings. In England, 41 churches were dedicated to him. Feast day 9 October.

denominations

A term for churches with specific names, or used to distinguish them from an established church. There has been great growth in their number during the 20th century. Western denominations have exported their peculiarities to the Third World, and many new movements have formed in the latter. It is estimated that in 1900 there were 1,900 Christian denominations, and that by 1985 the total had increased to 22,000.

Deo Gratias

Latin, 'thanks be to God'. It occurs in liturgies, and is used when receiving gifts, or even as a personal name.

descent into hell

More properly, into HADES. Based on 1 Peter 3:19, which states that Christ 'went and preached to the spirits in prison'; from the second century there was widespread belief that he delivered the righteous figures of the Old Testament from waiting in Hades and took them, like the penitent thief, to Paradise. The phrase found its way into the APOSTLES' and ATHANASIAN Creeds and into the third of the Thirty-Nine ARTICLES of the Prayer Book. (*See also* ADAM; HARROWING OF HELL.)

desert

Withdrawal to the wilderness inspired early ASCETICS, following the examples of Elijah and John the Baptist. The desert was thought to be full of evil spirits, to be conquered like physical desires. Monastic reform movements look back

to the desert ideal of separation from the world and often seek remote places. (*See also* ANTONY; CARMELITES; HERMIT.)

detachment

Non-attachment to material things or relationships. It is taught in the gospels (Mark 10:29 and parallels) and by Paul (Eph. 4:22f.). Monastics and mystics sought detachment as stripping oneself of everything that hinders the soul from the knowledge of God.

devil

The notion of a chief evil spirit appeared in the inter-testamental period and early Christianity, probably coming from Zoroastrianism. Jesus was seen in conflict with the devil, also called SATAN, and exorcisms were challenges to the power of evil. Paul wrote of 'rulers of darkness' and 'spiritual wickedness' (Eph. 6:12), and the APOCALYPSE is full of notions of 'the dragon, that old serpent, which is the Devil, and Satan' (Rev. 20). Such ideas persisted through history, with speculation about why the devil fell and if he could be saved. Protestants did not doubt the existence of the devil, until modern times, and Milton provided diabolical mythology in *Paradise Lost* (Book I). (*See also* BRAY, BILLY; DEMON; ZOROASTER.)

devil's advocate

Popular name for the Promoter of the Faith, an official of the Roman Catholic Church who investigates claims of virtues and miracles made on behalf of a candidate for beatification or canonization, in order to prevent rash decisions.

devotion

A general term for worship, prayer and dedication to God. In particular it may indicate withdrawal from normal concerns for the practice of contemplation. Modern Devotion (*Devotio moderna*) was a movement of mystical piety among lay people in the 14th century, beginning in the Netherlands and spreading to much of Western Europe. Houses were established of Brothers and Sisters (BRETHREN) OF THE COMMON LIFE, life in which was voluntary and not lifelong. The best-known writing of the movement was the IMITATION OF CHRIST by Thomas à KEMPIS. (*See also* RUYSBROECK.)

dialectic

Investigating and testing opinions and doctrines by logic and discussion. Dialectical theology has been especially associated with Karl BARTH and his followers. They rejected liberalism and mysticism alike, and sought understanding of God in biblical revelation, emphasizing transcendence. (*See also* EXISTENTIALISM; KIERKEGAARD.)

Diana

See ARTEMIS.

dianetics

See HUBBARD.

diaspora, dispersion

The dispersal of Jews from their homeland, beginning with that of the northern tribes of Israel to Assyria in 722 BCE, and then from Judaea in 587 BCE. Later, many Jews were diffused across the Middle East and Mediterranean lands. The modern return to Israel has affected both Jewish and Christian thought, notably in millenarian circles. 'Diaspora' is now also used of other religious groups away from their land of origin: Parsis, Sikhs, Hindus and Buddhists. (*See also* BRITISH ISRAELITES; GHETTO; JUDAISM.)

Diatessaron

Greek, 'composed of four': a combination of the four gospels into one narrative, made by a GNOSTIC writer, Tatian, about 150. This was used in churches until the fifth century, when it was replaced by the separate gospels. It was popular in Greek and Syriac versions, and shows the authority that the gospels had already at this early period.

Didaché

Greek 'Teaching' of the twelve APOSTLES, an early Christian writing, perhaps from the first century. The author and the place of writing are unknown. In 16 short chapters the Didaché gives instructions on Christian life and practice, baptism and the Eucharist, prayer and fasting, bishops and deacons, and travelling prophets.

Dies Irae

Latin, 'Day of Wrath': a hymn of 18 verses in the Mass for the Dead in the Roman Catholic Church. It has been rather poorly rendered as an English hymn.

Diggers

See LEVELLERS.

diocese

From Greek for 'keeping house': an administrative division, and specifically an area over which a bishop rules, with the help of other clergy or bishops. It is divided into smaller groups under rural deans and archdeacons; several dioceses form a province under an archbishop.

Dionysius

A convert of Paul at the AREOPAGUS in Athens (Acts 17:34). Nothing more is known of him, but about the year 500 some Christian Neoplatonic writings were ascribed to Dionysius the Areopagite, also called the Pseudo-Areopagite. The four works are: *The Celestial Hierarchy*, on angels; *The Divine Names*, on attributes of God; *The Ecclesiastical Hierarchy*, on the sacraments and three ways of spiritual life in purgation, illumination and union; *The Mystical Theology*, the ascent of the soul to God. These writings had great influence on medieval theologians and mystics. (*See also* CLOUD OF UNKNOWING; DENIS.)

diptych

From Greek for 'two folds', the name comes from a hinged board bearing names of living or dead persons for whom prayers were desired at the Eucharist. The word was used also for paintings with two leaves that closed like a book, such as the Wilton Diptych, a 14th-century painting by an unknown French artist, formerly owned by the earls of Pembroke at Wilton House. (*See also* TRIPTYCH.)

direction, spiritual

Pastoral guidance by counselling and prayer, by men and women appointed or recognized as having understanding as spiritual fathers or mothers.

dirge

From Latin *Dirige*, 'Lead me', in Psalm 5:8, in the Office for the Dead. Used of the commemoration of the departed, it is also used to mean lament in general.

Discalced

See CARMELITES.

discernment

Paul listed among the spiritual gifts 'discernment of spirits' (1 Cor. 12:10), a check against rash and even blasphemous cries that might be uttered in emotional outbursts, such as that Jesus is anathema (12:3). Later writers produced rules for discerning good and bad movements and activities of feelings and persons.

disciple

From Latin for a 'learner' or pupil, generally applied to a follower of a teacher or way of life. Any follower of Jesus, male or female, could be called a disciple, but the term came to be applied especially to the twelve APOSTLES.

Disciples of Christ

See CAMPBELL.

disciplina arcani

Latin, 'discipline of the secret' or 'hidden practice'. Persecution in the early Church, and the existence of mystery religions, led Christian leaders to conceal some of their rites and beliefs from outsiders or beginners. Catechumens were allowed to hear Scripture and sermon, but were dismissed before the Eucharist, until they were baptized.

In the 19th century some Anglo-Catholic leaders taught 'reserve' in religious teaching and practice, partly in reaction against the openness of evangelicals.

Dismas

From Greek for 'dying', this is the supposed name of the good dying thief crucified with Jesus (Luke 23:39ff). In an apocryphal Acts of PILATE the other thief was called Gestas.

dismissal

Sending out worshippers at the end of the service. From words of dismissal came the name of the Mass. (*See also* ITE, MISSA EST.)

Dissent

See FREE CHURCHES; MARRIAGE; TOLERATION, ACTS OF.

dissolution of the monasteries

From 1536 small and then large monasteries in England were closed by Henry VIII, aided by Thomas CROMWELL. Their property and contents were seized by the king for himself or his favourites. Some monasteries were spared to be parish churches, and some monks became parish priests or were given small pensions. No doubt there had been a decline in ideals, and some moral laxity, but the monasteries were centres of learning, the arts, agriculture and hospitality. The squires who took stones and goods for their country houses boosted their own wealth and position and reinforced class divisions. (*See also* ABBEY; CHANTRY; MONASTICISM; PILGRIMAGE OF GRACE.)

Dives

From Latin for 'rich', this title has been used for the unnamed rich man in the parable of the contrast between himself and the poor man LAZARUS (Luke 16:19ff).

Divine Comedy

See DANTE.

divine right

Belief in the absolute authority of the monarch deriving from appointment by God. Thus Charles I considered that the court had no right to try him, whereas Parliament thought that the king held his office by the consent of the governed. (*See also* KING'S EVIL; LAUD.)

divorce

The words of Jesus seem to imply the indissolubility of marriage: 'What God has joined together, let not man put asunder' (Mark 10:2ff), though there is a 'Matthean exception', allowing a 'cause of fornication' (Matt. 5:32). Protestants have permitted divorce on grounds of adultery and for other reasons, widely extended in recent years, and remarriage. The Eastern ORTHODOX churches have allowed divorce for various reasons, including incompatibility. The Roman Catholic Church has dissolved a marriage if it is declared not consummated, or if it is held that there has never been a true marriage. The Anglican Church seems the most rigid, refusing to allow remarriage of a divorced person during the lifetime of the previous partner. The question would be very problematic, despite the divorces and marriages of Henry VIII, if a divorced monarch who was head of the Anglican Church wished to remarry in church. (*See also* MARRIAGE; SEXUALITY.)

Docetism

From Greek to 'seem', this was an early GNOSTIC Christian view that the earthly life of Christ was mere appearance and that his humanity and sufferings were not physical and real, despite the biblical affirmations that the Word was 'made flesh' (John 1:14). Apocryphal writers had Jesus say, 'to the multitude I am being crucified ... but to you I speak' (Acts of John). A reflection of such Docetism may be found in the Muslim QUR'ĀN (4:156): 'they did not kill him, but it seemed to them as such.' (*See also* BARNABAS; IGNATIUS.)

Doddridge, Philip (1702–51)

Nonconformist minister. He refused to go to Oxford to train for Anglican orders and instead entered a theological academy at Kibworth in Leicestershire. His chief pastorate was at Castle Hill in Northampton, to which he transferred an academy for Dissenting ministers. He was ordained a presbyter to the Independent Congregation by eight ministers, five of them Presbyterians, and received a DD from Aberdeen University. His health was poor and he died in Lisbon seeking a warmer climate. Doddridge was a great preacher, letter- and hymn-writer. His hymns, including 'Hark, the glad sound' and 'O God of Bethel', have been sung in many churches.

dogma

Greek, meaning 'opinion' or 'judgement': the word is used for principles, tenets, or doctrinal systems. Especially it indicates a truth set forth as part of divine revelation, essential to belief. (*See also* ORTHODOXY.)

Dome of the Rock

The Muslim shrine in Jerusalem on the site of the old Temple; wrongly called the Mosque of Omar. Inside and outside the famous dome are inscribed many verses from the QUR'ĀN that refer to Jesus. (*See also* JERUSALEM; TEMPLE MOUNT MOVEMENT.)

The Dome of the Rock, Jerusalem: According to tradition, this was built in 691 CE. Inside the building is a bare rock, perhaps dating back to an old temple or altar; tradition says that marks in the stone are footprints of Muhammad.

Dominic, Dominicans

The Order of Friars Preachers (OP) has been known in England as the Black Friars, and in France as the Jacobins. Dominic (1170–1221), their founder in 1215, was a Spaniard who sold all his belongings to help the poor. He became head of a community of AUGUSTINIAN monks and set out several times to try to convert the ALBIGENSIANS in France, with little success. His order abandoned manual labour to concentrate on study and preaching, and produced thinkers like ALBERTUS MAGNUS and THOMAS AQUINAS. Dominicans were active in the CRUSADES, the INQUISITION, and missions. There is a second enclosed order for nuns and a third, more open, order. Dominic's feast day is 4 August. (*See also* ROSARY.)

Donation of Constantine

A ninth-century forgery, claiming that the Emperor Constantine had given the Pope primacy over the eastern patriarchs and the western provinces and cities. It was included in the false DECRETALS, but was proved spurious by NICHOLAS OF CUSA and others.

Donatism

Fourth-century persecution in North Africa led to divisions in the Church, with a strict party refusing to accept a new bishop of Carthage ordained by one who had surrendered scriptures to persecutors. A rival bishop was appointed, succeeded in 312 CE by Donatus after whom the schismatic movement was named. There were attacks on the Donatists, and on their side association with violent mobs. Despite repression, Donatism grew rapidly, disappearing only with the Islamic conquest of North Africa in the seventh century. (*See also* CONSTANTINE; CYPRIAN.)

Donne, John (1572–1631)

Poet and Dean of St Paul's Cathedral in London. He was brought up a Roman Catholic and became an Anglican in his twenties. He was Member of Parliament for Brackley in 1601, secretly married, had twelve children, was ordained in 1615 and became Dean in 1621. Donne was a colourful character and powerful preacher who is still remembered for his poetry and prose. His verse includes love poems in *Songs and Sonnets*, verse *Satires*, and *Holy Sonnets*.

Dorcas (Tabitha)

A woman disciple healed by Peter (Acts 9:36ff). She cared for the needy, and Dorcas Societies and Dorcas Baskets for similar good works were named after her.

Douai

A college in northern France founded in 1568 for exiled Roman Catholic priests in training for missionary activity in England. It was closed in the French Revolution and transferred to England in 1795. The Douai Bible (1582 and 1609) was prepared in opposition to English Protestant versions, but the translation was made from the Latin Vulgate and not the original Hebrew and Greek. Nevertheless its language influenced parts of the AUTHORIZED VERSION. (*See also* CAMPION; RECUSANCY.)

Doukhobors

A Russian religious movement of 'Spirit-fighters'. Of unknown origin, existing largely among peasants in the 18th century, it was also known as 'Christians of the Universal Brotherhood'. Some of their teachings resembled those of the Quakers; they refused military service and were persecuted by government and ORTHODOX clergy. Tolstoy and Quakers organized relief for them to emigrate to Cyprus and Canada. Doukhobors refused to own land, or send their children to school, where they might be taught militarism. In the 1960s some of them demonstrated naked in Canada, refusing to own land individually and to register births, marriages and deaths,

which led to imprisonment. They now number about 13,000. (*See also* FRIENDS.)

doxology

'Glory', from Greek *doxa*: a liturgical formula of praise to the TRINITY.

drama

The early Church opposed drama, since it was associated with pagan worship, mysteries, spectacles of gladiators or victims fighting or being thrown to beasts, and obscene comedies. Yet the Bible and the Christian story contained ample material for dramatic presentation, and the Eucharist was a supreme mystery. In the middle ages drama developed in mystery and miracle plays, performed in churches and cathedrals, and some of this survives in passion plays, notably at OBERAMMERGAU. Nowadays there are countless nativity and religious plays. (*See also* BECKET; DANCE.)

dreams

Visions, voices, predictions and inspirations have been experienced down the ages in sleep as well as in wakefulness. The Bible recounts many such incidents, from the self-centred dreams of Joseph in Genesis to dreams of the child Jesus by another Joseph recounted in Matthew's Gospel.

Drummond, Henry

See CATHOLIC APOSTOLIC CHURCH.

Dry Mass

See ANTE-COMMUNION.

dualism

Belief in the opposition of good and evil, light and dark, matter and spirit, developed especially in Zoroastrianism, which influenced early and medieval Christianity. (*See also* CATHARI; DEVIL; ZOROASTER.)

dulia

See HYPERDULIA.

Duns Scotus, Johannes
(1264–1308)

One of the greatest medieval school-men. Born near Roxburgh in Scotland, he became a Franciscan and lectured in Oxford, where it is said 30,000 students thronged to hear him. He went to Paris, and died in Cologne. He was a major critic of THOMAS AQUINAS, attacking the latter's rationalism and preferring to give primacy to love and the will. The Scotist system had great influence, but was criticized by humanists and reformers; the word 'dunce' was coined for the followers of Duns.

Dunstan (909–88 CE)

Son of a West Saxon noble, he became a monk at Glastonbury and later abbot. He introduced reform and the abbey became a teaching centre, Dunstan himself being a noted musician and painter. He was made Archbishop of Canterbury by King Edgar, and helped reform of Church and state. After Dunstan's death his cult spread rapidly; Canterbury had his body though Glastonbury claimed it. In London there are churches of St Dunstan-in-the-East and St Dunstan-in-the-West, by WREN and Shaw respectively, replacing earlier churches. Feast day 19 May. (*See also* GLASTONBURY.)

Durham

See BEDE; CUTHBERT; LINDISFARNE.

E

Easter

The English name is said by BEDE to derive from Eostre, the name of an Anglo-Saxon spring goddess. As with Christmas and the new year, so Easter celebrates spring, continuing old pagan festivals. This is appropriate since the CRUCIFIXION and RESURRECTION of Christ occurred at the Jewish PASSOVER, also a spring festival. In France it is Pâques, from the Hebrew Pesakh via Latin. The date of Easter is fixed, in the West, for the first Sunday after the first full moon, after the Spring equinox (21 March). Easter is the greatest Christian feast, prepared for by LENT and Passiontide and begun by all-night vigils in many places, East and West, and in many African and new churches. Easter gardens are models of the Holy Sepulchre, but Easter eggs are probably old pagan symbols of fertility. (*See also* PASCHAL.)

eastward

From the second century Christians turned eastwards in prayer, perhaps following ancient sun-worship, and writers said 'Christ is the true east, like the rising sun.' Churches were 'orientated', with the altar placed at the east end; people turned to it at the CREED, and priests faced east in the EUCHARIST. Protestants generally ignore orientation and ministers face the people. Early Islam followed the Christian eastward position in prayer, but changed it for the direction of the Ka'ba in Mecca.

Ebionites

From Hebrew *ebyonim*, 'poor people': a nickname given for several centuries to Jewish Christians who followed the old Law but believed in Jesus as the Messiah. They were also called NAZARENES, as all Christians were once; but the Ebionites held that Jesus was the natural and legitimate son of Joseph and Mary, denying the notion of a VIRGIN BIRTH. Following the Law the Ebionites kept to circumcision, and some were ASCETIC and VEGETARIAN. Their numbers declined with the dispersion of the Jews and growth of the gentile Church. (*See also* HEBREWS, GOSPEL ACCORDING TO.)

Ecce homo

'Behold the Man.' Latin version of the words of PILATE presenting Jesus (John 19:5). They have been used for lives of Christ, and for pictures of him wearing a crown of thorns.

ecclesia

From Greek, meaning 'called out', this word was used in Greek commonwealths for a general assembly of all free citizens. It was taken over by later brotherhoods and guilds, and by Jews for the congregation and community of Israel.

In the New Testament it was the regular word for the CHURCH, for gatherings for worship and for local communities. The French word *église* for church is derived from *ecclesia*.

Eckhart, John, 'Meister' (1260–1327)

German DOMINICAN mystic whose teaching of unity with God has influenced mystics ever since his time. Eckhart was a powerful preacher in both Latin and German. He supported the female BÉGUINES, criticized the 'merchant mentality' of rulers, and told peasants in the vernacular that they were 'aristocrats' because God made them beautiful. Eckhart spoke for a creation-centred spiritual tradition, on themes of blessing, beauty, healing and humour. Many of his writings were lost, but four volumes have been edited in German and Latin. (*See also* PANTHEISM; SUSO; TAULER.)

ecology

Concern for life and the environment is found in the Bible from the story of creation, where God told animals and human beings to be fruitful and replenish the earth (Gen. 1:28). Paul wrote of all creation travailing for a better future (Rom. 8:22). Christian theology tended to separate cosmic order and moral order, but the link between them has been reaffirmed in modern times, urging care for all creatures and avoidance of destruction. (*See also* ECKHART; HARVEST.)

ecstasy

From Greek for 'out of the senses'; used of mystical or prophetic trances. The Spirit of the Lord seized the prophets, Paul was rapt to the third heaven (2 Cor. 12:2), and TERESA's ecstasy led to divine union. Some have regarded ecstasy as pathological, but most mystics were active and rational people, without illness or degeneration in their experiences. (*See also* RAPTURE.)

ecumenism/oecumenism

From Greek for 'the whole of the world', this word has been much used in the twentieth century for moves towards church unity. It is said to have been a command of Christ, 'that they may all be one' (John 17:21), though this may be the reflection of the evangelist in face of Christian divisions. Ecumenical movements are dated from an Edinburgh Missionary Conference in 1910; 1948 saw the formation of the World Council of Churches, with Protestant and Orthodox members, and later Roman Catholic observers. Corporate union has been difficult to achieve, though some Methodists, Congregationalists and Presbyterians have amalgamated, and there were unions with episcopalians in South and North India. (*See also* CHURCH OF SOUTH INDIA; GENERAL COUNCILS; SCHISM.)

Eddy, Mary Baker

See CHRISTIAN SCIENCE.

edict

See MILAN; NANTES.

education

See RELIGIOUS EDUCATION.

Edmund (840–70 CE)

King of the East Angles, he was defeated by invading Danes and shot to death with arrows for refusing to abjure his Christian faith. His tomb at Bury St Edmunds became a great place of pilgrimage. Feast day 20 November.

Edward the Confessor (1003–66)

Last Anglo-Saxon king of the old line. His reign was marked by struggles between Saxons and Normans. He began the building of WESTMINSTER ABBEY and his piety brought later canonization.

Edward VI

See BOOK OF COMMON PRAYER; CRANMER.

Edwards, Jonathan (1703–58)

American Congregational minister. He became colleague to his grandfather at Northampton, Massachusetts. An extreme Calvinist, Edwards excluded the unconverted from Communion and had to resign his ministry. He went as missionary to Indians, and then to be president of Princeton College, but died of smallpox. Edwards was widely read in philosophy and theology and a leader in the 18th-century revival (See also GREAT AWAKENING.)

Église de Jesus-Christ

See KIMBANGU.

Egypt

See COPTIC.

elder

Anglo-Saxon equivalent of 'presbyter'; however, the latter term normally meant an ordained minister, whereas an elder in the Reformed tradition is a lay person. Elders belong to a board or session to govern the congregation, and may also sit or stand round the minister at the sacrament. (See also PRESBYTERIANISM.)

election

From Greek for 'choice'. In the Bible, Israel was the 'Chosen People', and this belief was taken over by Christians who saw themselves as 'a remnant according to the election of grace' (Rom. 11:5). Election and PREDESTINATION were often used indistinguishably by theologians, and Augustine argued that predestination to life implied an act of election by God.

elevation

See GESTURES.

Elim

The Elim Foursquare Gospel Church developed in Northern Ireland in 1914. It was led by George Jeffreys, who was later ordained minister by a Welsh Congregationalist. Elim comes from Exodus 15:27, meaning 'palm trees', where the Israelites found refreshment. The movement claims to stand 'foursquare' on the Bible, in the evangelical tradition; it is organized like METHODISM, but it is FUNDAMENTALIST, ADVENTIST and PENTECOSTAL. Much of its activity is in large cities, like London and Birmingham. (See also MCPHERSON.)

Eliot, John (1604–90)

Born in England, he migrated to Massachusetts and became a missionary to the Indians. He learned the Algonquin language, translated the Bible, and composed a catechism and grammar. He organized 14 separate communities for his converts, but they gradually declined after Indian uprisings. In old age Eliot turned his attention to black slaves.

Elizabeth I

See DE HAERETICO; TALLIS; THIRTY-NINE ARTICLES.

Elmo

Popular name for a legendary Erasmus, about the fourth century. He is said to have preached during a thunderstorm, unafraid of a thunderbolt nearby. St Elmo's Fire was the name given to electrical discharges at mastheads of ships after storms, to show the saint's protection. He is patron of sailors and his emblem is a windlass. Feast day 2 June.

Ember Days

Perhaps from the old English for 'period': the Wednesday, Friday and Saturday of four weeks in the year, originally three agricultural festivals at sowing, harvest and vintage. Ember Days are after 13 December (St Lucy), after Ash Wednesday, after Whitsunday and after 14 September (Holy Cross Day).

Emmaus

A village in Judaea to which two disciples were walking on Easter Day when they met the risen Christ (Luke 24: 13ff). *See also* CLEOPAS.

encyclical

A circular letter sent to churches by a leader or bishop; nowadays in Roman Catholicism used only for letters from the Pope. Anglican Lambeth Conferences have also sent out such circulars.

England, Church of

See ANGLICANISM.

enthusiasm

Late Greek for 'god-possession': used of divine indwelling in poets, prophets and mystics. Employed critically, doubting the inspiration, it has been applied to Montanists, Jansenists, Quakers, Anabaptists, Methodists, Pentecostals and Charismatics. (*See also* ECSTASY.)

Ephesians, Epistle to the

A letter from Paul to Christians at Ephesus in Asia Minor, modern Turkey. The absence of personal greetings, which occur in other letters, suggests that it was a circular letter. Like COLOSSIANS, Ephesians describes the person and work of Christ, and some regard it as a reworking of Colossians into a more systematic treatise.

Ephphatha

Aramaic for 'be opened': used by Jesus in healing a deaf and dumb man (Mark 7:34). It occurs in the baptismal ceremony of the Roman Catholic Church.

epiclesis

Greek 'invocation': in the Eucharist, a prayer for the descent of the Holy Spirit on the elements, that they may become to the recipients the body and blood of Christ.

Epiphany

Greek 'manifestation' or 'showing forth'. In Eastern churches it celebrated the baptism of Jesus, and in the West the manifestation of Christ to the gentiles, the visit of the wise men to the infant Jesus at Bethlehem (Matt. 2). Epiphany falls on 6 January. (*See also* MAGI.)

episcopacy, episcopi vagantes

See BISHOP.

Episcopalian, Scottish

See CHURCH OF SCOTLAND.

epistle

A letter, especially one ascribed to an APOSTLE, which is part of the CANON of Scripture. It is often the first biblical passage read at the EUCHARIST. A reader or chanter of the epistle was sometimes called the epistoler.

Erasmus, Desiderius
(1466–1536)

Dutch humanist, born at Rotterdam, who anticipated the REFORMATION. He was ordained priest, studied in Paris and visited England. He stayed with Thomas MORE and wrote a witty *Encomium Moriae*, 'Praise of Folly', a play on the name 'More' which resembles a Greek word for 'folly'. Erasmus was appointed to a new Lady Margaret chair at Cambridge, and completed the first printed edition of the New Testament in Greek in 1516. He attacked the corruptions of the Church and the monasteries, and introduced rational conceptions of doctrine. However, he did not become a Protestant and he disagreed with Luther on FREE WILL. He died at Protestant Basle; he was condemned at the Council of TRENT and his writings were placed on the INDEX.

Erastianism

The view that the STATE should be supreme over the Church, named after

German wood carving of Erasmus, Brussels: Erasmus was the most famous scholar of the 15th–16th centuries, a critic of abuses but a supporter of Church tradition.

Swiss theologian Thomas Erastus (1524–83). In England, Richard HOOKER maintained the supremacy of the state, but INDEPENDENTS sought complete freedom from it. The situation remains, in the establishment of the Church of England under the final authority of Parliament.

eros

See AGAPÉ; SHAFTESBURY.

eschatology

Greek, 'last words' or 'things': teachings about the end of the world, the final destiny of individuals and of humanity, including ideas of death, judgement, heaven, hell and the Second Coming of Christ. The term dates from the 19th century. Some theologians (notably SCHWEITZER) have interpreted all or most of the teaching of Jesus as determined by belief in the imminent end of the world. (*See also* ADVENTISM; APOCALYPSE; ARMAGEDDON; INTERIM ETHIC; MILLENNIUM; ZOROASTER.)

Essenes

Jewish ascetic groups (the name means 'pious ones') who flourished from the second century BCE to the first or second century CE. According to Josephus, the Essenes followed severe discipline, in temperance and mastery of passions. They were communistic, wore old clothing, bought and sold nothing, and worked at their own crafts. They scorned wedlock and brought up other people's children as their own. It has been debated whether the ruins of a settlement at Qumran by the Dead Sea were of an Essene community, and whether the famous scrolls were connected with them. (*See also* DEAD SEA SCROLLS.)

Establishment

See ERASTIANISM; STATE AND RELIGION.

eternal life

See IMMORTALITY; RESURRECTION.

Ethelbert

See AUGUSTINE OF CANTERBURY.

Ethiopian Church

Ethiopia was for a long time the only formally Christian country in Africa, the faith having been introduced in the fourth century. It took the form of COPTIC ORTHODOXY with MONOPHYSITE doctrine. For centuries the ruling patriarch, Abuna, was appointed from Egypt, and independence did not come till 1959. The Ethiopian (Abyssinian) Church has priests and monks, follows the Bible and some apocryphal books, and observes Jewish customs such as the Sabbath and circumcision. (*See also* AFRICA; HAILE SELASSIE; RASTAFARIANS.)

Eucharist

Greek, 'thanksgiving': a general term for the major Christian sacrament. The noun does not occur in the New Testament, which speaks rather of the LORD'S SUPPER, but it appears in early writings such as the DIDACHÉ. Later names for this sacrament are Holy Communion and MASS. The institution of the Eucharist by Jesus is recorded by Paul (1 Cor. 11:23ff) and the three SYNOPTIC GOSPELS, each with variants but containing the central elements of bread and wine given by the Lord and commanded as remembrance of him. The meanings of the Eucharist, and its sacrificial nature, have been constantly debated with wide differences between Catholic and evangelical writers. (*See also* AGAPÉ; WORSHIP.)

Eusebius (260–340 CE)

The 'Father of Church History', best known for his *Ecclesiastical History* (323 CE). He became bishop of Caesarea and proposed a compromise in the ARIAN controversy. His history is valuable in quoting from earlier writers, on the sources of the gospels, the work of the apostles, persecutions, controversies, and the peace of the Church under CONSTANTINE.

Euthanasia

Greek, 'easy death'. In voluntary form, it has been proposed by various legalization societies, with safeguards, giving a person the right to terminate his or her own life. It was condemned by the Popes from 1943, by the Anglican archbishops in 1936, and by the Protestant Episcopal Church in America in 1952, among others.

Eutychus

A young man who slept during Paul's sermon at Troas, fell down from a loft and was taken up as dead, but was restored to life by Paul (Acts 20:9ff).

Evangel

Greek, 'Gospel': the 'Good News' of the kingdom of God (Mark 1:14ff).

evangelical

A term applied to Protestant Reformers from their claim to base doctrine on the Gospel. The Lutheran Church in Germany is called the Evangelical Church. From the time of the Methodist movement in the 18th century, 'evangelical' was applied to those who stressed conversion, experience, 'evangelism' and mission. In the 19th century evangelicals were LOW CHURCH, as opposed to ANGLO-CATHOLICS and High Church. In the 20th-century 'evangelical' often indicates FUNDAMENTALIST interpretation of the Bible, as opposed to liberal or modernist. (*See also* CHARISMATIC; EXPERIENCE; HOUSE CHURCHES.)

Evangelium vitae

See ABORTION.

Evangelization

The evangelization of non-Christian peoples has been undertaken by nearly all churches, and has increased in the 20th century more than ever before. (*See also* MISSIONS.)

Eve

The first woman, in the Genesis myth, originally one being with ADAM. Her name meant 'life' and she was called 'the mother of all living' (Gen. 3:20). In the New Testament Eve is mentioned as an example of the status of man and woman in worship (1 Tim. 2:13). (*See also* FALL.)

Evensong

Old English name for an evening service of prayers, psalms, canticles and scripture readings. It combines the offices of VESPERS and COMPLINE. (*See also* MATINS.)

evolution

See DARWINISM.

ex cathedra

Latin, 'from the chair', a phrase describing solemn utterances by the Pope from his throne of authority, and held to be INFALLIBLE.

ex opere operato

Latin, 'from the action performed': the assertion that the efficacy of a sacrament comes from the correct performance of the ritual, and does not depend on the worthiness of the minister.

ex voto

Latin, 'out of a vow': an offering made in fulfilment of a VOW, a votive offering.

exaltation

See HOLY CROSS DAY.

Exclusive Brethren

See DARBY.

excommunication

An action by church authorities excluding from communion, either by denial of the Holy Communion, or more extensively from communion in all the life and worship of the Church. (See also ANATHEMA.)

exegesis

From Greek, to 'lead', and hence to explain or interpret: the exposition of biblical texts.

existentialism

A modern philosophical movement which concentrates on the existence of the individual, who is what he makes himself through development of his essence. Originating with Søren KIERKEGAARD, it has been espoused both by atheistic exponents, like Sartre, and by Christian writers who see it as leading to God.

exorcism

Jewish and pagan practices of casting out evil spirits by prayers and formulas were taken over by the early Church. The gospels describe Jesus exorcizing, and Paul practised this in the name of Christ (Acts 16:18). The power to exorcize was regarded as a CHARISMATIC gift, and priests received the 'order of exorcist'. For a long time baptism included casting out the evil spirit, but this was replaced by prayer for deliverance from sin. While some revivalists claim to cast out evil spirits, and even disease, general modern preference would be to seek medical and psychiatric help.

experience

All human experience may be significant, but need not be experience of God. Religious experience requires encounter with the 'holy', the 'tremendous and fascinating mystery'. Stress upon formality and orthodoxy in word may bring reaction to emphasize emotion and experience. (See also CONVERSION; EVANGELICAL; HOLY.)

expiation

The removal of offence, against God or neighbour, the former taken as effected by the death of Christ and applied to the believer. (See also ATONEMENT.)

exposition

The showing of the sacrament, in private in devotion or in public at the feast of CORPUS CHRISTI. Also used of the expounding of Scripture.

extempore prayer

'On the spur of the moment' or spontaneous prayer seems to be included in Paul's discrimination of prayers and tongues (1 Cor. 14:15ff). After the Reformation and production of revised prayer books, there were some who opposed all set forms in worship. Quakers and other Nonconformists objected to 'paper prayers', though much so-called 'free' prayer used traditional phrases and patterns of petition. Once the norm in Free Churches, extempore prayer has declined, but is revived in charismatic and evangelical groups.

extreme unction

See UNCTION.

F

Faber, Frederick William
(1814–63)

Born in Yorkshire, from a Calvinist background, he became an Anglican priest and then a Roman Catholic in 1845, influenced by J. H. NEWMAN. Faber wrote many hymns, such as 'Faith of our Fathers'.

faculty

An authorization or licence given by law or a superior for the performance of an action, or occupation of a position. Faculties are needed for alterations or additions to churches and churchyards.

faith

There is no verb 'to faith' in English, but we say 'I believe' or 'I have faith', or 'I make an act of faith.' Distinctions are made between 'the faith', as the body of Christian truth, and personal faith as one of the 'theological virtues': 'Faith, hope, love, these three' (1 Cor. 13:13). In general, Catholic theology stressed the intellectual side of faith as belief, while Protestant or evangelical theology emphasized personal faith as belief and trust. (*See also* GRACE.)

Faith-healing usually refers to the search for restoration of health by prayer and invocation of the Holy Spirit. (*See also* EXORCISM; HEALING.)

Faith Tabernacle

See CHRIST APOSTOLIC CHURCH.

Fall

The Genesis story of the disobedience of Adam and Eve in eating forbidden fruit, entailing a fall from innocence and expulsion from Eden, used to be taken literally. Jewish writers did not deduce original or inherited sin from it, or identify the snake with SATAN, and modern Christian commentators regard the story as symbolic of human selfishness and capacity for evil. Paul connected Adam's sin with death (Rom. 5:12) and later writers related this to ORIGINAL SIN. Further mythology added to the Fall the rebellion of Satan against God and his envy of God's power, entailing expulsion from heaven, as described at length in Milton's *Paradise Lost*. The liturgy of the Mass for Holy Saturday speaks of the 'necessary sin of Adam', and cries 'O happy fault [*O felix culpa*] that merited such a Redeemer.' (*See also* DEVIL; LUCIFER.

False Decretals
See DECRETALS.

Family of Love
See BERG.

fasting

Fasting was practised by Jesus and recommended by him (Matt. 4.2, 6:16ff). Weekly fast days were observed in the early Church, and later at LENT, EMBER

Detail from Michelangelo's painting on the ceiling of the Sistine Chapel showing the Fall. Female culpability is emphasized by also giving the serpent a woman's face.

weeks, and on the eves of great feasts like Christmas. Fasting could mean complete abstention from food for a period, or from flesh permanently. Apart from severe fasts in some religious orders, general fasting has now been relaxed. (*See also* ABSTINENCE.)

father

Jesus called God 'father', and no one else should have that title, according to one verse (Matt. 23:9). 'Fathers of the Church' was a term applied to early Christian writers, and to bishops who were later called Reverend Fathers in God. The Pope is popularly named Holy Father. The modern custom of calling Roman and Anglican priests 'father' came from Ireland in the 19th century. (*See also* ABBA.)

Father Divine (1889–1965)

Born George Baker, an African-American minister, he developed a theology of African, Catholic, Protestant and New Thought elements, to achieve health and salvation. He campaigned for civil rights and attracted both blacks and whites. His followers opened Peace Missions to help the poor and offer low-priced goods. (*See also* BLACK THEOLOGY.)

Fatima

Favourite daughter of the Prophet MUHAMMAD. A town in central Portugal was named after her during Moorish rule. On 13 May 1917 three illiterate Portuguese Christian children claimed to have had visions of a woman, who eventually declared herself to be Our Lady of the Rosary. Two of the children died but the third, Lucia Santos, became a Carmelite nun and wrote accounts of her visions, with promises of future secrets. She was still seeing visions in 1996 at the age of 89, at the Carmel in Coimbra. Fatima became a place of pilgrimage, where there are gatherings on the 13th of each month, awaiting further revelations.

Fawkes, Guy (1570–1606)

Born in York of Protestant parents, he became a Catholic and served in the Spanish army in the Netherlands. Back in England he joined the Gunpowder Plot to blow up the king and Parliament on 5 November 1605. He was caught and hanged. Guy Fawkes' Day on 5 November has been celebrated ever since with bonfires, perhaps a relic of old winter fires.

feasts

Church celebrations. The chief is the weekly Sunday, like the Jewish Sabbath and still called Sabbath in some places. Movable feasts depend on the date of EASTER. Immovable feasts, such as CHRISTMAS, EPIPHANY and saints' days, follow the CALENDAR. (*See also* OBLIGATION.)

felix culpa

See FALL.

female ordination

There is some evidence that there were female APOSTLES, for example Junia in Romans 16:7, yet ordination of women to the ministry in mainstream churches has only been achieved in the 20th century. Independent churches, Congregational and then Methodist, were the first to introduce it. When the Anglican Church in England debated the matter, it was shown that 16 churches in the universal Anglican communion already had women priests, with over 1,000 in the United States. Female ordination was approved for the Church in England in 1992 and three years later there were 1,400 women priests in this church. (*See also* WOMAN.)

feminist theology

Like most religions, Christianity in history and thought has been dominated by male concerns and interpretations, although it is remarkable that in both Western Catholicism and Eastern Orthodoxy the figure of MARY, mother of Jesus, has been central in worship and devotion. Further, there have been strong-minded women who have directed whole communities, such as HILDA and TERESA. Feminist theology, especially but not only in America, began with suffragist figures and developed in both Catholic and Protestant circles. Feminists made new interpretations of biblical texts and standard doctrines, criticizing the restriction of the priesthood to men, and offering new light on sin, salvation, the nature of Christ and social teaching. In particular, many efforts have been and are being made to make the language of worship more inclusive, and also in translations of Scripture. (*See also* ADONAI; GODDESS; HÉLOISE; WOMAN.)

Fénelon, François (1651–1715)

French Archbishop of Cambray, he met the QUIETIST Madame GUYON, and after hesitation accepted her teaching and practice of quiet and union with a God of pure love. But when this was condemned by Rome as dangerous, Fénelon accepted the decision and turned against JANSENISM. His *Maximes* remained popular in France and Britain.

Ferrar, Nicholas (1592–1637)

Cambridge scholar and businessman. He retired to Little Gidding in Huntingdonshire in 1625 to found a religious community of about 30 people, based on the Bible and Prayer Book. Criticized as an 'Arminian nunnery', the community fed the poor, taught children and farmed land. King Charles I visited the community twice, but it was ransacked by PURITANS in 1646. The memory of Little Gidding was revived in T. S. Eliot's *Four Quartets* in 1942.

festivals

See FEASTS.

Fid. Def.

See DEFENDER OF THE FAITH.

fideism

From Latin *fides*, 'faith': asserting the primacy of faith over reason, denying that truth of belief can be established by argument. The term was invented in the 19th century for a Protestant interpretation, 'the religion of the spirit'. It is now sometimes applied to the 'language-game', which holds that a theological system has its own rules of language and cannot be fairly criticized from the outside.

Fifth Monarchy

Millenarians of the 1650s sought a 'fifth monarchy' to succeed the empires of Assyria, Persia, Greece and Rome, following a prophecy of Daniel (2:44), and anticipating the 1,000-year rule of Christ and his saints (Rev. 20:4). They opposed both Cromwell and Charles II and after uprisings their leaders were executed.

filioque

Latin, 'and the Son': a phrase introduced into the Nicene Creed, to affirm the 'double procession', that the Holy Spirit 'proceeds from the Father and the Son'. Its use was rejected by ORTHODOX churches and claimed as the major cause of the division of East and West, though that may owe as much to the sack of Constantinople by Crusading armies. In modern times some Western churches have omitted the *filioque* clause. (*See also* CRUSADES; PHOTIUS; PROCESSION; SCHISM.)

finding of the Cross

See INVENTION OF THE CROSS.

Finney, Charles

See REVIVALISM.

first-fruits

See HARVEST; LAMMAS.

fish

See ICHTHUS.

Fisher, John (1469–1535)

Chancellor of Cambridge University, and bishop of Rochester, a fine scholar and popular preacher. Fisher gave the funeral oration for Henry VII but fell out with his son over the proposed divorce and refused to recognize Henry VIII as supreme head of the Church of England. The Pope created Fisher a cardinal, but Parliament condemned him to death and he was executed as one of the first martyrs for the old faith in the English Reformation. He was canonized in 1936. Feast day 22 June.

flagellants

From Latin for 'scourge'. The practice of self-scourging began as sharing in the Passion of Christ. A flagellant movement developed in the 13th century in Italy, stirred up by millenarian preachers like JOACHIM OF FIORE. There were further outbursts during the Black Death in the 14th century, and similar practices exist today in the Philippines. There is a close parallel with the annual flagellations during the Shi'a Muslim Passion Plays for the martyr Husain.

Fletcher, John William (1729–85)

Of Swiss origin, he settled in England and became vicar of Madeley in Shropshire. He joined the Methodist movement and supervised Lady HUNTINGDON's Methodist seminary. Fletcher's wife, Mary Bosanquet, was one of the first Methodist women preachers.

flight from the world

See ANTONY.

flight into Egypt

Journey of the Holy Family from Bethlehem to Egypt, according to Matthew (2:13ff). Luke (2:21ff), however, has them remaining near Jerusalem and being presented in the Temple. (*See also* HOLY INNOCENTS.)

Focolare

Italian, 'little fire': a revival movement within the Roman Catholic Church, founded by Chiara Lubich in 1945 as 'Works of Mary'. At first its members were all virgins; then married women and men were admitted and formed communities for Bible study and holy life. There are summer conferences, called 'Cities of Mary', and a journal, *New City*. Focolare claims to have revitalized parishes, colleges and religious orders, but it has aroused criticism as a church within the Church. (*See also* NEO-CATECHUMENATE; OPUS DEI.)

font

From Latins *fons*, 'a spring of water', the name is given to a stone or metal receptacle for the water of BAPTISM. From the third century, fonts were large basins in which the candidate stood for water to be poured over him or her. As baptism by full immersion declined (except among BAPTISTS), the fonts sometimes became smaller and cuplike. (*See also* BAPTISTERY.)

foot-washing

Jesus washed the disciples' feet and commanded them to do the same for one another (John 13:14). In the middle ages the washing was performed on MAUNDY THURSDAY by bishops and abbots, and by some monarchs, in England being replaced by distribution of Maundy money. Modern Popes continue the practice and so do some Protestant societies, including AMISH, MENNONITES, SEVENTH-DAY ADVENTISTS and AFRICAN groups.

forgiveness

Both a moral idea and a religious experience, forgiveness expresses a relationship to God which results in reconciliation between people. The SERMON ON THE MOUNT insists on human forgiveness so that divine pardon may follow, and in the LORD'S PRAYER, recited daily throughout most of the world, Christians pray: 'Forgive us our trespasses [or debts] as we forgive those who trespass against us.' The poet William Blake insisted that Jesus did not inculcate moral virtue but 'Forgiveness of Sins. This alone is the Gospel' (*The Everlasting Gospel*).

form-criticism

Early 20th-century analysis of scriptural texts, especially of the gospels, according to their form, whether as sermons, teaching or narration, and considering how far the material was shaped by the needs of the community and its liturgy. Distinctions have been made between miracle stories, pronouncements, preachings, parables, apocalyptic sayings, legends and myths.

Fortune, Dion (1890–1946)

Born Violet Mary Firth, of CHRISTIAN SCIENTIST parents, she became one of the leading modern occultists. She encountered THEOSOPHY and helped to form a Society of the Inner Light, with a Christian outlook.

Foursquare

See ELIM; MCPHERSON.

Fox, George (1624–91)

Founder of the Society of Friends (Quakers). He was born at Fenny Drayton in Leicestershire, son of a weaver. He left home and wandered round the country, Bible in hand, guided by the 'inner light'. Fox rejected formal religion, criticizing churches as 'steeple houses' and their ministers as 'professors'. He refused to take off his hat to kings or commoners or take an oath. He married Margaret Fell, widow of a judge, and travelled to Holland, Germany and America. Fox was outspoken, and sometimes incoherent, but he was devoted, and organized his society and the education of the poor. His *Journal* remains a classic. (*See also* FRIENDS.)

Foxe, John (1516–87)

Ardent Calvinist. Born at Boston in Lincolnshire, he took refuge on the continent during the reign of the Catholic MARY TUDOR. He published in Latin and English accounts of the sufferings of Protestant martyrs, which came to be known as *Foxe's Book of Martyrs* and took its place for centuries in many homes alongside the Bible and *Pilgrim's Progress*. Foxe's narratives are vivid and exaggerated, but contain valuable historical material.

fraction

Breaking of bread or wafer in the liturgy of the EUCHARIST before the Communion. The position of the fraction varies, and some modern liturgies are no clearer than older ones.

Francis of Assisi (1181–1226)

One of the most popular medieval saints, among Protestants as well as Catholics. Born Giovanni Bernardone, he used the language of the Troubadours and had the nickname of Il Francesco ('little Frenchman'). His father was a wealthy merchant at Assisi in central Italy, but after a serious illness Francis renounced everything, even his clothes, and lived as a HERMIT. Others were attracted and Francis drew up a simple rule of brotherhood, requiring chastity, poverty and obedience, which gained approval from the Pope. His followers took the names of 'friars minor' (*fratres minores*), and a parallel movement was founded for women. Francis also founded the TERTIARIES, the Third Order, for those who remained in the

Fresco of St Francis preaching to the birds, Little Kimble Church, Buckinghamshire: In the legendary Little Flowers, *written about a century after his death, Francis is said to have preached to the birds, telling the swallows to keep quiet until he had finished, when they flew away with his message.*

world but followed his ideals. In an ecstasy he is said to have received the STIGMATA, wounds of Christ. He died near Assisi and was canonized two years later. His *Canticle of the Sun* praises God in nature and the *Little Flowers of St Francis* gives stories of Francis and his followers.

The Franciscan Order became noted for preaching, and produced scholars such as the British DUNS SCOTUS and William of OCKHAM. Feast day 4 October. (*See also* CANTICLE; CAPUCHINS; CLARE; CRIB; CROSS.)

Francis of Sales (1567–1622)

French bishop and writer. Born at the family castle of Sales in Savoy, he was one of the leaders of the Counter-Reformation. He met Madame de Chantal and established an order of nuns under her direction. A society of Salesians, named after him, was founded in Italy in 1859 to train poor young men for the priesthood. Among his writings, *Introduction to the Devout Life* (1609) was especially popular in showing how the Christian life could be practised amid worldly occupations. Feast day 29 January.

Francis Xavier

See XAVIER.

Free Church of Scotland

See CHALMERS.

Free Churches

Modern name in England for churches formerly called Dissenting or Nonconformist. Baptists, Congregationalists, Presbyterians and Quakers had all refused to conform to the Established Church. Methodists arose within that church but formed their own societies and became the largest of the Free Churches. 'Free' did not imply any particular church organization, which varied considerably, nor a lack of discipline,

which was often firm. Unions of Free Churches and sharing of churches are increasingly common. (*See also* TOLERATION ACTS.)

free will

One of the great philosophical problems, difficult of proof or disproof, though Dr Johnson declared in the 18th century: 'We *know* our will is free, and *there's* an end on't.' In theology the debate has been between teachers of PREDESTINATION, such as Augustine and Calvin, and supporters of free will, like Pelagius and Arminius.

Freeman, Thomas Birch (1806–90)

Son of a freed black slave and the daughter of a farm labourer. Born near Winchester, he became an ardent Wesleyan Methodist and went as a missionary to the Gold Coast in 1838. Many missionaries had died of fevers, but Freeman's mixed blood perhaps enabled him to survive for over 50 years. He travelled to Ashanti, Dahomey and Abeokuta, putting Africans in charge of new congregations. The mission became nervous of his activity, and Freeman resigned for a time but returned to consolidate his work.

freemasonry

Called the world's largest secret society, it is condemned by the Roman Catholic Church and numerous Protestants. Masonry is claimed as religious, with belief in a Supreme Being and immortal souls, and many Protestants belong to it, including some at high levels in society. But the secrecy, and the exclusion of women, arouse suspicion.

friar

A 'brother', member of one of the medieval orders: Franciscans (Grey Friars), Dominicans (Black Friars) or

Carmelites (White Friars), from the colours of their habits. There were also Augustinian or Austin Friars, and Crutched or Crossed Friars.

Friday

Not only GOOD FRIDAY, for the annual memorial of the Crucifixion, but the weekly Friday was observed in commemoration of this event. It was formerly a day of fasting, or abstinence from meat, but both abstentions have now been relaxed.

Friends, Society of

The proper name for the Quakers. Founded by George FOX in 1668, they were called the Friends of Truth, who told magistrates to quake before God. The 'friendly persuasion' was taken to America by William PENN, who founded Pennsylvania on Quaker principles of consensus and fair dealing. By the doctrine of the inner light, women were on equal terms with men and slavery was opposed. Opposition to military service brought conflict with authority. The social and educational work of the Friends has been notable. The numbers of Friends are not great, but their influence has been much greater. Some 80 per cent are now in the USA. *See also* FRY.

Frith, John (1503–33)

Born at Westerham in Kent, he went abroad and helped TYNDALE translate the New Testament. Frith wrote tracts against PURGATORY and TRANSUBSTANTIATION, and on return to England he was arrested on the orders of Thomas MORE, tried and condemned for heresy, and burned at Smithfield.

fruits of the Spirit

These are nine, according to Paul, who lists them in Galatians 5:22–3: love, joy, peace, patience, kindness, goodness, faithfulness, gentleness, self-control.

Fry, Elizabeth (1780–1845)

Born at Norwich, third daughter of a rich Quaker banker, she married Joseph Fry, a London Quaker merchant, in 1800. She became a 'minister' and speaker among Quakers. She visited Newgate prison, was appalled at the condition of women and children there, and devoted her life to prison reform, aiming at separation of the sexes, female supervision of women, and adequate instruction. She founded hostels for the homeless, evangelized, and wrote *Texts for Every Day* as well as reports on social conditions.

fundamentalism

Belief in the literal truth and inerrancy of the Bible, against scientific or critical study and the theory of evolution. The terms 'fundamentals' and 'fundamentalist' have been used since the early years of the 20th century. Churches were torn by disputes, aggravated in 1925 by the 'monkey trial' of J.T. Scopes in Tennessee who taught evolution. Conservative political swings in recent decades have brought new attacks on evolution and liberalism. Fundamentalist interpretation of Scripture is often combined with ADVENTISM and millenarianism. Similar fundamentalist movements appear in the other religions of the Book, Judaism and Islam. (*See also* DARWINISM; EVANGELICALISM; MODERNISM.)

funerals

See BURIAL; DEAD, PRAYERS FOR THE.

G

Gabriel

See ANGEL; ARCHANGEL.

Galatians, Epistle to the

One of Paul's earliest letters, to Christians in Asia Minor. He declares his own apostleship, from God not man, and discusses disagreements with Peter, emphasis on faith rather than law, and the oneness of race, status and sex in Christ.

Galilee

Northern province of Palestine in Roman times, where most of the ministry of Jesus was passed, from his home in Nazareth to Capernaum and Bethsaida. It is hot and humid country by the lake, 600 feet below sea level, though tempered by winds from the Sea of Galilee or Tiberias.

'Galilee' was also a name given to a porch for penitents in some medieval cathedrals. Some modern Africans 'go to Galilee' for rejoicing after Easter Sunday.

Galileo (1564–1642)

Italian astronomer who taught the Copernican theory that the earth revolves round the sun, instead of vice versa. The papal office brought in the Inquisition, and under threat of torture Galileo was forbidden 'to hold, teach, or defend' the earth's motion. He submitted, but is said to have muttered 'Nevertheless, it does move' (*eppur si muove*). In 1992 the Vatican admitted its error and formally rehabilitated Galileo.

gallery

A balcony or platform projecting from the wall of a building. Galleries were used in fourth-century BASILICAS, providing space when the nave was occupied by clergy, and they also separated women from men as in Jewish synagogues. After the Reformation, galleries were often erected for singers, and in large Free Churches galleries on three sides brought worshippers nearer the preacher.

Gallican

Appertaining to the French Roman Catholic Church, which during the Great SCHISM of the papacy was independent of Rome. A Gallican Psalter was a version of the Psalms popular in Gaul, and Gallican rites were liturgies used there at different times.

Gamaliel

Jewish rabbi who counselled tolerance when Peter and others were arrested (Acts 5:34ff) and who was claimed by Paul as his teacher (Acts 22:3).

gambling

Something for nothing, or very little, is the principle. A game of chance, like cards, is not gambling if no money is involved. Many Christians have enjoyed mild forms of gambling, such as raffles, yet the 'work ethic' of Puritans often set them against it. The National Lottery in Britain has been opposed by Methodists and some black churches, seeing danger in excess. (*See also* MAMMON; WORK.)

Gandhi, Mohandas Karamchand (1869–1948)

The Indian national leader (called Mahatma, 'great soul') held that truth was God and non-violence was love. He used hymns and prayers from Christian and other religions in his services and writings. His non-violent teachings and actions were potent in struggles for racial justice in America and South Africa as well as India.

Garden of Eden

See PARADISE.

garden tomb

General C. G. Gordon, British warrior in China and the Sudan, spent the year 1883 wandering round Palestine and Jerusalem, Bible in hand, trying to identify sacred sites. Not content with the traditional shrines of the tomb and Calvary in the Church of the HOLY SEPULCHRE, Gordon found another place for Calvary outside the Damascus Gate of Jerusalem, and a tomb in a garden nearby for the burial of Jesus.

Garvey, Marcus Mosiah (1887–1940)

Born in Jamaica, he founded the Universal Negro Improvement Association in 1914. Garvey taught an economic, political and spiritual philosophy, applying Psalm 68:31: 'Ethiopia shall soon stretch out her hands to God.' He became the prophet of RASTAFARIANISM, and from 1927 declared that black people would be liberated by their Messiah, Ras Tafari, HAILE SELASSIE. (*See also* BLYDEN.)

Gaspar

See MAGI.

Geddes, Jenny

A vegetable-seller in Edinburgh. According to a shaky legend, when the hated Scottish Prayer Book was introduced at St Giles' Cathedral in 1637, Jenny threw her stool at Bishop Lindsay, shouting: 'Thou false thief, dost thou say mass at my lug?' (*See also* KNOX.)

Gehenna

'The valley of Hinnom': a rubbish dump outside the walls of Jerusalem, which had been a place of human sacrifice (2 Kgs. 23:10). In the gospels it is taken as a symbol of hell, with undying worms and unquenchable fire (Mark 9:43ff).

Gelasian

Ancient Roman missal, with feasts fitted to the church year, mistakenly ascribed to the fifth-century Pope Gelasius.

genealogies of Jesus

Matthew and Luke contain lists of ancestors of Jesus, both traced through JOSEPH as his father. Matthew (1: 1–17) goes back to Abraham, and includes four women of dubious behaviour, apparently to clear MARY of any similar suspicion in the virginal conception. Luke (3:23ff) returns to Adam, and interestingly does not include Solomon. The irreconcilable differences between the two genealogies indicate that they came from independent early Christian circles.

gender

See FEMINISM.

general councils

Gatherings of leaders of all the churches were held from early centuries to consider doctrine and discipline, though Article 21 of the Book of Common Prayer asserted that general councils 'may err, and sometimes have erred'. Two of the most important were at NICAEA in 325 and CHALCEDON in 451. Since the division between the churches of East and West, most churches have not recognized general councils, but there have been Vatican Councils and Ecumenical Councils of Protestant and Orthodox Churches. (*See also* CONCILIARISM; ECUMENISM; SCHISM; VATICAN.)

Geneva

Centre of REFORMED, as distinct from Lutheran, Protestantism, led by John CALVIN.

Geneva Bible

An English translation, published in Geneva in 1560, which became known as the Breeches Bible, because in Genesis 3:7 it said that Adam and Eve 'made themselves breeches', which the AUTHORIZED VERSION changed to 'aprons'. This Bible was popular because it had numbered verses and was in a small, handy format. (*See also* TREACLE BIBLE.)

gentile

A term variously used in English Bibles for nations, peoples, Hellenes and Greeks: in general, non-Jews. Mormons use it of non-Mormons. Traditional Jewish writings refer to the *goyim*, goys, which is Yiddish for gentiles. 'Righteous gentiles', in Jewish belief, are those who followed the Commandments and helped Jews in the times of persecution.

genuflection

From Latin for 'knee-bending'. A single genuflection is a brief kneeling on the right knee, before the sacrament or Cross, or during the creed. A double genuflection is on both knees before the exposed sacrament.

George

Patron saint of England since the 14th century. Little is known of him. The legend of St George and the dragon may have come from the ancient Greek story of Perseus delivering Andromeda from a dragon. George as a soldier-saint became popular during the CRUSADES, and was adopted as protector by Richard I. The red cross on a white background became a kind of military uniform and then the national flag. Some 200 churches in England are dedicated to George, but in the reform of the Roman calendar of saints in 1969 his cult was reduced to a local one. Feast day 23 April.

German Christians

'Deutsche Christen' were those who tried to reconcile Christianity and Nazism in the 1930s. Some wanted to reject the Old Testament and anything Jewish in the New, to 'complete' the Reformation. The Holy Land was said to be Germany and Evangelical Youth was to be incorporated into the Hitler Youth. There were strong protests from the CONFESSING CHURCH, but more than half of the country's Protestants supported the German Christians.

Gerontius

Both a Cornish and a Welsh saint are called Gerontius, Geraint or Gerent. In 1865 J. H. NEWMAN wrote *The Dream of Gerontius*, about a vision of a just soul leaving the body, with choruses of angels and demons; it was put to music by Edward Elgar. It contains the hymn 'Praise to the holiest in the height', though that is usually sung to a setting by J. B. Dykes.

Gestas

See DISMAS.

gestures

Natural movements which become stylized in worship. The SIGN OF THE CROSS goes back to the third century. Elevation is raising the sacramental host. Imposition or laying on of HANDS occurs in blessing, confirming, ordaining and healing. The peace, or kiss of peace, is an ancient practice revived in modern times.

Gethsemane

A garden at the foot of the Mount of Olives, with an ancient wine press and oil farm. There Jesus retired with his disciples after the LAST SUPPER, suffered agony and was arrested. At the modern site there are ancient olive trees and in a church is a rock said to be where Jesus prayed.

ghetto

From Italian *borghetto*, 'small borough': used of walled parts of towns where Jews lived in the middle ages.

Gidding, Little

See FERRAR.

gifts of the Spirit

See FRUITS OF THE SPIRIT.

giving

See ALMS.

Glastonbury

Perhaps the oldest English abbey. A Celtic foundation made into a Saxon monastery, it was destroyed by Danes and revived by DUNSTAN. In legend Joseph of Arimathea came here with the Holy GRAIL, having been sent by the apostle Philip to evangelize Britain. Other legends make it Avalon where King Arthur was buried. Glastonbury Tor is the old tower of a 13th-century St Michael's Church. Glastonbury Thorn is a hawthorn which flowers twice a year. Today Glastonbury is a place of pilgrimage for environmentalists and pop concerts.

glebe

From Latin for 'clod' or 'soil': land given to support the parson of a parish. It could be cultivated or let out to tenants. It has now been abolished. (*See also* TITHE.)

Gloria

The first Latin word of the DOXOLOGY, 'Glory be to God on high' or 'Glory be to the Father'.

glossolalia

From two Greek words, for 'tongue' and 'speaking'. Phenomena found in early and later PENTECOSTAL and CHARISMATIC Christianity, and in other religions. The account of PENTECOST in ACTS 2 speaks of both 'tongues' and 'dialect', and the author seems to think the apostles spoke the languages of all nations. But from Paul's instructions (1 Cor. 14:19) it appears that no one understood what speakers in 'tongues' were saying: 'I had rather speak five words with my understanding than ten thousand in an unknown tongue.' 'Tongues' may be ecstatic utterances, giving expression and relief to the speaker but not to others. There seems no clear evidence that they are foreign languages, and Pentecostals have to learn the hard way of study when abroad, or use interpreters.

Gnosticism

From Greek *gnosis*, knowledge. Gnosticism is a general term for religious movements that emphasized 'secret knowledge' enabling humans to escape from this evil world to the realm of the true God. There was a dualism between the world and God, and notions of a lesser deity, the DEMIURGE, who created the cosmos, along with DOCETIC views of the nature of Christ. Gnostic ideas have emerged down history, in MANICHAEISM, CATHARI and THEOSOPHY, and in writers like GURDJIEFF. (*See also* VALENTINIANS.)

God

The New Testament continues the teachings of the Hebrew prophets of one God, with emphasis upon his nature and relationship to humanity as Father. God may be envisaged or described in human terms, anthropomorphically, but this does not mean that God is a glorified male or female human being. The first of the THIRTY-NINE ARTICLES affirms that 'there is but one living and true God, everlasting, without body, parts, or passions.' Along with Judaism and Islam, Christianity is monotheistic, though in the early centuries there were many debates about the place of Christ and the doctrine of the TRINITY. (*See also* ARIANISM; CHRISTOLOGY; FILIOQUE; MONOTHEISM; PANTHEISM.)

goddess

Since God has no body or passions, there is no sex. 'He' is as much 'She', though beyond both. The early Church met goddess cults: 'Great is Diana [Artemis] of the Ephesians' cried the people there, but Paul would have none of it (Acts 19:28). Some have suggested that the Holy Spirit, which is neuter in Greek, could represent a female element in the deity, and others that the place is occupied by the Virgin MARY, who, though not strictly worshipped, receives countless honours and prayers. (*See also* HYPERDULIA.)

God-fearer

See PROSELYTE.

godparents

Since the second century godparents or sponsors have been required at BAPTISMS, especially of infants to answer on behalf of the child and ensure its Christian upbringing. At least one godfather and one godmother were needed for each child, and though parents might be sponsors they often took second place in baptismal promises. Sponsors should be communicants, especially important in newly evangelized places, or in secular society today where they should not be casual friends but church members.

Gog and Magog

Two powers doing battle under Satan (Rev. 20:8). They are taken from Ezekiel (38:2), where Gog is a prince and Magog his country. They appear in the QUR'ĀN (18:93) as Yajuj and Majuj, working corruption. As giants they are great wooden statues in the Guildhall in London.

Golden Legend

A 13th-century compilation, also called *Lombardica Historia,* by the Italian friar and archbishop Jacob of Voragine. It gave many early Christian apocryphal legends, especially those of PSEUDO-JAMES, and was very popular in art, literature and preaching. William Caxton printed an English version which was often reprinted. But the historicity of the Golden Legend was severely attacked by scholars from the 16th century onwards.

Golden Rule

The principle of doing to others as one would have them do to oneself. Often in a negative form, it is found in many places: in the Jewish Talmud and Islamic QUR'ĀN, in Plato and Confucius. The positive form occurs in both versions of Jesus' sermon, so it may be taken as a foundation statement: 'Whatever you wish that men should do to you, do so to them' (Matt. 7:12; Luke 6:31).

Golgotha

See CALVARY.

Good Friday

The FRIDAY of HOLY WEEK, before Easter, commemorating the CRUCIFIXION and death of Jesus. A day of fasting, even with some modern relaxation, it is really Sad or Holy Friday. This and the following Holy Saturday are the only days in the Roman Catholic Church when there is no celebration of MASS. Altars are stripped and no bells or organs are played. Other churches have 'Three Hours' services, processions or simple morning prayer. Though it is still a 'bank' holiday, many shops are now open on this most holy of days.

Good Samaritan

The foreigner in the parable of Luke 10:30ff, who had compassion on and cared for the wounded traveller when priest and Levite passed by on the other side. The name SAMARITAN has thus been given to hospitals and caring organizations.

Good Shepherd

A title of Christ from John 10:11, betokening a care also illustrated in the parable of the shepherd seeking one lost sheep (Luke 15:4ff). In the CATACOMBS Jesus is painted as the Good Shepherd with a lamb on his shoulder, and the theme often occurs in later art.

Gordon, General

See GARDEN TOMB.

Gospel

From Old English *godspel*, 'good tidings', though the first part was sometimes identified with 'God' and not with 'good'; later it was replaced with *evangelium*. (*See also* EVANGEL.)

grace

The love of God to humanity, as FAITH is the returning love. Grace is free and unmerited, the gift of God, not to be earned by one's own efforts. Prevenient grace is that which precedes conversion. Habitual grace comes through the sacraments; actual grace is for a special purpose; efficacious grace is that producing an effect.

Grace at meals follows the example of Jesus (Mark 6:41). Saying grace, once universally Christian, is now probably observed more by American than by European Protestants. John Wesley's grace, 'Be present at our table Lord', was printed on a teapot made for him by the potter Josiah Wedgwood.

gradual

From Latin for 'step', an ANTIPHON sung on altar steps during the liturgy.

Graham, William Franklin, 'Billy' (b. 1918)

American evangelist. Born to Scottish-Irish parents, he was ordained a Southern Baptist minister in 1934. Through his international crusades and radio and television addresses, he has become probably the best-known preacher ever. Criticized for conservative views and political naïveté, he has nevertheless hinted that Christians can learn from other religions, and he has co-operated with Roman Catholic and Orthodox organizations.

Grail

The Holy Grail figures in medieval legends of King Arthur and the Knights of the Round Table, first appearing with the French poet Chrétien de Troyes about 1180. Later the Grail was identified as the cup used at the Last Supper in which JOSEPH OF ARIMATHEA caught the blood of Christ from the Cross. The word Grail may be derived from Latin for a 'dish', though some think San Graal should be Sang Real, 'royal blood'. Thomas Malory wrote up the story in the 15th century and Tennyson in the 19th in *Idylls of the King*. (*See also* GLASTONBURY.)

Grande Chartreuse

See CARTHUSIANS.

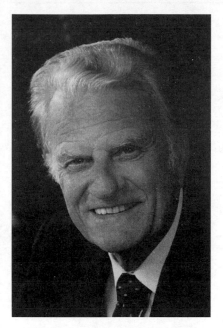

Billy Graham: The grand old man of moderate American evangelism, and friend of presidents of different parties.

Great Awakening

A religious revival in New England in 1725–60, marked by fiery preaching and emotional reactions. Calvinism and Anglicanism were revitalized by this experiential religion, which JONATHAN EDWARDS called the 'surprising work of God'. (*See also* BAPTISTS; REVIVALISM.)

Great Bible

See COVERDALE.

Gregorian calendar

See CALENDAR.

Gregory I, the Great

See AUGUSTINE OF CANTERBURY.

Gregory VII

See CANOSSA.

Gregory of Nazianus and Nyssa

See CAPPADOCIANS.

Griffiths, Bede (1906–93)

Roman Catholic priest and prior of Farnborough Abbey. In 1955 he went to India to live in Kerala and Tamil Nadu in Christian ASHRAMS. He aimed at a truly Indian Christianity, free from foreign associations, and adapted dress, worship and doctrine to Indian tradition. In his *Return to the Centre* he reached to the mystery to which all religions witness.

Groves, A.N.

See DARBY.

Guadalupe

See BLACK VIRGIN.

guardian angel

The belief that everyone has an ANGEL to guard him or her is found in Plato (*Phaedo* 108) and early Christian writers. Jesus spoke of children's angels in heaven (Matt. 18:10). A popular English rhyme, written down by Thomas Ady in 1656, confuses angels with the four evangelists:

> Matthew, Mark, Luke, and John,
> The Bed be blest that I lie on.
> Four angels to my bed,
> Four angels round my head.

Gunpowder Plot

See FAWKES.

Gurdjieff, Georgei Ivanovich (1877–1949)

Modern GNOSTIC of Armenian and Greek parentage. He travelled in the Middle East and Central Asia, studying with Sufis and Lamas. He married Countess Ostrowska, and founded an Institute for the Harmonious

Development of Man, first in Moscow and then, after the Russian Revolution, in France. Gurdjieff's basic teaching is that human beings need to be awakened from their sleep, and his teachings and techniques continue to be promulgated in small groups. (*See also* NEW AGE; OUSPENSKY.)

Gutiérrez, Gustavo (b. 1928)

Born in Lima, Peru, he studied medicine and trained for the priesthood. His *Theology of Liberation* (1973) was hailed as the charter of LIBERATION THEOLOGY. Coming from 'an authentic encounter with the Lord', it seeks to combine socialism and Christianity. (*See also* BOFF; CAMARA; LAS CASAS.)

Guyon, Madame (1648–1717)

French mystical writer. After an unhappy marriage, she devoted herself to the poor and the cultivation of spiritual perfection. She was twice imprisoned for teaching QUIETIST doctrines and for being in correspondence with MOLINOS, the Spanish Quietist, but was defended by Archbishop FÉNELON. She wrote an autobiography, letters, poems and a mystical interpretation of the Song of Songs.

Hades

In classical Greek, the name of the god of the underworld. In the New Testament it is the abode of departed spirits, similar to the Hebrew Sheol, a place of waiting or reward. In English, Hades features in an explanation of the phrase in the creed 'he descended into hell', since Christ was said to have 'preached to the spirits in prison' (1 Pet. 3:19). (*See also* ADAM.)

Hadrian IV

Nicholas Breakspear, the only English Pope (1154–9). In his novel *Hadrian the Seventh* (1904), F.W. Rolfe imagined himself as the second English Pope.

haeretico

See DE HAERETICO COMBURENDO; HERESY.

Hagia Sophia, Istanbul: Regarded as one of the most perfect examples of Byzantine architecture, its mosaics, damaged by iconoclasts, were restored in the 19th and 20th centuries.

Hagia Sophia

Greek, 'Holy Wisdom': the name of the great cathedral in Istanbul (Constantinople) dedicated to Christ as the Wisdom (Sophia) of God. It was built in 538 for the Emperor Justinian. Not attractive outside, one great feature is an enormous dome supported by piers and arches. Inside there are magnificent mosaics of Christ, not naked and dead on a cross as in the West, but alive on a throne teaching wisdom. When Constantinople was conquered by the Turks in 1453, the mosaics were plastered over and the church turned into a mosque, but they have been uncovered and restored in modern times. No longer a mosque, the building is a tourist attraction, though still with a numinous atmosphere under the glowing mosaics. (*See also* CRUSADES; ORTHODOX CHURCH.)

hagiography

Literature about holy men and women (Greek: *hagioi*) of Christian history. Much of it is legend, though often including historical and liturgical texts. Critical hagiography began in the 17th century; with the weeding out of much fanciful material, this enabled a revision of the CALENDAR of SAINTS in 1969.

Hail Mary

See AVE MARIA.

Haile Selassie (1892–1975)

Emperor of ETHIOPIA (1930–74). Known as Ras ('prince') Tafari, he assumed the titles of King of Kings and Lord of Lords, traced his lineage to Solomon and Sheba, and was head of the Ethiopian Orthodox Church. He tried to modernize his mountain kingdom but the Italians occupied it from 1934 to 1941. He returned to reign until 1974 when a Communist coup deposed him; he was murdered, while a palace prisoner, a year later. The growth of RASTAFARIANISM in the Americas made

him into a returned Messiah, and he was overwhelmed on a visit to Jamaica in 1966. (*See also* GARVEY; PRESTER JOHN.)

hallelujah

Hebrew, meaning 'Praise ye Yah [God]'. Often rendered in English as 'alleluia'. This expression of praise is common in the Psalms, but in the New Testament it occurs only in Revelation (19:1–6). It was soon adopted by the Church in hymns and liturgies. The Hallelujah Chorus in Handel's *Messiah* closes the first part of that oratorio; when it was first performed in London in 1743 George II and all the people present rose to their feet and remained standing to the end, a tradition that has continued since.

Hallelujah Movement

A revival among Carib people in South America from 1845, when a leader called Bichiwung said he had visited heaven in a dream and God had given him directions for Hallelujah and a way to gain medicines and wealth. Modern Hallelujah performs dances, some in church, some in the open air. It is claimed that whites have stolen Carib wealth and hidden the way to God, and Hallelujah is a way of getting them back. (*See also* CARGO CULTS.)

Hallowe'en

The eve of All Saints' Day, or All Hallows, celebrated on 31 October. Customs of fun, trickery and masks are said to have come from old Celtic winter rites, but many appear to be American developments from various traditions, re-imported into Europe. (*See also* ALL SAINTS; ALL SOULS.)

halo

A circle round the head of gods or demigods. From Greek via Latin for a disc of the sun or moon (as *nimbus* was Latin for a cloud). This feature came slowly into Christian art, first for Christ, then for Mary and the martyrs and saints. Christ's halo often bore the Greek letters ALPHA AND OMEGA. The halo was originally blue but came to be rainbow-coloured, or especially yellow and gold.

Hammarskjøld, Dag (1905–61)

Secretary-General of the United Nations, killed in a plane crash in Zambia. His manuscript *Markings* was published after his death in 1964, 'a sort of White Book concerning my negotiations with myself – and with God'. This work aroused some criticism in his native Sweden but was influential. He did not join any church but said: 'The lovers of God have no religion but God alone.'

Handel, G.F.

See HALLELUJAH.

hands, imposition/laying on of

Ancient GESTURE of blessing from early times in the Bible; used by Jesus (Mark 10:16) and the apostles (Acts 8:17). Placing the hands on a person's head was performed in blessing, transmission of power, healing, exorcism, confirmation and ordination.

Harris, Charles (b. 1931)

President of Australia's Uniting Aboriginal and Islander Christian Congress. From a Pentecostal tradition, he served as a 'worker priest' with other churches until he developed an Aboriginal Christian institution. His theology focuses on social justice, aiming at a Church sensitive to the needs of Aboriginal and indigenous peoples throughout the world.

Harris, Howel (1714–73)

Welsh Calvinistic Methodist. His preaching attracted great crowds and he founded 30 societies in south Wales. After separation from his partner, Daniel Rowlands, Harris withdrew to Trevecca

where he established a 'family' of over 100 people. He was supported by the Countess of HUNTINGDON who had a school for ministers nearby. At his death all Harris's property was left to the 'family', which eventually died out.

Harris, William Wadé (1865–1929)

Born in Liberia of the Grebo people, he worked as a seaman and then a teacher in an American Methodist mission school. Imprisoned for political activity, he planned an African mission. Dressed in turban and white robes, like a Muslim but carrying a cross, calabash and Bible, he entered the neighbouring French Ivory Coast in 1913 and preached against traditional images and rituals. He met with great success, making an estimated 120,000 converts, but the French authorities sent him back to Liberia, afraid of political unrest, as Harris preached in English. His converts waited ten years till the British Methodist Church sent workers and organized churches. Harris had little success in his own country and died there in poverty.

Harrists

Ivory Coast churches following William Wadé HARRIS but independent of the missions. Divided into several sections, their membership was estimated at over 100,000.

harrowing of hell

Medieval English term for the descent of Christ to HADES to defeat the powers of evil (1 Pet. 3:19). Chaucer wrote of 'him that harrowed hell' (*Miller's Tale*, l. 326). (*See also* ADAM; DESCENT INTO HELL.)

Harry

'Old Harry', like 'Old Nick', was a traditional English name for the DEVIL.

harvest

Christian harvest festivals are relatively recent, though LAMMAS ('Loaf Mass', for the first-fruits) was observed from Saxon times. Even in these industrial and urban days there are harvest festivals in Anglican and Free Churches, though few in the Roman Catholic Church. Perhaps partly because there is no religious feast day between Trinity and Christmas, but also through the enduring love of nature and the rise of Green parties and ecological movements such as Friends of the Earth, harvest festivals are popular. Churches are decorated with flowers, fruit and vegetables, which are later given to old people and charities. (*See also* ECOLOGY).

Hawker, Robert Stephen

(1803–75)

Eccentric Anglican vicar of Morwenstow on the Cornish coast. He shared many of the superstitions of his people and wrote Cornish ballads, of which the best known has the traditional refrain 'And shall Trelawny die?', referring to one of the bishops imprisoned by James II. As Hawker died at Plymouth he was admitted into the Roman Catholic Communion.

healing

Most religions have had healing practices and it was a major activity of the primitive Church, in which bodily and spiritual health were seen as linked. Healings, blessings, purifications and exorcisms have been common. Modern charismatic and Pentecostal movements give a large place to healing as one of the chief gifts of the Spirit, and many of the main churches have revived prayers for health, but co-operation with trained doctors has not always been practised. (*See also* UNCTION).

Heart of Africa Mission

See STUDD.

Heart of Jesus

See SACRED HEART.

heathen

See PAGAN.

heaven

It seems natural to look up to the sky for a superior world and being: 'When I consider thy heavens' (Ps. 8:3). Those who decry this transcendent symbolism tend to look spatially down, to the depths of our being. Heaven also symbolizes the goal of spiritual life and eternal bliss. The word 'heaven' is used as a substitute for God, in phrases such as 'Good heavens'.

Heaven's Magic

See BERG.

Heber, Reginald (1783–1826)

Second Anglican bishop of Calcutta and author of hymns including 'From Greenland's Icy Mountains' and 'Holy, Holy, Holy'. In his short life he travelled round India and, unlike some missionaries, noted the courage and vigour of Indians. Meeting the Hindu holy man Swami Narayan, Heber ruefully remarked that whereas he himself had a large bodyguard of soldiers who went with him because they were paid, the Swami's 200 companions followed their leader out of devotion. Heber's *Life*, his diary of letters to his wife, is still worth reading.

Hebrew Bible

Modern term for what Christians also call the Old Testament.

Hebrews, Epistle to the

Placed at the end of Paul's letters in the New Testament and formerly attributed to him, this epistle contains no name of either author or audience. The title, 'To the Hebrews', was probably deduced from its contents. It is very different in style and matter from Paul's letters; guesses as to its author have been made, including a woman, Priscilla, but without evidence. The epistle is a long argument for the finality of Christ, the New Covenant and dispensation, aimed at preventing its probably Jewish readers from slipping back into the old faith.

Hebrews, Gospel According to the

An APOCRYPHAL writing, known only in fragments, in Aramaic. Some have thought it the original of the Gospel of Matthew, preserved by Jewish Christians. (*See also* EBIONITES; MATTHEW; NAZARENES.)

Helena (255–330 CE)

Mother of the Emperor CONSTANTINE. She was an ardent Christian and toured the Holy Land, founding churches and looking for relics. (*See also* INVENTION; PILGRIMAGE.)

hell

The English word comes from a root meaning 'to hide'. It indicates the abode of the dead, or a place or state of misery. The former sense is rather HADES as a place of waiting till the final judgement, hell being the ultimate destiny of the damned. Some modern theologians say that after purgation all will be saved, that there is a hell but with nobody in it. (*See also* GEHENNA.)

Héloïse (1100–64)

French lover of ABELARD and nun. Nothing is known of her parentage; at the age of 17 she was in Paris under the care of her uncle Fulbert, being tutored by Abelard. They fell in love and she bore his child. After Abelard's castration she became a nun and eventually prioress of the Paraclete religious house, making it one of the most distinguished in France and founding six daughter houses. From their letters it is clear that Héloïse retained a passionate love for Abelard; she was buried alongside him and their ashes were interred together in the Père Lachaise cemetery in Paris.

Helvidius (fourth century)

Latin theologian who affirmed that the BROTHERS AND SISTERS of Jesus were further children of Joseph and Mary. This view was opposed to suppositions that they were children of Joseph by a previous marriage, or cousins rather than brothers and sisters. Helvidius sought to defend marriage against tendencies to prefer virginity or claim perpetual virginity for MARY.

Henry Suso

See SUSO.

Henry IV of France

See NANTES.

Henry VIII of England

See ANGLICANISM; ANNATES; CROMWELL; DISSOLUTION OF THE MONASTERIES; DIVORCE; MORE; TYNDALE; WOLSEY.)

Herbert, George (1593–1633)

Anglican clergyman and poet. Called 'Holy George Herbert', he was a model of piety. But his poems, for example 'I struck the board', 'With sick and famish'd eyes' and 'Love bade me welcome', reveal devotion and passion. His hymns included 'Teach me, my God and King'.

heresy

From a Greek word meaning 'choice', the term was used to denote exaggeration, distortion or denial of articles of faith. In opposition, the traditional party called itself CATHOLIC or ORTHODOX. 'Formal' heresy was wilful error, distinguished from 'material' heresy in holding false doctrines through no fault of one's own. (*See also* INFIDEL.)

Hermas

Author of a second-century treatise called 'The Shepherd'. Little is known of his life, but the book gives a picture of early Christianity in three parts – Visions, Mandates and Similitudes – and teaches Christian belief and behaviour.

hermeneutics

From Greek for 'interpretation', derived from the messenger god Hermes: the theory and practice of interpreting biblical and other texts, with special attention to language and literary and historical criticism.

Hermetica

Greek and Latin mystical writings of the early centuries, named after Hermes Trismegistus, 'Hermes the Thrice-Greatest'. These works mingle Platonic, Stoic and Neo-Pythagorean ideas. Notions from the Hermetica influenced Western Europe in occultism from the 15th century. A Hermetic Society and a Hermetic Order of the Golden Dawn were founded in England in the late 19th century. (*See also* GNOSTICS).

hermit

From Greek, a 'DESERT-dweller': an ASCETIC living a solitary life instead of in a community. (*See also* ANCHORITE.)

Herod

There were several Herods. Herod the Great was appointed by the Romans to rule the Jews from 37 to 4 BCE, and it is in his reign that Jesus is said to have been born (Matt. 2:1). One of his sons was Herod Antipas, tetrarch of Galilee (Matt. 14:1), who had John the Baptist beheaded. Herod the Great's grandson Agrippa I (called Herod in Acts 12:1) put James the apostle to death. His son Agrippa II was the king before whom Paul appeared (Acts 25:13ff).

The Herodians of the Gospels (Mark 3:6) seem to have supported the Herods who ruled in Galilee but no longer in Judaea, where PILATE was in charge during the ministry of Jesus.

Herrick, Robert (1591–1674)

From a wealthy family, after lavish living he was ordained an Anglican priest in 1623 and went to the country parish of Dean Prior in Devonshire. He was ejected by Parliament for refusing the SOLEMN LEAGUE AND COVENANT, but reinstated in 1662 and he died a bachelor in his parish. Herrick is most noted for his poems, chiefly secular and some erotic. His religious verse has been considered childish, though recent study sees it as idealizing childhood in face of Puritan emphasis on infant corruption and sin.

Hesychasm

From Greek for 'quiet' or 'tranquillity': a hesychast is one who lives in stillness, either by practising inner prayer or as a recluse. Monks of Mount ATHOS propagated Hesychasm, but were accused of superstition. They were defended in the 14th century by Gregory Palamas, and Hesychasm came to prevail throughout the Greek Church. (*See also* JESUS PRAYER.)

heterodoxy

See ORTHODOXY.

Hidden Christians

Jesuit missions had great success in Japan in the 16th century and by 1593 there were 300,000 baptized Christians. Then, with a change of rule, Christianity was prohibited and severe persecution followed. The faith survived in secret from 1638 to 1859, and when it was allowed again some believers joined the newly arrived Roman Catholic Church. Others preferred to remain independent and are called Kakure or Sempuku Kirishitan, 'Hidden Christians'; they are known to Catholics as Hanare

Church of Martyrs, Nagasaki, Japan: A modern commemoration of 26 martyrs crucified in 1597 of whom five were Europeans, the others Japanese. Their followers became the Hidden Christians.

Kirishitan, 'Separated Christians'. They number about 33,000 and have their own Christian rites incorporating some elements of Buddhism and Shinto. (*See also* XAVIER.)

Hieronymus
See JEROME.

High Church
See ANGLO-CATHOLICISM; EVANGELICAL.

High Mass
Solemn MASS, the normal form of the chief eucharistic liturgy for Sundays and great feasts.

Higher criticism
See CRITICISM.

Hilda (614–80)
Of royal descent, she was baptized at 13, became a nun, and by 649 was abbess of Hartlepool in northern England. In 659 she founded a famous monastery at Whitby, a double house for monks and nuns which she ruled until her death. A strong character, Hilda defended old Celtic customs, though after the SYNOD of Whitby in 664 she accepted Roman practice.

Hildebrand
See CANOSSA.

Hilton, Walter (d. 1396)
One of the 14th-century English mystics and writers, an Augustinian canon and head of a priory at Thurgarton, in Nottinghamshire. His *Scale* or *Ladder of Perfection* was published in 1494. In vigorous English, Hilton describes the soul's journey, from faith and feeling, through the DARK NIGHT, to the Spiritual Jerusalem. (*See also* CLOUD OF UNKNOWING; JULIAN; ROLLE.)

Hocus Pocus

Sham Latin phrase, used by conjurors in performing tricks. The words seem to date from the 17th century, though some think they were a parody of the words in the Mass, *Hoc est corpus*, 'This is my body.'

Hogmanay

See NEW YEAR.

Holiness Churches

In 18th-century Methodism there was emphasis on Christian PERFECTION or holiness, but in America some felt that this emphasis was waning and Holiness Churches were created to revive it. They were linked in a national movement, which in 1917 was the Christian Holiness Association.

Holocaust

From a Greek term meaning 'whole burnt': a sacrifice wholly consumed by fire (Lev. 1:9 etc.). The word came to be applied to slaughter of a large number of people, and especially to the massacre of up to 6 million Jews and others by the Nazis between 1939 and 1945. This is the Holocaust, or Shoah, the time of desolation, and it raises many problems: Where was God? Why did the innocent suffer? Why were prayers not answered? These questions are acute especially for Jews, but also for Christians, and post-Holocaust theology tries to face them and change attitudes to the Jews, the Old Covenant and the state of Israel. In 1965 a declaration of the Second Vatican Council, *Nostra Aetate* (Our Age), recognized the implication of the Church in ANTI-SEMITISM, acknowledged the validity of the Mosaic covenant, abandoned the term 'deicide' ('killing God') for crucifying Christ and directed the Church to changes in teaching and liturgy.

holy

At the heart of all religion, said the German writer Rudolf Otto, is 'the holy' (his 1917 book *Das Heilige* was translated into English as *The Idea of the Holy*, 1923). The holy is the 'tremendous and fascinating mystery' (*mysterium tremendum et fascinans*), the NUMINOUS power which transcends and draws us on. (*See also* EXPERIENCE.)

Holy City

A name for Jerusalem (Matt. 27:53), known in Arabic as al-Quds, 'the Holy'.

Holy Club

A group of young Methodists at Oxford with Charles WESLEY. When his brother John joined it in 1729 he was nicknamed 'curator of the Holy Club'. (*See also* METHODISM.)

Holy Communion

In the BOOK OF COMMON PRAYER the EUCHARIST is termed 'the Lord's Supper or Holy Communion'.

Holy Cross Day

14 September in the Prayer Book calendar. Also called the Exaltation of the Cross, it commemorated the exposition of the supposed True Cross in Jerusalem in 629, after its capture. (*See also* INVENTION.)

Holy Family

In much of Christian art the Holy Family is depicted as the infant Jesus, MARY his mother, JOSEPH, and sometimes his grandmother ANNE. But, like many Jewish families, the Holy Family may have been much bigger with nine or ten members. (*See also* BROTHERS AND SISTERS OF JESUS.)

Holy Father

A title of the POPE.

Holy Ghost

Old English term for HOLY SPIRIT.

Holy Innocents

All the baby boys in Bethlehem and neighbourhood were said by Matthew (2:16ff) to have been killed on the orders of HEROD in an attempt to destroy the child Jesus, but this story seems not to have been known to Luke (2:21ff). The event is commemorated on 28 December. *See also* FLIGHT INTO EGYPT.

Holy Island

See LINDISFARNE.

Holy Land

A name given in the middle ages to the country of Jesus and his followers. Some disillusioned pilgrims called it the 'stinking land'. It has been called Palestine (from Philistine) and is now incorporated in the State of Israel. (*See also* HELENA; PILGRIMAGE.)

Holy Office

Roman Catholic court charged with protecting faith and morals.

Holy Orders

See ORDERS.

holy rollers

Nickname for ecstatic American groups, who claim experience of the Spirit by jumping in the air and rolling on the ground.

Holy Saturday

The day after GOOD FRIDAY and before EASTER Sunday.

Holy See

The SEE of the POPE as bishop of Rome, but commonly used of the papacy in general.

Holy Sepulchre

In Jerusalem the Church of the Holy Sepulchre is a large, ancient building, many times rebuilt, which includes the supposed rock tomb where the body of Jesus was laid (Matt. 27:60). There is also a side chapel to stand for the place of the Crucifixion. (*See also* GARDEN TOMB.)

Church of the Holy Sepulchre, Jerusalem: The original church was built in 386 CE and often rebuilt. It claims to contain the Holy Sepulchre of Christ and the place of the True Cross.

Holy Shroud

See SHROUD.

Holy Spirit

The third person of the TRINITY in Christian theology. The descent of the

Spirit upon the apostles and others is described in graphic detail in Acts 2. The Spirit is spoken of many times in Paul's writings, as the Spirit of God, Spirit of Christ, Spirit of adoption; and in giving the first-fruits and making intercession (Rom. 8). The gifts of the Spirit are stated at length (1 Cor. 12–13). Doctrines of the nature and place of the Holy Spirit were worked out slowly over the centuries. (*See also* FILIOQUE; GLOSSOLALIA; PENTECOST.)

holy war

See CRUSADES; JUST WAR; PACIFISM; TEMPLE MOUNT.

holy water

Water that has been blessed is placed at the entrance to Catholic churches, in a stoup or niche, from which people cross or sprinkle themselves. Blessed water is also used at dedications and funerals. (*See also* ASPERGES.)

Holy Week

The week before EASTER. Each day is allocated prayers and meditations, with suitable ceremonies. (*See also* GOOD FRIDAY; MAUNDY THURSDAY; PALM SUNDAY.)

holy year

A year of INDULGENCE or JUBILEE, granted by the Pope to those who visit Rome.

homily

From Greek for 'discourse', a homily may be a short explanation of a Bible text or a longer sermon. Books of homilies were issued to help the clergy under Edward VI and Elizabeth I. 'Homiletics' is the study of the preparation and delivery of sermons.

homoousion

Greek, 'of one substance': a term used to express the relationship of Christ with the Father in the Nicene Creed. Some writers preferred the term *homoiousion*,

'of like substance', as allowing for distinctions in the TRINITY. Edward Gibbon in his *Decline and Fall of the Roman Empire* (ch. 21) derided 'the furious contests which the difference of a single diphthong excited between the Homoousians and Homoiousians'. But it was an essential difference for CHRISTOLOGY. (*See also* NICAEA; SEMI-ARIANS.)

homosexuality

Church attitudes have tended to be condemnatory, though some distinguish between the condition of born homosexuals and the genital practice. Some refer to the prohibition in Leviticus (20:13), but would hardly agree with the death penalty prescribed. The Gospel accepts that there is a natural condition of eunuchs 'so born from their mother's womb' (Matt. 19:12). In the middle ages homosexuality was associated with heresy: the CATHARI were accused of it, and the association with Bulgaria, where the Cathari originated, gave rise to the word 'bugger'.

Hooker, Richard (1554–1600)

Anglican clergyman and theologian, defender of the Church of England as reformed but continuous with the medieval Church. In his *Laws of Ecclesiastical Polity* Hooker attacked Puritans who took Scripture as the sole guide of conduct and he propounded a theory of natural law, coming from God, to which both Church and STATE are subservient. On another topic Hooker was less acceptable to the Church, denying the need for episcopal ordination. But in the main his writing, in seven books, gave tone and direction to Anglican theology, expressed in masterly prose. (*See also* ERASTIANISM.)

hope

A universal human aspiration, looking to a future object or goal. It is one of the three theological virtues, alongside faith and love (1 Cor. 13:13).

Hopkins, Gerard Manley
(1844–89)

A High Anglican, after studying at Oxford he became a JESUIT priest in 1877 and professor of Greek at Dublin. Hopkins was a striking and original poet, but burnt some of his writings on his conversion. Other poems went to Robert Bridges, later Poet Laureate, who was puzzled by their 'oddity' and strangely did not publish most of them until 1918, 30 years after the death of their author. Hopkins is now recognized as a major English poet. Among his great works is 'The Wreck of the Deutschland'.

hosanna

Hebrew, 'Save, we beseech thee', cried at the entrance of Jesus to Jerusalem on PALM SUNDAY (Mark 11:9 and parallels), quoting the Pilgrim Psalm 118:25. The word was early taken into Christian liturgies and hymns. *Hosanna in excelsis*, from the Latin rite, was rendered in English as 'Hosanna in the highest'.

Hospitallers

An order of knights at a hospital in Jerusalem in the 12th century, later becoming the Knights of Rhodes and Knights of Malta. (*See also* TEMPLARS.)

host

From Latin for a 'victim', this is the consecrated bread or wafer in the EUCHARIST, regarded as the sacrifice of the BODY of Christ.

hot cross buns

Special buns made for GOOD FRIDAY, supposedly made of the dough for the HOST and marked with a cross. There were similar crossed cakes in ancient Greece, Egypt and Mithraism.

hours

Canonical times for daily prayers, in the West reckoned as seven: Matins and Lauds as one, Prime, Terce, Sext, None, Vespers and Compline.

house churches

Evangelical and charismatic fellowships, independent of organized churches. These groups have mushroomed in recent years. Their publication *Bodybook* lists 402 house churches in Britain in 1988, rising to 743 in 1995. (*See also* CHARISMATIC; CLASS MEETING; EVANGELICAL.)

Howard, John (1726–90)

English prison reformer and Nonconformist evangelical. A short captivity in France showed him the harsh treatment meted out to prisoners of war, and later as High Sheriff of Bedford he visited many prisons seeing appalling conditions. Largely through him, two Acts of Parliament were passed in 1774, securing fixed salaries for gaolers to lessen corruption and enforcing cleanliness. He travelled on the continent; in Russia he caught fever from a prisoner and died. Howard wrote on *The State of the Prisons* and *The Principal Lazarettos in Europe*.

Hubbard, Lafayette Ronald
(1911–86)

Founder of Scientology. Born in Nebraska, in 1950 he published *Dianetics*, a system for the control of human thought. The Church of Scientology was founded in 1954. There have been debates on whether it is a religion, and could benefit from rate exemption, or a CHURCH, a distinctively Christian title. Hubbard and his movement have been surrounded by controversy: against claims that they are only interested in money, they counter-claim that they have benefited many people.

Hügel, Baron Friedrich von
(1852–1925)

Of Austrian and Scottish descent, he was a learned lay theologian and devout

Roman Catholic who supported the modernist movement. He wrote *The Mystical Element in Religion* (1908) on CATHARINE OF GENOA. In 1904, with the Jewish Biblical scholar Claude Montefiore, he founded the London Society for the Study of Religion, the oldest inter-religious society in Britain, which still flourishes.

Hugh (1140–1200)

Born in Burgundy, he joined the severe Carthusian Order and became bishop of Lincoln in 1186. He defended the rights of the people against the king and was revered for his sanctity and care of lepers. He was canonized in 1220 and his tomb at Lincoln became a place of pilgrimage.

Another Hugh of Lincoln (1246–55) was a boy supposedly murdered by Jews, a libel repeated in Chaucer's *Prioresses' Tale*. (*See also* WILLIAM OF NORWICH.)

Huguenots

A nickname for French Protestants, of debatable origin, perhaps from German *Eidgenossen*, 'confederates', or from a medieval romance about a King Hugo. A major early influence was CALVIN, and although he fled to Geneva, a Protestant Synod in Paris in 1559 accepted Calvinistic teaching. In the 16th century there existed virtual civil war in France between Protestants and Catholics; many of the former died in the Massacre of St Bartholomew in 1572. The Edict of NANTES in 1598 gave Protestants freedom of worship, but was revoked by Louis XIV in 1685. Many Huguenots were forcibly converted and others fled to Holland, England and America. There was rebellion by CAMISARDS and others, with many martyrdoms. Huguenots welcomed the French Revolution and gained legal status. Internal divisions erupted in 1872, between liberal *Réformés* and traditional *Évangéliques*. Reunion has come in recent times, to include the smaller Lutheran and Methodist groups. (*See also* COLIGNY.)

humanism

A term often used for non-religious beliefs and values, and secular alternatives to religion, such as utilitarianism and Marxism. These have often had a semi-religious character, with ethical societies, and even humanist churches and Sunday Schools, near-infallible books and millenarian belief in a coming perfect society. (*See also* CHURCH; COMMUNISM; SECULARISM.)

humility

A moral attitude and practice; part of the cardinal virtue of temperance. Humility towards others and God, resignation to his will, have been taught, but with warnings against undue self-abasement.

humour

Etymologically connected with 'humid', it suggests freshness of mind, or support for the small against the great. It is in the teaching of Jesus, for example in imagining a devout man straining at a gnat but swallowing a camel.

Huntingdon, Selina Hastings, Countess of (1707–91)

A 'Lady Bountiful' and an early Methodist. After her husband's death in 1746 she devoted herself to social and religious work. In 1768 she opened a Methodist seminary with John FLETCHER as president, founded chapels, and formed them into a 'connexion'. She supported the Calvinism of WHITEFIELD against WESLEY and became trustee of Whitefield's foundations in America. Some of Lady Huntingdon's chapels still exist, some 20 holding an annual conference and continuing mission work in Sierra Leone. (*See also* HOWEL HARRIS; PERRONET; WESLEYAN REFORM.)

Huss, John (1369–1415)

Czech reformer, son of a Bohemian peasant. He became rector of Prague University, a priest and a popular preacher. Charged with heresy for supporting WYCLIFFE's teachings, he was nevertheless re-elected rector. Summoned to a general council at CONSTANCE, despite a 'safe conduct' from the emperor he was thrown into prison. Brought to trial, Huss was not allowed a defender or to speak freely, and refusing to recant he was burnt at the stake in 1415. The anger of his followers led to two bloody Hussite wars. The present Bohemian Church continues Huss's tradition. (*See also* MORAVIANS.)

Hutterites

A Moravian ANABAPTIST, Jacob Hutter (or Huter), was executed in 1536 as a heretic and his followers took his name. They migrated through Eastern Europe and arrived in America in the 1870s. Like the AMISH, they hold goods in common, but use modern farm equipment. Some went to the Canadian prairies and there are now about 300 Hutterite family settlements. (*See also* MENNONITES.)

Huxley

See WILBERFORCE, SAMUEL.

hymns

Sacred songs have been part of most Christian worship, beginning with the Psalms. In fourth-century controversies hymns were sung like rival football songs today. Reformation hymns resembled creeds, and Luther's 'A Safe Stronghold' has been compared to the Marseillaise. Isaac WATTS and Charles WESLEY gave Free Church worship depth and popularity with their hymns, and 19th- and 20th-century revivals produced their own expressions. Some free worship has been called a 'hymn-sandwich', a liturgy dominated by hymns, but its form may be traced back to the synagogue. (*See also* SPIRITUALS; WORSHIP.)

Hypatia

See CYRIL.

hyperdulia

From Greek, meaning 'more than veneration': used to describe devotion paid to the Virgin Mary, above the *dulia* given to other saints, but below the *latria*, the worship due to God alone.

hypostasis

Greek 'substance', used in CHRISTOLOGICAL discussions for a 'person', though that term can be taken too individually. At the Council of Constantinople in 381 the orthodox Trinitarian formula was accepted of 'three hypostases in one Being' (*ousia*). (*See also* HOMOOUSION.)

I

ichthus

Greek for 'fish', a common symbol for the name and titles of Christ in the early centuries, often found in the CATACOMBS. It is an acrostic on the first letters, in Greek, of the words Iesous, CHristos, THeou (of God), Uios (son) and Soter (Saviour), thus giving *ichthus*, fish. As a secret or mystical symbol the fish was easily recognized, and it has become popular again in recent times.

Fish symbol with basket of bread, S. Cellisto, Rome: The fish symbolizes Christ, the bread his body; together they represent the Lord's Supper.

icon

Greek 'image' or 'likeness', in two dimensions, painted on wood or other materials. The Bible said: 'You shall not make any graven image' (Exod. 20:4), and this would seem to prohibit rounded three-dimensional images as used in the Western Roman Catholic world. In Eastern ORTHODOXY churches are lavishly decorated, but with flat icons. In the eighth and ninth centuries there were iconoclastic controversies, partly due to the growth of Islam which forbade any imagery. A second Council of NICAEA in 787 decreed that icons were to be used 'not to pay them actual worship' but 'to recollect the originals'.

iconostasis

Greek, 'icon-station'. In Orthodox churches it is the SCREEN which separates the sanctuary from the nave and on which ICONS are placed, with five rows depicting sacred history. There are three doors, the central or royal door giving admittance to the altar.

Identity Christianity

See BRITISH ISRAELITES.

Ignatius (35–107)

An early bishop of Antioch. Most knowledge of him comes from seven letters that he wrote on the way to Rome, where he was thrown to the beasts in the amphitheatre. Two of his chief concerns are the authority of bishops and the reality of the life, death and Resurrection of Christ, against those who said he 'suffered only in semblance'. Feast day 1 February. (*See also* DOCETISM.)

Ignatius Loyola (1491–1556)

Founder of the JESUIT Order. Born of a noble family at Loyola in Spain he became a soldier, was laid up with a leg wound, read lives of Christ and resolved to become a soldier of the Lord. He went to Rome with several companions and formed the Society of Jesus, which was sanctioned by the Pope in 1540. Ignatius wrote a devotional manual, entitled SPIRITUAL EXERCISES, and spent the rest of his life organizing the Order. Feast day 31 July. (*See also* XAVIER.)

IHS

The first three letters of the name JESus in Greek. The monogram is put in church decorations, and given various interpretations, but the Greek letters are the origin.

Illuminati

Name given to various bodies which maintained that they alone had the 'illuminating' grace of Christ. ROSICRUCIANS and some masonic organizations claimed the title.

image

See ICON.

imago Dei

The 'image of God' (Latin) in which humanity was created (Gen. 1:27): 'in the image of God, he created them male and female', perhaps an original male–female or androgynous being. Theologians have debated in what the image of God consists, and whether it was obscured but not lost in the FALL. The divine image may be seen in human reason, or in FREE WILL and moral responsibility. (*See also* ADAM; EVE.)

imitation of Christ

A Christian ideal, though not a literal copying of the dress and life of Jesus *The Imitation of Christ* is a famous book of devotion written by a German monk, Thomas à KEMPIS, which affirms that we ought to imitate the 'life and manners' of Christ and meditate upon his life. This monastic work, full of self-abnegation, has been popular among Protestants. John WESLEY circulated it among his preachers, and George Eliot in *The Mill on the Floss* (1860) wrote of it as 'a secret of life'.

Immaculate Conception

Not the VIRGIN BIRTH, though sometimes confused with it. This DOGMA, declared by Pope Pius IX in 1854, affirms that 'from the first moment of her conception the Blessed Virgin Mary was . . . kept free from all stain of ORIGINAL SIN.' This had been long debated, THOMAS AQUINAS and others holding that as MARY was conceived in the natural way she was not exempt from original sin. (*See also* ASSUMPTION; OLD CATHOLICS.)

immanence

The presence of the divine throughout the universe. It is distinct from PANTHEISM, if held with the parallel doctrine of divine transcendence.

Immanuel/Emmanuel

Hebrew, 'God with us'. First used in the Bible by Isaiah (7:14), where the prophet assured King Ahaz that a child to be born would bear this name as sign of God's presence. This was perhaps the good king Hezekiah. The verse is quoted in Matthew (1:23) of the birth of Jesus, fulfilling prophecy. Immanuel was adopted as a name of Christ in writings and hymns. (*See also* VIRGIN BIRTH.)

immersion

Partial or complete submerging in water of the body of a candidate for BAPTISM.

immortality

Not dying, or surviving death. Belief in life after death is found in most, if not all, religions in one form or another. Greeks, like Hindus, often thought that an immortal soul existed before birth (pre-existence) as well as after death (post-existence). Christian belief is in the creation of souls before or at birth, and survival after death to be gained from union with Christ in his RESURRECTION. Paul expounded this (1 Cor. 15) as the spiritual body coming from the Lord in heaven. (*See also* REINCARNATION.)

impassibility

The belief that God does not suffer, for that would imply limitation and fallibility. Yet faith in a God of love, revealed in the suffering of Christ, makes impassibility seem cold and unfeeling. Modern writers have argued both for and against such views. BONHOEFFER held that 'only the suffering God can help' (Letter to Bethge, 16 July 1944). (*See also* PATRIPASSIANISM; PROCESS.)

imposition of hands

See GESTURES; HANDS.

imprecatory

Modern term for Psalms which express vengeance, such as 137:9. John WESLEY in his revised Prayer Book omitted such verses as 'not proper for the mouths of a Christian congregation', and their use is made optional in modern prayer books.

imprimatur

Latin, 'let it be printed.' An official licence to print works sanctioned by a 'censor' of the Roman Catholic Church.

imputation

Belief in the substitution of the righteousness of Christ for that of a sinner, so that God can regard the latter's wrongs as covered by the Saviour. Especially important in Lutheran theology. (*See also* JUSTIFICATION.)

in hoc signo vinces

Latin, 'by this sign you will conquer': said to be words which CONSTANTINE saw in the sun before the battle of Milvian Bridge at which he defeated his rival Maxentius and became the champion of Christianity.

incarnation

From Latin *carnis*, flesh, this doctrine of the nature and work of Christ is rooted in the Johannine affirmation that 'the Word was made flesh' (Greek: *sarx*). It taught that Christ was truly human, against DOCETIC notions that he appeared only in 'semblance' and did not really suffer. This was asserted again in the Nicene creed, which stated that 'he became incarnate' and 'was made man'. (*See also* AVATAR.)

incense

Aromatic substance. It was used in the Temple in Jerusalem and referred to in visions of heaven (Rev. 8:3). The evidence for Christian use of incense is late, but it became normal in Catholic and Orthodox services. Abolished at the Reformation, incense was re-introduced in the ANGLO-CATHOLIC movement.

incumbent

A holder of a church BENEFICE, a RECTOR or VICAR.

Independents

In modern AFRICA the term 'Independents' is used of churches separate from those of missionary foundation, sometimes called SECTS or just 'Africans'. (*See also* CONGREGATIONALISM.)

Index

A list of books prohibited to Roman Catholics. The Index Librorum Prohibitorum was first issued by the INQUISITION in 1557. It came to include many famous works, and modern novels, but was suspended after the Second Vatican Council in 1966. (*See also* ERASMUS.)

indulgence

Remission of punishment for sin, a power claimed by the Roman Catholic Church in the middle ages. Those who went on the CRUSADES were offered plenary or full indulgences. There was abuse by 'pardoners' who sold indulgences, and reaction against them was a major cause of the Reformation in Germany. Indulgences are still offered for piety and good works, plenary or partial, for living people or souls in purgatory. Indulgences may be attached to specially blessed medals, crucifixes or rosaries. (*See also* LUTHER; TETZEL.)

inerrancy

See FUNDAMENTALISM.

infallibility

Dogma defined by papal authority. The First Vatican Council in 1870 declared that 'the Roman Pontiff, when he speaks *ex cathedra* . . . is endowed with infallibility . . . in defining doctrine concerning faith or morals.' Some German, Austrian and Swiss Catholics refused to accept this dogma and separated from Rome. (*See also* OLD CATHOLICS.)

infant baptism

See BAPTISM.

infidel

One who is unfaithful, or an unbeliever in religion. The old Prayer Book Collect for Good Friday used to lump together 'Jews, Turks, Infidels and Heretics', but this has been changed. In South Africa the Arabic word *kafir* for an unbeliever has been used of black people, though many were and are devout Christians.

inner light

The Holy Spirit within the believer, apart from Church or Bible. Belief in the inner light as the source of guidance is held by the Society of FRIENDS, and was put forward by BARCLAY in his *Apology*. (*See also* FOX; FORTUNE.)

Innocents

See HOLY INNOCENTS.

Inquisition

Body set up to examine suspects for HERESY, begun by Pope Gregory IX in 1232. The new orders of Dominicans and Franciscans questioned those suspected of false doctrine; and torture was authorized by Pope Innocent IV in 1252. The so-called Spanish Inquisition was directed particularly against converted Jews and Muslims (MARRANOS and Moriscos), and in the 16th century turned against Protestants. It was suppressed in 1820. The Inquisition was responsible for cruelty and executions, but during the witch fevers which convulsed much of Europe the Inquisitors in Spain found most accusations to be worthless and acquitted the victims. (*See also* MALLEUS; TORQUEMADA.)

INRI

The first letters in Latin of words on the Cross of Jesus: Iesus Nazarenus Rex Iudaeorum, 'Jesus of Nazareth, King of the Jews', said in John 19:20 to have been in Hebrew, Greek and Latin.

Institutes of the Christian Religion

Theological work by John CALVIN, published in Latin in 1536 and in French in 1541. It is in four parts, discussing God as Creator, Redeemer and Holy Spirit, with the Church and means of grace.

intention

In morals, responsibility for an act may depend on whether it is done intentionally, as 'actual', willed with conscious intention, or 'virtual', from a previous decision. In prayers of intercession the 'intention' is the object for which prayer is offered.

intercession

PRAYER for another person, group, or even the whole world, undertaken for particular needs such as sickness, or more generally for peace.

interdict

In the Roman Catholic Church a ban imposed by the Pope on persons or peoples, excluding them from various activities. (*See also* CANOSSA; EXCOMMUNICATION.)

interim ethic

A term used by Albert SCHWEITZER for the moral teaching of Jesus, given for a time but restricted in view of the coming end of the age.

Inter-Varsity Christian Fellowship

An evangelical student movement, which spread from Cambridge, England in 1927 to many campuses in the USA and Canada.

introit

From a Latin root 'to go', the opening phrase of the MASS: *Introibo ad altare Dei*, 'I will go unto the altar of God' (Psalm 43:4). The choir may sing the introit, sometimes a whole Psalm. Since the 19th century, introits by a choir have been sung in many churches.

invention of the Cross

Formal phrase for the 'finding' (Latin: *inventionem*) of portions of the true Cross by HELENA, mother of Constantine, in 326. This may have occurred during excavations preparatory to building the Church of the Holy Sepulchre in Jerusalem. Perhaps 'invention' is a suitable word, since shiploads of fragments of the 'true Cross' were sent all over Europe. (*See also* HOLY CROSS DAY.)

investitures

Medieval controversies between Church and state, over claims that kings and other rulers could invest a bishop or abbot with his ring and staff and receive his homage, before he was consecrated by the Pope. There were quarrels with Germany in the 11th–12th centuries, and in England ANSELM refused to do homage to Henry I. (*See also* CANOSSA.)

Iona

A small island off Mull in western Scotland, where COLUMBA went in 563 to found a monastery as centre for his work. Many times plundered and rebuilt, the monastery was closed down at the Reformation in 1561. The cathedral and other buildings have now been restored, after the founding of the Iona Community in 1938, by George Macleod with ministers and laity of the Church of Scotland. (*See also* AIDAN; LINDISFARNE.)

iota

The English word 'jot' comes from this small Greek letter. TYNDALE translated Matthew 5:18: 'One jot or one tittle of the law shall not scape.'

Irenaeus (130–200 CE)

One of the first Christian apologists, his *Against Heresies* attacked forms of GNOSTICISM. Born in Smyrna, he studied in Rome and became bishop of Lyons. Irenaeus was a disciple of POLYCARP and others who had seen John the apostle, and provided a link with them and with the Church which was growing despite persecution. Feast day 28 June.

Irving, Edward (1792–1834)

Scottish Presbyterian minister, he was called to the Caledonian Church,

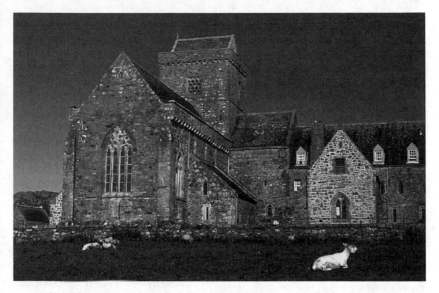

Iona: The 13th-century cathedral of St Mary has been restored and enlarged. The cemetery is said to have contained the remains of 46 Scottish kings.

Hatton Garden, London, and was a popular preacher. He announced the imminent Second Coming of Christ, and also speculated on the nature of Christ, declaring it to be sinful. Ejected from a new church in Regent Square, he was associated with the CATHOLIC APOSTOLIC CHURCH; his followers were called Irvingites, though he died soon after.

Isaiah, Ascension of

A Jewish–Christian writing of the second century, which shows beliefs of that time in the Incarnation, Resurrection and Trinity. Written in Greek, it survives only in fragments in Latin and Ethiopic.

Iscariot

See JUDAS.

Islam and Christianity

Islam arose in the seventh century in Arabia when Christianity was well established in many neighbouring lands, but with only scattered centres in Arabia. Islam's holy book, the QUR'ĀN (5:85),

speaks of Christians as being 'nearest in love' to Muslims, and reveres Jesus as a prophet of God. But like other family relations, Christians and Muslims have often quarrelled and misunderstood each other. Today there has been impartial study and appreciation of each religion, but FUNDAMENTALISTS on both sides hinder reconciliation. (*See also* Introduction; MUHAMMAD.)

Israel

Used to mean the Hebrew people, descended from Jacob surnamed Israel (Gen. 32:28). In modern times the title has been taken by the Jewish State of Israel. Paul began the transfer of this name to the Church as 'the Israel of God' (Gal. 6:16).

Istanbul

See CONSTANTINE.

Ite, missa est

Phrase at the end of the Roman Catholic MASS, meaning 'Go, you are dismissed.'

J

Jacobites

In the sixth century MONOPHYSITES (holding to the belief of 'one nature' in Christ), opposed to the Council of CHALCEDON, were led in Syria by Jacob Baradai, who consecrated bishops and priests for his Jacobite churches. By the 18th century pressure from Muslims led the Jacobite Patriarch of Antioch to seek help from Rome, and the Jacobites were split into a UNIATE Church in communion with Rome and Jacobite independents, each group now numbering about 80,000 members. (*See also* MALABAR.)

Jairus

A ruler of a synagogue who came to Jesus for help when his daughter lay dying (Mark 5:22ff).

Jamaa

Founded by a Belgian priest, Placide TEMPELS, this is a 'family' movement in the Roman Catholic Church of Katanga in the Republic of Congo, which teaches married love as the ideal of the Christian community. Declared unorthodox, the movement went underground, still teaching the union of physical and spiritual, of human beings and God. (*See also* KAGAME.)

James (1)

Apostle, son of Zebedee, one of the first disciples of Jesus, called with his brother John; as James is always named first, it is assumed he was the elder. He appears at key occasions in the gospels, such as the TRANSFIGURATION and in GETHSEMANE, but James is not noted in Acts until his execution by order of HEROD Agrippa I in the year 44 (Acts 12:2). (*See also* COMPOSTELA.)

James (2)

Brother of Jesus (Mark 6:3 etc.). He plays no part in the gospels but emerges in Acts and the epistles as head of the Church in Jerusalem (Acts 12:17, 15:13). Traditionally he was its first bishop. He was more conservative than Paul, leading Jewish Christians who observed the Law. JOSEPHUS called him 'the most righteous of men', and said he was killed by a high priest, Ananus in 62 (*Antiquities*, 20. 197). To this James has been attributed the Epistle of James, though this has been disputed. The epistle has parallels with the SERMON ON THE MOUNT. (*See also* BROTHERS AND SISTERS OF JESUS; NAZARENES.)

A Book of James, or Protevangelium, is wrongly attributed to this James; *see* PSEUDO-JAMES.

James (3)

Son of Alpheus, one of the 12 disciples (Mark 3:18), about whom nothing more is known, unless he is James the Less, or Younger (Mark 15:40).

James I

See AUTHORIZED VERSION.

Jansenism

A rigorist movement within the Roman Catholic Church, named after a Belgian theologian, Cornelius Jansen (1585–1638). His work *Augustinus* (1640) taught absolute PREDESTINATION and irresistible GRACE. The Jansenists were strongly opposed to the JESUITS, regarding them as morally lax, and were supported by the philosopher PASCAL. Jansenists were condemned by the Popes and were persecuted in France, many taking refuge in the Netherlands. (*See also* OLD CATHOLICS; PORT ROYAL.)

Januarius (Gennaro)

Legendary saint and patron of Naples, where his blood, preserved in a glass phial, is supposed to liquefy at his three feasts every year.

Japan

See HIDDEN CHRISTIANS; KAGAWA; UCHIMURA; XAVIER.

Jeanne d'Arc

See JOAN OF ARC.

Jeffreys, George

See ELIM.

Jehovah

See ADONAI.

Jehovah's Witnesses

A millenarian movement begun by Charles Taze Russell (1852–1916) of Pittsburgh, who predicted that Christ would return secretly in 1874 and the end of the world would come in 1914. He and his successor, Judge J. R. Rutherford, adjusted the dates of their prophecies but had a large following. The Witnesses emphasize the Old Testament Jehovah, deny the Trinity, refuse military service and blood transfusions, and do not salute the flag. They were fiercely persecuted by the Nazis in Germany. Their headquarters are in Brooklyn, New York; they meet in Kingdom Halls, and carry out door-to-door evangelism, selling their magazine *The Watch Tower*.

In Nigeria a breakaway Witness movement, called God's Kingdom Society, was founded by Gideon Urhobo (1903–52). Since his death the movement has continued to grow.

Jerome (Hieronymus) (342–420)

Monk and biblical scholar. Born in Dalmatia, he studied in Rome and learned Greek and Hebrew to study the scriptures in the original languages. He settled in Bethlehem and began producing a Latin text of the whole Bible, later called the VULGATE. Jerome wrote many biblical commentaries and other works, threw himself into controversy and was noted for his difficult temperament. In art he is often shown, wrongly, with a red cardinal's hat, or in a cave with a lion at his feet. (*See also* SEPTUAGINT.)

Jerusalem

The gospels say that Jesus made short visits to Jerusalem and spent the last week of his life in the Holy City, where his Crucifixion and Resurrection took place. The apostles stayed there for a time and JAMES, brother of Jesus, became head of the Jerusalem Church. The city was destroyed by the Romans in 70, and while Christian churches were built the site of the old Temple was derelict until the building of the Muslim shrine of the DOME OF THE ROCK, which remains today. (*See also* GARDEN TOMB; HELENA.)

Jerusalem, Council of

A public gathering of early Christians to decide whether gentile converts should be circumcised. There are two accounts of this Council (Acts 15, Gal. 2), which despite variations show that Paul won as apostle to the gentiles. (*See also* JAMES (2); PAUL.)

Jesse

See DAVID.

Jesuits

The Society of Jesus was founded by IGNATIUS LOYOLA in 1540 to provide a religious army for the papacy and do missionary work in the world which was opening up in America, Asia and Africa. Jesuits attacked Protestants and JANSENISTS and were suspect outside Italy as a foreign influence, giving more loyalty to the Pope than to national interests. They were expelled from various countries, though they recovered. Today the Jesuits are found in most lands, with universities and schools, and bringing out important publications. (*See also* PASCAL.)

Jesus Christ

The personal name 'Jesus' is from the Greek form of the Hebrew Joshua, meaning 'Yah saves', not an uncommon name. 'Christ' is a title, the Greek version of the Hebrew Messiah, 'Anointed One'. It is said that Jesus was born 'in the days of Herod the King', who died in 4 BCE (Matt. 2:1). For his birth, *see* VIRGIN BIRTH. He grew up in Nazareth in Galilee, with JOSEPH and MARY and the family of which he was the first-born. Jesus is once called 'the carpenter' (Mark 6:3). After baptism by John the Baptist he began his own preaching of the imminent kingdom of God. He was a charismatic preacher and healer, remarkable for peaceableness and commensalism, eating with 'publicans and sinners'. He chose 12 disciples, like the 12 tribes, and sent them out to announce God's kingdom. After one or three years he went to Jerusalem, where he challenged the authorities by cleansing the Temple of commerce. He was arrested and crucified as a potential rebel, condemned by both the high priest CAIAPHAS and the Roman procurator PILATE. Very soon after his death, the disciples became convinced that Jesus was alive and telling them to continue his work. He was now openly the Messiah, Jesus Christ, and as the Church spread it developed doctrines of his nature and universal claims. (*See also* BROTHERS AND SISTERS OF JESUS; CALENDAR; CHRIST; CHRISTOLOGY.)

Mosaic of the infant Jesus with his mother Mary, from St Sophia, Istanbul: Jesus is alert, the 'Wisdom' (Sophia) of God; his mother is the 'God-bearer'.

Jesus People

An evangelical youth movement of the late 1960s, opposing the spread of Asian ideas and proclaiming dedication to the 'one way' preserved in the gospels. (*See also* BERG.)

Jesus Prayer

The prayer said in frequent repetition in Eastern Orthodoxy: 'Lord Jesus Christ, Son of God, have mercy on me.' (*See also* HESYCHASM.)

Jewish Christians

See JAMES (2); NAZARENES.

Jews

See JUDAISM.

Jews for Jesus

Founded in San Francisco in 1973, this movement seeks to persuade Jews that Jesus is their still-expected Messiah. It may be anti-semitic in attacking normal Judaism, and millenarian in seeing the conversion of the Jews as a preliminary to the Second Coming of Christ.

Joachim

The father of MARY, mother of Jesus, is not named in the Bible, but in the book of James in the second century he is introduced as Joachim, 'very rich'. In the Old Testament apocryphal Story of Susanna there was one Joakim, 'very rich'. In Christian tradition Joachim does not appear much till the middle ages. Feast day 16 August. (*See also* PSEUDO-JAMES.)

Joachim of Fiore (1132–1202)

Italian monk and visionary. He wrote of a threefold pattern of history: the Age of the Father up to the end of the Old Testament; the Age of the Son in the New Testament and for 42 generations; and the Age of the Spirit from about 1260, lasting till the Second Coming of Christ. The last stage aroused millenarian hopes, spread by pseudo-Joachimite prophets. (*See also* FLAGELLANTS.)

Joan, Pope

Female Pope, alleged to have reigned as John VII for two years (855–7) after which she gave birth to a child and died. There is no truth in this fantasy, first circulated in the 13th century, though it was widely believed.

Joan of Arc (1412–31)

'La Pucelle', the 'Maid of Orléans', was born at Domrémy in eastern France. At the age of 13 she heard voices from Saints Catharine, Margaret and Michael, telling her to save France from English domination. Accepted by King Charles VII, Joan dressed in white armour and forced the English to retire from Orléans, and then took Charles to be crowned at Rheims cathedral. In a new campaign she was captured and sold to the English. Tried by the bishop of Beauvais (Cauchon) for witchcraft and heresy, Joan first recanted and then reaffirmed her 'voices' and was burnt in the marketplace in Rouen. She was canonized in 1920 and declared second patron of France (*see* DENIS). George Bernard Shaw's play *Saint Joan* (1924) brought her story alive for English-speaking people. Feast day 30 May.

Jocists

An organization of Catholic factory workers, Jeunesse Ouvrière Chrétienne (JOC), which originated in Belgium in 1924. The aim was to practise Christian principles in industry, and keep young people in the Church. The movement spread rapidly in France, and later to Britain, the Commonwealth and America. (*See also* WORKER PRIESTS.)

John

Apostle, son of Zebedee and younger brother of JAMES, he was one of the first disciples in an inner circle with Jesus. He and James were called Boanerges, 'sons of thunder' (Mark 3:17), suggesting impetuous character, but they offered to suffer with their Master (Mark 10:39). After Pentecost, John went with Peter to prison and before the SANHEDRIN, and he met Paul at the council of Jerusalem (Gal. 2:9). Then John disappears from certain sight; some say he was martyred, and others that he lived till old age at Ephesus. John is never mentioned by name in the Fourth Gospel, but many have thought he was the disciple 'whom Jesus loved' (John 13:23) at the Last Supper and the Resurrection, though some suggest this was Lazarus. Tradition made John the author of the Fourth Gospel and Johannine epistles, even of Revelation, but all these claims are questionable. Feast day 27 December. (*See also* JAMES (1); JOHN, GOSPEL AND EPISTLES OF.)

John, Gospel and Epistles of

The fourth gospel is very different from the first three (SYNOPTIC) GOSPELS. Comparison of synoptic teachings of Jesus in sermons and parables with the long Johannine discourses suggests that the latter are meditations and elaborations on the person and work of Christ. There are important differences of detail also: the length of the ministry of Jesus is one year in the synoptic gospels but three in John; and in John the Last Supper occurs before and not during PASSOVER. Critical scholars date this gospel at or after the end of the first century, by which time the Church was largely gentile. The Gospel is late, sophisticated and critical of Jews; yet it claims to contain memoirs of the disciple whom Jesus loved (21:24). It was probably written about 90–100 CE. Whether the Johannine epistles are by the same hand as the gospel is debated, but the author calls himself an 'elder' (2 John 1; 3 John 1).

The Book of REVELATION is certainly by a very different author, though he was later called John the Divine, meaning 'theologian'. The style and fantastic contents of this work are in such contrast to the Gospel that they cannot have come from the same person. (*See also* APOCALYPSE.)

John the Baptist

Luke's Gospel begins with birth stories of John the Baptist, the son of ZACHARIAH, a priest, and Elizabeth, a cousin of MARY, mother of Jesus. In all four gospels John the Baptizer appears at the river Jordan, calling people to prepare the way of the Lord and baptizing them on repentance. John baptized Jesus, then was imprisoned by HEROD Antipas, and sent two of his disciples to ask whether Jesus was the Coming One. John was beheaded by Herod, but his influence continued and people at Ephesus had experienced his baptism (Acts 18:25; 19:3), and perhaps that was why the Gospels stressed John's role as forerunner. The Baptist is still revered by the MANDEANS in Iraq. Feast day 24 June. (*See also* SALOME.)

John of the Cross (1542–91)

Spanish mystic and founder with Teresa of the Discalced (barefoot) CARMELITES. He was imprisoned because of his support for the Carmelite reform, escaped and lived in illness at a monastery where he died. John was a poet and influential mystical writer, his texts consisting of poems and long commentaries. His *Ascent of Mount Carmel* and *Dark Night of the Soul* tell of purgation, suffering in the 'night of the spirit' and rising to the goal of divine union. Feast day 24 November. (*See also* TERESA.)

John Paul II (Karol Wojtyla) (b. 1920)

Pope from 1978. Formerly Archbishop of Cracow; the first Polish Pope, and the first non-Italian since 1522. (*See also* ABORTION; BIRTH CONTROL; BISHOP; HOLOCAUST; KNOCK; MODERNISM; ULTRAMONTANE)

John XXIII (Angelo Giuseppe Roncalli) (1881–1963)

Pope. Born of a peasant family in northern Italy, he served as a chaplain in the First World War and was papal nuncio to liberated France in the Second, then Patriarch of Venice. Elected Pope on the 12th ballot (*see* CARDINAL), he convened the Second VATICAN Council to bring reform and revival to the Church. He was followed by Popes Paul VI, John Paul and John Paul II.

Johnson, James (1835–1917)

Anglican priest in Nigeria. Mission policy at the time was against African leadership and Johnson waited a long time for advancement, but in 1890 he was made assistant bishop, or 'half-bishop' as he called it. Subsequently he worked for the independence of the African Church. (*See also* CROWTHER.)

Jones, James Warren, 'Jim' (1931–78)

Born to a poor family in Indiana, he ran a community for blacks and whites. In 1965 he founded a People's Temple in California, and some claimed he healed the sick and raised the dead. In 1977 he moved to 'Jonestown' in the jungle of Guyana, and when Congressman Leo Ryan went to investigate complaints he and some of his party were shot dead. Shortly thereafter Jones and 900 followers committed suicide or were murdered. The events at Jonestown remain obscure.

Jordan, River

In a deep valley, 700 feet below sea level, the river divides towns and people, though in the dry season it is only a small stream. John the Baptist preached there and Jesus was baptized in its waters. In Christian story the Jordan becomes the water between heaven and earth, and crossing over Jordan brings liberation and final bliss.

Josaphat

See BARLAAM.

The River Jordan, site of Christ's baptism: The Jordan is a small river, in the dry season quite narrow, but it divides the country and has been famous for baptisms.

Joseph

Described negatively by some writers as 'spouse of the BVM', Joseph is referred to in the Gospel of Luke (2: 48) and in John (1: 45, 6:42) as father of Jesus. He lived at Nazareth in Galilee and is once called a carpenter (Matt. 13:55), but little else is known of him. The genealogies of Matthew and Luke give different names for his father, and only agree in claiming descent from DAVID. Since Joseph is not mentioned later in the gospels, or anywhere else in the New Testament, it is assumed that he died before Jesus began his ministry. In the Roman calendar Joseph is patron of workers, with a feast on 1 May. (*See also* BROTHERS AND SISTERS OF JESUS; GENEALOGIES; VIRGIN BIRTH.

Joseph of Arimathea

Nothing is known of him before the Crucifixion, when he went to beg the body of Jesus from Pilate and buried it in a rock sepulchre (Mark 15:43ff). In medieval legend Joseph brought the GRAIL to England and built the first church at GLASTONBURY. Feast day 17 March.

Josephus, Flavius (37–100 CE)

Jewish historian, contemporary with the growing Church. He has been said to refer to Christ as 'a wise man, if indeed one should call him a man', but this is now regarded as a Christian interpolation in his writings. The only sure reference to Christian matters that Josephus makes is to the martyrdom of 'James, the brother of Jesus who was called the Christ' (*Antiquities* 20:197). This passage is generally accepted as authentic and suggests that Jesus was known to the historian's readers. (*See also* JAMES (2).)

Juan Santos Atahualpa (1712–56)

Peruvian religious leader who claimed descent from Inca emperors and led a rebellion against the Spanish. He called himself Messiah and Son of God, come to deliver his children from slavery. Spanish forces went into the jungle against him, but his followers said he ascended into heaven. His tomb was for many years a centre of devotion.

Jubilate

Latin for the first word of Psalm 100, 'O be joyful', and a CANTICLE at morning prayer. Recently the word has become popular again, in Latin, in modern hymns sung at TAIZÉ and elsewhere.

jubilee

The Bible said: 'You shall hallow the fiftieth year . . . it shall be a jubilee to you' (Lev. 25:10); slaves were given freedom and land reverted from tenants to its owners. In the Roman Catholic Church there is a similar year of remission and indulgence every 25 years. (*See also* HOLY YEAR.)

Judaism

Modern name for the religion, and also the culture, of the people known variously as Hebrews, Israelites and Jews. Although all the first Christians were Jews, later relationships between Jews and Christians deteriorated, with extreme persecutions during the CRUSADES and the HOLOCAUST. (*See also* ANTI-SEMITISM.)

Judas Iscariot

Disciple who betrayed Jesus (e.g. Mark 3:19). John (12:6) suggests that he was a thief. But what did Judas betray, and why? Did he hope that the arrest would force Jesus' hand and make him declare a revolution? Judas came from Kerioth in southern Judea, while most of the disciples were Galileans, and there may have been rivalry and plotting. Judas remains a mystery. There are two versions of his suicide (Matt. 27:3ff; Acts 1:16ff).

Jude

One of the brothers of Jesus (Mark 6:3); he may have been in Jerusalem at Pentecost (Acts 1:14). Little is known of him, but the strange one-chapter Epistle of Jude has traditionally been ascribed to this Jude, and some modern scholars agree. The letter is an apocalyptic fantasy, rather similar to the Second Epistle of Peter. Feast day, with Simon, 28 October.

judgement, general/last

Christian writers have anticipated a final general judgement. The Apostles' and Nicene CREEDS speak of Christ coming 'to judge the quick and the dead', based on the parable of the judgement (Matt. 25:31ff). Theologians have also considered 'particular' judgement at death, but whether this is followed by purgatory or sleep, awaiting a final judgement, is not universally agreed. (*See also* ADVENTISM; APOCALYPSE.)

Julian, Flavius Claudius (the Apostate) (332–63 CE)

Nephew of CONSTANTINE, he became emperor in 361 and sought to re-establish the old Roman religion and degrade the Church. Julian wrote against Christian doctrine, but sought to purify public morality. He was killed in a campaign in the east, but the story that Julian died saying 'Thou hast conquered, O Galilean', was a later invention.

Julian of Norwich (1342–1413)

English mystic. Very little is known of Mother or Lady Julian, except that she lived as a strict recluse in the east part of St Julian's Church, Norwich. She is famous for her book *The Sixteen Revelations of Divine Love*, which speaks of God as 'our very Mother', and of the world as 'a hazel-nut, in the palm of my hand'. (*See also* CLOUD OF UNKNOWING; HILTON; KEMPE; ROLLE.)

just war

The notion of a 'holy war' was against Christian principles, though the CRUSADES seemed to be that to their participants. Conditions for a 'just war' were slowly developed, THOMAS AQUINAS giving three: (1) it must be waged by proper authority; (2) the cause must be just; (3) the intention must be to suppress evil and establish good. A fourth was added later: that war must be waged by rightful means. Some modern writers develop this, or add as a fifth that any kind of atomic or nuclear warfare must be ruled out as indiscriminate and genocidal. Modern views of non-nuclear war, or 'limited war', in some ways resemble restatements of the concept of the 'just war'. (*See also* CONSCIENCE; PACIFISM.)

justification

Paul spoke of being 'justified freely by [God's] grace' and 'justified by faith without the deeds of the law' (Rom. 3:24ff). This is taken to mean that God forgives human beings and 'pronounces them righteous'. For LUTHER and many Protestants, justification by faith alone meant that salvation depended entirely on the GRACE of God and not on human actions.

Justin Martyr (100–65 CE)

Christian philosopher. Born in Samaria to parents of Greek origin, he taught in Ephesus and Rome wearing a philosopher's cloak, but on refusing to offer sacrifice he was beheaded. Justin wrote *Apologies* and a *Dialogue with Trypho*, a Jew. He argued that Christ was the LOGOS in which every race shared, and those who lived before Christ, like Socrates, were Christians if they lived according to reason. Feast day 14 April.

Justinian

See HAGIA SOPHIA.

K

kabbalah

In the middle ages, knowledge of Jewish *kabbalah* (Hebrew, 'tradition') and of the Hebrew language persuaded some Christian thinkers that these mystical teachings attested the divinity of Christ, the ATONEMENT and the TRINITY, but with better knowledge of language and doctrine few later scholars followed the notion that *kabbalah* 'proved' Christianity. (*See also* PARACELSUS.)

kafir

See INFIDEL.

Kagame, Alexis (b. 1912)

Catholic priest, poet and philosopher, from the Tutsi people of Rwanda. He developed African beliefs in a 'life force' (Muntu) propounded by Placide TEMPELS, and pleaded for the harmony of Catholic teaching and his own tradition. (*See also* JAMAA.)

Kagawa, Toyohiko (1888–1960)

Japanese Christian social reformer. Educated in a Buddhist monastery, he became a Christian and a Presbyterian minister. After study in America he took up social work, though he suffered from tuberculosis, and founded Labour and Peasant unions. He started a National Anti-War League in 1928 and was imprisoned as a pacifist during the Second World War, but he was a member of the cabinet which negotiated Japan's surrender. He helped form the Socialist Party and was a pastor in Tokyo till his death. Kagawa wrote books which were widely translated, including *Christ and Japan*.

Kakure

See HIDDEN CHRISTIANS.

Keble, John (1792–1866)

Anglican priest. After university he assisted his father in a country parish, published poems in the *Christian Year* (1827) and became professor of poetry at Oxford University. A leader of the Oxford Movement, Keble preached in 1833 on 'National Apostasy' on a plan for the suppression by the state without consulting the Church of ten Irish Anglican bishoprics, and wrote for *Tracts for the Times*. After NEWMAN's defection to Rome in 1845, Keble worked with PUSEY to keep the High Church movement within the Anglican Church. Keble College, Oxford, was founded in his memory in 1870. (*See also* ANGLO-CATHOLICISM; TRACTS.)

Kells

See BOOK OF KELLS.

Kempe, Margery (1373–1438)

Born at Lynn in Norfolk, she married a burgess of the town and bore him 14 children. Her *Book of Margery Kempe* is claimed as the first autobiography in English, the people of Lynn not knowing much Latin or French. Visiting Canterbury, Margery reproved the monks, denounced pleasure and was accused of LOLLARDY. She went on pilgrimage to the Holy Land, to COMPOSTELA and to Mother JULIAN at Norwich. Her book is emotional, a work of story and exhortation rather than mysticism, but invaluable as a picture of her time. (*See also* ROLLE.)

Kempis, Thomas à (1380–1471)

Born Thomas Hemerken, at Kempen near Cologne, he was educated by the BRETHREN OF THE COMMON LIFE, entered a house of AUGUSTINIAN CANONS in 1399 and lived there for the rest of his life. He wrote several books, of which the most famous is the IMITATION OF CHRIST. (*See also* RUYSBROECK.)

Ken, Thomas (1637–1711)

Anglican priest, chaplain to Charles II and bishop of Bath and Wells. Refusing to swear allegiance to William III, as a NON-JUROR, he was deprived of his SEE and lived in retirement. He wrote the hymn, 'Glory to Thee, My God, this Night'.

kenosis

Greek, 'emptying', a concept derived from Paul's statement that Christ 'emptied himself, taking the form of a servant' (Phil. 2:7). Kenosis has been explained as showing that in the INCARNATION Christ became a true human being. (*See also* PHILIPPIANS.)

Kensit

See PROTESTANT TRUTH SOCIETY.

kerygma

Greek, 'preaching'. In worship and theology, distinct from *didaché*, 'teaching'. (*See also* PREACHING.)

Keswick

A convention centre in the Lake District of England for annual gatherings of evangelicals, with Bible study, prayer and preaching.

keys

See ABSOLUTION; KINGDOM OF GOD.

Kierkegaard, Søren Aaby (1813–55)

Danish philosopher who inspired the development of EXISTENTIALISM and DIALECTICAL theology. Brought up in a devout Lutheran family, he attacked the Church for worldliness and PANTHEISM. He stressed faith against reason and the position of the individual soul before God. His books translated into English include *Philosophical Fragments* and *Sickness unto Death*.

Kimbangu, Simon (1889–1951)

Born in Zaïre (Congo) and educated by the Baptist Missionary Society, after teaching he began a mission of healing and preaching. His great success alarmed the Belgian colonial authorities, and he was arrested and sentenced to death in 1921. Reprieved by the King of Belgium after appeal by missionaries, Kimbangu's sentence was commuted to life imprisonment and he died in captivity 30 years later. Kimbangu's church developed underground, became the national church at the independence of Zaïre in 1960, and was the first of the new African churches to join the World Council of Churches. Under the title L'Eglise de Jésus-Christ sur la Terre par le Prophète Simon Kimbangu, it now has some 4 million members. (*See also* HARRIS.)

kindred and affinity, table of

List in the BOOK OF COMMON PRAYER stipulating whom a man or a woman may not marry. It begins: 'A Man may not marry his Grandmother.' Published in 1563, it was based on prohibitions in Leviticus 18. It has been amended to allow the marriage of cousins, or of a deceased wife's sister.

King, Martin Luther, Jr
(1929–68)

African-American Baptist minister and civil rights leader. Born in Atlanta, Georgia, he studied sociology and theology, and became pastor at Montgomery, Alabama. He led protests and boycotts against racial segregation in public transport. In Washington in 1963 he delivered his famous 'I have a dream' speech at the Lincoln Memorial, and in 1964 received the Nobel Peace Prize. An admirer of Gandhi, King insisted on non-violence, but was assassinated in Memphis, Tennessee, on 4 April 1968. A national holiday is held on 15 January to honour him.

King James Version

American title of the AUTHORIZED VERSION of the Bible.

Kingdom of God

Also Kingdom of Heaven, avoiding use of the divine name: a concept central to Christian teaching. It was proclaimed by John the Baptist to be at hand; Jesus began his ministry with the same message, and many of his parables refer to the Kingdom. How far it is present and how far future has often been debated. The Church has always prayed, 'Thy kingdom come.' It is said that Jesus preached the Kingdom and the Church emerged instead, though the promise of the 'keys of the Kingdom' to Peter seems to reflect the evangelist's view of the Church as ruled by Peter and his successors (Matt. 16:18–19). (*See also* ABSOLUTION; EVANGEL.)

Kingdom Hall

See JEHOVAH'S WITNESSES.

King's Evil

Scrofula, swelling of the lymph glands of the neck from tuberculosis. This condition was supposed from Saxon times to be curable by the royal touch. The Stuarts encouraged the notion and Charles II touched 100,000 persons. Dr Johnson as a child was taken to Queen Anne, 'his mother yielding to the superstitious notion . . . as to the virtue of the regal touch'. But it was 'without any effect' (J. Boswell, *Life of Samuel Johnson*, 1, year 1712).

Kingsley, Charles (1819–75)

Anglican priest and social reformer. Educated at King's College, London, and at Cambridge, he became a country vicar and an early CHRISTIAN SOCIALIST. He also wrote novels such as *Westward Ho!* and *The Water-Babies*. Rashly criticizing J. H. NEWMAN, he provoked the notable *Apologia* from the latter.

Kirchentag

German, 'Church Day': lay people's rally of German Christians meeting every three years for several days since the Second World War. It helped to unite the churches after the Nazi regime and the division between East and West. In 1997 it was held at Leipzig in the East for the first time. Average attendance is 120,000.

kirk

See CHURCH.

kirk-session

See CONSISTORY; ELDER.

kiss of peace

See GESTURES.

kneeling

See BLACK RUBRIC.

knights

See HOSPITALLERS; TEMPLARS.

Knock

A village in western Ireland, now a town with a basilica and an airport. Visions of MARY and miraculous cures were reported here from 1879. It became a popular place of pilgrimage and was visited by Pope John Paul II in 1979 at the centenary of the first visions.

Knox, John (1513–72)

Scottish priest, an ardent reformer and chaplain to Edward VI in England. When Mary became Queen of Scots he fled to Geneva, to be influenced by CALVIN. Knox wrote *The First Blast of the Trumpet against the Monstrous Regiment of Women*, criticizing the regent Mary of Guise. On return to Scotland he led the reformers and preached to Mary of Scots against celebration of MASS in Holyrood Chapel. When she abdicated he preached at the coronation of James. Knox with others drew up the Scottish Confession and the Book of Common Order. He died in Edinburgh and was buried at St Giles. (*See also* GEDDES.)

koinonia

A New Testament Greek expression for communion or fellowship, union with God or participation in a community. It is the word used in the blessing, 'the fellowship of the Holy Spirit'.

Koran

See QUR'ĀN.

Koresh

See BRANCH DAVIDIANS.

Krishnamurti

See BESANT.

Küng, Hans (b. 1928)

Swiss Catholic theologian and prolific writer. His criticisms of the Vatican led to his being barred from the Catholic Faculty at Tübingen, but he continued at the Ecumenical Institute there. His best-known writing in English translation is *On Being a Christian* (1976).

Kyrie Eleison

Greek, 'Lord, have mercy': a brief prayer which has been used in the liturgy since the early centuries. In its Greek form it is used in the Mass; it was dropped from the Book of Common Prayer in 1552, but has been restored in modern times, in Greek or English. (*See also* LITANY.)

L

labarum

Imperial standard adopted by CONSTANTINE, probably with traditional emblems replaced by the Greek letters X and P, the Chi Rho, first two letters in Greek of CH-R-ist. The origin of the Latin word *labarum* is unknown; possibly it indicated a standard or banner. (*See also* IN HOC SIGNO VINCES.)

ladder

An emblem for progress towards union with God, based on Jacob's ladder connecting earth and heaven (Gen. 28:12). Eastern Orthodox writers indicate a *Ladder of Divine Ascent*, and a well-known text in English is Walter HILTON'S *Scale of Perfection*.

Lady

'Our Lady' is a common title of MARY, mother of Jesus. Lady Day is the feast of the ANNUNCIATION on 25 March.

laity

The people: members of the churches who are not ordained clergy. The distinction between the two is most marked in Catholic and Orthodox churches, while Protestants emphasize the priesthood of all believers (1 Peter 2:5, 9), and Quakers have no ordained ministry.

lamb

See AGNUS DEI; GOOD SHEPHERD.

Lambeth

Lambeth Palace in London is the official residence of the Archbishop of Canterbury. It dates from the 13th century, and the architectural historian, Nikolaus Pevsner, writes that 'Londoners would flock to see it, if only it were not so near' (*London*, 2:281). Lambeth Conferences of bishops of the worldwide Anglican Church have been held about every ten years since 1867. Lambeth Articles have been propounded stating essentials for a united Christian Church. (*See also* ANGLICANISM; CANTERBURY.)

Lammas

Old English, 'loaf mass': celebrated on 1 August, when the first-fruits of the corn harvest were consecrated in the middle ages. Now celebrated only in Scotland, it is one of the quarter-days – the four times in the year for celebration of the Lord's Supper or Holy Communion. (*See also* HARVEST.)

language-game

See FIDEISM.

Laodicea

A city in Asia Minor to which Paul says he wrote a letter, which has not survived (Col. 4:16). In the book of Revelation (3:14ff) the Laodiceans are said to be 'neither cold nor hot', and so the name is applied to those who are indifferent in religion or politics.

Las Casas, Bartolomé de (1474–1566)

Spanish Dominican missionary to South America. He championed the rights of Indians and wrote an account of *The Destruction of the Indies* (1552). He won the backing of the papacy, influenced missions also in the Philippines, and is honoured today for his 'theology from below'. (*See also* LIBERATION THEOLOGY.)

last judgement

See JUDGEMENT.

Last Supper

The final meal of Jesus with his disciples, to be distinguished from the LORD'S SUPPER, which is a commemoration of that meal. The SYNOPTIC GOSPELS say this was a PASSOVER meal (Mark 14:12ff), but John situates it before the Passover (John 13:1), perhaps to make the

Passover and the Crucifixion coincide. Whether the Last Supper was a *seder*, a Passover eve ritual, has been much debated; the rites of that time are not clearly known. Nor is it known whether the Last Supper table bore more than bread and wine. And where were the women, who would be present at a family meal? But our Gospel accounts record what would interest the later Church, with its celebration of the Lord's Supper.

Lateran

The cathedral Church of Rome stands on the site of an ancient palace on the Lateran hill. Councils were held here from the 7th to the 18th century. A Lateran Treaty was signed in 1929 to establish the VATICAN City as a sovereign state.

Latimer, Hugh (1485–1555)

Born near Leicester, he was a university preacher in Cambridge and attacked the

The Last Supper, from the Oberammergau Passion Play. An impressive rendering, with Christ and the disciples appearing in traditional costume and speaking with formal dialogue.

reformer Melanchthon, for at that time, he says, he was 'as obstinate a papist as any in England'. Then he 'began to smell the Word of God' and became a zealous Protestant preacher. He was chaplain to Anne Boleyn and supported the royal divorce. Under Mary Tudor, Latimer was found guilty of heresy, along with RIDLEY and CRANMER, and was burned with Ridley opposite Balliol College in Oxford, saying, according to FOXE: 'Be of good comfort, Master Ridley, we shall this day light such a candle by God's grace in England as I trust shall never be put out.'

Latitudinarian

Allowing latitude or freedom of thought in religious matters. It was applied to Anglican divines of the 17th century who accepted episcopacy and the liturgy, but regarded them as of minor importance.

Latter-Day Saints

See MORMONS.

Laud, William (1573–1645)

Archbishop of Canterbury, favourite of Charles I and fierce opponent of Calvinism. He introduced High Church customs, proclaimed the DIVINE RIGHT of kings, branded the Puritan PRYNNE with hot irons on the cheeks and was attacked by him in turn. He was impeached by the Long Parliament for 'endeavouring to overthrow the Protestant religion', and executed on Tower Hill.

Lauds

Morning prayer, named from Psalm 148: 'Praise ye', in Latin 'laudate'.

law

See JUSTIFICATION.

Law, William (1686–1761)

Anglican spiritual writer, a NON-JUROR who refused to swear allegiance to

George I. He retired to his birthplace at Kingscliffe in Northamptonshire, with rich lady friends, and organized schools and almshouses. Law was influenced by German mystics and wrote much. His *A Serious Call to a Devout and Holy Life* affected many people, notably Dr Johnson and the WESLEYS.

Lawrence

See BROTHER LAWRENCE.

lay reader, lay preacher

In the Church of England a lay person who is authorized to conduct morning and evening prayer and to preach and teach, but not to celebrate Holy Communion. (*See also* LOCAL PREACHER; PREACHING.)

Lazarists

See VINCENT OF PAUL.

Lazarus

Mentioned only in JOHN's Gospel (11:1ff), as brother of Martha and Mary, 'he whom you [Christ] love' died and was raised up. Nothing else is known of him, though some have identified him with the disciple Jesus loved at the Last Supper and Resurrection. Medieval legend took him to Cyprus, Constantinople and Marseilles.

Another Lazarus, hardly similar, died and went to Abraham's bosom while the rich man was in Hades (Luke 16:19ff). He became patron of lepers.

lectern

A reading stand for books, from Latin *legere*, 'to read'. A lector is a reader, of Scripture or parts of the liturgy.

Lee, Ann (1736–84)

Prophetess of the SHAKERS or Shaking Quakers, known as Mother Ann. She joined the Quakers at the age of 22, gave enthusiastic witness, and was imprisoned in harsh conditions in Manchester. There she had an intense experience, convinced that the Second Coming was already happening. With eight companions she went to America to found a Shaker Church, where worship involved dancing. Shaker common life was disciplined and celibate, and the members produced goods renowned for their functional beauty.

legate

A representative of the Pope for special missions, from Latin for 'commission'.

legend

See MYTH.

Legio Maria/Maria Legio

An African INDEPENDENT Church from a Roman Catholic background, founded in Kenya in 1963. It combines Catholic and African features, carries out healings and exorcisms, and claims 80,000 adherents.

Leibniz

See THEODICY.

Lenshina, Alice (1924–78)

Prophetess of the Lumpa (Visible Salvation) Church in Zambia. Lenshina, whose name means Regina or Queen, was a Presbyterian who led her own movement and attracted many followers in a fight against witchcraft. Refusing to pay taxes, her church clashed with the Zambian government in 1964 and 700 people were killed. Alice was arrested and died in detention. Her church was banned, but it still exists as an underground movement.

Lent

Perhaps from the 'lengthening' of the days in spring, this time begins on ASH WEDNESDAY and continues till Easter Eve. A fast of 40 days was taken from that of Jesus (Matt. 4:2). The FASTING

was formerly severe, though it is now much relaxed. Special services may be confined to HOLY WEEK.

Levellers

A radical movement in 17th-century England. Its members were opposed to monarchy, arguing for religious toleration, abolition of tithes and a parliament elected by universal male suffrage. Their leader was John Lilburne, who was whipped and imprisoned by order of the Star Chamber, and died in 1657. Cromwell was suspicious of the Levellers and after the restoration of Charles II the movement faded away. A group of Levellers, nicknamed Diggers, led by Gerrard Winstanley, advocated cultivation of common land and a COMMUNIST commonwealth.

Levi

See MATTHEW.

levirate marriage

From Latin *levir*, meaning a husband's brother, a type of marriage mentioned by Sadducees to Jesus (Mark 12:18ff) in which the brother of a man who died without children married the widow so that they should not be without descendants.

Levites

Descendants of the priestly tribe of Levi, acting as servants in the Temple. One is mentioned in the parable of the GOOD SAMARITAN (Luke 10:32).

Liberal Catholic Church

Founded in England in 1915, this movement gathered more supporters in America and Australia. It seeks to combine traditional emphasis on episcopacy and the sacraments with THEOSOPHICAL teachings.

liberation theology

After the Second Vatican Council in the late 1960s, South American priest-theologians began criticizing social injustice, poverty and oppression. Some used Marxist economic analysis, provoking criticism, not least from the VATICAN; but they spoke of the judgement of God on the rich. Liberation theology spread throughout the world, adapting itself to particular conditions. In South Africa it attacked APARTHEID, and in Asia it is called Minjung or 'poor people theology'. (*See also* BOFF; CAMARA; CARDENAL; GUTIÉRREZ; SEGUNDO; TORRES.)

lich

See LYCH-GATE.

Lilburne

See LEVELLERS.

limbo

From Latin for 'border' or 'edge': in Roman Catholic teaching, the place where unbaptized babies and righteous people born before Christ go after death. In DANTE's *Divine Comedy* limbo is the first circle of hell, for those who had not had baptism, among whom was his guide Virgil. People in limbo did not suffer, except from the hope of seeing God. (*See also* AVERROES.)

Lindisfarne

Also called Holy Island: an island off the coast of Northumberland, where AIDAN arrived from IONA in 635 CE and made a centre for founding churches in England and Scotland. The Lindisfarne Gospels, in an Irish style from about 700 CE, are in the British Museum in London, but in 1997 there was pressure for this manuscript to be sent to Durham Cathedral as nearer its place of origin. (*See also* BOOK OF KELLS; COLMAN; CUTHBERT.)

litany

From Greek for 'supplication': a series of prayers or biddings, to which people respond 'Kyrie Eleison', or 'Lord, have mercy.' In the BOOK OF COMMON PRAYER the Litany was appointed to be sung or said on Sundays, Wednesdays and Fridays. Litanies may also be lists of invocations to the Trinity, prophets, apostles and saints.

Little Flower

A name for THÉRÈSE OF LISIEUX. The Little Flowers (Fioretti) of St FRANCIS OF ASSISI is a collection of legends about the saint and his companions, dating from about a century after his death and giving in Italian a picture of the early Franciscans.

Little Gidding

See FERRAR.

Little Office

An abbreviated sequence of prayers for the Virgin Mary, dating from the 10th century, which declined and then revived in popularity as vocal prayer in female congregations.

Liturgical Movement

A revival of lay participation in the liturgy in the 20th century, renewed after the Second Vatican Council in a Constitution of the Sacred Liturgy, using the vernacular. A continental Liturgical Movement, especially prominent in France, had parallels with ANGLO-CATHOLICISM, and also with Reformed and Protestant movements, notably in the CHURCH OF SOUTH INDIA and at TAIZÉ.

liturgy

Greek, 'people's work', applied to that of the Temple. The word is used of all the services of the Church, and particularly of the eucharistic worship of Eastern Orthodox churches as distinct from the Roman Mass. (*See also* WORSHIP.)

Livingstone, David (1813–73)

Scottish missionary and explorer. He worked in a cotton factory, studied medicine in Glasgow and joined the London Missionary Society. He went to southern Africa in 1841, and after a time in the mission he travelled across Africa unarmed, then turning north to discover the great lakes and find the sources of the Nile. He published *Missionary Travels* on his adventures. Lost to the world, Livingstone was found at Ujiji in Tanzania by Stanley, and died shortly after in Zambia. His attendants carried his body to the coast and it was buried in Westminster Abbey.

local preacher

METHODIST term for a lay preacher in a locality or 'CIRCUIT', distinct from ordained 'travelling' preachers who minister anywhere in the country. (*See also* BIBLE CHRISTIANS; CLASS MEETING.)

Locke, John (1632–1704)

English liberal philosopher. He disliked the Puritan intolerance of Oxford theologians and was not ordained. He dabbled in medicine and travelled as secretary with Lord Shaftesbury. Locke championed freedom of thought and wrote *Letters Concerning Toleration* and *The Reasonableness of Christianity*, aiming at the reunion of the churches.

Logia

Greek, 'sayings'. An early church writer, PAPIAS, said that MATTHEW compiled the 'sayings' in the Hebrew language, but what these were is uncertain. Our Gospel of Matthew is in Greek but it, along with Luke's, probably used a collection of words of Jesus which may have been these Logia. (*See also* Q.)

Logos

Greek, 'word' or 'reason'. A term from philosophy for divine creative and controlling power. It is expressed in the prologue to John's Gospel: 'In the beginning was the Logos . . . The Logos was made flesh.' This concept was not developed in the rest of the gospel, but it was taken up in Christian theology of the person of Christ, the divine reason and incarnate, not a simple idea but a human being. (*See also* CHRISTOLOGY; INCARNATION; JUSTIN MARTYR; PHILO; TRINITY.)

Loisy

See MODERNISM.

Lollards

A nickname, said to mean a 'mumbler of prayers', applied to the followers of the reforming John WYCLIFFE in 14th- and 15th-century England. Cherishing the Bible, which Wycliffe and his followers translated into English from Latin, the Lollards attacked clerical celibacy, INDULGENCES, pilgrimages, transubstantiation, prayers for the dead and clerical wealth. They were opposed by vicious laws, with the burning of heretics being introduced for the first time in England, but these 'poor preachers' carried their message throughout England to Scotland and Bohemia, and prepared the way for the Reformation. (*See also* DE HAERETICO COMBURENDO; HUSS; KEMPE.)

Lombardica Historia

See GOLDEN LEGEND.

London Society for the Study of Religion

See HÜGEL.

Lord's Day

The name occurs in the book of Revelation (1:10). Early Christians observed the Saturday SABBATH, and the Lord's Day on Sunday as celebration of the Resurrection and Pentecost. The Lord's Day Observance Society, founded in 1831, wages a battle against Sunday opening of shops, on the principle that the Sabbath was made for humankind and should guarantee rest from work.

Lord's Prayer

There are two versions of the prayer which Jesus taught his disciples: Matthew 6:9–13 and Luke 11:2–4. Luke's is shorter, though the Authorized Version added lines from Matthew. The DOXOLOGY in Matthew, 'Thine is the kingdom . . . Amen', is not in the oldest manuscripts and was appended later. Visitors to Scots kirks note that they say 'debts' instead of 'trespasses', and it has to be admitted that they are right, for the text says that. 'Trespasses' seems to have been taken up from a later verse. The Lord's Prayer is taken as a summary of the Gospel, for spiritual and material needs, and it is used in English daily by both Catholics and Protestants. (*See also* ROSARY; SERMON ON THE MOUNT.)

Lord's Supper

Paul wrote of eating 'the Lord's supper' (1 Cor. 11:20), his name for the commemoration of the LAST SUPPER historically held by Jesus with his disciples. The title is used still, especially by Protestants, for the Holy Communion or EUCHARIST.

Loreto

The house where Jesus lived in Nazareth is said to have been carried through the air to Loreto in Italy, though the story is questioned by Catholic and other writers. (*See also* WALSINGHAM.)

lottery

See GAMBLING.

Lourdes

See BERNADETTE.

Love, love feast

See AGAPÉ.

Low Church

In the Church of England, contrasted with High Church, which stressed episcopacy and priesthood. Today 'EVANGELICAL' seems to be a more commonly used term than Low Church, and indicates that large part of Anglicanism that insists on the primacy of the Bible sometimes, but not necessarily, interpreted in FUNDAMENTALIST fashion.

Low Mass

A liturgy celebrated by a priest without assistants, on weekdays, to fulfil the requirement of a daily EUCHARIST.

Low Sunday

The Sunday after EASTER, so-called in contrast to the high celebrations of Eastertide.

Lucifer

Latin for 'light-bearer'; Venus, the morning star. Similar imagery is applied to Christ as the Daystar (2 Pet. 1:19; Rev. 22:16). Then by a strange reversal it was applied to the DEVIL, the rebel archangel whose fall from heaven was supposed to be referred to in Isaiah 14:12: 'How art thou fallen from heaven, O Lucifer, son of the morning?' (Authorized Version). This demonic reference was developed by early writers, and also by Milton in *Paradise Lost* (7:131).

Lucy

A third-century martyr from Sicily, famed for giving her goods to the poor and guarding her virginity. Many legends grew up around her. She was popular in both East and West, and her feast day on 13 December is celebrated in Europe in preparation for Christmas.

Luke

Probably the only non-Jewish writer in the Bible, he is held to be author of both his Gospel and the ACTS OF THE APOSTLES. Paul called him 'the beloved physician' (Col. 4:14), and so Luke has been taken as patron of doctors. He is also patron of artists, from a later tradition. Luke went with Paul on his second and third missionary journeys, and on to Rome with him. He gathered material for his gospel from many sources and wrote in good Greek, though the Jewish Josephus wrote better. Tradition said that Luke was not married and died aged 84.

Luke, Gospel According to

Like Matthew, Luke used the Gospel of Mark and also the Sayings in Q. But he had other sources too and wrote them up skilfully, so from him we have stories not known elsewhere: the GOOD SAMARITAN, the Prodigal Son, the Rich Man and LAZARUS, Zacchaeus, the walk to EMMAUS, and many others. Like Matthew, Luke begins with two chapters on the infancy of Jesus, but they are quite different from Matthew's and disagree on some points. Luke parallels, but again differs from, Matthew on the SERMON on the Plain, the BEATITUDES and the LORD'S PRAYER. His Passion and Resurrection narratives vary and add to the other

gospels. Luke has an attractive style and an ability to compress his stories, a care for women and strangers, and emphasis on Christ as Saviour. This gospel was probably written about 80–5 CE. (*See also* ACTS; MARK; MATTHEW; Q.)

Lull, Ramon (1235–1315)

A Franciscan TERTIARY, lay follower, from Spain, noted for attempts to spread Christianity in the Islamic world. He spent nine years studying Arabic language and philosophy, made several journeys to India and North Africa, and is said to have been imprisoned and stoned to death at Bougie in Algeria. Lull wrote poetic, mystical and philosophical works in Catalan, Latin and Arabic.

Lumpa Church

See LENSHINA.

Luther, Martin (1483–1546)

Born at Mansfeld in Saxony, he entered an Augustinian monastery and was ordained priest. He lectured at

Luther, Melanchthon and other reformers.

WITTENBERG, where in 1517 he nailed 95 Theses against INDULGENCES on the door of the Schlosskirche. Writing on *The Babylonian Captivity of the Church*, in Latin and German, Luther criticized many church practices and abuses, and he was excommunicated in 1521. Under princely protection he returned to lecturing, discarded his priestly habit, and married a former Cistercian nun, Katharine von Bora. He disputed with ZWINGLI on the Eucharist, and contradicted Henry VIII of England on the seven sacraments.

Luther made a great German translation of the Bible, and wrote many hymns, including that known as 'A Safe Stronghold' in English translation. His *Table Talk* was lively and revealing, often using coarse expressions, attacking the papacy, theological opponents, and the Jews and their synagogues. His theology was pessimistic, holding the TOTAL DEPRAVITY of humankind, and utter dependence on God. (*See also* CONSUBSTANTIATION; JUSTIFICATION; WORMS.)

Lutheranism

LUTHER's protests aroused enthusiasm in Germany, along with abandonment of many Catholic beliefs and practices. Lutherans produced the AUGSBURG CONFESSION, largely the work of MELANCTHON. Disputes arose after Luther's death, which were settled in a *Formula* and *Book of Concord* (1577, 1580). In the following centuries Lutheran orthodoxy tended to be intellectual, and reaction came with PIETISM. Domination by the state, and divisions between the Lutheran and Reformed churches, provided a background to modern divisions between CONFESSING and GERMAN CHRISTIANS.

Lutheranism became the state religion in Scandinavia, and in America German and Scandinavian Lutherans had their own synods, but formed the Evangelical Lutheran Church together in 1987. Throughout the world Lutheranism is estimated to have 60 million members.

Luwum, Janani (1922–77)

Ugandan archbishop and martyr. He joined in the BALOKOLE revival but entered the Anglican Church and was ordained in 1955, becoming the first bishop from the Acholi people and archbishop in 1974. Along with Roman Catholics, Luwum protested against the massacres enacted by Idi Amin, and he was taken from a meeting of bishops and shot.

LXX

See SEPTUAGINT.

lych-gate

From old English for a 'corpse', the lich- or lych-gate is a shelter at the entrance to a churchyard, where coffins are set down as the minister arrives.

M

Macaulay, Zachary (1768–1838)

Anglican evangelical and slave abolitionist, father of the historian T. B. Macaulay. He was governor of Sierra Leone for six years, a member of the CLAPHAM SECT, and a founder of London University.

Machiavelli

See BORGIA.

Maciel

See CANUDOS.

Mackenzie

See ROSICRUCIANS.

McLeod

See IONA.

McPherson, Aimee Semple (1890–1944)

American evangelist, converted to Pentecostalism by Robert Semple. The couple married and went as missionaries to China, where they lived until his death in 1910. Two more marriages ended in divorce, and in 1917 Aimee began evangelistic campaigns in the United States. At Los Angeles she built an Angelus Temple, launched the first church-owned radio station, and formed the International Church of the Foursquare Gospel. At her death there were 400 congregations in the USA and 200 foreign missions (See also ELIM; TELEVANGELISM.)

Macumba

A Brazilian new religion, combining Brazilian, African and Christian traditions. It spread across Brazil in the 1970s, despite government repression, but has met rivalry from UMBANDA and Protestant missions. (See also VOODOO.)

Madonna

Italian for 'My Lady', a title used especially of pictures and statues of MARY with the infant Jesus.

Magdalene, Mary

Mary from Magdala in Galilee. The only reference to her before the Crucifixion is in Luke's Gospel (8:2), where it is said that 'from her seven demons had gone out', a reference to an unrecorded healing. There is no evidence at all for the later notion that Magdalene was a prostitute; that came perhaps from confusion with the story in the previous chapter of a woman who was a sinner (Luke 7:37ff). Mary Magdalene witnessed the Crucifixion (Mark 15:40) and with other women went to the tomb on Easter Day. According to John (20:11ff), Jesus then appeared to her alone. Mary Magdalene appears no more in the Bible, but later legend took her to Ephesus and even to France. In the middle ages the Magdalenes, or White Ladies, were communities of reformed prostitutes. Feast day 22 July.

magi

Called *magoi* by Matthew (2:1ff), this word has been translated 'wise men' or 'astrologers' in English Bibles. But the true magi were priests from Persia (Iran), and helped to transmit ideas from Zoroastrianism to the West. The visit of the magi to Judaea does not appear in Luke's parallel infancy stories, but even if legendary it may witness to Persian influence on Judaism and early Christianity, showing gentiles coming to Christ. The Gospel does not state that there were three magi, but names were invented for them in the sixth century: Gaspar, Melchior and Balthasar. They were claimed as saints and their relics are said to be in Cologne Cathedral. (*See also* ZOROASTER.)

Magnificat

The song of Mary (Luke 1:46ff). The title is taken from the Latin version, 'Magnificat anima mea Dominum', 'My Soul Magnifies the Lord'. Mary's song closely resembles that of Hannah (1 Sam. 2) and it has been used from early times as a CANTICLE in church worship.

Magog

See GOG AND MAGOG.

Magus

See SIMON MAGUS.

Mahomet

See MUHAMMAD.

Maitreya

See TARA CENTERS.

Malabar Christians

Christians in Malabar, Madras and neighbouring regions in south India claim origin from the apostle THOMAS,

Monaco, The Adoration of the Magi.

his supposed grave being in Madras, of disputed date. Probably Syrian missionaries brought the faith, their descendants being divided between JACOBITES and the Malankarese Uniate Church in communion with Rome.

Malleus Maleficarum

The 'Hammer of Witches': a handbook for inquisitors produced in 1486 in Germany by Dominican preachers Henry Kramer and James Sprenger. An evil work, it recommended torture and burning at the stake for victims, mainly women, convicted in trumped up charges of WITCHCRAFT. (*See also* INQUISITION.)

Malta, Knights of

See HOSPITALLERS.

Mammon

Aramaic for 'wealth' or 'gain'. The word occurs four times in the Greek gospels, e.g. 'you cannot serve God and mammon' (Matt. 6:24). Mammon was used of property, but a negative meaning was 'unrighteous mammon', applied to riches and greed, and some writers personified it as a demon. Mammon is still a symbol for worldly possessions, sometimes ill-gotten. (*See also* GAMBLING.)

Mandeans

Deriving their name from Aramaic for 'knowledge', these are small GNOSTIC groups surviving in Iraq. They claim descent from John the Baptist but believe in a DUALISM of light and dark and imprisonment of the soul in the world. They look for a coming Saviour to guide souls to heaven. Rituals are of repeated baptisms in flowing water.

Mani, Manichaeism

Mani was born in Babylonia in 216 CE, had early visions and later taught the fulfilment of Zoroastrian, Buddhist and Christian beliefs. He taught the DUALISM of God and the devil, the evil of matter,

and the need for ASCETICISM and CELIBACY. After a time living under royal protection, he was put to death in 277 CE. Mani's teachings spread to the Roman Empire; AUGUSTINE was a Manichaean before he became Christian, and notions of the evil of matter affected Christianity. The medieval Church used the label 'Manichee' for any dualists, such as the CATHARI and ALBIGENSES.

maniple

From Latin, 'hand': originally a handkerchief carried in the left hand, it became a eucharistic VESTMENT, a strip of silk on the left arm.

manna

Food supplied to the Israelites in the wilderness (Exod. 16), of obscure meaning and nature. Christ is called the true bread from heaven (John 6:50ff), and the hidden manna is promised in Revelation (2:17). Manna was later taken as a symbol of the EUCHARIST, the living and eternal bread.

Manning, Henry Edward
(1808–92)

Roman Catholic Archbishop of Westminster and CARDINAL, he began as an evangelical Anglican but became a Tractarian and Roman Catholic in 1851. He became prominent in social work and mediated in a dock strike in 1889; he supported papal infallibility, but differed strongly from his fellow convert and cardinal, NEWMAN.

manse

House of a minister in the FREE CHURCHES in England or the Church of Scotland.

Manson, Charles Miles
(b. 1934)

Leader of the 'Manson Family', a paramilitary mystical sect in California. He called himself both Jesus and the devil, persuaded himself that he could do anything, and in 1969 ordered the ritual murder of film star Sharon Tate and several others, for which he is serving a life sentence. (*See also* SATANISM.)

Maori churches

See RATANA.

Maranatha

An Aramaic expression used by Paul (1 Cor. 16:22), meaning either 'the Lord is coming' or 'O Lord, come.'

Maranké, Johane (1912–63)

Founder of the African Apostolic Church of the Shona people of Zimbabwe. Born a Methodist, he had visions in youth and set up his own church, preaching and healing. Despite schism after the prophet's death, this is the largest of the indigenous Zimbabwean churches, with over 100 branches.

Marburg Colloquy

See ZWINGLI.

Marcion (d. 160 CE)

A wealthy shipowner, he went to Rome and organized his own church and scriptures. Marcion rejected the Old Testament as the work of a DEMIURGE, a 'craftsman' who was a tyrannical God of Law. Only Paul understood this, and Marcion accepted ten of Paul's epistles. His followers suffered in persecutions and some were absorbed into MANICHAEISM. A positive result of Marcion's work was that he obliged the orthodox to formulate the CANON of scripture and reject DOCETIC and GNOSTIC writings. (*See also* POLYCARP.)

Marcus Aurelius (121–80 CE)

Roman emperor. A Stoic and deeply religious, his *Meditations* record attempts to lead a good life amid the strains of office, and a number of Christian writers addressed 'Apologies' to him.

Mardi Gras

See CARNIVAL; SHROVE TUESDAY.

Maria Legio

See LEGIO MARIA.

Mariology

Study of the person and place of Mary, mother of Jesus. Mariolatry is the wrongful rendering to Mary of that worship (*latria*) which belongs to God alone. (*See also* HYPERDULIA.)

Mark

Evangelist. He travelled with PAUL and BARNABAS, separated from Paul for a time but was useful to him later (2 Tim. 4:11). According to PAPIAS, Mark was PETER's interpreter and after his death 'wrote down carefully, but not in order, all that he remembered of the Lord's sayings and doings'. Mark's Gospel was probably written about or just after the fall of Jerusalem to the Romans in 70 CE. Tradition said that Mark went to Alexandria and was its first bishop. His remains were moved to Venice, and the Lion of St Mark is the emblem of Venice.

For long the Gospel According to Mark was regarded as secondary, shorter than the other gospels, and omitting much of the teaching of Jesus. Modern study regards Mark's as the first written gospel; all of it except a few verses is reproduced in Matthew and Luke, but Mark is fresh and 'immediate' (one of his favourite words). He sketches the works of Jesus, his healings and parables. Jesus is SON OF MAN, but Peter confesses him as Messiah, and they go to Jerusalem where the Crucifixion follows. In the last chapter women go to the tomb, but after seeing a young man they flee and say nothing, 'for they were afraid'. Mark ends with this brief statement, the last verses (16:9–20) coming from later writers. Mark gives light on early teaching, with Jesus as MESSIAH and SON OF GOD and the KINGDOM expected shortly. (*See also* COPTIC CHURCH; MATTHEW; Q.)

Maronites

Prominent in Lebanon in recent years, the Maronite Church claims to go back to a fourth-century Maro, and can be traced clearly from the seventh century. Followers of MONOTHELITE doctrine, asserting that there was only 'one will' in Christ, they were expelled from Syria in 680 and settled in the Lebanese hills. In the 12th century they became a UNIATE Church in communion with Rome. Maronites have a patriarch in Antioch and colonies elsewhere in the Orient and USA.

Marprelate Tracts

PURITAN writings attacking episcopacy, under the name of Martin Marprelate, in 1588–9.

Marranos

From Spanish for 'swine', a term used of Spanish Jews who were forcibly converted to Christianity, but continued Jewish practices in secret, lighting Sabbath eve candles and fasting on the Day of Atonement. All professing Jews were expelled from Spain in 1492, and the Inquisition turned against the Marranos. Some fled to more tolerant countries where they were welcomed back into Judaism. (*See* INQUISITION; TORQUEMADA.)

Marriage

Instituted by God and blessed by Christ, marriage is a SACRAMENT, 'an outward and visible sign of an inward and spiritual grace' (Prayer Book Catechism). Strictly speaking, no church or priest was necessary for this sacrament to be valid, the two parties ministering it to each other before God and two witnesses. On this principle, a civil or 'native' marriage may be just as valid as a church ceremony, and this is as important in newly evangelized countries as in long-established Christian societies. From the human pattern, divine union is described by mystical writers as 'spiritual marriage'.

In England, even after the Toleration Act of 1689, Nonconformists still had to get married in the Established Church, until the Dissenters' Marriage Act of 1826 allowed other places of worship to be registered, or a registry office to be used. Now any place may be used provided it is registered. (*See also* MONOGAMY.)

Martha

In Luke's Gospel (10:38ff), Martha is the active sister of the contemplative Mary. In John (11) she is sister of Mary and LAZARUS, believer in the Resurrection and confessor of Christ. Medieval legend took the three of them to the south of France.

Martin

In legend this fourth-century Roman soldier gave half his cloak to a beggar at Amiens, had a vision of Christ, and became a monk and finally bishop of Tours. Martin's story is recorded in stained glass in churches in France and England. Armistice Day is on the feast of this soldier-saint, 11 November, Martinmas. (*See also* CHAPEL.)

Martin, William Keble
(1877–1969)

Anglican priest, serving in industrial parishes and as chaplain to the forces. After the First World War he moved to Devon and pursued his life's passion for botany. His *Concise British Flora*, lavishly illustrated with his own drawings of 1486 species, was a best-seller in 1965 and has had many editions. (*See also* WHITE.)

Martyn, Henry (1781–1812)

Born in Truro, Cornwall, he served as chaplain to the East India Company in Calcutta. In a short life he did valuable linguistic work, translating the New

Testament into Hindustani, Persian and Arabic. On his way home from Persia he died of fever at Tokat in Asia Minor, but his work of evangelism and translation made him popular in Britain. Martyn disputed with Muslims, but in rather medieval polemic. A Henry Martyn Institute of Islamic Studies was founded at Lahore in 1930 and is now at Hyderabad, Andhra Pradesh.

martyr

Greek 'witness': used of disciples who had witnessed the life of Christ (Acts 1:8), and then of those who witnessed with their lives during the persecutions of the early centuries, with a 'baptism of blood'. The tombs of martyrs became places of commemoration, and in Roman Catholicism every altar should contain RELICS of a martyr. (*See also* FOXE; HIDDEN CHRISTIANS; SAINTS; WESTMINSTER ABBEY.)

Mary

Mother of Jesus, she is central to the Annunciation and Nativity stories in Luke's Gospel. Nothing is said of her parents. During the ministry of Jesus, Mary seems not to have understood his actions (Mark 3:31ff), but she followed him to the Cross and was present with his brothers at Pentecost (Acts 1:14). Mary appears no more in the New Testament, and both Jerusalem and Ephesus claimed to be the place where she died. Devotion to Mary grew slowly, as she was not a MARTYR. The title 'God-bearer' (THEOTOKOS) was used from the fourth century, 'Ever-virgin' from the fifth and 'Mother of God' from the sixth. Her IMMACULATE CONCEPTION was made a dogma only in 1854, and her ASSUMPTION in 1950. Popular devotion to Mary, however, a potent symbol of a mother protecting her children, became fervent and widespread much earlier. Even in Islam Mary is held to be sinless, like all prophets, and she is the only woman named in the QUR'ĀN, where she

Modern representation of Mary with the baby Jesus, Henry Moore, 1944, in St Matthew's Church, Northampton.

is mentioned 34 times. (*See also* ANNE; ANNUNCIATION; JOACHIM; NESTORIUS; VIRGIN BIRTH.)

Mary Tudor

See BUCER; CRANMER; DE HAERETICO COMBURENDO; LATIMER; RIDLEY; TALLIS.)

Mass

Catholic name for the EUCHARIST, deriving from Latin *missa*, to send or dismiss, the dismissal ending the liturgy. (*See also* ITE, MISSA EST; EUCHARIST.)

Matins/Mattins

Latin, 'morning'. In medieval times it denoted prayers recited at midnight, but also at daybreak. In the BOOK OF COMMON PRAYER the corresponding service was called Morning Prayer, and was traditionally the normal Anglican Sunday morning service.

matrimony

See MARRIAGE.

Matthew

Tax-collector, so-called in Matthew's Gospel (9:9), but called Levi by both Mark (2:14) and Luke (5:27). Little is known about him otherwise, though legend made him a martyr. The first gospel in the canon is named after Matthew, though it is in Greek and PAPIAS said that Matthew wrote 'the Sayings in the Hebrew tongue'. Perhaps he wrote Q, but as an apostle he would hardly have copied Mark, which this gospel did; so the author of our first gospel remains unknown. Like Luke, this gospel includes long discourses from Q, as well as material from other sources. His matter is organized in blocks, which has made it a favourite with church teachers: three chapters of the SERMON ON THE MOUNT, a long collection of parables in ch. 13, and others later. This gospel has been regarded as the most Jewish, relating the Gospel to the Law, and Peter and the Church have special places in it (16:16ff; 18:15ff). It is dated about 80–5. Feast day 21 September. (*See also* MARK; Q.)

Matthias

Disciple, chosen by lot to take the place of Judas (Acts 1:23). Matthias was not named among other disciples in the gospels and nothing else is known about him.

Maundy Thursday

The English name comes from Latin, *mandatum novum*, a 'new commandment', from the story of Jesus washing the disciples' feet (John 13:4ff). The commemoration is on the Thursday before Easter. (*See also* FOOT-WASHING.)

Maurice, Frederick Denison

(1805–72)

Anglican minister and professor at King's College, London. He was forced to resign in 1853 after rejecting belief in everlasting damnation. A CHRISTIAN SOCIALIST, he started a working men's college. Tennyson supported him, as did the agnostic George Eliot, and he became a professor at Cambridge. Maurice wrote many books, notably *The Kingdom of Christ*. (*See also* COLENSO.)

Mayflower

See CONGREGATIONALISM.

meditation

Common in Hinduism and Buddhism, in the Christian tradition meditation has been especially concerned with repetition of words and phrases, aloud or silently, from Scripture or hymns. (*See also* MENTAL PRAYER.)

Medjugorge

Site of reported appearances of the Virgin MARY in Bosnia-Herzegovina from 1981. It became a popular place of pilgrimage until the Yugoslav civil war of the 1990s.

meeting house

Usual name for the place where FRIENDS (Quakers) gather for worship. The building is bare, with no minister; members speak when prompted by the Spirit. Other Nonconformist places might be called meeting houses, but John WESLEY said that he 'particularly objected' to the term for his chapels.

Melanchthon, Philip

(1497–1560)

His surname is a Greek form of his original German name, Schwarzerd, 'black earth'. Professor of Greek at WITTENBERG, he became a colleague of LUTHER, wrote on Reformed doctrine, translated parts of the Bible and composed the AUGSBURG CONFESSION. Of a conciliatory and scholarly spirit, he was more humanistic than most Reformers.

Friends' Meeting House, 1710, at Come-to-Good, Cornwall: This large, white-washed thatched cottage housed stables for worshippers' horses under the same roof. Inside are plain benches and a raised gallery.

Melchior

See MAGI.

Melchites/Melkites

From Syriac via Greek for 'imperial', the term was used of Syrians and Egyptians who followed the imperial see of Constantinople, rejecting the local MONOPHYSITE doctrine.

Melchizedek

This king and priest of Salem (Gen. 14:18) was taken by the epistle to the Hebrews to be a type of Christ who is there described as 'high priest for ever after the order of Melchizedek' (6:20). From such authority the name of Melchizedek was introduced into the canon of the Mass.

mendicants

Literally 'beggars', Latin name given to members of those religious orders who were forbidden to own property in common. Originally these were Franciscans and Dominicans, but the title of mendicant friars was extended to other orders.

Mennonites

Followers of Dutch reformer Menno Simons (1496–1561). At first a Catholic priest, he joined the ANABAPTISTS and organized his own peaceful companies. After early persecutions Mennonites became most numerous in Holland, but many migrated to America, where they included AMISH and HUTTERITES. Mennonites have independent congregations and refuse to bear arms or swear oaths. Their communities are often called 'peace churches' or 'believers churches'.

mental prayer

An exercise of the mind, silent rather than vocal, personal or turned towards others. Sometimes identified with MEDITATION, it is more active and worshipful, not mere stillness but looking to a divine object. (*See also* JESUS PRAYER.)

Merton, Thomas (1915–68)

Born in France, he went with his parents to New York. He became a Roman Catholic in 1938 and soon joined the TRAPPISTS, the Cistercian Order of Strict Observance. Despite the practice of silence, Merton wrote extensively. His works include spiritual studies and treatises against nuclear arms and the Vietnam War, and for black civil rights. He was attracted to Hindu and Buddhist spirituality, especially ZEN meditation. He died by accidental electrocution in Thailand.

Messiah

Hebrew, 'Anointed One'. In the New Testament the Hebrew word (as Messias) occurs only twice (John 1:41, 4:25), being normally replaced by the Greek Christos. (*See also* CHRIST; CHRISTOLOGY.)

metanoia

See REPENTANCE.

metempsychosis

See REINCARNATION.

Methodism

Largest of the English FREE CHURCHES and third largest American denomination. Methodism was a product of the industrial revolution of the 18th century, an evangelistic movement taking the Gospel to unchurched communities in mining and industrial towns. 'The harmless nickname of Methodist' was given first to Charles WESLEY when a student at Oxford, and applied to study and religious exercises. His brother John drew up 'Rules for the People called Methodists' of religious and moral practice. Although Methodism was a 'society' within the Church, John WESLEY's ordination of preachers brought virtual separation.

The major body was Wesleyan Methodist, but there came secessions in the Methodist New Connexion, Primitive Methodists, Bible Christians and Wesleyan Reform, most of them joining together in 1932 in the British Methodist Church. In North America there was a Methodist Episcopal Church in 1784, but various groups merged in a United Methodist Church in 1968. There are other movements of FUNDAMENTALISM and African American Methodism. In 1992 American Methodism had over 50,000 churches and 13 million members; in Britain numbers of full members were less than half a million. (*See also* AGAPÉ; ASBURY; BIBLE CHRISTIANS; COKE; HOLY CLUB.)

metropolitan

A title for a bishop who has powers over a province with more than one diocese. In Eastern ORTHODOXY the name is used for diocesan bishops.

Michael

ARCHANGEL, mentioned twice in the New Testament (Jude 9; Rev. 12:7). He became popular as a super-saint and defender of individuals and the Church. Michaelmas Day on 29 September was roughly the equinoctial quarter day and a popular feast. The restored Coventry Cathedral has a large figure of Michael with drawn sword over Satan.

Milan, Edict of

The emperors CONSTANTINE and Licinius met at Milan in 313 and decreed that 'Christians and all others should have freedom to follow the kind of religion they favoured; so that the God who dwells in heaven may be propitious to us.'

millennium

A thousand-year kingdom, when the DEVIL will be bound and the saints rule with Christ, is predicted in Revelation 20. Some regard this as general prophecy of the end of all things, but pre-millennialists place the Second Advent of Christ before the millennium, while post-millennialists expect the Advent after the thousand-year span. There have always been groups with millennial expectations, medieval enthusiasts awaiting at the end of the first millennium from the birth of Christ. With the ending of the second millennium such expectations will strengthen. (See also ADVENTISM.)

Miller, Millerites

See SEVENTH-DAY ADVENTISTS.

minister

Latin 'servant': person who works in the Church for God and the community. In the Prayer Book the officiant is regularly called the minister, though some Anglicans prefer the title PRIEST. FREE CHURCHES use the word 'minister' for pastors and preachers, also speaking of 'presbyteral ministry', and there has been a revival of the use of 'minister' in Roman Catholicism. (See also ORDERS.)

Minjung

See LIBERATION THEOLOGY.

minor orders

The major orders of ministry are bishops, priests and deacons; below them are the minor orders of lectors (readers), exorcists and acolytes.

minster

Abbreviation of 'monastery'. The name is applied to a monastery church or to a CATHEDRAL. York Minster is a cathedral and Beverley Minster is a church. WESTMINSTER ABBEY is a Royal Peculiar, independent of London and a centre for great occasions of state. (See also ABBEY.)

miracle

An event provoking wonder, ad-*mira*-tion. In the Bible and church history,

miracles were regarded as acts of God, superseding the normal run of nature. Today, a miracle may be considered as breaking or suspending the laws of nature, or as demonstrating some unknown laws. Protestants generally tend to consider the miraculous as limited to Scripture, while Catholics claim continuing miracles in saints and apparitions. (See also PROVIDENCE; THEOLOGY.)

misericord

Latin, 'mercy': used for the underside of a choirseat, often beautifully carved, in churches and cathedrals. (See also PEWS.)

Misrule, Lord of

A Lord, Abbot, Master or King of Misrule in medieval and Tudor times presided over festivities and horseplay at Christmas, first parading in church with hobby-horses, dragons and musicians. The pageantry is said to derive from Roman Saturnalia. (See also BOY BISHOP.)

missions

Having originated as a Jewish sect, Christianity became international with Paul preaching to and eating with gentiles, and Peter accepting the foreign Cornelius (Gal. 2; Acts 10). Missionaries spread throughout the Roman Empire and beyond, NESTORIANS going to India and China. There were waves of activity: preaching orders were highly successful, though less so at the Reformation; new outbursts began after the evangelical revival, and TELEVANGELISM continues today. In 1980 it was estimated that there were 249,000 foreign missionaries at work, but including national workers Christian personnel amounted to more than 3 million. Some 25 countries were closed to foreign missions and another 40 restricted. There are missions, usually less organized, of other religions, notably Islam and Hinduism. The attitudes of Christian missionaries towards other religions varied; Pentecostal and evangelical types opposed or failed to understand them, while older churches had made long study of them, and some held that other religions should be helped to face secularism. (*See also* STATE AND RELIGION.)

Missionaries of Charity

See TERESA, MOTHER.

Mithraism

The cult of the Persian and Indian sun god Mithra was popular in the Roman Empire and a rival to Christianity. It had a temple at Hadrian's Wall in the north of England, and the Church of San Clemente in Rome was built over a Mithraic temple, of which the altar survives showing Mithra slaying a sacred bull. Mithraism slowly declined with the growth of the Church.

mitre

From Greek for 'turban': a bishop's head-dress, shaped like a shield with a cleft at the top. It dates from the 11th century, but was rarely used in England after the Reformation until its revival in modern times.

mixed marriages

Union of two people of different churches or religions: what Jews call 'marrying out'. It causes problems for religious minorities. In France couples often agreed that boys would follow their father's religion and girls their mother's. Until the Second VATICAN Council in 1965, the Roman Catholic Church used to insist that all children of a Catholic parent must become Catholics, but much depended on the strength of conviction of the non-Catholic partner. (*See also* MARRIAGE.)

Moderator

Not a mediator, but the presiding minister in Presbyterian church courts, first among equals. The Moderator of the

General Assembly of the Church of Scotland is elected for one year and receives the courtesy title of Right Reverend.

Modern Devotion

See DEVOTION.

modernism

A term used of both Roman Catholic and Protestant liberal theologies, seeking to reconcile Christian theology with other disciplines. The critical study of the Bible, widely accepted outside the Roman Church, was championed within it by Loisy (1857–1940), Tyrrell (1861–1909) and others, but condemned by Pope Pius X in 1907 as the 'synthesis of all heresies'. After some decline it may be said that modernism prevailed at the Second VATICAN Council, though Pope John Paul II has done his best to reverse the tide, and Protestant FUNDAMENTALISM has grown. (*See also* CRITICISM; HÜGEL; POST-MODERNISM.)

Mohammedanism

See ISLAM; MUHAMMAD.

Molinos, Miguel de (1640–97)

Spanish priest and mystic, teacher of QUIETISM in his little book, *The Spiritual Guide, which Disentangles the Soul.* Molinos taught the abandonment of effort for union with God, and nuns whom he directed gave up their rosaries, pictures and confessions. He was condemned to life imprisonment, despite recantation, but maintained his serenity, and his influence spread to France and Italy. (*See also* GUYON.)

Monarchians

See PATRIPASSIANISM.

monasticism

From Greek *monos*, 'alone', the term was used for celibates and solitaries, a monastery being a house where celi-

Greek Orthodox monastery of Mar Saba, Judean desert.

bates could live in community. Christian monasticism began with ANTONY in Egypt, and monasteries became both refuges from the world and centres of learning, with hospitals and hostels. Monastic rules became necessary for large communities. (*See also* BENEDICT; DISSOLUTION; PACHOMIUS.)

Monica (331–87 CE)

Mother of AUGUSTINE OF HIPPO, she prayed for her son's conversion from immoral living, followed him to Milan, and saw him become a Christian. Their shared prayers and meditations are described in Augustine's *Confessions*.

monk

See MONASTICISM.

monkey trial

See FUNDAMENTALISM.

monogamy

The union of one man and one woman in marriage is taken for granted as Christian practice, though some Africans have pointed out that the New Testament ruled only that bishops and deacons should be 'husbands of one wife' (1 Tim. 3:2, 12). Old Testament patriarchs were polygamous, but by New Testament times most Jews were probably monogamous. The early Church interpreted the above texts as forbidding a second marriage if the first wife died. Monogamy remains the Christian ideal, and with the balance of the sexes being about equal, it can claim to be the natural condition. (*See also* MARRIAGE.)

Monophysitism

Belief in one nature (Greek *physis*) in Christ. The Council of Chalcedon in 451 CE gave the orthodox (duophysite) doctrine that in Christ there were 'two natures', divine and human. After long debates breaks came with Monophysite churches established in Syria, Armenia, Egypt and Ethiopia. (*See also* JACOBITES; MELCHITES; MONOTHELITISM.)

monotheism

Belief in one GOD is characteristic of the three Semitic religions: Judaism, Christianity and Islam. Modern apologists for the TRINITY insist that understanding between these religions can only proceed on acceptance of the biblical teaching that 'the Lord our God, the Lord is one' (Deut. 6:4).

Monothelitism

Belief in one will in Christ (from Greek *thelein*, 'to will'). This was a seventh-century development of MONOPHYSITISM, but the orthodox insisted on Christ's dual nature and will, divine and human, and this was confirmed at a Council of Constantinople in 680 CE. (*See also* MARONITES.)

monstrance

From medieval Latin for 'showing': a vessel used for displaying the eucharistic HOST for veneration. It is usually a frame of gold or silver rays, with a glass window, carried in procession. (*See also* CORPUS CHRISTI.)

Montanism

A second-century prophet named Montanus claimed that the New Jerusalem would descend from heaven to Phrygia in Asia Minor. With two prophetesses, Prisca and Maximilla, an enthusiastic movement attracted many, including the church writer TERTULLIAN, who criticized Church laxity and favoured the pneumatics or spirit-filled. Like other revivalist movements, Montanism flourished for a time and faded away.

Monte Cassino

See BENEDICT.

Moody, Dwight Lyman
(1837–99)

American revivalist from Massachusetts. After a successful business career, he worked in Sunday Schools and YMCA. He met Ira David Sankey (1840–1908), with whom he went on evangelistic tours, and they composed the *Sankey and Moody Hymn Book* (1873). Moody's fundamentalism was developed in his Chicago Bible Institute. (*See also* YMCA.)

Moon, Sun Myung (b. 1920)

North Korean businessman and founder in 1954 of The Holy Spirit Association for the Unification of World Christianity, known as the Moonies. In his book *Divine Principle* he states that the family is the basis of true society and the Messiah will be born in Korea, now declared to be Moon himself. Moon has organized many businesses and scholarly conferences, and his anti-communist stance gained him followers.

Moral Rearmament (MRA)

See BUCHMAN.

Moravians

Successors of the BOHEMIAN BRETHREN, the Unitas Fratrum ('Unity of the Brethren'). Founded in 1467, they sought to follow the SERMON ON THE MOUNT. A revival came at Herrnhut in 1722, led by Count ZINZENDORF, and they became the Moravian Church. Ardent missionaries, they influenced the WESLEYS. More than half of them now live in America.

More, Hannah (1745–1833)

Social reformer and writer. She wrote sacred dramas, tracts and moral sketches. She came into contact with the CLAPHAM SECT, and travelling with William WILBERFORCE she established schools, training and friendly societies. Accused by landowners and some of the clergy of Methodist leanings, she persevered and her schools survived.

More, Thomas (1478–1535)

Chancellor of England and friend of continental scholars. On an envoy to Flanders he wrote *Utopia*, 'No-where', a prophecy and satire, depicting natural law and religion. More opposed LUTHER's teachings and persecuted Protestants, but he disagreed with Henry VIII over his divorce and the Act of SUPREMACY, and consequently was imprisoned in the Tower of London and executed. He was canonized in 1935. Feast day 9 July. (*See also* ERASMUS; FRITH.)

Mormons

Popular name for the Church of Jesus Christ of Latter-day Saints. In 1827 Joseph Smith (1805–44), at Manchester, New York, said he was told by an angel of the prophet Moroni (son of Mormon who died about 400) of records hidden on gold plates, which Smith published as the *Book of Mormon* in 1830. Smith was murdered by a mob while in jail, and Brigham Young led the Saints to Salt Lake Valley, where a temple was built. There was conflict with the government over polygamy, begun by Smith, forbidden since 1890, though a few still practise it. Mormons do genealogical research and teach pre-mortal existence and marriage for eternity. They are active in education and welfare and are keen proselytizers, with 4.5 million followers in the USA and 2.5 million abroad; about 170,000 in Britain.

mortal sin

'There is a sin unto death' says the epistle (1 John 5:16). In Church teaching such a sin is conscious and deliberate, but it can be overcome by repentance and absolution. Venial sin (from Latin *venia*, 'pardon') is the 'sin not unto death', one that does not deprive the soul of GRACE but still needs repentance. (*See also* PURGATORY.)

mortification

'Mortify your members', said Paul (Col. 3:5), and while he had in mind impurity and greed, some later Christians went to excesses in repressing their, partly sexual, desires. Some stood in cold water, did not wash, wore hair shirts or carried crosses with nails. Milder were the practices of ABSTINENCE and renunciation of luxuries on FRIDAYS and during LENT, though even that may be declining. (*See also* SUSO.)

Moses

The great biblical leader and prophet appears in the New Testament representing the Law (Mark 9:4), and for Paul he is virtually identical with it: 'when Moses is read' (2 Cor. 3:15).

Moses, David

See BERG.

Moshoeshoe (1786–1870)

Southern African chief, founder of Lesotho, he sought to identify Molimo, his people's supreme God, with the God of the Bible, but ancestor veneration and polygamy kept him from Christian conversion. The leading INDEPENDENT Church of Lesotho, named after him, perpetuates the fusion of African and Christian belief.

Mother Ann

See LEE, ANN.

Mother of God

See MARY; NESTORIUS.

Mothering Sunday/ Mother's Day

The fourth Sunday in LENT, traditionally called Mid-Lent or Refreshment Sunday from the Gospel for the day which is the feeding of the five thousand, and on which some relaxation of Lenten FASTING might be allowed. People visited their mothers, or mother church. The day has been subject to great commercialization in recent years.

movable feasts
See CALENDAR.

Mow Cop
See PRIMITIVE METHODISTS.

Mozarab
A corrupt form for 'would-be Arabs', indicating Christians under Moorish rule in Spain, who gave allegiance to the rulers but followed their own religion. The Mozarabic liturgy was the rite of the Spanish Church from early times till the 11th century.

Muggletonians
Group in London. Ludowick Muggleton (1609–98) and his cousin John Reeve were hailed as the two witnesses of Revelation (11:3) who would prophesy for over 1,000 days. They claimed the final revelation and condemned formal religion. As a select movement in the UK it lasted till the 19th century. (*See also* MILLENNIUM.)

Muhammad (570–632 CE)
The prophet of Islam. Born in Mecca, he grew up an orphan, married a rich widow, Khadija, and had seven children by her. There were few Christians in Arabia, but Khadija's cousin Waraqa was a Christian and welcomed Muhammad's visions and voices. Misunderstood and maligned in the Christian world until the 20th century, Muhammad is now recognized by many Western scholars as a prophet, monotheist, and founder of a great Semitic religion, alongside Judaism and Christianity. (*See also* ISLAM; QUR'ĀN.)

Music
See ANTHEMS; BELLS; CANTICLES; CAROLS; CHOIR; DANCE; HYMNS; ORGANS; PRECENTOR.

mysterium
See HOLY.

mystery
'Behold I show you a mystery,' said Paul of the life to come (1 Cor. 15:51). The mystery religions were secret or semi-secret cults, often representing dying and rising agriculture, and bringing union with the deity, notably in Eleusinian and Dionysiac mysteries.

In Christian usage the mysteries are the seven SACRAMENTS, the EUCHARIST, and subjects of meditation in the ROSARY. Mystery plays in the middle ages developed from the liturgy, and were extended to Bible stories, Nativity and Passion Plays. (*See also* DRAMA.)

mysticism
The word derives from 'MYSTERY' and is used of unutterable experiences such as Paul's (2 Cor. 12:4). Distinction has been made between pantheistic and theistic mysticism, the latter being union but not identification with God. There have been countless Christian mystics, specialists in religious life, but there is no clear break between their mysticism and normal Christian experience in prayer and communion. (*See also* PANTHEISM; SPIRITUALITY.)

myth
From Greek 'tale' or 'speech': a myth is an account of supernatural or unhistorical beings, whereas a legend is about human beings, saints or heroes. The early stories of Genesis may be myths, while the gospels may contain legendary elements. (*See also* BULTMANN; STRAUSS.)

N

Nag Hammadi

Town in Upper Egypt near which papyrus texts have been discovered since 1945. These are Coptic translations of Greek originals, dating from about the fourth century, and contain GNOSTIC writings, including a Gospel of THOMAS.

Nag's Head

See PARKER.

name of Jesus

The apostles performed signs in the name of Jesus, that is, by his power (Acts 4:30). In the middle ages there developed a Litany of the Holy Name, and a feast of the Holy Name in January. Protestant hymns include 'None other Name', and 'How Sweet the Name'.

Nantes, Edict of

In 1598 Henry IV of France, who had been a Protestant but thought 'Paris well worth a Mass', issued this edict permitting 'those of the so-called Reformed Religion to live and abide in all the towns and districts of this our Realm . . . free from inquisition, molestation or compulsion'. This tolerant law was revoked by Louis XIV in 1685, bringing persecution. (See also BOSSUET; HUGUENOTS.)

Nathanael

A disciple of Jesus praised for having 'no guile' (John 1:47ff). Later it was said

that he came from Cana in Galilee (John 21:2), but nothing else is known of him. (See also BARTHOLOMEW.)

national apostasy

See ANGLO-CATHOLICISM; KEBLE.

Native American Church

Since 1918 the name of Amerindians who combine use of the peyote cactus drug with rituals of Christian singing, praying and preaching. Adepts invoke peyote as mediator of divine action, treat illness by both botanical and spiritual medicines, and require chastity and family solidarity.

Nativity

See CHRISTMAS.

natural law

Paul said that gentiles had no law, but did by nature the things of the law (Rom. 2:14), though modern writers would credit all peoples with laws and morality. THOMAS AQUINAS said that rational creatures participate in eternal reason, and 'such participation in the eternal law is called natural law.' (See also REVELATION.)

nave

Perhaps deriving from a word for a ship, or for a temple, this is the main body of a church, sometimes separated from the chancel and choir by a screen.

Nazarene, Nazareth

Jesus was called a Nazarene, or of Nazareth, from this Galilean village where he grew up (Matt. 26:71; John 19:19). Nazareth was not mentioned in the Old Testament (despite Matt. 2:23). The modern town is on a hill, now overbuilt with houses and shrines, and overlooks a busy international highway.

Early Christians were called Nazarenes (Acts 24:5), but after gentile congregations were called Christians the name Nazarene came to be applied to Jewish Christians, groups of whom existed for centuries. (*See also* CHRISTIANS; EBIONITES.)

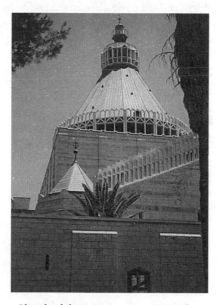

Church of the Annunciation, Nazareth: A modern building built on the foundations of a crusader church excavated in 1908. It is held to be the place where the Annunciation of the birth of Jesus was made by Gabriel to the Virgin Mary.

Nazarene Church

American Protestant denomination founded in 1895, with Methodist teachings of Christian perfection but reformed in the HOLINESS tradition, emphasizing healing.

Nazirites

Jewish 'consecrated ones' (Num. 6), who seem to be those to whom Paul joined, purifying himself in fulfilment of vows (Acts 21:23ff).

Neo-Catechumenate

A Roman Catholic revival movement, founded by Spanish artist Kiko Arguello and former nun Carmen Hernandez in 1964. It prepares people for commitment to the Church, like the catechumen period before baptism. It is said to have half a million members around the world, but there has been criticism of FUNDAMENTALISM and emotional manipulation in group meetings, and of the movement as a church within the Church. (*See also* FOCOLARE; OPUS DEI.)

Neo-Platonism

Movement among late Greek philosophers, developing and adding to ideas from Plato, different from but influential upon Christian thinkers and mystics. (*See also* DIONYSIUS; PLOTINUS; PORPHYRY.)

Neri

See ORATORIANS.

Nero

See ANTI-CHRIST.

Nestorius (d. 451 CE)

Syrian theologian and Patriarch of Constantinople, he opposed the use of the term God-bearer (Greek, THEOTOKOS) or Mother of God for MARY, since the LOGOS existed before the INCARNATION and Mary could not be mother of the Godhead. He preferred Man-bearer (Anthropotokos) or Christ-bearer (Christotokos). Nestorius was condemned at a council at Ephesus in 431 CE, rigged by CYRIL of Alexandria. He was banished to Egypt and died some years later. Nestorian churches were formed in Mesopotamia and Persia, and their missionary efforts took them to CHINA where inscribed monuments have been found testifying to the first Christian mission to the Far East. Small Nestorian churches survive in Iraq and Kurdistan, known as Assyrians and CHALDEANS, and they have some churches in the United States. (*See also* ANATHEMA.)

New Age

A term for a number of modern movements inspired by hopes of social and world renewal. In 1970 John Bennett (1897–1974) prepared for the New Age with an International Academy at Sherborne in the Cotswolds. Others have adopted elements from India, Africa and native America into Christian or more general religious beliefs. New Agers have been condemned by some evangelicals as heretical, but they demonstrate millennial hopes. (*See also* AETHERIUS; AQUARIUS; THEOSOPHY.)

New Church

See SWEDENBORG.

New Covenant

See COVENANT; NEW TESTAMENT.

New Jerusalem

In APOCALYPTIC literature, the hope of a celestial city comes from Rev. (21:2ff), which refers to 'the holy city, new Jerusalem, coming down from God out of heaven'.

new religious movements

Preferred term for what have been described as CULTS or SECTS, indicating secessions from or revivals within traditional churches and societies, or completely independent movements. (*See also* PAGAN.)

New Rome

A name for Constantinople. (*See also* CONSTANTINE.)

New Testament

Paul wrote of reading the 'old testament', or 'old covenant', meaning the Hebrew scriptures (2 Cor. 3:14). From the second century the term New Testament came into use for the accepted Christian scriptures of gospels, Acts, epistles and Revelation. (*See also* CANON; OLD TESTAMENT.)

new year

Christmas is a New Year festival, the old pagan feast of the winter solstice. But in the Julian and Gregorian CALENDARS the New Year began formally on 1 January, though the date had no religious significance. The Scottish Hogmanay, a word of unknown origin, is celebrated on New Year's Eve when traditionally children demanded gifts of cake.

Newman, John Henry (1801–90)

Anglican priest and later Roman cardinal. He wrote many of the *Tracts for the Times*, number 90 especially interpreting the Anglican THIRTY-NINE ARTICLES in a Catholic sense, and he became a Roman Catholic in 1845. He was a fine preacher and writer, his *Apologia pro vita sua* (1864) not only demolishing KINGSLEY's arguments but making enjoyable reading. Newman clashed with H.E. MANNING and became a cardinal after him in 1879. His *Essay on the Development of Christian Doctrine* (1845) was influential in both Anglican and Roman churches. (*See also* ANGLO-CATHOLICISM; GERONTIUS; MANNING; TRACTS.)

Newton, John (1725–1807)

Slave trader in West Africa, though he tried to treat slaves 'with as much humanity' as possible. Converted, he became an evangelical Anglican and rector of a London city church. He was a friend of the poet William COWPER and co-operated with him in *Olney Hymns* and with WILBERFORCE in fighting slavery.

Nicaea/Nicene

A town in Asia Minor to which CONSTANTINE in 325 CE summoned the first ecumenical council of the Church to settle the ARIAN dispute. 318 bishops attended, mostly from the east. An Arian CREED was rejected, with ANATHEMAS, and a first short Nicene creed accepted. What came to be known as the Nicene Creed, used in liturgies, was approved by the Council of CHALCEDON in 451 CE. (*See also* CONSTANTINE, FILIOQUE, HOMOOUSION.)

Nicholas

Legendary saint from Myra in Asia Minor who was said to have given bags of gold to three girls as dowries, to save them from prostitution. This tale is said to have been the origin of the trademark of three golden balls used by pawnbrokers as their sign. Nicholas became patron saint of Russia and had 400 churches dedicated to him in England. In America he became Santa Claus, bringing gifts to children on 6 December, his feast day.

Nicholas of Cusa (1400–64)

German philosopher and cardinal, born at Cusa on the Moselle. Of a conciliatory spirit, he tried to restore the Hussites to the Church and bring about union between East and West though both projects failed. He exposed the False DECRETALS and DONATION, and supported science, teaching the movement of the earth round the sun. His ecumenical attitude extended to other religions, especially to Islam after the fall of Constantinople to the Turks in 1453. (*See also* HUSS.)

Nicholls, Douglas Ralph
(1906–88)

A pastor of the Australian Aboriginal Church of Christ, fighting for social rights. He protested against atomic explosions near Aboriginal homelands, and opposed the 150th Australia Day celebrations in 1938. He was knighted in 1972 and became Governor of South Australia for a year, but ill health forced his retirement.

Nicodemus

Mentioned only in John's Gospel, as a PHARISEE and ruler who came to Jesus by night. He refused to condemn Jesus, and with JOSEPH OF ARIMATHEA helped to bury him (John 3:1ff, 7:50ff, 19:39).

Niebuhr, Reinhold (1892–1971)

American minister at Bethel Evangelical Church in Detroit, and Professor at Union Theological Seminary, New York in 1928. Influenced by Karl BARTH, Niebuhr was also involved in socialism and pacifism. He wrote on *Moral Man and Immoral Society*.

Niemöller, Martin (1892–1984)

A German U-boat commander in the First World War, he became a Lutheran pastor. At first attracted to National Socialism, he opposed its paganism and supported the CONFESSING CHURCH. His anti-Nazi activities led to his incarceration in a concentration camp from 1937 to 1945, where he remained despite offers of release. After the war Niemöller became first President of a new Evangelical Church and served as President of the World Council of Churches from 1961 to 1968.

Niles, Daniel Thambyrajah
(1908–70)

Methodist minister in Ceylon (Sri Lanka) who became President of the Methodist Church of Ceylon and of the World Council of Churches. He was active in the STUDENT CHRISTIAN MOVEMENT and the International Missionary Council, travelling, lecturing and writing as representative of Asian churches.

nimbus

See HALO.

Ninian (360–432 CE)

Son of a converted chief in northern England, he became a priest and bishop and set out to evangelize the Scots. BEDE says Ninian founded a church at Whithorn in Wigtownshire called the White House (Candida Casa), as a centre for missions to the Picts. Ninian's tomb in the church was a place of pilgrimage and many Scottish churches are dedicated to him. Feast day 16 September.

Nobili

See DE NOBILI.

No-Church

See UCHIMURA.

Nonconformist conscience

When in 1890 Methodist minister Hugh Price Hughes called for the resignation of Irish leader Charles Parnell for adultery, a letter in *The Times* said that 'nothing less will satisfy the Nonconformist conscience'. The term has been used since for the religious scruples of evangelicals. (*See also* CONSCIENCE.)

Nonconformity

See FREE CHURCHES.

non-jurors

After the English Revolution of 1688 eight bishops and 400 clergy of the Church of England refused to swear allegiance to William and Mary, because they had given their oath to the refugee James II. The bishops were deprived of

their offices, but most non-jurors were absorbed into the national Church in the following century. (*See also* KEN.)

non-violence

See PACIFISM.

North India

See CHURCH OF SOUTH INDIA.

Nostra Aetate

See HOLOCAUST.

Nostradamus

Latinized name of French physician and astrologer Michel de Notre Dame (1503–66). He published prophecies in ambiguous language, with several meanings or unintelligible. His *Centuries* were condemned by the papacy.

Novena

From medieval Latin for 'nine', a series of prayers or services for nine successive days. Introduced as special devotion in the 17th century, novenas may be for particular needs or recurrent devotions.

Novice

A 'new' convert or person received into a monastic community on probation. A novice has normally previously been a POSTULANT, wears the dress of the order, and may leave or be dismissed at any time.

Nowell

See CHRISTMAS.

Noyes

See ONEIDA.

nullity

A contract, especially a marriage, may be declared null and void if some impediment can be proved, such as the parties being related to one another; non-consummation of the marriage; insanity or epilepsy; venereal disease; the wife's pregnancy by someone other than the husband.

Number of the Beast

See ANTI-CHRIST.

numinous

In his book *The Holy* (1917) Rudolf Otto said, 'I adopt a word coined from the Latin *numen*. *Omen* has given us *ominous* and there is no reason why from *numen* we should not similarly form a word "numinous".' *Numen* meant divine will or assent; 'numinous' referred to the presence and power of the divine. (*See also* HOLY.)

nun

From the female form of Latin *nonnus* for a monk or elderly person: a woman member of a religious order, often called 'sister'.

Nunc Dimittis

The Song of SIMEON, Luke 2: 29–32, named after its first words in the Latin Vulgate version, meaning 'Now you dismiss your servant in peace.' (*See also* CANDLEMAS.)

nuncio

Latin, 'messenger': a papal ambassador at a foreign court.

nuptial Mass

A Mass following a wedding, giving a blessing on the marriage. A service of Holy Communion may be provided for church members in non-Roman Catholic churches.

O Sapientia

Latin, 'O Wisdom': opening words of the first of seven ANTIPHONS sung in the week before Christmas Eve, each of which begins with O.

Oates, Titus (1649–1705)

Son of an ANABAPTIST preacher, and himself an Anglican naval chaplain and JESUIT seminarian, he became notorious for concocting the POPISH PLOT. A popular hero for a time, he was imprisoned for perjury and calling the Duke of York a traitor, pilloried and flogged. Titus was released after the 1688 revolution and given a pension.

oath

'Swear not at all' said the Gospel (Matt. 5:34ff). Some have taken this literally, refusing to take an oath in court: Quakers, Waldensians, Mennonites and some Baptists. Other Christians take the prohibition to be against casual swearing or foul-mouthedness. Objection to radio or television programmes is more often made on the grounds of bad language than the actual pictures.

oath of allegiance

See NON-JURORS.

Oberammergau

A town in southern Germany where a PASSION PLAY has been held every ten years, with some breaks, in thanksgiving for the ending of a plague in 1634. The actors come from the locality and men grow beards for the occasion. The scenes, in German, are somewhat stilted, and formerly there were objections to anti-Semitism in the script, but revisions have toned this down.

Oberammergau Passion Play: A formal scene where Jesus is condemned although Pilate declares him innocent and washes his hands of the affair.

oblation

Offering of bread and wine in the EUCHARIST, distinguished from gifts of money by the phrase 'our ALMS and oblations'.

obligation

Christian laity as well as clergy have an obligation to worship and abstain from work on Sundays and major feasts. Holy Days of Obligation on working weekdays are now generally being transferred to Sundays. (*See also* FEASTS.)

obscurantism

See FUNDAMENTALISM.

Occam

See OCKHAM.

occasional

Occasional services are those held for special occasions, as distinct from regular worship, such as baptism, confirmation, matrimony, visitation of the sick and burial of the dead. Occasional petitions are prescribed in prayer books, mostly for social concerns.

occult

'Hidden' beliefs or activities: a term loosely applied to matter outside formal Christian or other teaching, such as astrology, THEOSOPHY, or some of the NEW RELIGIOUS MOVEMENTS.

Ockham/Occam, William of (1300–49)

English philosopher, from Ockham in Surrey. He joined the Franciscans, studied at Oxford and Paris, and led a revolt against Pope John XXII who had attacked evangelical poverty. Ockham revived nominalism, the doctrine that universal ideas are merely names. He applied 'Occam's razor', claiming that 'beings should not be multiplied without necessity'. In separating faith from reason, and the papacy from temporal authority, he prepared the way for the Reformation.

octave

The 'eighth day' after a feast, as Low Sunday is the octave of Easter.

odium theologicum

Latin, 'theological hatred': a term used for disputes and insults in theological matters.

oecumenism

See ECUMENISM.

offertory

A term loosely used for collection of money. The Offertory in the BOOK OF COMMON PRAYER begins with biblical sentences, reception of ALMS, and offering of the bread and wine for the Eucharist.

office

Prayers to be recited in daily services, preparation for the Eucharist, or occasional services, such as the Office for the Dead. The office may comprise psalms, hymns, lessons, versicles and prayers.

OFM

The Franciscan Order of Friars Minor.

Olaf/Olave II (995–1030)

King and patron saint of Norway. He fought in England against the Danes, became a Christian and returned to Norway, using persuasion and force to make it Christian. He was exiled and, trying to return, was killed at the battle of Stiklestad. His tomb became a place of pilgrimage where miracles were reported. Many churches and schools were called after Olaf, including 40 in Britain. Feast day 29 July.

Olcott, Henry Steel (1832–1907)

American Civil War colonel and lawyer, he was first president of the Theosophical Society which he founded in New York with Helena BLAVATSKY in 1875. In 1882 he established the Society's headquarters at Adyar, Madras, in India. In numerous visits to Ceylon (Sri Lanka) Olcott helped Buddhists found schools and colleges, to counteract Christian mission schools, and he wrote a *Buddhist Catechism*. (*See also* BESANT; THEOSOPHY.)

Old Believers

Russians who split from the Orthodox Church when Patriarch Nikon in 1652 tried to bring Russian liturgical practices into line with those of the Greeks. The Old Believers had no bishops, and they split into two groups, the Popovtsy who sought to retain a priesthood (also called Old Ritualists), and the Bezpopovtsy who rejected it. The former increased in numbers and were recognized by the state in 1881, while the latter divided into sects and remained a small minority.

Old Calendarists or Authentic Orthodox

Greek ORTHODOX who rejected the change in 1924, by the Ecumenical Patriarch, from the Julian to the Gregorian CALENDAR. The total community in Greece in 1985 numbered 218,000 compared with nearly 9 million professing Orthodox.

Old Catholics

Groups of churches which separated from Rome independently from the Reformation. The first was the Church of Utrecht which rejected papal condemnation of JANSENISM in 1723. The largest body was of churches, chiefly German, Austrian and Swiss, which denied papal INFALLIBILITY at the First Vatican Council in 1870. A Declaration of Utrecht was drawn up in 1889, repudiating infallibility and the dogma of the IMMACULATE CONCEPTION. Old Catholic priests and bishops may marry, they have been in full communion with the Church of England since 1932, and in 1996 ordained women priests. Some national groups, including Slav and Croat, have also established themselves as Old Catholic churches, the largest being the Polish National Church with 350,000 members in America.

Old Testament

Christianity is the only major religion which accepts and uses the scriptures of its parent religion, Judaism, as inspired and canonical. Old Testament is the Christian name for the Hebrew Bible, regarded as preparatory to the New, but nevertheless true revelation. The two are bound up in one Bible and used in all churches. (*See also* CANON; NEW TESTAMENT.)

Olives, Mount of

A hill to the east of JERUSALEM, traditionally the site of the Ascension; a church at the summit claims to have a footprint of Christ. According to Luke (19:37ff), Jesus beheld the city from there and wept over it, lamenting that it did not know the things which belonged to its peace.

Omar, Mosque of

See DOME OF THE ROCK.

Omega

See ALPHA.

Omen

See NUMINOUS.

Oneida Community

A communistic society founded at Oneida, New York, in 1848 by John Humphrey Noyes (1811–86). He taught that the Second Coming had already been realized and that perfection was attainable. Known also as Perfectionists, members engaged in complex, non-monogamous marriages, allowing communal experimentation. Occupied in agriculture and industry, the community became prosperous; its factories are now owned by a joint stock company.

Onesimus

See PHILEMON.

ontological argument

See ANSELM.

OP

The Dominican Order of Preachers.

open-air meeting

Public preaching and teaching in the open air go back to the biblical prophets, the teachings of Jesus and the apostles, and continued among the medieval friars, early Quakers, Methodists and the Salvation Army. Such meetings have become more effective with loudspeaker systems, used for example by Billy GRAHAM, Martin Luther KING, the German KIRCHENTAG and French TAIZÉ ecumenical youth gatherings. (*See also* PREACHING; TELEVANGELISM.)

opium of the people

Karl Marx in *Critique of Hegel's Philosophy of Right* (1844) said that 'Religion is the sob of the oppressed creature, the heart of a heartless world, and the soul of soulless conditions. It is the Opium of the People.'

Opus Dei

Latin, 'work of God': a description of the office of prayer and worship. In 1928 the title was adopted by a conservative Roman Catholic organization, established in Madrid by José Maria Escriva de Balaguer. Opus Dei has been approved by the Pope, but criticized for ruthless methods and for functioning as a church within the Church. (*See also* CARDENAL; FOCOLARE; NEO-CATECHUMENATE.)

Oratorians

The Italian Oratory of Philip Neri was a community of popular preaching priests,

Chapel at Gwennap pit, near Redruth, Cornwall, which is an amphitheatre formed by mining subsidence and still used for special open-air services.

made into a congregation in 1575, and introduced to England by J. H. NEWMAN. The French Oratory of Pierre de Bérulle, founded in 1611, concentrates on training priests and popular devotion.

oratorio

See CANTATA.

orders, ordination

The Christian ministry began with Jesus choosing twelve APOSTLES to preach and heal (Mark 3:14); after PENTECOST they led the community (Acts 2:14). Later SEVEN DEACONS were appointed to assist them (Acts 6:5). Then there were 'elders' or 'presbyters' and 'overseers' or 'bishops', though the terms seem interchangeable. By the second century there were three orders: bishops, presbyters and deacons. In Roman Catholicism ordination is one of the seven SACRAMENTS, but the Anglican Article 25 in the Book of Common Prayer spoke of things 'commonly called Sacraments', including Orders, which 'are not to be counted for Sacraments of the Gospel'. Ordinal is a word dating from about 1600 to indicate the 'Manner of Making, Ordaining and Consecrating Bishops, Priests and Deacons' (Book of Common Prayer). (*See also* MINISTER; PRIEST.)

organs

Keyboard instruments can be traced back to the ancient Greeks, and by the middle ages there were organs in cathedrals and many churches. Some Puritans distrusted music in Church and the issue caused division in early Methodism and Scottish Presbyterianism. Fine organ music was written by Bach, Purcell, Samuel Sebastian WESLEY and many others.

orientation

See EASTWARD.

Origen (185–254)

Egyptian theologian. He led an ASCETIC life and took literally the verse about becoming a eunuch (Matt. 19:12). From Greek philosophy, he taught the eternity of creation and the pre-existence of souls. He gave ALLEGORICAL interpretations of scripture, as 'figurative statements', 'mysterious truths by seeming history'. In a vicious persecution by Decius, Origen was tortured and died. He left many followers, as well as opponents. His teachings, and variant interpretations, were condemned at a Second Council of Constantinople in 553 CE, and this original thinker was never canonized. (*See also* CLEMENT; PHILO; REINCARNATION.)

original sin

Paul stated that 'by one man [Adam] sin entered the world' (Rom. 5:12), and this was taken by AUGUSTINE to mean that Adam's 'guilt' was transmitted to all his descendants; but this was much debated and denied from PELAGIUS to ABELARD and the moderns, although the myth of Adam's fall and transmission of guilt by CONCUPISCENCE was held by THOMAS AQUINAS and the Reformers. Many modernist writers have abandoned the notion of original or inherited sin. (*See also* FALL; SIN; TAYLOR.)

Orthodox Church

A title used primarily for East European churches which developed from the Byzantine Church. At present there are 15 'autocephalous' or self-governing churches, including four ancient patriarchates of Constantinople, Alexandria, Antioch and Jerusalem. The PATRIARCH of Constantinople is known as Ecumenical Patriarch, as first among equals. Churches of Russia, Serbia, Georgia, Romania and Bulgaria also have patriarchs, while others are led by METROPOLITANS or archbishops. Other churches also call themselves Orthodox: these include Nestorians, Syrian

Jacobites, Egyptian and Ethiopian Copts, Armenians and Indians.

The Orthodox maintain the doctrine and discipline of the ecumenical councils up to Nicaea II (787CE), and they separated from Rome in the SCHISM of 1054. Their central worship is the Liturgy (EUCHARIST), and a distinctive feature is the use of ICONS. Priests may marry but bishops must be CELIBATE. (*See also* ATHOS; FILIOQUE; HESYCHASM; ICON; MARONITE; OLD CALENDARISTS; UNIATE; VLADIMIR.)

orthodoxy

Greek 'right opinion', a term adopted by claimants to true belief, as opposed to HERESY. Bishop Warburton (1698–1779) said, 'Orthodoxy is my doxy; heterodoxy is another man's doxy.' Doxy also meant paramour. The title is used especially of the Eastern ORTHODOX churches, called 'holy, orthodox, catholic, apostolic'. (*See also* CATHOLIC; CULT; PAGAN; SPARTAS.)

OSB

Order of Saint BENEDICT.

osculation

A formal kiss. (*See also* GESTURES.)

Oswald (605–42)

Northumbrian king. Converted to Christianity by monks at IONA, he was given AIDAN to establish the faith. Oswald was killed in battle, praying for the souls of his bodyguard. He was honoured as a martyr, 62 churches in England being dedicated to him.

Otto, Rudolf

See HOLY; NUMINOUS.

Our Father

See LORD'S PRAYER.

Ouspensky, Pyotr Demianovich (1878–1947)

Born in Moscow, he became interested in the OCCULT and travelled to Egypt and India. He met GURDJIEFF in 1915 and expounded his meetings and techniques in his *In Search of the Miraculous*. He left Russia in 1919, went to London and bought a farm in Surrey, where he died.

Oxford Group

See BUCHMAN.

Oxford Movement

See ANGLO-CATHOLICISM.

Oxyrhynchus

An ancient Christian centre in Egypt where thousands of fragments of papyri have been discovered since 1897, with apocryphal writings including two series of sayings of Jesus.

P

Pachomius (290–346 CE)

Egyptian monk and founder of communal or COENOBITIC MONASTICISM, which
was so attractive that by his death there
were nine monasteries for men and two
for women. He governed by a Rule, of
which no original survives, which combined prayer and work. (*See also*
ANTONY; BENEDICT.)

pacifism

A term first used early in the 20th century as 'anti-War-ism', rejecting violent
action to solve disputes; also called
pacificism. Early Christians, oppressed
by the state, repudiated force and the
tradition persisted, so that the notion of
a 'holy war' in the CRUSADES was an
innovation. Many reforming bodies
rejected war, including Lollards,
Mennonites, Quakers, Jehovah's
Witnesses. There have been pacifist
movements in most churches, small but
often potent minorities. (*See also* JUST
WAR; SHEPPARD.)

Padre Pio

See STIGMATA.

paedo-baptism

BAPTISM of infants.

paedophile

See CHILDREN.

pagan

Latin 'peasant' or 'villager': the word is
used in derogatory ways of non-
Christian or 'primitive' religions. Even
the sophisticated Greek sages used to be
called 'pagan philosophers'. The word
'heathen', strictly a dweller on a 'heath',
a rustic, was also formerly used but is
now to be avoided, and a hymn line on
'the heathen in his blindness' is generally
omitted. Yet by a curious reversal there
are groups which rejoice in the name of
pagan religions, inventing or claiming to
have pre-Christian or anti-Christian
beliefs and rituals. (*See also* BLACK MASS;
SATANISM; WITCHCRAFT.)

Palamas, Gregory

See HESYCHASM.

Paley, William (1743–1805)

Anglican priest and apologist, his
Natural Theology argued that as from
finding a watch we would infer a watch-
maker, so from the human body we infer
an almighty designer. This mechanical
demonstration of God lost much of its
force with the theory of evolution. (*See
also* DARWINISM.)

palimpsest

Greek, 'rub again': a manuscript from
which the writing has been rubbed out
and the surface used for another text.
Some such manuscripts of the Bible can

be read in the original by means of chemical agents and photography.

pall, pallium

The principal use of pall is for a cloth, usually black, put over a coffin. A pall or pallium is also a woollen VESTMENT worn by the Pope and some archbishops.

Palm Sunday

The Sunday before Easter, commemorating the entry of Jesus into Jerusalem, when people 'took branches of palm trees' and went to meet him, laying some on the road (John 12:13; Mark 11:8). There are still processions with palm branches on this day, along with blessing and distribution of palms or palm crosses. Palm Sunday introduces HOLY WEEK. (*See also* HOSANNA.)

Pancras

Apart from a reputed martyrdom in Rome in the fourth century, little is known of him. Six churches in England were dedicated to St Pancras as a martyr, one in Canterbury by AUGUSTINE, and one in London from which a railway terminus takes its name.

panentheism

See PANTHEISM.

pantheism

Greek 'all-God-ism': belief that the universe and God are identical, or that God suffuses all things. A variation upon this is pan-en-theism: that all is in God, but the universe does not exhaust his being. A further term was coined by R.C. Zaehner in his *Mysticism* (1957), Pan-en-hen-ism meaning 'all-in-one-ism', without reference to God. Some Christian mystics have been criticized for pantheism, notably Meister ECKHART, yet belief in divine TRANSCENDENCE and the TRINITY, and devotional movements, have helped to preserve understanding of the union but not identity of humanity

and deity. (*See also* IMMANENCE; PROCESS THEOLOGY; THEISM.)

Pantokrator

Greek 'All-ruler': a title of Christ and his representation in Eastern Orthodox icons and mosaics.

Pantokrator of Christ from the Kariye Museum, formerly St Saviour Church, Istanbul.

papacy

The office and power of the Roman Catholic POPE. (*See also* VATICAN.)

Papias (60–130 CE)

A bishop in Asia Minor of whom little is known, but who preserved the traditions of the early Church. His *Expositions of the Oracles of the Lord* survived only in quotations in IRENAEUS and EUSEBIUS, but said that MARK was the interpreter of Peter, and that Matthew wrote the 'sayings' (LOGIA) in Hebrew.

parable

Greek 'comparison'. The parables, such as the Sower, the Good Samaritan, the

Prodigal Son, and over 30 others, are characteristic of the teaching of Jesus in the synoptic gospels. John's Gospel has no parables, though references to Christ as the Good Shepherd or True Vine are similar.

Paracelsus (1493–1541)

A name coined for himself (meaning 'superior to Celsus', a first-century physician) by Swiss physician Von Hohenheim, who developed a mystical philosophy with NEO-PLATONIC and kabbalistic elements. He taught that as we know nature from our own nature, so we know God in so far as we are God. (*See also* KABBALAH; PANTHEISM.)

Paraclete

Greek 'advocate' or 'counsellor', translated 'comforter' in old versions. The word is used of the Holy Spirit in John (14:16) and of Christ in 1 John (2:1). (*See also* HÉLOÏSE.)

paradise

Persian for 'garden', the abode of the blessed in Zoroastrianism. In Christianity and Islam it is identified with heaven or the celestial Garden of Eden. The word appears three times in the New Testament: 'today you will be with me in Paradise' (Luke 23:43) were the words of Jesus to the penitent thief; here 'paradise' is usually interpreted as HEAVEN or LIMBO. See also 2 Corinthians 12:4 and Revelation 2:7, both referring to paradise as heaven. (*See also* ZOROASTER.)

pardon, pardoners

See FORGIVENESS; INDULGENCES.

parish

From Greek via French for a district round a dwelling or church, indicating the area under the care of a curate or church incumbent. In the middle ages landowners had to provide a place of worship and a priest for tenants, and countries were divided into parishes, with many new ones added as towns spread. On 'beating' the parish bounds, *see* ROGATION DAYS.

Parker, Matthew (1504–75)

A moderate reformer, he married under Edward VI, became Dean of Lincoln, was deprived by Mary and made Archbishop of Canterbury by Elizabeth. A libellous story of the 17th century said that Parker was consecrated at the Nag's Head Inn in Cheapside because he could not receive Catholic consecration. Parker sought a religious settlement in England, getting the THIRTY-NINE ARTICLES approved and helping to compile the revised English scriptures known as the Bishops' Bible.

parousia

Greek, 'presence', 'arrival', 'advent' or 'coming': a term used in the New Testament to indicate 'the coming of the Son of Man' (Matt. 24:27). The senses of *parousia* have been interpreted as the presence of Christ at Pentecost, in the Church, and at the end of all things. Some Christians have expected a visible *parousia* almost hourly; the vast majority have regarded it as a spiritual or far distant event. (*See also* ADVENTISM; MILLENNIUM.)

parson

The 'person' or clerical incumbent of a parish: a word used loosely of any clergyman. Chaucer's poor 'persoun' taught Christ's lore, but 'first he followed it himselve' (*Canterbury Tales*, Prologue, l.527).

Particular Baptists

See BAPTISTS.

Pascal, Blaise (1623–62)

French mathematician and philosopher. His sister entered a JANSENIST convent at PORT ROYAL. Pascal himself had a midnight revelation in 1654. A statement found sewn into his coat at his death stated: 'Fire. God of Abraham . . . not of philosophers and scholars.' He went to Port Royal and attacked Jesuits who denounced Jansenists as heretics. His 18 *Provincial Letters* criticized JESUIT CASU-ISTRY and laxity; his later *Thoughts* (*Pensées*) were fragments for the defence of Christianity against indifference.

Paschal

To do with PASSOVER, or EASTER, from Hebrew *pesakh*. The Paschal Vigil is held on the Saturday night and Sunday morning of Easter. A large Paschal Candle is lit from new fire on Easter Eve, all other lights having been put out on MAUNDY THURSDAY. Paschal Controversies took place in the early Church, concerning whether Easter should be on a fixed day of the lunar month as in Jewish custom, or on the following Sunday. There were differences between Eastern and Western churches, which in Britain were solved when the Synod of Whitby in 664 accepted the Roman custom.

Passion

Term used for the suffering of Christ during the last week of his life, especially at GETHSEMANE and CALVARY. Passion Sunday is the fifth in LENT, introducing Passion Week, before Palm Sunday and HOLY WEEK. 'Passiontide' extends over these two weeks.

Passion plays

See OBERAMMERGAU.

Passover

The English word 'Passover' was coined by William TYNDALE in his translation of Exodus 12:11, 'it is the Lord's passover', for Hebrew *pesakh*, which had formerly been rendered *pasch* or variants. (*See also* PASCHAL.)

pastor

Originally a shepherd; in the Church, 'some are pastors', or shepherds (Eph.

4:11). The term is used of Protestant ministers, to avoid the sacrificial implication of PRIEST, and in a general sense of all pastors or guardians of a congregation.

pastoral epistles

Three letters addressed ostensibly by Paul to Timothy and Titus. They indicated the pastoral characteristics needed in church workers and members. There has been much discussion whether they are by Paul, or some later unknown authors, or contain fragments of Paul's writing. (*See also* TIMOTHY.)

paten

From old French or Latin for a plate: the dish to contain the bread or wafers at the EUCHARIST.

Pater Noster

Latin, 'Our Father'. *See* LORD'S PRAYER.

Patmos

A small island off the coast of Asia Minor on which the 'JOHN' of the book of REVELATION (1:9) said he wrote his work. (*See also* APOCALYPSE.)

patriarch

A term used of 'fathers' in Scripture, Abraham, Isaac and Jacob, and also of David (Acts 2:29). In the sixth century the title patriarch was applied to bishops of five principal sees: Rome, Antioch, Alexandria, Constantinople and Jerusalem. Some other ORTHODOX bishops have also been given the title of patriarch.

Patrick (389–461 CE)

Born in the west of Britain or Gaul, he was taken by pirates to Ireland. He escaped to France and trained for the priesthood, returning to Armagh, organizing the Church and founding monasteries. Legend said that Patrick expelled all the snakes in Ireland, perhaps meaning pagan religions, and he explained the Trinity from trefoil shamrock leaves. His BREASTPLATE is said to have been used against Druids. He became patron saint of Ireland with a feast on 17 March.

patripassianism

The 'suffering of the Father' seemed to be implied by the doctrine of the Trinity. Early Monarchians held to the Unity or Monarchy of the Godhead, so that the Father suffered as the Son. They were criticized by TERTULLIAN, who said 'they put to flight the Comforter and crucified the Father.' (*See also* IMPASSIBILITY; SABELLIANISM.)

patristics

Study of the writings of the Church fathers (*patres*).

Paul (d. 64–5 CE)

The apostle of the gentiles, called the second founder of Christianity, who took the Church from being a Jewish sect and made it an international religion. First named Saul, born of Jewish parents at Tarsus in Asia Minor, and a Roman citizen, he insisted on his Jewishness while criticizing rigid adherence to the Mosaic Law. After persecuting Christians he was converted by a vision on the Damascus road, and retired to work out his understanding of the new faith. After missionary journeys he was arrested in Jerusalem and on his appeal sent to Rome. Tradition says he was executed during persecution of Christians by Nero.

Paul was the greatest single writer of the New Testament. His letters are arranged roughly in order of length in the CANON. ROMANS is the only attempt at a doctrinal thesis, but other letters contain teachings on CHRISTOLOGY, GRACE, FAITH, PREDESTINATION and FREE WILL. These and his social and marital injunctions have influenced all later Christian ages. Feast day, with Peter, 29 June. (*See also* ACTS;

CIRCUMCISION; CONVERSION; HEBREWS; PHILIPPIANS; THECLA.)

Paulinus

Several saints bear this name. One was sent to England by Gregory in 601 and became first bishop of York. Back in Kent he became bishop of Rochester, and five ancient churches were dedicated to him. Feast day 28 January. (*See also* AUGUSTINE OF CANTERBURY.)

pax

Latin 'peace'. See GESTURES.

peace

See PACIFISM; JUST WAR.

peace missions

See FATHER DIVINE.

Peculiar People

From verses that call Christians a chosen or 'peculiar people' (1 Pet. 2:9, AV) a small group of faith-healers was founded at Plumstead in London in 1838; also called the Plumstead Peculiars, they had branches elsewhere. Rejecting usual medicines, they relied on prayer and anointing with oil. They were restricted congregations, strongly evangelical, and now seem to have disappeared.

Pelagius (360–420 CE)

A British or Irish monk who was shocked at AUGUSTINE's words that human actions were predestined, which seemed to undermine the moral law. Pelagius declared that all good and evil is 'done by us, not born with us'. Augustine accused Pelagius, and his disciple Celestius, of denying ORIGINAL SIN, and got them excommunicated in 418 CE. Pelagius died in Palestine and his teachings were summarized by Celestius: that Adam's sin injured himself alone and not the human race, that the Law as well as the Gospel leads to the Kingdom, that there were men without sin before the coming of Christ, and that infants are innocent as Adam was before the FALL. Although condemned, many thought Pelagians were right to affirm human responsibility and the need to co-operate with GRACE. Semi-Pelagianism (a modern term) was held for some centuries by opponents of extreme PREDESTINATION.

penance, penitence

Penance is one of the seven SACRAMENTS in medieval and Roman Catholic teaching, and includes contrition, CONFESSION, satisfaction and ABSOLUTION. Penitents in churches often wore special robes, had their hair cropped, and were not allowed to marry or be soldiers while the penance lasted. Penitential books gave lists of sins, with suitable penances. (*See also* FORGIVENESS; REPENTANCE.)

Penn, William (1644–1718)

Son of an admiral, he was sent down from Oxford for having become a Quaker. Attacking orthodox doctrines of the TRINITY and ATONEMENT, he was imprisoned in the Tower of London and wrote *No Cross, No Crown* (1669). After his father's death he was granted land in America, called Pensilvania in his father's honour, and with emigrant Quakers established the colony with tolerance of all forms of worship. He returned to England to get 1,200 Quakers released from prison, went back to America and tried to soften the evils of slavery. He died in England and was buried at Jordans, near Chalfont St Giles. Penn wrote many books and pamphlets, notably *The Fruits of Solitude*. (*See also* FOX; FRIENDS.)

Pentateuch

Greek 'five books': the Hebrew written Torah, consisting of Genesis, Exodus, Leviticus, Numbers and Deuteronomy.

Pentecost

Greek '50th day', from Hebrew Shavuot, 'weeks'. The Jewish Feast of Weeks fell on the 50th day after PASSOVER, for the first-fruits of the corn harvest. In Acts 2 the disciples were assembled in Jerusalem on this day when the Holy Spirit descended on them. The name Pentecost, in English popularly called WHITSUNDAY, celebrates this event.

Pentecostals

Modern evangelical movements stressing gifts of the Spirit, especially speaking in tongues and healings. Their origins were mainly in revivals within or separations from METHODIST and HOLINESS reforms, seeking a 'second blessing' and 'baptism in the Spirit'. Pentecostal activities produced the Foursquare Gospel and ASSEMBLIES OF GOD, and recently TELEVANGELISM and CHARISMATICS. The worldwide membership of such churches has been estimated at many millions. (*See also* ELIM; GLOSSOLALIA.)

People's Temple

See JONES.

perfection

The exhortation 'Be perfect, as your heavenly Father is perfect' (Matt. 5:48) provided an ideal, pursued by Catholic and Protestant spirituality. John Wesley said, 'By perfection, I mean the humble, patient, gentle love of God and our neighbour.' The dangers of perfectionism were in self-depreciation, scrupulosity, and individual rather than social concern. (*See also* HOLINESS; SUPEREROGATION.)

pericope

Greek, 'section': a portion of Scripture prescribed to be read in a church service. The Pericope Adulterae in John's Gospel (7:53–8:11) concerns the woman taken in adultery, not found in the older manuscripts of John, undoubtedly genuine but perhaps taken from elsewhere.

Perronet, Vincent (1693–1785)

Vicar of Shoreham in Kent. He befriended Charles and John WESLEY and was called 'the archbishop of Methodism'. Two of his sons became Methodist preachers and he supported John Wesley against the Calvinistic Countess of HUNTINGDON.

persecution

Christianity began with the Crucifixion of Jesus and his followers were persecuted for three centuries for refusing to worship Roman emperors. Persecutions were not constant; the worst trial was under the emperor Decius (250 CE), when many apostasized. Toleration came with CONSTANTINE, but there have been many persecutions down history. (*See also* COMMUNISM; CYPRIAN; HUGUENOTS; INQUISITION; MILAN; TORQUEMADA.)

Peter

The Greek name means 'rock', as does the Aramaic Cephas, a nickname given to Simon. John says he and his brother came from Bethsaida in Galilee. Peter is always named first in lists of disciples. He tried to defend Jesus at his arrest and followed him to the trial, but denied him. Paul (1 Cor. 15:5) puts a resurrection appearance of Christ to Peter first, but the SYNOPTIC GOSPELS give no account of this experience. In ACTS, Peter and John are prominent at Pentecost, being imprisoned and released, and Peter later baptizing the gentile Cornelius. Tradition said that Peter went to Rome and was crucified head downwards. Jerome said Peter was first bishop of Rome. Peter was married (Mark 1:30), and Paul says Peter took his wife on his travels (1 Cor. 9:5). Eusebius, quoting Clement of Alexandria, said that Peter's wife was martyred with him: 'When blessed Peter saw his wife led away . . . he said, "My dear, remember the Lord." Such was the marriage of the blessed.' (*See also* MARK; PAPIAS; QUO VADIS?)

Peter's Pence

A tax on English houses, or hearth tax, paid to the Pope in the middle ages. Also called Romescot, it was fixed at £200. Unpopular as a foreign levy, it was abolished by Henry VIII in 1534.

pews

From Latin and Greek for 'pedestal', these are benches, seats with backs, or enclosed compartments in churches. In Eastern Orthodox churches the people stand or kneel, but in the West seats were provided for the aged or infirm, at first fixed to walls or columns in the nave, and finally right across it. Pews were often finely carved, and some remain where they have not been destroyed in restorations. (*See also* MISERICORD.)

Peyotism

See NATIVE AMERICAN CHURCH.

Pharisees

From Aramaic for 'separate ones' or 'interpreters', they were prominent from the time of the Maccabees in the second century BCE till the fall of Jerusalem in 70 CE. After this time Pharisaic Judaism was followed by most Jews, their teachers called RABBIS. The Gospels (especially Matt. 23) tend to read back into the time of Christ later opposition by the Pharisees when the Church was breaking away from Judaism, and from this came denigration of Pharisees, in dictionaries unfairly described as 'hypocrites'. The gospels, notably Mark and Luke, do not implicate the Pharisees in the trial and death of Jesus, but show these events to be the responsibility of leading SADDUCEE priests and Roman rulers.

Philemon, Epistle to

Shortest of Paul's letters, addressed to a Christian of Colossae of that name. His slave Onesimus had run away and found his way to Paul. Paul 'the aged' pleads with Philemon for his 'son', in his own writing. No more is known of this matter, but it showed how relationships could be changed within the community. (*See also* SLAVERY.)

Philip

Named in the SYNOPTIC GOSPEL lists of disciples. Only John gives any details of this Philip: his birthplace at Bethsaida, bringing Nathanael to Jesus, questioning at the feeding of the five thousand, and asking to be shown the Father (14:8). Nothing further is known.

Another Philip was one of the SEVEN DEACONS (Acts 6:5) who met and baptized the Ethiopian eunuch (Acts 8:26ff). He settled at Caesarea, where he is called an evangelist with four daughters who prophesied (Acts 21:8–9).

Philippians, Epistle to the

A short but important epistle of PAUL, generally accepted as genuine, and probably sent from Rome, one of the 'captivity epistles'. Apart from personal greetings and exhortations, there is the 'KENOSIS' passage describing Christ 'emptying himself', becoming man and exalted with the name of Lord (2:5ff). In the next chapter Paul insists on his own Jewish birth, pharisaism, persecuting zeal, renunciation, suffering and rising with Christ.

Philippine Independent Church

Peasant protests against Spanish Catholics took place from 1840, and by 1970 there were over 330 indigenous churches in the Philippines, some groups mixing Christian and tribal traditions. The largest was founded in 1890 by a Catholic priest and national leader, and at one time attracted nearly half the Catholic community. It is estimated that by the year 2000 independent Filipino churches will have about 12 million

members, and Roman Catholics 70 million. (*See also* FLAGELLANTS.)

Philo (20 BCE–50 CE)

From a Jewish priestly family in Alexandria, he became an expositor of the Bible and of Greek philosophy. His attempted synthesis appealed more to Christian than to Jewish thinkers, especially the Alexandrine school of CLEMENT and ORIGEN. Philo gave a central place to the LOGOS, and this has been held to have influenced the first chapter of John's Gospel.

Philokalia

Greek, 'love of the beautiful' or 'good'. A Philokalia of ORIGEN gave extracts from his writings. A Philokalia of Macarius and Nicodemus came from an 18th-century Greek Church movement for spiritual renewal, with extracts from mystical writers. (*See also* HESYCHASM; JESUS PRAYER.)

phoenix

Greek mythical bird which burned itself to ashes and came back to life. Christian writers and artists used it as a symbol of the Resurrection.

Photius (810–95 CE)

Made Patriarch of Constantinople while still a layman; his appointment was declared invalid by the Pope of Rome. This and doctrinal arguments prepared the way for the final split between East and West, creating a Photian SCHISM. Photius not only challenged the rights of Rome over Eastern patriarchs, but accused Rome of innovation in the FILIOQUE clause in the Nicene Creed.

phylactery

An amulet, from Greek meaning 'guard', it represents the Hebrew *tefillin*, leather boxes containing scriptural verses which were tied to the forehead and forearm during Jewish prayer. Their ostentatious use is criticized in Matthew 23:5.

Orthodox Jews wearing tefillin *at the Western Wall, Jerusalem:* Tefillin *are known as phylacteries in the Greek of the New Testament.*

pietism

A movement in 17th-century Germany against rationalism in Lutheranism. It emphasized experience and emotion, formed circles for prayer and Bible study, and held the priesthood of all believers. Pietism was criticized for irrationality and praised for sincerity and missionary work. It influenced French QUIETISM and British METHODISM. (*See also* LUTHERANISM; SPENER; ZINZENDORF.)

Pilate, Pontius

Roman governor of Judaea from 26 CE to 36 CE. Josephus depicts him as shrewd but ruthless, the SYNOPTIC GOSPELS show him as impartial, and John adds his question, 'What is truth?' (John 18:38). Legend said that Pilate committed suicide and in the Coptic Church he is regarded as a martyr. There is an apocryphal Acts of Pilate from the fourth century, showing the trial of Jesus and how all Pilate's images bowed down before him. Much later Francis Bacon wrote: 'What is Truth? said jesting Pilate; and would not stay for an answer' (*Essays*, 1597).

Pilgrim Fathers

Radical PURITANS who sailed from Plymouth in England in 1620 on the *Mayflower* and founded Plymouth Colony in Massachusetts. (*See also* CONGREGATIONALISM.)

pilgrimage

RITES of passage, rituals of historical or devotional importance to holy places, have been common to most religions. Visits to the Holy Land were encouraged by HELENA, mother of Constantine, seeking RELICS, and interruption of pilgrimage by the Turks was one cause of the CRUSADES. Other pilgrimage centres were Rome, Constantinople, real or imagined sites of saints like Compostela, or places of apparitions, such as Lourdes. Modern tourism extends pilgrimage.

Pilgrimage of Grace

Risings in the north of England in defence of the monasteries and against government policies were led in 1536 by Robert ASKE, who negotiated with Henry VIII. The rebels then dispersed peacefully, but a further outbreak gave an excuse for repression and Aske was executed at York in 1537. (*See also* DISSOLUTION.)

Pilgrim's Progress

John BUNYAN's allegory of Christian's journey from the City of Destruction to the Heavenly City, published in 1678. Partly written in prison, its simplicity and colourful incidents and characters made it famous worldwide, translated into countless languages; it was once found with the Authorized Version of the Bible in most Protestant homes.

pillar saints

Called Stylites from Greek for a pillar, in early Eastern Christianity some ascetics lived on the top of pillars of varying heights, up to 20 metres. A pillar might have a platform and a small hut, but all food had to be drawn up by rope. People came to admire and consult the ascetic and he tried to resolve personal, civil and theological disputes. (*See also* SIMEON STYLITES.)

plainchant
See CHOIR.

Plato, Platonism
The supreme Greek philosopher. His influence on Christian thought has been profound and constant, and it has been said that European philosophy consists of footnotes to Plato. The early Church fathers and apologists, mystics and schoolmen, humanists, romantics, and many others came under the Platonic spell. (*See also* ARISTOTLE, NEO-PLATONISM; PLOTINUS.)

plenary
See INDULGENCES.

Plotinus (205–70 CE)
First of the NEO-PLATONISTS through whom Platonic thought came to dominate the medieval West. His teachings on God and the soul were assimilated into Christian teachings, and description of the ascent of the soul was compared with Christian experience of seeking God.

Plumstead
See PECULIAR PEOPLE.

Plunket, Oliver (1629–81)
Irish Roman Catholic. Of a noble family, he studied at Rome, became a priest and in 1669 was Archbishop of Armagh. He reorganized the diocese but persecutions developed and, in the scare of the POPISH PLOT, Plunket was arrested, taken to London and executed at Tyburn. (*See also* OATES.)

Plymouth Brethren
See DARBY.

pneuma
Greek, translated variously, as in 'the wind [*pneuma*] blows where it will . . . so is everyone born of the spirit [*pneuma*]' (John 3:8). Pneumatology is the doctrine of the HOLY SPIRIT.

Polycarp (69–155 CE)
A leading early Christian in Asia Minor, providing a link with the first Christians. Irenaeus said Polycarp had been taught by the apostles and many that had seen Christ. Polycarp became bishop of Smyrna and called MARCION 'the first-born of Satan'. Polycarp lived a long life, and travelled to Rome; but returning to Smyrna during a pagan festival, he refused to take part in it and was burned to death.

polygamy
Having more than one marriage. More than one wife is polygyny and more than one husband polyandry. Although against Christian tradition, there have been exceptions and Luther approved of the bigamous marriage of his supporter Philip of Hesse. Polygamy has been a problem in modern African Christianity, being against some indigenous practice. (*See also* COLENSO; MARRIAGE.)

polyglot
In several languages; used of an edition of the Bible with parallel texts in more than one language, such as Hebrew, Greek and Latin, or in various English translations.

polytheism
Worship of two or more deities, as distinct from the MONOTHEISM of the Semitic religions, Judaism, Christianity and Islam.

Pontifex Maximus
Originally a title of the chief priest at Rome, perhaps derived from Latin *pons*

for a bridge, or *puntis* for a propitiatory offering. Play has been made with a suggestion of a Great Bridge-builder. The title was used by some bishops and taken over by the Pope. The Supreme Pontiff 'pontificates' from Rome and issues pontifical encyclicals.

Pontius Pilate

See PILATE.

Poor Clares

See CLARE.

Pope

From late Greek 'papa' for father, the title is used for the bishop of Rome as head of the Western Church. In Eastern Orthodoxy 'Pope' or 'Papa' is a common term for a parish priest. Popery is an English term for Roman Catholicism, used since the time of TYNDALE. 'No Popery' has been a cry of Protestants in fear of Roman domination. (*See also* CARDINAL; JOHN PAUL II; ROMAN CATHOLICISM; VATICAN.)

The Palace of the Popes, Avignon: The residence of the Popes when in exile from Rome in the Babylonian Captivity (1309–77).

Pope Joan

See JOAN.

Popish Plot

In 1678 Titus OATES claimed to have discovered a plot to murder Charles II and put his brother James, a known Catholic, on the throne. There was public hysteria, in which 24 Catholics were killed, and Parliament tried to exclude James from the succession. Charles dissolved Parliament and rode out the crisis. (*See also* PLUNKET.)

Porphyry (232–303 CE)

NEO-PLATONIST philosopher, noted for opposition to Christianity in a treatise of 15 books, which survive only in fragments. He criticized inconsistencies in the gospels, and attacked church leaders for lack of patriotism in rejecting cults of Roman emperors.

Port Royal

A convent of Cistercian nuns south of Paris, founded in 1204, and attaining notoriety in the 17th century when it became a centre of JANSENISM. The nuns refused to accept papal condemnation of Jansenists. Their house was divided into two and those who continued to reject the ban were finally dispersed. (*See also* PASCAL.)

post-modernism

Confusing, since it should refer to an unknown future, the term post-modern has been used since the late 19th-century of art criticism, architecture, literature and philosophy. Post-modern theology considers the effect of evolution (a 19th-century problem) on religious thought, relativity, indeterminacy and uncertainty, all scientific concepts affecting theological statements. The existence, nature and activity of God are hotly debated. (*See also* DARWINISM; DEATH OF GOD; MODERNISM.)

postulant

From Latin for 'demand': a candidate demanding admission to a religious order, undergoing testing before acceptance as a NOVICE.

poverty

For many, poverty is deprivation and suffering, but 'holy poverty' has been welcomed as freedom from wealth and avarice, provided that, as Buddhists say, there is 'a village nearby for support'. Protestants have regarded religious poverty as stewardship of wealth. The Rule of TAIZÉ (1961) says 'the spirit of poverty is to live in the gladness of today.'

Practice of the Presence of God

See BROTHER LAWRENCE.

praemunire

Latin, 'warning' a person to appear in an English court, and not a papal court. From 1353 several acts forbade referring English cases to Rome, but they were not regularly enforced until Henry VIII asserted his royal SUPREMACY. (*See also* ANNATES.)

prayer

There are several kinds of prayer, for example adoration of God, confession of sins, intercession for others, petition for needs, thanksgiving for benefits. Christian prayer is addressed to God the Father, through our Lord Jesus Christ, and although there is often confusion in popular prayers this pattern can be seen in the collects of the Book of Common Prayer. Prayer meetings are held for communal praise and petition. (*See also* DEAD, PRAYERS FOR; JESUS PRAYER; LORD'S PRAYER; MENTAL PRAYER.)

prayer beads

See ROSARY.

preaching

The Hebrew PROPHETS had a 'call' to preach, as did Jesus and the apostles. The SERMON or preaching from Scripture is a central feature of much Protestant worship, coming from conviction and experience. BUNYAN said, 'I preached what I felt, what I smartingly did feel' (*Grace Abounding*, 1666). (*See also* KERYGMA; LAY READER; OPEN-AIR.)

prebend

Part of the revenue of a cathedral or collegiate church granted to a prebendary canon as stipend. It was normally the TITHE from land belonging to the cathedral.

precentor

A cleric in charge of musical services in a cathedral. In Presbyterian and some other churches, the precentor leads the singing; this was formerly an important role when many people could not read and needed direction in words as well as music.

predestination

From Latin for 'fore-ordaining': the chief biblical support is in Romans (8:29–30), 'those whom he foreknew he also pre-destined ... and those whom he predestined he also called.' The question whether good for some implied damnation for others divided Christendom with, for example, AUGUSTINE, CALVIN and WHITEFIELD against PELAGIUS, ARMINIUS and WESLEY. The Book of Common Prayer took the positive view that 'Predestination to Life is the everlasting purpose of God' (Article 17). (*See also* FREE WILL; JANSENISM; WESTMINSTER CONFESSION.)

pre-existence

See IMMORTALITY.

preface

Words introducing the central part of the Eucharist, beginning with 'Lift up your hearts.' (*See also* SURSUM CORDA.)

prelate

In the Anglican Church a term used only of bishops, but in Roman Catholicism applied to several officials of the VATICAN. Prelacy has been employed in a critical sense of government by bishops.

pre-sanctified

A liturgy of the 'previously consecrated', using elements from an earlier service. It is celebrated on certain days in LENT in Orthodoxy, now restricted to GOOD FRIDAY in the West, with Communion from a SACRAMENT reserved from MAUNDY THURSDAY.

presbyter

Greek, 'elder'. Milton said that 'New Presbyter is but old Priest writ large' (*On the New Forcers of Conscience under the Long Parliament*, 1646), since both words come from the same root, but he also meant that presbyters were as dominant as former PRIESTS. New Testament presbyters seem to have been virtually identical with 'overseers', *episcopoi*, BISHOPS, but by the second century different offices had evolved. Since the Reformation Presbyterian church government has been established in many places, and other churches speak of the presbyteral ministry or presbyterate to distinguish it from that of DEACONS or diaconal ministry. (*See also* MINISTER; SUPERINTENDENT.)

Presbyterianism

A type of church government by 'elders' in the Reformed tradition, derived especially from CALVIN, ZWINGLI and KNOX. In Scotland the Presbyterian is the state church, but with independence from the Crown. In the USA a merger of northern and southern churches into the Presbyterian Church adopted a new statement of faith in 1991. (*See also* CHURCH OF SCOTLAND; ELDER; WESTMINSTER CONFESSION.)

presbytery

A term used in several ways: for the sanctuary of a church beyond the choir; for a priest's house in Roman Catholicism; for a Presbyterian church court above the KIRK SESSION.

Presentation

See CANDLEMAS.

Prester John

Presbyter or Priest John, in a medieval story that there was a Christian priest-king of 'the Indies' who had defeated the Muslims and would liberate the Holy Land. Perhaps this was a NESTORIAN legend from their missions in the Far East, but more likely it refers to the Christian priest-king of Ethiopia, the vague geography of the time situating the story in 'the Indies'. (*See also* HAILE SELASSIE.)

prevenient grace

GRACE 'coming before', predisposing us to seek God. That God is first active, seeking the lost, is basic to the doctrine of grace.

prie-dieu

French 'pray God', a prayer desk, with a kneeler and a shelf for books.

priest

From the same root as PRESBYTER, meaning 'elder'. In the New Testament Church MINISTERS were called elders and overseers, and the sacrificial or sacerdotal office of Old Testament priests was not applied to them. The sacerdotal priesthood developed slowly in the Church, with the EUCHARIST as the Christian SACRAMENT and sacrifice. In the middle ages the supernatural powers of priests were emphasized, offering sacrifice and giving absolution. The Reformers reacted against such powers and functions, preferring to speak of presbyters or ministers, though the ANGLO-CATHOLIC movement made the title 'priest' common again in Anglican churches.

Priestley, Joseph (1733–1804)

Trained at a dissenting academy at Daventry, he became a Presbyterian minister. As a chemist he was one of the discoverers of oxygen. Priestley taught UNITARIANISM in his chapel at Leeds, publishing the *History of the Corruptions of Christianity*. He went to America and died in Pennsylvania. Despite his unorthodoxy in other matters, Priestley expected the Second Coming of Christ.

primate

A bishop of a 'first see', a METROPOLITAN or PATRIARCH. Rivalry for primacy between the Archbishops of Canterbury and York raged for centuries, until Pope Innocent VI (1352–62) decided that the Archbishop of York should be called 'Primate of England', but then said that Canterbury was to be styled 'Primate of All England'.

Prime

'First': the office for the first hour of the day in monastic rule, 6.00 a.m.

Primitive Methodists

A group which broke from the major Wesleyan METHODIST Church in England in the early 19th century in order to return to 'primitive' open-air gatherings. Hugh Bourne began an evangelistic movement at Mow Cop in Staffordshire in 1800, introducing American-style CAMP MEETINGS. He was expelled from the Wesleyans as 'highly improper', and joined with William Clowes to form the Primitive Methodists in 1811. The new society gave itself to evangelism, and undertook missions in Africa and Australia. In 1932 the 'Prims' joined with Wesleyan and United Methodists to form the present Methodist Church in Britain. (*See also* BIBLE CHRISTIANS; RANTERS.)

prior

Head of a religious house or order: one who is 'prior' as earlier or greater in importance. A prioress directs a house of nuns. A priory is a religious house under prior or prioress. (*See also* ABBEY.)

Prisca/Priscilla

Usually mentioned first with her husband Aquila, she seems to have been the dominant partner. With other Jews they were expelled from Rome, met Paul at Corinth and stayed with him since they also were tentmakers (Acts 18). They went to Ephesus and back to Rome where Paul said they risked 'their own necks' for him (Rom. 16:4). Feast day 8 July.

probabilism

The principle that if there is any doubt of the lawfulness of an action, then it is permissible to follow the probable opinion. 'A doubtful law does not oblige.' After long debates probabilism became dominant in the Roman Catholic Church, safeguards against laxity insisting that the probable opinion must be 'solidly' probable. (*See also* ALPHONSUS LIGUORI; CASUISTRY.)

process theology

Modern teaching that to be real is to be in process, developing in response to the environment. Not only human beings, but God himself is thought to be affected by all other entities. In contrast to a transcendental theism, with its distinct and IMPASSIBLE God, process theology is panentheistic, holding that God embraces all things and leads them to fulfilment. (*See also* PANTHEISM; TRANSCENDENCE.)

procession, processional

Processions take place in church, before or after services, or in the open air as acts of witness, especially on GOOD FRIDAY or at ROGATIONTIDE. Processionals are books with hymns and prayers to be used during processions.

procession

As a theological term, the doctrine as stated in the Nicene Creed, that the Holy Spirit 'proceeds' from the Father and the Son, which was disputed by ORTHODOX churches. (*See also* FILIOQUE.)

profane

The natural, everyday world, contrasted with sacred reality. From Latin 'before' or 'outside the temple', the term may include BLASPHEMY, lack of reverence, esoteric knowledge, or exclusion from religious rites. (*See also* HOLY; SACRED.)

profession

Taking religious vows before entering an order, normally after a novitiate or training period of some years.

prohibited degrees

See KINDRED AND AFFINITY.

Propaganda

A Roman Catholic Congregation – the 'Sacred Congregation of Propaganda' – founded in the 16th century at the Counter-Reformation, to seek to regain Protestant lands and also foster missions to non-Christian countries.

Prophet, Mrs Elizabeth Clare (b. 1940)

Born in New Jersey, she attended churches and synagogues, Christian Science and theosophical meetings. She married Mark Prophet in 1963 and they published teachings of the Ascended Masters. After his death she established centres of the Summit Lighthouse, regarded as the true Church of both Christ and Buddha. From headquarters in Montana, 'Guru Ma' sends out weekly letters.

prophets

In the early Church prophets were listed after apostles (1 Cor. 12:28). The evangelist Philip had four daughters who prophesied (Acts 21:9). These were inspired speakers, and they seem sometimes to have been elders or DEACONS. In the later Church, friars or lay preachers might prophesy spontaneously or give prepared addresses. (*See also* PREACHING.)

proselyte

Greek for 'one who has arrived', a 'stranger', and in the Bible a convert to Judaism. Proselytes would be circumcised, unlike 'God-fearers' who were interested in but not members of the Jewish religion. In later times 'proselyte' was applied to converts from any religion.

Protestant Episcopal Church

The ANGLICAN Church in the United States, in communion with the See of Canterbury and a leader in the Lambeth Conferences. By 2000 it should have over 11 million members.

Protestant Truth Society

A movement of opposition to Roman Catholicism and Anglo-Catholicism, and 'ritualism' in the Church of England. Its secretary from 1890 was John Kensit, who ran a Protestant publishing house. He and his followers caused disturbances at various 'High' churches and after a meeting in Birkenhead Kensit was wounded in the eye. He died in hospital of pneumonia, his followers claiming him as a martyr.

Protestantism

The term Protestant was first used in Germany in 1529 by those who protested against a ban from the Diet of Speyer against each principality or city determining its own faith. It was soon applied to all who had broken from Roman Catholicism, chiefly Lutherans, Calvinists and Baptists, and developing from them the Reformed, Presbyterian, Congregational, Methodist, Unitarian and Quaker churches. The position of the Church of England is disputed; at the coronation the monarch as head of the Church vows to maintain the Protestant Reformed religion, but ANGLO-CATHOLICS reject the name Protestant and insist on the Catholic nature of their Church. There are over 2,000 Protestant groups in the USA. (*See also* REFORMATION; SUPREMACY.)

Protevangelium

See PSEUDO-JAMES.

providence

From Latin for 'foresight': the word would strictly indicate God's 'provision', prior knowledge of human affairs, rather than his action in the world, but in practice both of these meanings are included in the notion of providence. 'General providence' is seen in divine blessing, sending rain on the just and the unjust (Matt. 5:45), and 'special providence' when God is believed to speak to a PROPHET or work through a MIRACLE. Modern theologians tend to regard nature and history as independent, seeing special providences as concerned only with persons.

province

A group of DIOCESES forming a unit, such as Canterbury or York.

provincial

A ruler of a religious order in a certain area, though not necessarily in the same province.

Prynne, William (1600–69)

PURITAN barrister. He wrote veiled attacks on Charles I and his queen, was fined and had his ears lopped off. After a further attack on Archbishop LAUD he was branded on both cheeks, and not surprisingly was a bitter prosecutor of Laud when the latter was attainted for treason. Prynne became a Member of Parliament but was 'purged' and imprisoned in 1650.

He criticized Cromwell's regime, but was appointed Keeper of the Tower Records by Charles II. He denounced the reviving Anglican Church and the Book of Common Prayer.

Pseudo-Dionysius

See DIONYSIUS.

Pseudo-James

An apocryphal book of the second century, claiming to be by James, Jesus' brother, but he died in 62 and this book partly follows Matthew's Gospel, which was written about 85. A modern title for it is Protevangelium, meaning 'original gospel', an unfortunate name since it is clearly later than the canonical gospels. Pseudo-James gives names for Mary's parents, JOACHIM and ANNA, Mary being brought up in the temple, Joseph an old man, and contains the first mention of a virginal birth as well as conception. The book became popular, inspiring other APOCRYPHA, and providing material for story and art, but historically it seems worthless. (*See also* VIRGIN BIRTH.)

psychical research

See SPIRITUALISM.

pulpit

Latin, 'platform': a raised stand in wood or stone in church or chapel, from which the PREACHER delivers his SERMON. The word 'pulpit' is sometimes used for the preacher, his message or sermons.

purgative way

See CATHARSIS; JOHN OF THE CROSS.

purgatory

A condition or place of purification, in Roman Catholic teaching, for souls that need to expiate venial or MORTAL SINS before admission to PARADISE. The pains of purgatory may be described as literal or figurative fire, and DANTE in his

Dante at the foot of Purgatory by Domenico di Michelino, 15th century, in Church of Santa Maria del Fiore, Florence.

Purgatorio gives many details. The Roman Church developed masses for souls in purgatory, along with INDULGENCES, PRAYERS and ALMS. Protestants generally rejected the notion of purgatory, but Anglo-Catholics defend belief in an intermediate state, between heaven and hell, after death.

Puritans

Protestants in the Church of England in the 16th and 17th centuries, dissatisfied with moderate reforms and calling for theology and worship along the lines of Calvin's Geneva. After the Civil War and Restoration, some were expelled and joined Dissenting groups, while others conformed to the Established Church. Puritans who went to America founded four 'Holy Commonwealths' in New England, which gradually became CONGREGATIONALIST. (*See also* PILGRIM FATHERS.)

Pusey, Edward Bouverie (1800–82)

Theologian and professor of Hebrew at Oxford. He joined NEWMAN in *Tracts for the Times*, writing on baptism and the Eucharist, and was condemned for error by the university. When Newman went over to Rome in 1845, followed by MANNING, Pusey became leader of the High Church party, holding that the Anglican was part of the Holy Catholic Church, separated from Rome not so much by doctrine as by popular practices, but he was disappointed by the new Roman dogma of papal INFALLIBILITY in 1870. He died at Ascot Priory and was buried at Christ Church Cathedral, Oxford. (*See also* ANGLO-CATHOLICISM; KEBLE; TRACTS.)

pyx/pix

Greek, 'box-wood vessel': a receptacle, usually metal, containing consecrated elements for carrying to the sick.

Q

Q

This letter is used for the source of sayings of Jesus found in both Matthew and Luke, perhaps the LOGIA, words of Jesus which PAPIAS said were written by Matthew in Hebrew. Q is a modern symbol, said to come from German *Quelle*, 'source'. Some scholars dispute the existence of such a document, but the many resemblances of the sayings in the Gospels of Matthew and Luke have to be explained in one way or another.

Quadragesima

From Latin for '40': the first Sunday in LENT, 40 days before Easter.

Quakers

See FRIENDS.

Quarr Abbey

A modern Benedictine monastery near Ryde in the Isle of Wight. Consecrated in 1912, built in red brick, it is recognized

Quarr Abbey, Ryde, Isle of Wight: Dom. Paul Bellot (d. 1943) built many buildings in Holland, Belgium, France and Canada and is regarded as a pioneer of 20th-century Expressionism. Quarr Abbey is considered his most outstanding work.

by discerning critics (such as Pevsner) as 'outstanding' and 'original'.

Quasimodo

A title for LOW SUNDAY in the Roman Catholic Church, taken from the Latin opening words at MASS, *Quasi modo geniti infantes*, 'As new-born babes' (1 Pet. 2:2).

Queen Anne's Bounty

See ANNATES.

Quicunque vult

Opening words of the ATHANASIAN Creed in Latin, 'Whosoever would' be saved.

Quietism

A MYSTICISM which inculcates a passive attitude, stressing contemplation and abandonment of the will. It is particularly connected with Miguel de MOLINOS, in his teaching that union with God may be achieved by removing all mental images, dispensing with outward aids and actions. (*See also* FÉNELON; GUYON.)

Quinquagesima

From Latin '50': the Sunday before LENT, 50 days before Easter.

Quire

Old spelling for choir, used in the Book of Common Prayer: 'Quires and Places where they sing' (rubric after the third collect).

Qumran

See DEAD SEA SCROLLS.

Quo vadis?

A legend in an APOCRYPHAL Acts of PETER, written in Greek about 200 and translated into Latin, says that Peter was fleeing from persecution in Rome when he met Christ and asked him, 'Domine, quo vadis?' ('Lord, where are you going?'). Christ replied that he was going to be crucified in Peter's place, so the abashed apostle turned back and insisted on being crucified upside down. But Peter would not have spoken to Jesus in Latin or Greek, instead of their own Aramaic, and the story is probably a development of Peter's denial. A more reliable tradition does indeed place him in Rome and going to his death, with his wife, in the Neronian persecution.

Qur'ān

The sacred scripture of Islam, also spelt Koran in English, and formerly Alcoran. Although written down in Arabic in the seventh century, it was not translated into English until 1734. Qur'ān means 'reading' or 'recitation', and it is regarded by Muslims as the very Word of God. It respects other revelations, naming the Torah and the Gospel. It speaks of Jesus in 93 verses, always with reverence, relates his birth twice, names his mother Mary, but denies the Crucifixion, apparently with intent to defend Jesus against those who thought they could kill the Messiah. (*See also* ALCORAN; DOME OF THE ROCK; ISLAM; MARY; MUHAMMAD.)

R

rabbi

Hebrew for 'my Master', it came into general use for Jewish teachers after the fall of Jerusalem in 70. It is notable that this title, along with 'Rabboni', Aramaic for 'my rabbi', is applied to Jesus especially in the fourth Gospel (John 1:38 etc.).

race relations

As an international religion, Christianity should be a force for racial harmony. Paul wrote that in Christ there is 'neither Jew nor Greek, neither slave nor free, neither male nor female' (Gal. 3:28). Missionary movements have sought to bring diverse races into the Church, but religious history has been marred by racial prejudice. Recently, both the VATICAN and the World Council of Churches have taken firm stands for racial understanding and equality. (*See also* ANTI-SEMITISM; APARTHEID; HOLOCAUST; MISSIONS.)

Racovian Catechism

See SOCINUS.

Radio Church of God

See WORLDWIDE CHURCH OF GOD.

Rahner, Karl (1904–84)

German Jesuit priest and theologian, who re-interpreted the authoritative teachings of the Roman Catholic Church for contemporary life, and was criticized for his work in preparing for the Second Vatican Council. His long series of essays was collected in 16 volumes, published from 1954 to 1984 as *Theological Investigations*. (*See also* SACRED HEART.)

Raikes, Robert (1735–1811)

Born in Gloucester, he was struck by the neglect and ignorance of children and started a Sunday School in 1780 to teach reading and behaviour. He was opposed by strict Sabbatarians, and others who thought education led to revolution. Raikes persisted and before his death saw Sunday Schools opened in many parts of the country and himself recognized as founder of the movement. Sunday Schools lost part of their original purpose with universal education, and have been further weakened by the secularization of Sunday. (*See also* LORD'S DAY; SABBATH.)

Ram Mohun Roy (1772–1833)

Hindu religious reformer who had close links with Christian UNITARIANS. The Brahmo Samaj ('Theistic Society') which he founded was also called Hindu Unitarianism. He used the Bible in debates with missionaries and wrote *Precepts of Jesus* to show from the gospels the moral rather than doctrinal teachings of Christ.

ransom

See ATONEMENT.

Ranters

A term applied pejoratively to ANTINOMIANS of the 17th century accused of revolutionary or immoral teachings, sometimes associated wrongly with Quakers. Later it was used of PRIMITIVE METHODISTS, Hugh Bourne saying that his people singing in the streets after prayer meetings 'procured for them the name of Ranters'.

rapture

Religious ecstasy, as when Paul was 'caught up to the third heaven' (2 Cor. 12:2). Rapture, or being rapt, derives from the same root as rape, the difference being in willing abandonment to love of God. (*See also* ECSTASY; TERESA.)

Rastafarians

When HAILE SELASSIE became emperor of Ethiopia in 1930, some Jamaicans took his name Ras Tafari for a religious revival, hailing him as the African Messiah who

Haile Selassie: Emperor of Ethiopia (1930–74) and Messiah to the Rastafarians.

would lead black people to the promised land. Rasta has no organized movement or creeds, but beliefs concern messianic hopes and black–white relations. Since the death of Haile Selassie there has been less emphasis on his role and more on pan-Africanism. *Reggae* music (meaning unknown, but Jamaican), the use of *ganja* (marijuana) and wearing of long hair in dreadlocks give distinctiveness to Rastas. They refuse to be counted, but numbers are estimated at hundreds of thousands, in the Caribbean, USA, and Europe. (*See also* GARVEY.)

Ratana, Tahupotiki Wiremu (1873–1939)

Maori founder of the Ratana Church of New Zealand. Following dreams and healings people came to him, but he insisted they must give up *tapu* (taboo) and rely on God alone. A temple was built in Ratana village and members were encouraged to stand for Parliament, capturing the four Maori seats. Membership of the Ratana Church is said to be about 20,000 but some Maoris refuse to declare their religion.

reader

See LAY READER.

real presence

Used of the belief in the actual, rather than symbolic, presence of the body and blood of Christ in the Eucharist. (*See also* EPICLESIS; TRANSUBSTANTIATION.)

Rechabites

A group of people in ancient Israel who refused to drink wine (Jer. 35). Their name was adopted in 1835 by some modern Christian total abstainers from alcohol. (*See also* TEMPERANCE.)

recluse

From Latin for 'shut'. One who lives in seclusion or retirement, as a religious discipline. (*See also* ANCHORITE; COENOBITE.)

rector

In the Anglican Church, the incumbent of a parish who receives its tithes or equivalence. The title also is given to the heads of Exeter and Lincoln Colleges in Oxford, and in Scotland to headmasters of some schools and universities. Leaders of Jesuit houses are also called rectors.

recusancy

From Latin, 'refuse': applied to Roman Catholics in the 16th century who refused to attend services of the Anglican Church. When Elizabeth I was excommunicated, and Jesuit missions infiltrated England, recusancy was considered dangerous, with widespread fears of Roman Catholic plots. Penal laws imposed heavy fines, which were relaxed in the late 17th century and disappeared with CATHOLIC EMANCIPATION in 1829. (*See also* DOUAI.)

red letter day

In church calendars and prayer books, important feasts and saint's days may be printed in red ink. In the Prayer Book, feasts with collect, epistle and gospel were also called red letter days.

Redeemer, redemption

In the Bible redemption was setting free by repaying or releasing, used of animals, slaves, and the captive people. Paul linked forgiveness with the death of Christ: 'in him we have redemption through his blood' (Eph. 1:7). Later writers saw redemption as removal of ORIGINAL SIN and restoration to righteousness; some held it to be for the elect, but ARMINIANS said it was universal. (*See also* ATONEMENT; SALVATION.)

Redemptorists

See ALPHONSUS LIGUORI.

Reformation

A general term for movements in West European Christianity from the 14th to the 17th century. Beginning with LOLLARDS and Hussites, changes developed in Lutheran and Calvinist, Anglican and Scandinavian churches. Theological leaders rejected the corruptions of the medieval Church and sought return (reform) to what was thought to be the purity of primitive Christianity. Some reformers wanted purification within the Church, others rejected the papacy and all its ways. At the same time political forces led to the formation of national churches separate from Rome. LUTHER won the support of German princes, CALVIN established a theocracy in Geneva, and the English Reformation led to a national church but in time conceded toleration to Nonconformists. The variety of PROTESTANT expression was carried over and developed in North America, while Latin America, with Spanish and Portuguese languages and cultures, remained largely Roman Catholic. *See also* ANGLICANISM; ERASMUS; HUSS; REFORMED CHURCHES; WYCLIFFE; ZWINGLI.)

Reformed Churches

Those derived from the Calvinistic stream of the Reformation, as distinct from Lutherans. French Huguenots, German Reformed, Presbyterian and Congregational denominations were, in the main, Calvinistic or Reformed. Migrants to America continued the tradition, with the Dutch Reformed Church of America being formed in 1628 and the German Reformed Church in Philadelphia in 1747. A World Alliance of Reformed Churches was founded in 1975, with headquarters in Geneva, from 86 countries representing some 70 million people. (*See also* CALVIN; LUTHER; PROTESTANT; ZWINGLI.)

Refreshment Sunday

See MOTHERING SUNDAY.

regeneration

Spiritual rebirth. (*See also* BORN AGAIN.)

Regina coeli

Latin, 'Queen of Heaven': opening words of an Easter anthem to the Virgin Mary, from the 12th century.

regular

From Latin 'rule': a name given to clergy who follow a rule and live in community, as distinct from 'secular' priests who live in the world.

reincarnation

Also called metempsychosis: belief in the passing of souls from one body to another, held by Greeks and Indians. There is little trace of it in the Bible, apart from occasional verses such as the blind man responsible for his condition (John 9:2). Josephus said the Pharisees held that 'the souls of good men pass into other bodies' (*Jewish War* 2:165). ORIGEN thought that souls pre-existed, but this idea was attacked by AUGUSTINE, who believed in the creation of souls at birth. In modern times reincarnation has been taught by spiritualists and theosophists, but it is generally held to be at variance with belief in creation and RESURRECTION. (*See also* IMMORTALITY.)

relics

Venerated physical remains or possessions of holy people. The practice is found in many religions. The cult of relics grew rapidly in the early Church, with belongings of martyrs treasured in the CATACOMBS, and the Second Council of Nicaea in 787 CE ruled that no church should be without a relic. Countless relics were exported to the West during the CRUSADES, kept in reliquaries and carried in processions. The Reformation destroyed many false relics, and some genuine works of art and history. Even among Protestants relics may be revered, such as John WESLEY's Bible, passed down

yearly to his successors. (*See also* ALTAR; HELENA; INVENTION; MARTYR; SHROUD.)

religion

Defined in various ways: the Epistle of James (1:27) saw it as visiting the needy and keeping pure from the world. The term 'religion' is used in different senses: as personal piety, as a system of beliefs and practices, as a general term for spiritual activity.

religious

A religious is a member of an order, usually living in community and following a rule of life. (*See also* REGULAR.)

religious education

Keenly debated, between those who consider religion essential to culture, and those who seek the completely secular. Some schools are run by religious bodies: Anglican, Roman Catholic, Jewish. State regulations in Britain require teaching of a 'broadly Christian' nature, while in the USA school prayers and the teaching of evolution are highly contentious matters.

Religious Tract Society

See TRACTS.

reliquary

See RELICS.

remonstrance

See ARMINIUS.

renegade

From Latin, 'denial': one who changes his or her religion. Hakluyt wrote of 'a Renegado, which is one that first was a Christian and afterwards becometh a Turk' (*Voyages*, 1599).

renunciation

Self-denial is commanded in the Gospel: 'deny oneself' (Mark 8:34). The old and revised Books of Common Prayer asked godparents at baptism to 'renounce the devil and all his works', but recent revisions have made this more positive, in requiring Christian upbringing. (*See also* ABSTINENCE; FASTING.)

reordination

Once ordained, always ordained, is a common belief. Reordination may question the validity of the previous consecration, a sore point in discussions on church union, and for Anglican priests entering the Roman Catholic Church. Some have held it to be conditional ordination, not necessary if the original ordination could be found valid.

repentance

The Greek word *metanoia* means a change of mind, and so of life. John the Baptist preached 'repentance for the remission of sins' (Mark 1:4ff), and Jesus said 'Repent, and believe the Gospel' (Mark 1:15). Repentance includes change or amendment, whereas penitence extends to penance, penalty and reparation. (*See also* CONVERSION; PENANCE.)

Requiem

Latin, 'rest': used of a Mass for the departed, *Requiem aeternam*, eternal rest. Requiem Masses are held on the day of death or BURIAL, and on anniversaries and ALL SOULS' Day.

reredos

Word of mixed English–French derivation, 'rear' for behind and *dos* for back, indicating a decoration or screen at the back of an altar. A reredos might be painted wooden panels, fixed or as a TRIPTYCH, or in wood or stone with figures of saints.

reservation

Reserving the bread, and sometimes the wine, from the EUCHARIST for administration to the sick or those at a distance. Its carrying about for display was condemned in Article 28 of the Book of Common Prayer. (*See also* MONSTRANCE.)

response

See VERSICLE.

Resurrection of Christ

This is attested by Paul, all four Gospels, and Acts, with differences of detail. Paul (in 1 Cor. 15) says that he 'received' that Christ died and rose, puts an appearance to Peter first, includes James the Lord's brother, and finally Paul himself. MARK (16) has the empty tomb and a promised appearance in Galilee. Matthew adds details to both of these. Luke (24) has the walk to EMMAUS and ASCENSION at Bethany. Acts has the ascension and goes on to Peter's sermon that Jesus had been raised up and exalted. Belief in the Resurrection of Christ changed the bewildered disciples into public preachers of this faith, even to critical Greeks (Acts 17:18). (*See also* EASTER.)

resurrection of the dead

There is little about life after death in the Old Testament, but many Jews in the time of Christ believed in survival and heaven for the righteous. The gospels speak of Abraham's bosom, life with the patriarchs, and PARADISE. Paul (1 Cor. 15) affirms the resurrection, not in a physical but in a spiritual body, incorrupt and immortal. The Apostles' Creed affirmed 'resurrection of the flesh' (Greek *sarx*), but this was rendered 'the body' in English, perhaps with the spiritual body in mind. Generally it has been held in the Church that all the dead will survive, some to JUDGEMENT, and some to eternal life. (*See also* EASTER; HADES; HEAVEN; HELL; IMMORTALITY.)

retreat

A period of silence, meditation, instruction or spiritual exercises, under a leader who gives counsel and directs discussion. Retreats were introduced by Jesuits in the 17th century, adopted by Anglo-Catholics, and have become popular in other churches.

reunion

See ECUMENISM.

revelation

Some writers distinguish between natural religion, based on spiritual power in nature, and revealed religion as a call from God or in a sacred book. But an eminent anthropologist (E. E. Evans-Pritchard in *Theories of Primitive Religion*, 1965, p. 2) holds that 'all religions are religions of revelation', because all spring from belief in experiences of divine encounter. (*See also* BUTLER; NATURAL LAW.)

Revelation, Book of

'Apocalypse' in Greek: the last book of the New Testament, by an unknown JOHN, from the island of Patmos, sending messages to seven churches in Asia Minor. There are visions, of God, of the Lamb-Lion, of elect tribes, of angels, of a woman in heaven, of war between Michael and Satan, of the great beast, of the New Jerusalem, and of Jesus coming quickly. Much of the imagery is lurid and fantastic, arising out of PERSECUTION, probably that of Domitian (81–96 CE). The APOCALYPSE was not admitted till late into the CANON of Scripture. It has furnished material for ADVENTIST and millenarian speculations down the ages. (*See also* ANTI-CHRIST.)

Reverend

Title of ministers of religion since the 15th century. Archbishops are called Most Reverend, other bishops Right Reverend, deans Very Reverend. Nuns who have the title Mother may be Reverend. The Moderator of the Church of Scotland is Right Reverend.

British Free Church ministers use the title Reverend, since a legal case allowed this in 1876.

Revised Version

The AUTHORIZED or King James Version of the Bible in English held sway from 1611 to 1881, though there were some private revisions, John WESLEY publishing his version of the New Testament with notes in 1755. Changes in language, and knowledge of ancient codices, with better texts, especially Sinaiticus and Vaticanus, indicated the need for a thorough revision. Scholars from various churches produced the revised New Testament in 1881 and Old Testament in 1885. Since then there have been many other translations; a Revised Standard Version was published in 1952. (*See also* CODEX.)

revivalism

A feature of Protestant life since METHODISM and the SALVATION ARMY, though its origins go back to the friars of the middle ages, and eventually to PENTECOST. A GREAT AWAKENING in America in the years 1725–60 was followed by another in the 19th century, and revivalism continues with preachers like Billy GRAHAM, Billy Sunday and Oral Roberts, in radio and television religion. (*See also* TELEVANGELISM.)

Ricci Matteo (1552–1610)

Italian Jesuit missionary to China, welcomed because he had clocks and scientific instruments. Ricci adopted Chinese dress and manners, and allowed converts to continue veneration of ancestors and Confucius. Dominican missionaries, jealous of Jesuit success, referred his adaptation of Chinese rites to the Pope in a Rites Controversy, though it was not decided till 1742 when Jesuit practice was forbidden and hopes of a widespread Christian appeal to China were dashed. Ricci was buried outside the walls of

Peking and his grave was restored in 1980. (*See also* CHINA; DE NOBILI.)

Ridley, Nicholas (1500–55)

After study at Cambridge and abroad, he became firmly Protestant under Edward VI and was appointed bishop of London. Ridley's moderation and learning were notable and he helped CRANMER prepare the ARTICLES of Religion. Under Mary Tudor he was sent to the Tower, tried at Oxford with LATIMER, and burnt with him outside Balliol College.

rings

Betrothal and wedding rings go back to Roman times and were early adopted by Christians for wearing on different fingers. Episcopal rings date from the seventh century and are worn on the right hand. Nuns are given a ring at their profession. The Fisherman's Ring, engraved with Peter in a boat fishing, is placed on the Pope's finger by a cardinal. The Coronation Ring is placed on the fourth finger of the monarch's right hand by the Archbishop of Canterbury as sign of dignity and faith. (*See also* DEFENDER OF THE FAITH.)

rites, ritual

A rite is a formal act of religious observance, such as the eucharistic rite. Ritual refers to the prescribed form of words for the act of worship; ceremonial indicates the actions, though the two are often treated as the same. 'Rites of passage' was a term invented by Arnold van Gennep in 1909, for those rites where one passes from one stage of life to another, such as initiation, marriage or funeral. The Congregation of Sacred Rites was established in 1588 to ensure uniformity of worship as decreed by the Council of TRENT.

Rites Controversy

See RICCI.

Rogation Days

From Latin 'asking'. On the Major Rogation, processions went through the cornfields on 25 April, praying for preservation against mildew. There were Minor Rogations three days before Ascension Day; also at this time the Beating of the Bounds took place, with willow rods, to indicate parish limits. Rogation ceremonies have been suppressed and revived at various times, with prayers also for the sea harvest and industry.

Rolle, Richard (1295–1349)

Known as the Hermit of Hampole in Yorkshire, he made a hermit's habit of his father's rain-hood and two of his sisters' frocks. Richard was noted not only as a mystic but as one of the first religious authors to write in English as well as Latin, and has been called by C. Horstmann (*Yorkshire Writers*, 1895) 'the true father of English literature'. He wrote *Meditations on the Passion* and *The Forme of Perfect Living*. His many works were popular and used by the LOLLARDS. (*See also* HILTON; KEMPE; WYCLIFFE.)

Roman Catholicism

A term used especially since the Reformation for those in communion with the Pope of Rome, distinct from other 'catholics'. The Roman Catholic Church is by far the largest and most complex world organization, found in nearly every country, with an estimated membership of almost 1,200 million. As well as a hierarchy of bishops and priests under the POPE, this Church has multitudes of male and female religious, teachers, hospital, social and other workers. Its buildings, in cathedrals, churches, colleges, schools, hospitals, orphanages and the like represent colossal achievement. In doctrine the Church presents a military conformity, contrasting with the fissiparous nature of

Protestantism, but revealing since the Second VATICAN Council many strains and variations. Roman Catholicism has suffered persecution but has also expanded enormously, so that this Church is not only the dominant Christian organization but a formidable influence in international affairs.

Romans, Epistle to the

The longest of PAUL's writings, so placed first in the CANON. A doctrinal thesis rather than a letter, it begins with the broad view of the universality of sin and the need for justification, with baptism as dying to sin and rising with Christ, struggles against the flesh being won by the Spirit of Christ which bears us through all travail. The epistle was sent to a church that Paul had not yet visited, and it includes at the end salutations to many known and named Roman Christians.

Rome

Centre of the Roman Catholic Church and seat of the POPE. A tradition said that PETER went to Rome, became its bishop and was martyred there. More surely Paul arrived (Acts 28:16) and suffered in the Neronian persecution. Roman Christians persevered and after

St Peter's Basilica, Rome: One of the largest churches in Christendom, begun in 1506 and consecrated in 1626. It replaced a basilica built by Constantine.

Constantine the Church began to take over the role of the Roman Empire. Many famous churches remain, St Peter's basilica being rebuilt by 1614. (*See also* VATICAN.)

Romero, Oscar Arnulfo
(1917–80)

Archbishop of El Salvador in 1977. He seemed a safe conservative, but, touched by the murder of a priest and the treatment of peasants, he spoke at 'the disposition of the poor'. The military regime was outraged and assassinated Romero at the altar of a hospital. Since then he has been revered as the outstanding episcopal 'voice of the voiceless'.

rood

Old English rod or pole, formerly used of the cross of Christ and for a crucifix in the middle of the 'rood-screen', a wooden or stone screen separating the chancel of a church from the nave. People swore 'by the rood' but the word is archaic and the rood replaced by a cross or crucifix.

rosary

Latin 'rose-garden', applied to a book of devotion and to sets of devotions on prayer beads. Repetitive prayers on beads came from Hinduism and Buddhism, were adopted by Muslims in India and introduced to the West by missionary Dominicans in the 15th century. Prayers on the rosary are 15 decades (groups of ten), each decade preceded by 'Our Father' and followed by 'Glory be to the Father'. One-third of the rosary, a chaplet, is said at one time. It is divided into mysteries, events in the life of Jesus and his Mother: 15 subjects in all, divided into three groups: Joyful, Sorrowful and Glorious. (*See also* AVE MARIA; LORD'S PRAYER.)

Rosicrucians

Members of the Order of the Rosy Cross, a mystical brotherhood in

Germany founded by a supposed Christian Rosenkreutz in the 17th century who had learned the occult wisdom of the East and invited men of goodwill to join the Order. There was much literature, and several organizations claimed to come from the Rosicrucians. In England, Kenneth Mackenzie said he had joined a Rosicrucian masonic order in 1872, and in 1915 Arthur Waite developed his own Rosy Cross Fellowship. In California a recent organization is the Ancient and Mystical Order Rosae Crucis, teaching doctrines by correspondence.

rostrum

From Latin for beak of a bird, the word was used of the beak-like prow of a ship, and then for a speaker's platform in the Roman forum which was decorated with the prow of a captured ship. Thence the word was applied to any platform for addresses or lectures.

Roy

See RAM MOHUN ROY.

rubric

A ceremonial direction for the conduct of a service, in medieval books instructions being written in 'red' (Latin *ruber*) to distinguish them from the text of the

services. (*See also* BLACK RUBRIC; RED LETTER DAY.)

rule

See BENEDICT; GOLDEN RULE.

rural dean

In the Anglican Church, the head of a group of parishes called a rural deanery. He presides over a ruridecanal chapter of the clergy.

Russell, Charles Taze

See JEHOVAH'S WITNESSES.

Russia

See BERDYAEV; BULGAKOV; COMMUNISM; ORTHODOX CHURCH; SERGIUS; VLADIMIR.

Rutherford, Joseph Franklin

See JEHOVAH'S WITNESSES.

Ruysbroeck, Jan van
(1293–1381)

Flemish mystic. Prior of AUGUSTINIAN CANONS, he wrote many books in Flemish on the spiritual life. Ruysbroeck led a movement of modern DEVOTION (*devotio moderna*), which meditated on the life and death of Christ and included such writers as Thomas à KEMPIS.

S

Sabaoth

Hebrew 'hosts' or 'armies', untranslated in two New Testament references in the Authorized Version (Rom. 9:29; James 5:4), and in the traditional form of the canticle TE DEUM, in the phrase 'Lord God of Sabaoth'.

Sabbatarianism

Strict observance of Sunday rest in PURITAN circles.

Sabbath

From Hebrew Shabbat, 'cessation' of labour on the seventh day of the week, as God rested then from creation (Gen. 2:2). The choice of seven days probably came from phases of the moon, after which the 'month' was named. Jesus said 'the sabbath was made for man, and not man for the sabbath' (Mark 2:27), allowing good activities and protecting workers. The first Christians, as Jews, observed the Saturday Sabbath, but since both Resurrection and Pentecost took place on the first day of the week they observed Sunday also and in time abandoned the Saturday rest. The re-adoption of the Sabbath on a Saturday is a modern practice of SEVENTH-DAY ADVENTISTS or 'Saturday Sundays' as they are known in parts of Africa. (*See also* CALENDAR; LORD'S DAY.)

Sabellianism

Theories of Christology taught by Sabellius, who lived in Rome about 215 CE. Father, Son and Holy Spirit were said to be all one and the same, each revealing a character (*prosōpon*) of creator as Father, of redeemer as Son, and now as the Spirit. This identification was rejected by the orthodox, but the implication of equality between members of the Trinity influenced theology. (*See also* PATRIPASSIANISM.)

sacerdotal

From Latin for PRIEST: attributing sacrificial functions or supernatural powers to priests, or claiming excessive authority for them.

sacrament

Defined in the Prayer Book Catechism as 'an outward and visible sign of an inward and spiritual grace', in the middle ages there were said to be seven sacraments: baptism, confirmation, Eucharist, penance, extreme unction, orders and matrimony; but reformers said that only two were 'Sacraments of the Gospel', BAPTISM and the EUCHARIST.

Sacramentals are minor practices and objects, such as the SIGN OF THE CROSS, grace at meals, STATIONS OF THE CROSS, Angelus, ROSARY, CHURCHING OF WOMEN, and so on. (*See also* MARRIAGE.)

sacred

From Latin for 'HOLY': the NUMINOUS, divine; and by extension persons, places or things set apart and given respect and worship. (*See also* PROFANE.)

Sacred Heart

Devotion to the Sacred Heart of Jesus developed from meditation on the WOUNDS of Christ in the Western Church from the 12th century, and was stressed by writers like JULIAN OF NORWICH and FRANCIS OF SALES. In parallel, devotion to the Sacred Heart of Mary grew up from the 17th century. Some popular DEVOTION appears sentimental, but theologians like Karl RAHNER have looked beyond that to the vision of God in the wounds of Christ.

sacrifice

From Latin 'to make holy': an offering to a deity, and figuratively an act of prayer or the EUCHARIST. Paul wrote that 'Christ our passover is sacrificed for us' (1 Cor. 5:7), and in time the Crucifixion of Jesus and the eucharistic sacrament were regarded as sacrifices, though the Book of Common Prayer insisted that 'the offering of Christ once made is that perfect redemption', denying that masses were sacrifices which priests offered (Article 31). Christian theology held that when the believer offers himself or herself to God, that is a sacrifice united with the sacrifice of Christ.

sacrilege

From Latin for 'one who steals sacred things': taking what is consecrated, committing outrage on sacred persons or things, violating sacramental obligation, or whatever is under the protection of the Church, especially treating the sacraments irreverently. (*See also* BLASPHEMY.)

sacring bell

Bell rung at MASS to call attention, especially at the elevation of the elements. Also called the Sanctus bell.

sacristy

A room for VESTMENTS and vessels of a church. It may be separate from the vestry in churches with many liturgical objects. A sacristan is in charge of vessels and vestments, though the title is sometimes used of a SEXTON.

Sadducees

Temple priests, called after Zadok, a priest in the reigns of David and Solomon. Mainly upper-class and Judaean, they were not popular, and the picture of them given by Josephus agrees with the New Testament; both sources state that they rejected the immortality of the soul. Along with PILATE, their leader CAIAPHAS was responsible for the crucifixion of Jesus. (*See also* PHARISEES; SANHEDRIN.)

Sadhu Sundar Singh
(1880–1929)

The title Sadhu means 'holy' man; it was given to this Sikh convert to Christianity in 1904. In traditional robes he preached the Gospel in Indian ways, and in the West he was regarded, like some later gurus, as a Christ-like figure. In 1929 he went on a last mission to Tibet and no more was heard of him.

Saint Sophia

See HAGIA SOPHIA.

saints

Members of the early Christian community were 'called to be saints' (1 Cor. 1:2). Others were notable for sacred power or holiness, particularly the martyrs, 'the souls of those slain for the word of God' (Rev. 6:9). From there, saints were venerated in Catholic and Orthodox churches, their RELICS, tombs, feasts and pilgrimages revered and their intercession invoked. Distinction was made between 'devotion' (*dulia*) given to saints, and 'worship' (*latria*) offered to God. Prayers for the dead led on to veneration and invocation of saints, and to their canonization and inclusion in the CALENDAR of saints. (*See also* DEAD, PRAYERS FOR; HYPERDULIA; MARTYR.)

Salesians

See FRANCIS OF SALES.

Salome

Not named in the gospels but mentioned by Josephus: the daughter of Herodias (Mark 6:22) who danced before HEROD Antipas for the head of John the Baptist. Another Salome is named in Mark 15:40, but nothing more is known about her.

salvation

'What must I do to be saved?' asked the Philippian jailer (Acts 16:30), and the concept of salvation is found many times in the epistles, with the answer: 'Believe in the Lord Jesus Christ.' Salvation though faith, with remission of sins, led some ascetics to flight from the world, but in the Bible it was followed by good works in this present life. (*See also* ATONEMENT; REDEMPTION.)

Salvation Army

A worldwide organization, founded in 1865 on a military pattern with privates, officers and a general at the head, and with uniforms, flags and bands. OPEN-AIR services, emotional appeals for conversion, and visits to public houses, led on to care for the destitute, drunkards and criminals, with hostels for the homeless, night shelters and soup kitchens. The Army is strongly evangelical, akin to METHODISM, from which it began, but it does not celebrate baptism or the Lord's Supper. (*See also* BOOTH; CHURCH ARMY; REVIVALISM.)

Salve regina

Latin, 'Hail, O Queen': one of the most popular Roman Catholic devotions,

The Salvation Army: The SA has three main elements – ritual in costume and music; the preaching of sin and conversion; and social service in helping the needy and others in accidents.

recited at the end of prayers and sung in processions.

Samaritans

Mixture of races in the northern kingdom of Samaria led to conflict with Jews returning from exile. John's Gospel (4:9) remarked that Jews had no dealings with Samaritans, and the parable of the GOOD SAMARITAN in Luke (10:33ff) was like praising a good enemy. There is still a Samaritan community at Nablus in central Palestine, whose scripture is only the five books of the Torah ascribed to Moses.

In 1953 an Anglican minister, Revd Chad Varah, founded a charitable organization called the Samaritans, to help people in social and psychological troubles, or contemplating SUICIDE.

sanctification

Making holy: purification or beatification. 'Entire sanctification' is a concern for PERFECTION emphasized by HOLINESS churches.

sanctuary

Roman temples gave refuge to fugitives and this practice was taken over by the Church. In England a person could claim sanctuary in eight 'cities of refuge', but these were abolished in 1623. Popular feeling still regards a church as a place of refuge, but sanctuary for immigrants was broken in England in 1994 and in France in 1996.

Sanctus

Latin 'Holy': the threefold repetition at the preface to the Eucharist originates from Isaiah 6:3. (*See also* SACRING BELL.)

Sanhedrin

Hebrew and Aramaic form of a Greek word for a council: the supreme Jewish religious and judicial body, said to have had 70 or 71 members. The gospels show this council, under CAIAPHAS,

condemning Jesus (Matt. 26:59), with a sentence confirmed by PILATE. (*See also* SADDUCEES.)

Sankey

See MOODY.

Santa Claus

See NICHOLAS.

Santa Sophia

See HAGIA SOPHIA.

Santeria

Spanish, 'the way of the saints': name of a mixture of West African (Yoruba and Benin-Dahomey) religion with popular Catholicism in the Caribbean and southern USA. The basic unit of the Santeria is the *ile*, Yoruba for house or community, but there is no overall organization and estimates of numbers are difficult. Priests and priestesses are probably in the tens of thousands and active devotees in hundreds of thousands. (*See also* CANDOMBLÉ.)

Satan

From Hebrew for 'adversary' or 'opponent'. Satan appears as a tempting servant of God in the late Old Testament (Job 1:6 etc.). In the New Testament there is a more Zoroastrian identification with evil and the DEVIL (Matt. 4:10, etc.), to be met with opposition and EXORCISM. (*See also* ZOROASTER.)

Satanism

As reaction against Christianity, this was thought to exist in the middle ages, but there is little evidence for it. Modern claims for Satanism come from OCCULT practices, revived or invented. A Church of Satan was founded in San Francisco in 1966 by Anton LaVey, who sought to channel lust into self-affirmation. The MANSON family claimed to worship both Christ and the DEVIL. (*See also* BLACK MASS; WITCHCRAFT.)

satisfaction

That the death of Christ was a vicarious satisfaction was propounded by ANSELM, and reflected in the Prayer Book liturgy: 'a full . . . satisfaction for the sins of the whole world'. But the legalistic notion that God required such satisfaction was rejected by other theologians, from ABELARD to the moderns, and the term does not appear in recent eucharistic prayers.

Saturday

See HOLY SATURDAY.

Saviour

See REDEEMER.

Savonarola, Girolamo (1452–98)

Italian Dominican monk and fiery preacher against vanity and vice in Florence, where huge bonfires destroyed women's costly ornaments. He claimed the gift of prophecy and was called to Rome for heresy; but he refused to go, was forbidden to preach and disregarded the order. Savonarola's rigorism made many enemies, and he was hanged and burned with two disciples in the market-place of Florence. George Eliot's novel *Romola* gives a fair picture of the man and his times. In 1996 the Dominican Order began a case for the beatification of Savonarola.

sayings

See LOGIA; Q.

scapular

From Latin for 'shoulder-blades': a short cloak worn by monks over the shoulders, hanging down at front and back.

schism

Greek for 'tear' or 'rent': a term used of division within or separation from the Church. In 1054 there came a breach between the ORTHODOX East and CATHOLIC West, first over the FILIOQUE clause in the CREED; a later rift was caused by the sack of Constantinople in the Fourth Crusade in 1204. A schism within the papacy came with the 'BABYLONIAN CAPTIVITY', the exile of the Popes at Avignon in France from 1309 to 1377 with antipopes continuing in Avignon when the papal court had returned to Rome. The Reformation was a schism of much of northern Europe from Rome, and the term has been used also of divisions within Protestantism. (*See also* APOSTASY; CONSTANCE; ECUMENISM; PHOTIUS.)

Schleiermacher, Friedrich Daniel Ernst (1768–1834)

The most influential German theologian of the 19th century, whose definition of religion as 'the feeling of absolute dependence' reacted against orthodox rigidity and rationalism. Opposition to his 'feeling' came with Karl BARTH and others. (*See also* STRAUSS; ZINZENDORF.)

scholasticism, schoolmen

Medieval theologians who set about systematizing Christian truths, using the concepts and methods of philosophers, especially those of ARISTOTLE. (*See* ALBERT THE GREAT; DUNS SCOTUS; OCKHAM; THOMAS AQUINAS.)

Schweitzer, Albert (1875–1965)

German theologian, organist and mission doctor. In 1906 his book, translated into English as *The Quest of the Historical Jesus*, argued that Jesus expected an early end to this world order, and when that failed tried to bring it by his own death. In 1913 Schweitzer and his wife left for Lambaréné in Gabon, having raised funds by organ recitals, and founded a hospital where they served for 50 years. He received the Nobel Peace Prize in 1952, though his paternalistic methods brought criticism from some visitors to his hospital.

Science, Christian

See CHRISTIAN SCIENCE.

Scientology

See HUBBARD.

SCM

See STUDENT CHRISTIAN MOVEMENT.

Scopes, J.T.

See FUNDAMENTALISM.

Scotland

See CHURCH OF SCOTLAND.

screen

A partition of wood or stone dividing the chancel of a church from the nave. (*See also* ICONOSTASIS; ROOD.)

scriptures

See BIBLE; CANON.

scruples

From Latin for 'pebble' or 'sharp stone': a doubt or hesitation from fear of sin. Scrupulosity is obsession with trivial wrongs, or over-use of the confessional. (*See also* PERFECTION; SUPEREROGATION.)

Second Adam

See ADAM.

Second Coming

See ADVENTISM; PAROUSIA.

secret

Of prayer, one said silently; in the Eucharist, an offertory prayer by the celebrant.

sect

A term used, often in a derogatory manner, of a group separate from the dominant or established church. Puritans and enthusiasts might be called sectaries. (*See also* CULT; NEW RELIGIOUS MOVEMENTS.)

secular

The 'secular arm' refers to the exercise of the law, the power of the state or a lay organization interfering with or appealed to by the Church. In the middle ages a church court might examine an offender, but hand him over to secular authorities for punishment. Secular clergy are ministers living in the world, distinct from REGULAR clergy who belong to an order and follow a rule of life.

secularism

A term first used by G. J. Holyoake (1851) of the 'practical Philosophy of the People'. It indicated a practical and ethical element 'which the terms "Infidel", "Sceptic" and "Atheist" do not express'. (*See also* AGNOSTIC; HUMANISM.)

secularization

This occurs where the functions of religion are taken over by the state, as in education and social affairs. Some theologians argue that since we live in a secularized world we must find religion there, cherishing the secular and seeing God in it. So BONHOEFFER wrote of Christian life in a 'religionless world', speaking 'in a secular way' about God. (*See also* BULTMANN.)

see

From Latin for 'seat': primarily the official throne of a bishop. By extension, the place or town where a CATHEDRAL is situated is known as the bishop's see.

Segundo, Juan Luis (b. 1925)

Jesuit priest in Uruguay, a pioneer of LIBERATION THEOLOGY. A prolific writer, his books include *The Liberation of Theology* and *A Theology for Artisans of a New Humanity*.

Seicho No Ie

Japanese, 'the Household of Growth', founded by Taniguchi Mahasaru (1893–1985). It claims that all religions are the same in essence and should be respected, though Seicho No Ie alone has revealed the fundamental reality. The teaching includes ideas from Buddhism, Christianity, Christian Science amd Freudian psychology.

Semi-Arians

A group of fourth-century theologians who proposed a middle way between Arianism and orthodoxy. (*See also* ARIUS; HOMOOUSION.)

Semi-Pelagians

See PELAGIUS.

Sen, Keshub Chunder (1838–84)

Indian teacher who worked for social reform and the abolition of caste privileges. He lectured on *Jesus Christ: Europe and Asia* (1866), suggesting that Indians understood Jesus better than the British. He belonged to the Brahmo Samaj, 'Society of Brahman [God]', but split away to form a Church of the New Dispensation. (*See also* RAM MOHUN ROY.)

Separatists

See BROWNE.

Septuagesima

Latin, '70th' day before Easter, third Sunday before Lent.

Septuagint

Latin, '70': the Greek translation of the Hebrew Bible, said to have been produced by 72 translators about 270 BCE in Egypt. Abbreviated to LXX in references, this was the Bible used by the early Church. This is sometimes vital for exposition, as in Matthew 1:23 where the Hebrew word from Isaiah 7:14 meant a young woman, but Matthew used the Greek for 'virgin'. Although the Septuagint Greek Bible was widely used, JEROME's VULGATE went back to the Hebrew, and later TYNDALE and the AUTHORIZED VERSION used the Hebrew of the Old Testament and Greek of the New.

Sepulchre

See HOLY SEPULCHRE.

Seraphim

Angelic creatures in Isaiah 6, above the divine throne. The word is also used of fiery serpents. Christian writers regarded the seraphs as angels, counterparts of the Cherubs. (*See also* CHERUBIM.)

Sergius (1314–92)

Regarded as the greatest Russian saint. He was born in Rostov and his family fled to live near Moscow, where Sergius founded a famous monastery of the Holy Trinity and 40 others. He re-established communal life in the Russian Church, went into seclusion himself but stopped four civil wars, and inspired Prince Dmitri to resist Tartar incursions. Feast day 25 September.

sermon

The speech or written discourse which holds a central place in much Protestant worship, but less where there is a Eucharist. PREACHING a sermon in a service goes back to synagogue practice, and later there were prophets and preachers in the Church, and the bishop himself might preach a sermon.

Sermon on the Mount

'Seeing the multitudes Jesus went up the mountain . . . and opened his mouth and taught them.' Following these words Matthew introduced some of the basic teachings of Jesus, in three chapters (5–7). This was a valuable collection for instruction and has been used down the ages. Luke has a parallel but shorter collection (6:17–49), sometimes called the Sermon on the Plain. The sermon opens with the BEATITUDES, goes on to the Law on murder, adultery, divorce, swearing and love of enemies, and gives the LORD'S PRAYER, words on fasting, anxiety, judging, the GOLDEN RULE, the narrow way, and hearing and doing the word. (*See also* Q.)

server

An assistant at church services, especially the Eucharist. It used to be said that a server could be a man or boy but not a woman, but that has changed and in most churches now women fulfil many roles.

Servetus, Michael (1511–53)

Spanish theologian and physician who discovered the pulmonary circulation of the blood. Biblical studies led him to deny the Trinity and the divinity of Christ. His book on the errors of the Trinity was attacked by the Inquisition, and Servetus, not being himself within its grasp, was burned in effigy. But when Servetus went to Geneva for refuge, CALVIN had him arrested, tried and burned as a heretic. (*See also* SOCINUS; UNITARIANS.)

Servus servorum Dei

Latin, 'Servant of the servants of God': a title used by the POPES of Rome since its adoption by Pope Gregory the Great in the sixth century to express his humility.

Seven Churches

The bodies to which the Book of REVELATION was addressed: Ephesus, Smyrna, Pergamum, Thyatira, Sardis, Philadelphia amd Laodicea (Rev. 1:11).

Seven Deacons

The men appointed to help the apostles were STEPHEN, PHILIP, Prochorus, Nicanor, Timon, Parmenas and Nicolas (Acts 6:5). (*See also* DEACON.)

Seven Deadly Sins

Identified in Christian teaching as pride, covetousness, lust, envy, gluttony, anger and sloth (ACCIDIE).

Seven Gifts of the Spirit

These, based on a list in Isaiah (11:2), are wisdom, understanding, counsel, fortitude, knowledge, piety and fear of the Lord.

Seven Sacraments

See SACRAMENT.

Seven Sleepers

From the sixth century a story was told that during the Decian persecution (in 250) seven young Christians in Ephesus were walled up in a cave and awakened only 200 years later, thus proving the resurrection. The legend was so popular that it found its way into the Muslim QUR'ĀN (18:12–25) where seven men and their dog were in the cave 'three hundred years and nine more'. In later Islamic tradition the Seven Sleepers will arise with the Messiah and finally die as martyrs in Jerusalem. A shrine and tomb at the supposed site were visited by pilgrims and survived Turkish and secularist rule; the pilgrimage continues.

Seven Sorrows

The sorrows of the Virgin Mary are the prophecy of Simeon, the flight into Egypt, the temporary loss of the Holy Child, meeting the Lord going to Calvary, standing at the foot of the Cross, taking Christ down from the Cross (deposition) and the burial of Christ. (*See also* STATIONS OF THE CROSS.)

Seven Virtues

These consist of three theological virtues – faith, hope and love (charity) – and four cardinal virtues – justice, prudence, temperance and fortitude.

Seventh-Day Adventists

American millenarian movement, founded by Mrs Ellen Gould White (née Harmon, 1826–1915). Born a Methodist, she joined the Millerites, followers of William Miller who predicted the Second Coming of Christ in 1844. When this failed, she claimed a vision of the heavenly judgement already begun. She adopted the Jewish Sabbath and forswore alcohol, meat and drugs. In 1846 she married James White and they set up the Seventh-Day Adventist Church in 1855. They travelled widely and after White's death in 1881 Ellen went on missions to Europe and Australia. Her many writings are held to be divinely inspired. Seventh-Day Adventism became intensely missionary, with educational and health organizations. (*See also* ADVENTISM; MILLENNIUM; SABBATH.)

Sexagesima

From Latin for '60th' day before Easter: second Sunday before Lent.

Sext

The office of the 'sixth' hour, recited at noon.

sexton

From Latin for 'sacristan', an official caring for the church and churchyard, often a parish clerk and grave-digger. (*See also* SACRISTY.)

sexuality

Sex and religion have been two major concerns of humanity, yet often opposed to each other, flesh against spirit, as when Paul said that 'the flesh lusts against the spirit' (Gal. 5:17). Yet Genesis (1:27) said that God created male and female and told them to be fruitful and multiply. Monastic movements, pressure on priests and monks to be CELIBATE and the exaltation of virginity meant that sex was downgraded. At the Reformation priests began to marry, but little was done to provide a theology of sexuality. Only now, with better knowledge of physiology, can variant needs and problems be discussed. (*See also* DIVORCE; HOMOSEXUALITY; MARRIAGE; TAYLOR; WORLD.)

Shaftesbury, Lord: Anthony Ashley Cooper (1801–85)

Seventh earl of Shaftesbury, philanthropist and factory reformer. He piloted through Parliament bills regulating hours and conditions in factories and coal mines, prohibiting underground work for women and children under 13, providing lodging-houses and protecting chimney sweeps. He was chairman of the Ragged School Union and helped Florence Nightingale in army welfare. Strongly evangelical, he opposed both rationalists and ritualists, but worked with trade unions for factory reforms. The figure of the boy Eros at the end of Shaftesbury Avenue in London was erected as a memorial to him in 1892.

Shakers

An offshoot of the Quakers, led by Jane and James Wradley in Manchester in 1747. The nickname came from their shaking in ecstasy and dancing. Their own name was the Millennial Church. They were strictly celibate but saw the Female Principle and the Second Coming in Mother Ann LEE.

An American Indian Shaker Church was founded in 1881 at Puget Sound in Washington State, following revelations to John Slocum and his wife Mary. He claimed to have died and been resurrected with shaking and incomprehensible speech. This church spread to the north-west and claims some 20 congregations with 2,000 adherents.

Shema

Hebrew, 'hear': the confession of faith from Deuteronomy (6:4), recited daily by Jews and used and quoted by Jesus as the first commandment of all (Mark 12:29).

Shembe, Isaiah (1870–1935)

Zulu leader of one of the largest INDEPENDENT churches in South Africa and revered as a Black Messiah. In 1911 he founded the Nazirite Baptist Church or AmaNazaretha, and established a holy village at Ekuphakameni near Durban. Shembe was imprisoned and died in captivity, but the Nazirites built a great mausoleum and regard him as still alive, since it is claimed that he composed some popular hymns after his resurrection. Leadership of the Church passed to his son Johannes (d. 1976).

shepherd

See GOOD SHEPHERD; HERMAS.

Sheppard, Hugh Richard Lawrie (1880–1937)

Preacher and PACIFIST, 'Dick Sheppard' was a pioneer of religious broadcasting and vicar of St Martin-in-the-Fields, London. He founded the Peace Pledge Union in 1936, vowing never to support another war, directly or indirectly, though the menace of Nazism was growing rapidly in Europe.

shrine

From Latin, 'chest': the word was used of a casket for RELICS, then of a tomb of a saint, an altar or chapel, and broadly for any place hallowed by memory. (*See also* WALSINGHAM.)

Shroud, Holy

A purported winding-sheet of Jesus (Mark 15:46), kept since the 14th century in the Cathedral of Turin. A stained image on the cloth revealed in photographic negative a male body with marks of nails, and aroused great excitement. But tests in 1988 suggest that the RELIC dates from the late middle ages. Even if it were genuine, the relic would prove no more than that Jesus died, which nobody doubts.

Shrove Tuesday

The day before LENT, when the pious English were 'shriven' by confession and absolution. The French enjoyed themselves by feasting, calling it Mardi Gras, 'fat Tuesday'. A pale copy of that was the English practice of making pancakes, thin batter cakes, and so the day was also called Pancake Day. A pancakes race is still held at Olney and at Westminster School.

Sibylline Oracles

Pre-Christian books preserved utterances of sibyls, inspired women, which were consulted by the Senate in ancient Rome. Jewish and Christian authors made collections of similar oracles to gain converts. Although imitative and apologetic, these books were accepted by Church writers in the defence of the faith.

Sicilian Vespers

A massacre of some 4,000 French in Sicily, on 30 March 1282, signalled by tolling a bell for vespers or evening prayer.

sign of the Cross

From early times this 'sign of the Lord', recalling his passion, has been used by many Christians. In baptism 'the priest shall make a Cross upon the child's forehead' (Book of Common Prayer), and in BLESSINGS the sign is made over congregations, persons and things. In Eastern Orthodoxy the cross-stroke is from right to left, but in the West it goes from left to right. (*See also* CROSS; GESTURES.)

silence

In the middle ages 'SECRET prayers' and private devotions were added to the liturgy. Quakers make regular use of silence, and this practice has extended with the knowledge of silence in Asian religions. At TAIZÉ silence is observed after reading Scripture, and the same is done in other communities. The Practice of the Presence of God (*see* BROTHER LAWRENCE), interior prayer and waiting on God all stress the value of quiet. (*See also* MENTAL PRAYER.)

Siloam

A pool in Jerusalem where Jesus told a blind man to wash to regain his sight (John 9:7). One still shown to visitors is down a flight of steps. A further reference to a tower in Siloam (Luke 13:4) may indicate part of the city wall.

Simeon

A devout man in Jerusalem who hailed the child Jesus as 'a light to lighten the Gentiles' (Luke 2:25ff). (*See also* NUNC DIMITTIS.)

Simeon Stylites (390–459 CE)

The first of the 'PILLAR' ascetics, an ANCHORITE near Antioch, who built a pillar to sit on, gradually increasing its height to 20 metres; here he spent the rest of his life. Streams of pilgrims came for counsel, and he set a fashion for pillar practice. Tennyson's poem *St Simeon Stylites* (1842) imagined the penance and pains of this practice. Feast day 5 January.

Simon

See PETER. Another Simon is named in three lists of the disciples, called the Canaanean or the Zealot (Mark 3:18; Luke 6:15). He may have been a political zealot or zealous for the Law.

Simon Magus

A magician in Samaria (Acts 8:9ff) who was baptized by Philip; when Peter and John laid hands on converts to receive the Spirit, Simon offered them money that he might have 'this power'. Some later writers named Simon as 'the father of all heresy' who met Peter again at Rome, tried to show his magical powers by flying, fell down and died. The term 'simony' was used for buying and selling

spiritual things or advancement in the Church, and an English oath of 1604 required ordinands to state they had not obtained their office by money.

Simon of Cyrene

See STATIONS OF THE CROSS.

sin

Variously defined as transgression against divine law, disobedience to the known will of God, action detrimental to self or neighbour, or 'missing the mark' (literal meaning of Greek, *hamartia*, for fault or sin). Common elements are awareness of what is done, and that it is wrong before God. A crime is an offence against the law of the state, but sin implies responsibility to God. Much discussion of sin is negative and legalistic, but it needs to be seen in relationship to God and understanding of his purposes for individuals and society. (*See also* ORIGINAL SIN; SEVEN DEADLY SINS; SUICIDE.)

sister

See NUN.

Sisters of Charity

See TERESA, MOTHER; VINCENT OF PAUL.

Sistine Chapel

Chapel in the VATICAN built for Pope Sixtus IV (d. 1484), famous for the frescoes on the walls and ceiling by Michelangelo. The chapel is used by the CARDINALS for the election of a new Pope.

Six Articles

'The Whip with Six Strings', imposed by Henry VIII in 1539 to counteract Protestantism. They affirmed TRANSUBSTANTIATION, communion in one kind, clerical CELIBACY, monastic vows, private Masses and confession. There was some opposition, but the Articles were widely ignored. (*See also* TEN ARTICLES; THIRTY-NINE ARTICLES.)

SJ

Title of a member of the Society of Jesus. (*See also* JESUITS.)

slavery

Paul said that in Christ 'there is neither bond nor free' (Gal. 3:28), and though he did not condemn slavery, his letter to PHILEMON spoke of the returning servant as 'a beloved brother'. Among early writers, Gregory of Nyssa in the fourth century asked, 'Who can buy a man, who can sell him, when he is made in the image of God?' Those who engaged in the mass slavery trade from Africa to America from the 16th century, like NEWTON, were sometimes touched by scruples, and religious orders and Quakers set up colonies without slaves, but it needed the work of people like CLARKSON, WILBERFORCE and BUXTON to bring about abolition from 1833 onwards. (*See also* PENN.)

Slessor, Mary (1848–1915)

A factory worker in Aberdeen, she went as missionary to Calabar in West Africa for the United Presbyterian Church. She survived when many Europeans died of fevers, pioneered work into the interior, fought against slavery and exposure of twins; appointed Vice-Consul in 1892, her decisions were accepted by chiefs and people. A massive cross of Scottish granite marks her grave in Calabar.

Slocum, John

See SHAKERS.

sloth

See ACCIDIE; SEVEN DEADLY SINS.

Smith, Joseph

See MORMONS.

Sobornost

From Russian for 'assembly' or 'synod', an ambiguous term expressing conciliation and collaboration, especially co-operation in the liturgy. Sobornost is claimed by the Orthodox as their corporate working together, contrasted with Roman Catholic authoritarianism or Protestant individualism.

social gospel

See CHRISTIAN SOCIALISM; LIBERATION THEOLOGY.

Society of Friends

See FRIENDS.

Society of Jesus

See JESUITS.

Socinus, Faustus (1539–1604)

Italian theologian, his name Sozzini being Latinized as Socinus and his UNITARIAN teachings known as Socinianism. He wrote on John's Gospel and denied the divinity of Christ and the natural immortality of the soul, though outwardly he conformed to Catholic orthodoxy and opposed Protestant teachings. He spent much of his life in Poland, spreading Unitarian views among the upper classes. His ideas were expressed in a Racovian Catechism published at Racow in 1605. (*See also* SERVETUS.)

sola scriptura

Latin, 'scripture alone': a phrase used by some Protestants claiming the Bible as sole authority for belief and conduct, denying that Church tradition is also a source of revelation.

Solemn League and Covenant

An agreement for military and religious alliance between English and Scots during the Civil War in 1643. Parliament agreed to pay the Scottish army, abolish episcopacy and reform the Church of England 'according to the word of God', The Covenant was accepted by the Scottish Assembly, but ignored in

England after Cromwell came to power. (*See also* COVENANT; HERRICK.)

solifidianism

Justification by 'faith alone' (Latin, *sola fides*) without the merit of good works. The principle is derived from Lutheran interpretations of Rom. 3:28, 'justified by faith apart from works of law'.

Son of God

A title of Jesus as the Christ. (*See also* CHRISTOLOGY; FILIOQUE; TRINITY.)

Son of Man

A title used only in the gospels, and only by Jesus, with the sole exception of Stephen in Acts (7:56). It has been much debated whether Jesus used the title of himself, or of a Coming One, and reference is made back to Daniel (7:13), which describes a son of man coming on the clouds, quoted in Mark (13:26 and parallels). Interpretations of the Son of Man as emphasizing Jesus' humanity have to consider that the title is used also of his exaltation.

Song of Solomon, Song of Songs or Canticles

This collection of love lyrics, probably from ancient love feasts, in the Hebrew Bible, was interpreted symbolically by Jews and Christians. BERNARD of Clairvaux explained that the bride was the Church and the lover was Christ; Puritans and page headings in the Authorized Version took the kisses as symbols and parts of the beloved body as graces of the Church. (*See also* ALLEGORY.)

Sophia

Greek, 'wisdom'. (*See also* BULGAKOV; HAGIA SOPHIA; WISDOM.)

soteriology

From Greek for 'salvation': the theology of the saving work of Christ. (*See also* ATONEMENT; SALVATION.)

Soubirous

See BERNADETTE.

soul

The Bible describes man being made from dust and God breathing life into him, 'and man became a living soul' (Gen. 2:7). Paul speaks of 'spirit and soul and body' (1 Thess. 5:23), and later writers often confused the first two. The scholastics emphasized the unity of soul and body, the creation of each soul for the body, and its survival of death. (*See also* IMMORTALITY; ORIGEN; RESURRECTION.)

soutane

See CASSOCK.

South India

See CHURCH OF SOUTH INDIA.

Southcott, Joanna (1750–1814)

A farmer's daughter from Devon, she joined the Methodists and in 1792 startled them by claiming to be the woman of Revelation 12, 'clothed with the sun and the moon under her feet'. She began to seal 144,000 elect (Rev. 7:4) – certificating individuals with a red seal, at charges from 12s to 21s – and later said she would give birth to the Prince of Peace, but she fell into a trance and died of brain disease. For a long time Joanna's followers demanded that the Archbishop of Canterbury should open her box, but when this was finally done in 1927 it only contained a woman's nightcap and a lottery ticket. Jezreel's Tower at Gillingham in Kent, built by Joanna's disciples to anticipate the Second Coming, was demolished in the 1960s.

Southwell, Robert (1561–95)

Jesuit priest and poet. He was educated at DOUAI and Paris and sent on the English mission. After success underground he was betrayed, imprisoned for three years and then executed. Southwell's poems, written mostly in prison, are short lyrics, with a long sequence on Mary and Christ, and have been appreciated by both Catholics and Protestants. Feast day 21 February. (*See also* CAMPION.)

Spartas, Reuben Makasa
(1899–1982)

Founder of the African Greek Orthodox Church in Uganda. Brought up an Anglican, he strove to assert African independence, but in 1946 his church was admitted to the Greek Orthodox communion. A sportsman and politician, Spartas was imprisoned and then served in the Ugandan parliament. Conflict arose with the Greek Church over financial support, and his church broke away but remained orthodox in faith and liturgy.

SPCK

The Society for Promoting Christian Knowledge, founded in 1698 for educational and missionary work, and now concerned especially with publishing religious literature.

Spener, Philipp Jakob
(1635–1705)

German theologian and a leading PIETIST. As minister at Strasbourg and Frankfurt he revived evangelical fervour in the Lutheran Church, holding house meetings and giving the laity a fuller part in church life. He was opposed by some theologians but supported by rulers, and pietism became established, with insistence on personal religious life continuing to influence German Protestantism.

SPG

The Society for the Propagation of the Gospel in foreign parts. An Anglican organization founded in 1701 for missionary work, especially of the High

Church kind. (*See also* CHURCH MISSIONARY SOCIETY.)

Spirit

See HOLY SPIRIT.

Spirit, Brethren of the

See BRETHREN OF THE COMMON LIFE.

spiritual direction

See DIRECTION.

Spiritual Exercises

A manual of religious meditations and rules composed by IGNATIUS LOYOLA in 1522–41. Divided into four sections called Weeks, the First Week is on sin and its consequences, the Second contemplates the life of Christ, the Third Christ's sufferings and death, and the Fourth Week his resurrection.

spiritual healing

See HEALING; UNCTION.

spiritualism

In New England in 1848 the Fox sisters claimed to be able to communicate with the dead. Spiritualist societies grew up, especially in the Anglo-Saxon world, and some spiritualist churches claim to be orthodox Christian. A Society for Psychical Research was founded in London in 1882 to investigate mediumistic experiments; the results were inconclusive. Spiritualism has been denounced by most established churches, especially Roman Catholic.

spirituality

Formerly indicating the clergy as an order of society, and then distinguishing the spiritual from the material, spirituality in modern religious terms indicates rather the life of prayer and discipline, perhaps with MYSTICAL elements.

spirituals

Spiritual hymns and songs have been claimed as products of the evangelical revival, as protests against injustice, as adapted African songs, and as blending European and African rhythms. Whatever their origins, spirituals include different styles of jazz, suited to both black and white traditions, and there are attempts at adaptation to church music. The main force of spirituals is in American Baptist and Pentecostal churches. (*See also* HYMNS; REVIVALISM.)

sponsor

See GODPARENT.

Spurgeon, Charles Haddon (1834–92)

English Baptist minister. In 1854 he was called to Southwark, London, and drew such crowds by preaching that a large Metropolitan Tabernacle was built for him. He ministered there until his death, with a college for preachers, an orphanage and a centre for religious literature. He published 3,000 sermons and had over a million readers. Spurgeon was a strict Calvinist, and left the Baptist Union in 1887 through his opposition to biblical CRITICISM and liberal theology. (*See also* CLIFFORD.)

state and religion

Attitudes of governments towards organized or popular religion have varied considerably in the 20th century. In 1900 there were 145 governments which regarded their countries as religious, 78 nominally secular, and none admittedly atheistic. By 1980 the number of religious countries had decreased to 101, and atheistic governments numbered 30. However, the collapse of COMMUNISM in Eastern Europe in the 1980s brought a decline in militant atheism and religious influence grew, even when not officially established. (*See also* MISSION.)

Stations of the Cross

Fourteen pictures or carvings round the walls of Catholic churches, for devotions during Lent and Passiontide. They depict incidents from the passion of Christ: (1) Jesus condemned to death; (2) Jesus receiving the Cross; (3) Jesus falling under its weight; (4) Jesus meeting his mother; (5) Simon of Cyrene carrying the Cross; (6) the face of Jesus wiped by VERONICA; (7) a second fall; (8) meeting the women of Jerusalem; (9) a third fall; (10) Jesus is stripped; (11) Jesus is nailed to the Cross; (12) Jesus dying on the Cross; (13) the body taken down; (14) the body laid in the tomb. (*See also* SEVEN SORROWS; WESTMINSTER CATHEDRAL.)

Steiner, Rudolf (1861–1925)

Born in Hungary, he used scientific terms for new ideas. Secretary of the Theosophical Society in Germany, he broke with it by proclaiming ANTHROPOSOPHY, giving a central place to humanity and seeking OCCULT powers by MEDITATION. Steiner's system rejected the AVATARS of THEOSOPHY and was more clearly Christian. His ideas have been applied in agriculture and in schools for the disabled.

Stephen

First DEACON and martyr (Acts 6–7), 'full of faith and the Holy Spirit', appointed by the apostles to 'serve tables' but performing wonders. The long speech attributed to him in Acts 7 gives a Christian interpretation of Hebrew history, ending with the persecution of the prophets and the 'Just One'. His enraged hearers, without formal trial, cast him out and stoned him. Dying, Stephen said he saw the SON OF MAN at the right hand of God. Then 'he fell asleep', rendered bluntly 'died' by unimaginative modern translators. Saul consented to his death, which made such an impression that he soon became PAUL. Stephen has always

*Two Stations of the Cross from Lourdes: top, Station 8, meeting the women of Jerusalem,
below, Station 10, Jesus is stripped.*

been a popular saint, the day after Christmas being 'the feast of Stephen'.

stigmata

Greek, 'marks': the prints of the nails and spear in the body of the crucified Jesus, said to have been reproduced in various medieval and modern saints. The first reported appearance of the stigmata was on FRANCIS OF ASSISI, then on women such as the CATHARINES OF SIENA and GENOA, and in modern times on the Italian priest Padre Pio. (*See also* WOUNDS.)

stole

From Greek, 'robe': a long thin strip of silk or cloth, worn by priest and deacons, the COLOUR varying with the occasion.

stoup

See HOLY WATER.

Strauss, David Friedrich
(1808–74)

German Protestant theologian and biblical critic. In 1836 he interpreted supernatural elements in the Gospel as 'myth' in his *Leben Jesu* (translated into English as *The Life of Jesus* by the novelist George Eliot in 1846). Strauss lost his university post at Tübingen, and finally denied Christianity in favour of scientific materialism. Though largely negative, Strauss's work had a profound effect on biblical study. (*See also* BULTMANN; MYTH; SCHLEIERMACHER.

Studd, Charles Thomas
(1862–1931)

A noted cricketer, he was one of the Cambridge Seven who volunteered for missionary work and went to China in 1885 with the evangelical China Inland Mission. Bad health forced him to return home in 1894, and six years later he went to India but again had to come back through sickness. Against medical advice he went to central Africa in 1910

and stayed for over 20 years. Studd founded the Heart of Africa Mission and planned a world strategy for unevangelized countries.

Studdert-Kennedy, Geoffrey Anketell (1883–1929)

Anglican chaplain in the First World War whose nickname of Woodbine Willie, from the Woodbine cigarettes he distributed, made him popular in the forces and at home. His unconventional views, work with the Industrial Christian Fellowship, and light religious poetry gave him wide influence.

Student Christian Movement (SCM)

Developing from movements at Cambridge, England, at the end of the 19th century, through groups, conferences, and a publishing house, the SCM sought to interpret the Christian faith for the modern world and encourage missionary work. Interdenominational, it helped the ecumenical movement and the World Student Christian Federation. With a peak in the early years of the 20th century, and despite developments in Asia and Africa, it has been overshadowed by FUNDAMENTALIST and CHARISMATIC organizations. (*See* ECUMENISM.)

stylite

See PILLAR SAINTS; SIMEON STYLITES.

suffering servant

A figure identified in four passages in Isaiah, 'my servant whom I uphold' (42:1–4, 49:1–6, 50:4–9 and especially 52:13–53:12), called by commentators the suffering servant. Jewish interpretation identifies this figure with Israel, and Christians with the suffering Christ.

suffragan

From medieval Latin for an assistant: a bishop appointed to help a diocesan bishop, and also any bishop asked to assist his archbishop.

suffrages

From Latin via French for prayers seeking support or favour: these are petitions or intercessions in general or particular terms. Suffrages are normally versicles with responses, including the Lord's Prayer and ending with a collect.

suicide

This was long regarded as a sin against the Creator and an offence against society. Suicides were forbidden Christian funerals and burial in consecrated ground. Modern psychopathology has shown the irrelevance of criminal law to the action; restrictions have been relaxed, and treatment provided to those tempted to suicide. (*See also* SAMARITANS.)

Summa theologica

The chief work of THOMAS AQUINAS, written between 1265 and 1274. The *Summa* is in three main parts. The first considers God and all creatures proceeding from him. The second discusses God as the end of man, and human movements to God, with theological and cardinal virtues. The third was designed to deal with sacraments and last things, but was left unfinished.

Summit Lighthouse

See PROPHET, ELIZABETH.

summum bonum

Latin, 'chief good': the goal or final principle in an ethical system.

Sundar Singh

See SADHU.

Sunday

In English the word Sun-day translated the Latin *dies solis*, for the day anciently consecrated to worship of the sun. In Christian usage it referred to Christ as the Sun of Righteousness and was called the Day of the Lord. (*See also* LORD'S DAY; SABBATH.)

Sunday Schools

See RAIKES.

supererogation

Doing more than duty requires: counsels of perfection. In the middle ages it was thought to set up a reserve fund of merit that could be drawn on by sinners. The notion was rejected at the Reformation, Article 14 of the Book of Common Prayer asserting that 'Works of Supererogation cannot be taught without arrogancy and impiety.' (*See also* PERFECTION; SCRUPLES.)

superintendent

The Greek term *episcopos* meant 'overseer' or 'superintendent', and became 'bishop'. To avoid prelatical suggestions, German Lutherans and Scottish Presbyterians adopted the word 'superintendent'. The Methodist Church later took it over for a senior minister in charge of a circuit. (*See also* BISHOP; CIRCUIT; PRELATE; PRESBYTER.)

Supremacy, Act of

In 1534 Henry VIII assumed the title of 'the only supreme head in earth of the Church of England'. Repealed by Mary, the Act was restored by Elizabeth I in 1559, claiming that the monarch was 'the only supreme governor of this realm . . . in all spiritual or ecclesiastical things or causes as temporal'. (*See also* PRAEMUNIRE, PROTESTANTISM.)

surplice

From medieval Latin, 'over a fur garment': a white linen vestment originally worn over the fur coats of the clergy in cold northern countries. Now worn generally over the CASSOCK by clergy and choir, its use in preaching was much debated in earlier times.

Sursum corda

Latin, 'lift up your hearts': ancient phrase in the liturgy of the EUCHARIST just before the preface. The use of these words can be traced back to the third century.

Suso, Henry (1295–1366)

German Dominican monk and mystic, a pupil of Meister ECKHART, whom he defended. His autobiography, *The Life of the Servant*, describes self-tortures, pricking the name of Jesus, IHS, over his heart till the blood flowed, and later wearing a hair garment with sharp nails and carrying a cross with nails. He continued these masochistic exercises till angels told him God did not wish him to keep on, and he 'threw everything into the river'.

swastika

From Sanskrit, 'well-being', this ancient Indian symbol spread across the world, to ancient Europe, Africa and America. It was probably a symbol of the sun, the arms as rays. The adoption of the swastika by the Nazis was a late distortion of its symbolical and magical use.

Swedenborg, Emanuel (1688–1772)

Swedish scientist. He expounded mystical 'correspondences' between material and spiritual, and re-interpreted the Trinity: the Father as love, the Son as wisdom, the Spirit as energy, set forth in his *Divine Love and Wisdom* (1763). Swedenborg applied his ideas through a New Church, not an organization but a fellowship of like thinkers. He spent much of his life in Sweden, Holland and England, and died in London though his remains were transferred to Stockholm. Some of his followers founded the Church of the New Jerusalem in 1787, and in America the General Convention of the New Jerusalem is the oldest of Swedenborgian churches there.

Swift, Jonathan (1667–1745)

Anglican Dean of St Patrick's in Dublin, best known for his writings, most published anonymously. *A Tale of a Tub* (1704) was a satire on 'corruptions in religion and learning', while *Gulliver's Travels* (1726) satirized political and religious dissension and became world-famous.

Swiss Guard

Soldiers at St Peter's basilica in Rome and the Papal Palace. They were introduced in the 16th century and now number about 100 men from all the Swiss cantons, with red, yellow and blue uniforms designed by Michelangelo.

The Swiss Guard: Founded in the 16th century by Pope Julius II, 100 men from all the Swiss cantons act as guardians of the papal palace.

Swithin (d. 862)

Bishop of Winchester, he wished to be buried in the churchyard so that the 'sweet rain' might fall on his grave; but the monks put his body in the choir on 15 July and it rained for 40 days, according to legend. There are several versions of a popular rhyme: 'If St Swithin's day do rain, for forty days it will remain. If St Swithin's day be fair, for forty days 'twill rain nae mair.' His day is still 15 July.

Syllabus of Errors
(Syllabus errorum)

Eighty theses attacking supposed modern errors, issued by Pope Pius IX in 1864. They considered pantheism, rationalism, socialism, communism, liberalism and other subjects. There was widespread protest, led by Gladstone in England, and a ban on publication in France.

synagogue

Greek for a Jewish 'meeting place' for worship. Established after the return of the Jews from exile in the sixth century BCE, some synagogues probably replaced older local 'high places' for those who could not travel to Jerusalem frequently for temple worship. Synagogues at Nazareth and Capernaum are mentioned in the Gospels.

synod

From Greek, 'meeting of ways': a term used of councils of clergy and laity, usually on a regional basis, to regulate church life, doctrine and discipline.

synoptic gospels

From Greek, 'seeing together': a term applied to the first three gospels, of Matthew, Mark and Luke, which give a general survey of the life of Jesus, contrasted with John, which is more in the nature of discourses. The 'synoptic problem' is the relationship of these three gospels to one another, the primacy of Mark and its use by the other two. There is also non-Markan material from the sayings of Q, and separate sources of Matthew and Luke, sometimes called M and L. (*See also* Q.)

Syrian churches

See MALABAR; MELCHITES; MONOPHYSITISM; THOMAS.)

syzygy

Greek, 'pair', yoked together, conjunction or opposition: a word used by GNOSTICS for cosmic opposites, male and female, like Chinese yang and yin.

T

tabernacle

In Roman Catholic churches, a receptacle for the elements of the Eucharist. (*See also* PYX.)

table

The Book of Common Prayer refers to the Table or Lord's Table and this term, or Communion Table, is used by LOW CHURCHES and in the FREE CHURCHES. High Church Anglicans prefer the term ALTAR.

taboo

See RATANA.

Taizé

A small village in central France where a Swiss Protestant minister, Brother Roger Schulz, settled in 1940 to found an ecumenical community of reconciliation and peace. It is near the great Benedictine monastery of CLUNY and has evolved a liturgy from both Reformed and Catholic traditions. Taizé became popular with young people and there are

Community centre, Taizé: An international youth community in central France, with an emphasis upon a common liturgical life of worship and mission.

annual gatherings at its great church, reconciling French and German, black and white, parents and children, husbands and wives. (*See also* POVERTY; SILENCE.)

Tallis, Thomas (1505–85)

Organist and musical composer, called the 'father of English Cathedral Music'. Reflecting Catholic and Reformed traditions, he composed liturgical settings in Latin and anthems for Anglican services, and was patronized by both Mary and Elizabeth I.

Taniguchi Masaharu

See SEICHO NO IE.

Tara Centers

Organized since 1980 to spread the teachings of Benjamin Creme (b. 1922). A Scottish artist and a student of BLAVATSKY, Creme claims to have received messages from spiritual masters. In 1982 he advertised in newspapers in London that Christ or Maitreya (the next Buddha) would make himself known in two months. When that failed the cause was given as public apathy, but Creme promises that Christ-Maitreya will soon appear.

Tate, Nahum (1652–1715) and Brady, Nicholas (1659–1726)

Irish Anglican clergymen who put the Psalms into rather artificial verse, altered some of Shakespeare's plays, and wrote the libretto for Purcell's *Dido and Aeneas*.

Tatian

See DIATESSARON.

Tauler, John (1300–61)

German mystic. He became a Dominican at Strasbourg and was influenced by ECKHART and SUSO. Known chiefly for his sermons, Tauler stressed the dwelling of God in the soul, which

should abandon itself to the divine will and live in charity and self-sacrifice.

Taylor, Jeremy (1613–67)

Anglican bishop, theologian and moralist. His devotional works, *Holy Living* and *Holy Dying*, were popular for their graceful style and moderate content, though Taylor was accused of minimizing ORIGINAL SIN. He showed rare understanding of sexual relationships, placing married life above celibacy as 'a union of all things excellent', and recommending intercourse 'to endear each other'.

Te Deum

'Thee, O God': a Latin CANTICLE from the fourth century. The first part is to the Father, the second to the Son, and closing lines were added later. The Te Deum was part of MATINS, and remained in daily use, in English, in the Book of Common Prayer. (*See also* SABAOTH.)

teacher of righteousness

The DEAD SEA SCROLLS refer to a teacher raised up to guide the community who knew 'all the mysteries of the prophets'. He forecast the end of the world and, being persecuted by a wicked priest, had to flee into exile. Some writers identify him with Jesus, but the description could fit other figures.

teaching of the twelve apostles

See DIDACHÉ.

teetotalism

See TEMPERANCE.

Teilhard de Chardin, Pierre (1881–1955)

French priest, scientist and philosopher. From Paris he went to China for 20 years, doing research near Peking and sharing the discovery of the 200,000 year-old Peking Man. Back in France he was refused permission by his

JESUIT order to apply for a university post or publish papers on evolution. He moved to New York and died there four years later. None of his books were published during his life, but he became famous with *The Phenomenon of Man* (1959).

teleology

Greek 'doctrine of the end', arguing for the existence of God on the basis of the design and purpose of the world. Coming from Greek philosophy the argument has been attacked by evolutionists, but in a modified form it is maintained that the existence and survival of life give evidence of an intelligent Creator.

televangelism

Modern term for the use of radio and television for religious preaching. From the 1970s American preachers, sometimes only loosely connected with churches, had their own stations and following, notably Pat Robertson, Jerry Falwell, Jim Bakker and Jimmy Swaggart. Transmitted to Africa and other continents, such programmes had huge audiences, though how far they could build up church communities remained an open question. (*See also* MCPHERSON; WORLDWIDE CHURCH OF GOD.)

Tempels, Placide (1906–77)

Belgian Roman Catholic missionary and writer who sought to adapt mission teaching to African thought forms. His book *Bantu Philosophy* (in English from Flemish and French) expounded the concept of 'vital force', but was disapproved of by his superiors and Tempels was kept away from the Congo for three years. On return he founded JAMAA, 'family', a union of Christ and family. Tempels was sent home for good but Jamaa survives underground. (*See also* KAGAME.)

temperance

One of the CARDINAL VIRTUES, and taught by Plato and the Stoics as fundamental. In the modern West it has been particularly associated with temperate or total abstinence from alcohol. Temperance unions were founded in Britain from 1826, an Independent Order of Good Templars in New York in 1851, and a Swiss Blue Cross from 1872. The churches have varied in their attitudes, the SALVATION ARMY strictly forbidding alcohol but most others leaving it to the individual conscience. (*See also* RECHABITES.)

Templars, Knights Templar

After the capture of Jerusalem by the First Crusade in 1099, King Baldwin founded the 'Poor Knights of Christ' to defend the city from the Muslims. They received support from the West, adopted a form of monastic rule and spread to most countries in Europe. They built monasteries and castles, but did not prevent the recapture of Jerusalem by Saladin in 1187. The Templars became wealthy, but were charged with immorality and heresy and the order was suppressed in 1312. The Temple Church in London is a round building modelled on the Church of the Holy Sepulchre in Jerusalem. (*See also* BERNARD; CRUSADES; HOSPITALLERS.)

Temple Mount Movement

A term including Israeli and other Jews, and some American Christian fundamentalists, who seek the rebuilding of the Temple in Jerusalem, which would cause a holy war because the site is occupied by the Muslim shrine of the DOME OF THE ROCK. The Temple Mount Faithful attempted in 1990 to lay a temple cornerstone, which caused a riot in which 19 Muslims were killed by Israeli soldiers. The Jerusalem Temple Foundation (JTF) was most active in the 1980s as a link between Jewish philanthropists and Christian evangelicals who believe that the restoration of the Temple must precede the Second Coming of Christ.

Ten Articles

Moderate reforms proposed by the Church Convocation in 1536 at the wish of Henry VIII. They upheld the SACRAMENTS of baptism, penance and the Eucharist, but did not mention TRANSUBSTANTIATION. (*See also* SIX ARTICLES; THIRTY-NINE ARTICLES.)

Ten Commandments

See COMMANDMENTS.

Tenebrae

Latin, 'darkness': morning prayers for the last three days of HOLY WEEK, during which lights are extinguished one by one. The service ends with the Penitential Psalm 51.

Teresa, Mother

Agnes Gouxha Bojaxhiu (1910–97). From Yugoslavia of Albanian parents,

Mother Teresa on a visit in 1993 to the Missionaries of Charity, who have opened a house in Edinburgh.

she joined a congregation in Bengal and taught in Darjeeling and Calcutta. After brief medical training she founded the Missionaries of Charity, with houses in Calcutta ministering to the sick and dying, lepers and the starving. In 1979 she received the Nobel Peace Prize, and in 1996 her Sisters of Charity had 4,000 workers. She was succeeded by Sister Nirmala.

Teresa of Avila (1515–82)

From an old Spanish family, she entered the CARMELITE nunnery at Avila in 1533, and after some illness she undertook reforms by founding houses for monks and nuns of the primitive rule of Discalced Carmelites. Of strong character and practical ability, she was helped by JOHN OF THE CROSS, as also in her mystical life. She wrote *The Way of Perfection*, spiritual direction for her nuns, an autobiography and *The Interior Castle* describing her own experiences and 'spiritual marriage'. Feast day 15 October. (*See also* RAPTURE.)

Teresa of Lisieux

See THÉRÈSE.

tertiary

A member of a 'THIRD ORDER' of Franciscans, Dominicans or Carmelites.

Tertullian, Quintus Septimius Florens (160–220 CE)

Born in Carthage in North Africa, after legal education he became a Christian and joined the MONTANIST apocalyptic movement. He was the first theologian to write in Latin, and also the first to use the term 'Trinity'. He spoke of martyrdom as a 'second baptism', using a phrase which has been rendered as 'the blood of the martyrs is the seed of the church.' Tertullian was generally orthodox and anticipated AUGUSTINE as an African Latin theologian.

testament

See NEW/OLD TESTAMENT.

testimony

In some evangelical churches public testimony is given by members of the congregation after their CONVERSION.

Tetragrammaton

See ADONAI.

Tetzel, John (1465–1519)

German Dominican preacher. When in 1516 INDULGENCES were offered by the Pope for building the Church of St Peter in Rome, Tetzel went round Germany extracting payments in the crassest terms. This roused LUTHER, whose Ninety-five Theses condemned 'those who assert that a soul straightway flies out [of purgatory] as a coin tinkles in the collection box'. Tetzel replied with counter-theses, but the Pope's NUNCIO disowned him and tried to persuade Luther to keep silent.

Thaddeus

One of the apostles named by Mark (3:18) and Matthew, also called Lebbaeus in some texts. He is not mentioned by Luke who has Judas son of James in his place (6:16). Nothing more is known of him.

Thecla

A second-century apocryphal Greek book, Acts of Paul, or Paul and Thecla, provided romantic interest for Paul. It is said that Thecla was a virgin who 'yearned after Paul and sought him', dressing herself as a man. Paul sent her to Iconium to preach, and a long appendix says she lived to the age of 90 and was hidden in a cave against evildoers. A church was built over her tomb near Seleucia and Thecla was venerated in East and West, notably at Tarragona.

theism

A term first used by the Cambridge Platonist Cudworth in 1678, denoting belief in God: the opposite of atheism and distinct from other forms of belief. (*See also* CAMBRIDGE PLATONISTS; DEISM; PANTHEISM.

theocracy

Greek, 'government by God': a term used by Josephus for the rule of the Hebrew people from Moses to the monarchy. Theocratic rule was claimed by medieval Popes, by CALVIN at Geneva, by Cromwell's Commonwealth, and by Scottish Presbyterians. Vestiges of theocracy remain in those states, including Britain and the USA, which recognize God as the source of their authority.

theodicy

Greek for 'God's justice', a word coined by the German philosopher Leibniz in 1710 to defend divine justice and goodness in face of evil and suffering. The optimism of Leibniz was ridiculed by Voltaire in *Candide* (1759), which mockingly suggests that 'all is for the best in the best of possible worlds.'

Theodosius

Roman emperor who in 380 CE established Christianity as the state religion, ruling that 'all the various nations which are subject to our Clemency and Moderation, should continue in the profession of that religion which was delivered to the Romans by the divine Apostle Peter . . . and assume the title of Catholic Christians.' But heretics should be 'entirely excluded'. Theodosius himself was disciplined by Bishop AMBROSE for harshness in battle.

Theologia Germanica

An anonymous mystical book of the late 14th century. In 54 short chapters it teaches the way of perfection, by three stages of purification, enlightenment and union with God. It follows the mystical tradition of ECKHART and TAULER, and was admired by LUTHER and the PIETISTS, and many others.

theological virtues

Faith, hope and love (1 Cor. 13:13), regarded as the gifts of grace, in distinction from the natural or CARDINAL VIRTUES.

theology

Greek, 'doctrine of God'. In Christian usage, natural theology deals with the knowledge of God gained from nature and reason; revealed theology is the study of divinely revealed truths in the Bible, from the story of divine creation to that of redemption in Christ. Protestant theology has tended to concentrate on the Bible, whereas Catholic theology sees REVELATION also in Church tradition. Liberal theology seeks confirmation in conscience and reason. (*See also* MIRACLE.)

theophany

From Greek, 'appearance of God', as to Moses on Sinai, or in the Transfiguration of Christ. In early times theophany was used of the EPIPHANY, the manifestation of Christ to the gentile MAGI.

theosophy

Greek, 'divine wisdom': a term formerly and generally applied to natural and PANTHEISTIC MYSTICISM, in Hinduism or Buddhism, Hellenistic GNOSTICISM, Jewish KABBALAH, and writers such as BOEHME and SWEDENBORG. Since the 19th century the word has been used of the Theosophical Society, founded in New York in 1875, with its mixture of Eastern and Western ideas. (*See also* AETHERIUS; ANTHROPOSOPHY; BESANT; BLAVATSKY; NEW AGE; OLCOTT.)

Theotokos

Greek, 'God-bearer': a title of the Virgin Mary, affirmed by councils at Ephesus in

431 CE and CHALCEDON in 451 CE. (*See also* NESTORIUS.)

Thérèse of Lisieux (1873–97)

Thérèse Martin was born in northern France to devout parents who had nine children, four of whom died in infancy; the other five girls all left their widowed father to enter the cloister. Thérèse went to a strict Carmelite convent at Lisieux, where she developed tuberculosis but was not allowed warmth. She had intense consciousness of the divine presence and wrote *L'histoire d'une âme* (*Story of a Soul*), before her early death. A large traditionalist basilica was erected for the many pilgrims for the cult of 'the little Flower'. She was canonized in 1925.

Thessalonians, Epistle to the

PAUL visited Thessalonica, modern Salonika, and the two canonical epistles to the Church there are probably his earliest letters, sent from Corinth. The first gives assurances and exhortations and speaks of the Second Coming. The second seeks to correct notions about it and is more like an APOCALYPSE, reminiscent of the book of REVELATION, ending with commendations.

third orders

Organizations of religious societies, especially Franciscans and Dominicans, distinguished from fully professed members of first or second orders. In a third order one may live in the world, or in community taking vows, devoted to teaching, nursing, or mission. (*See* TERTIARY.)

Thirty-Nine Articles

Approved by Convocation under Elizabeth I in 1563 and 1571, these statements of doctrine were composed in the light of Roman Catholic and Protestant controversies, and seem intentionally ambiguous on some points, All Anglican clergy had to sign, or later affirm, the

ARTICLES, and while they were not imposed on most laity, until the 19th century they were enforced on those wishing to enter the only two English universities, Oxford and Cambridge, thus excluding Nonconformists, Free Church and Roman Catholic. (*See also* NEWMAN; SIX ARTICLES; TEN ARTICLES; WESTMINSTER CONFESSION.)

Thomas

Apostle, named in all four Gospels, but in John called Didymus, 'twin'. In John also he offered to die with Jesus (11:16); he has been rather unfairly called 'Doubting Thomas' from his first questioning and then fully confessing the risen Christ (John 20:24ff). Legend said he went to India as a slave and was martyred there. Indian Syrian Christians call themselves 'Christians of St Thomas' and assert that he was buried at St Thomas's Mount, near Madras, an improbable site, still shown, near a famous Hindu temple. Feast day 21 December. (*See also* MALABAR; NAG HAMMADI.)

Thomas, Gospel according to

Formerly known only in fragments and brief references, the text of a Gospel of THOMAS in Coptic translation was found at NAG HAMMADI in 1945. It dates from the fourth century, based on a Greek original probably of the second century. This apocryphal Gospel speaks of the Kingdom of God as both outside and inside, and of Jesus as passing understanding, and it considers that women must become male to enter the Kingdom. Some have suggested that this gospel contains traditions as old as the canonical works, but it is derivative and speculative, certainly not by the apostle Thomas but reflecting the thought of some early GNOSTIC Christians. An Acts of Thomas is later, in Greek and Syriac, recounting this apostle's supposed missionary activities in Syria and India and his martyrdom. (*See also* MALABAR.)

Thomas à Becket

See BECKET.

Thomas à Kempis

See KEMPIS; IMITATION OF CHRIST.

Thomas Aquinas (1225–74)

Italian Dominican theologian, called the 'Angelic Doctor', born in a family castle near Aquino. He studied under Albertus Magnus in Paris, and back in Rome conceived his great SUMMA THEOLOGICA, completing the second part in 1272. He previously wrote a *Summa contra Gentiles* to help missionaries in Spain and North Africa. On the way to a council at Lyons he had an accident, was taken to a monastery and died a few days later. Thomas's writings, his masterly systematization of medieval Catholic thought, became the basis for later theology, and as THOMISM guaranteed his place as the most important and influential medieval theologian. Feast day 7 March. (*See also* ALBERT THE GREAT.)

Thomism

Systematic expression of theological doctrine by THOMAS AQUINAS and his successors.

thurible

See CENSER.

Tilak, Narayan Vaman (1862–1919)

Born to an Indian priestly family near Bombay, he wrote poetry in Marathi. By chance he received a copy of the New Testament which confirmed his views which were going beyond Hinduism. He was baptized in 1895 and for a time was a Presbyterian minister, but he followed the unattached life of a poet and sought the indigenization of Christianity. He wrote hundreds of hymns in Marathi; 'One Who is All Unfit to Count' was translated into English and set to music. (*See also* NILES.)

Tillich, Paul (1886–1965)

German Protestant pastor and theologian. In the First World War he was an army chaplain. He held several university chairs, but criticized National Socialism, supported the Jews and was dismissed from his post. He went to New York in 1933 and was professor at Columbia, Union, Harvard and Chicago. Tillich wrote many books, including *Systematic Theology*, and popular sermons in *The Shaking of the Foundations*.

Timothy

Disciple and companion of Paul, son of a Jewess, Eunice, and a Greek, he was circumcised by Paul to placate critics (Acts 16:3). Paul sent Timothy to Ephesus, and according to Eusebius he became first bishop there. He is said to have been martyred for opposing licentious festivities of Artemis.

Letters to Timothy and Titus are called the PASTORAL EPISTLES, and were probably written in the last year of Paul's life. The first to Timothy sets out the duties and qualities of bishops and deacons, encourages elders and widows, and insists on sound doctrine. The second letter provides encouragement, warns against false teachers, and gives personal news.

Tischendorf

See CODEX.

tithe

From old English for 'tenth': a payment of a tenth part of produce of the land to support the clergy and church. A money payment was often made in its place, and later tithes were replaced by an annuity on land paid to the state tax department. Some evangelical churches practise tithing to support the Church, and with Mormons it is a strict obligation.

Titus

A companion and disciple of Paul, who called him 'my true child in a common faith' (1:4). Paul sent him on missions to Corinth and Crete, and according to Eusebius he was first bishop of Crete. The Epistle to Titus is the shortest of the PASTORAL EPISTLES, dealing with the duties of elders, bishops, old men, women and servants, exhorting to virtue and the avoidance of foolish questions. Feast day 6 February. (*See also* TIMOTHY.)

Toc H

Named after Talbot House (Toc from signallers' code for T): a club for soldiers in the First World War, founded in 1915 by an Anglican chaplain Neville Talbot and T. B. ('Tubby') Clayton. It developed a number of houses, and after the war spread widely with members doing social service.

Toleration Acts

In 1689 Dissenters in England were allowed to license meeting houses and maintain preachers and teachers, provided they took the oaths of allegiance and supremacy to William III, against the Roman Catholic James II. A Scottish Act in 1712 gave similar freedom to dissenters from the Church of Scotland. Non-Trinitarians were not given such rights until 1812. (*See also* CATHOLIC EMANCIPATION; FREE CHURCHES; NONJURORS.)

Tolpuddle Martyrs

Six agricultural workers at Tolpuddle, Dorset, five of them Methodists led by local preacher George Loveless. In 1833 they organized a trade union, were charged with administering illegal oaths, and sentenced to seven years' transportation to Australia. There were nationwide protests and after two years the labourers were pardoned and returned to England.

tongues

See GLOSSOLALIA.

tonsure

From Latin for shaving: the crown of the head of clergy is shaved in Roman Catholicism and the whole head in Eastern Orthodoxy, but clergy in some Western countries are exempt from this tonsure.

Toplady, Augustus Montague

(1740–78)

Anglican clergyman; he became a Methodist but developed extreme Calvinist views and attacked WESLEY and ARMINIANISM in the Church of England. He is best known for his hymn, 'Rock of Ages'.

Torah

See PENTATEUCH.

Toronto Blessing

In 1995 at the Airport Vineyard Church in Toronto, Canada, REVIVALISM produced a 'blessing' of laughing, crying, shaking, fainting and animal noises. These were held to bring heightened spiritual powers and healings. Such phenomena spread to other parts of the world and were claimed as new spiritual graces, but similar manifestations had occurred in previous revivals. (*See also* CAMP MEETING; SHAKERS.)

Torquemada, Tomás de

(1420–98)

Grand Inquisitor of Spain from 1483. He sought out Jews and Muslims who practised their faith secretly, and had Jews who refused baptism expelled from Spain in 1492. He wrote a manual for inquisitors, giving the methods to be used, and was responsible for some 2,000 burnings as well as torture and loss of property for thousands more. (*See also* INQUISITION; MALLEUS; MARRANOS.)

Torres, Camilo (1929–66)

Born in Bogotá, Colombia, he studied modern Catholicism and Marxism at Louvain. Back lecturing at Bogotá, he organized students as social workers and began a school and farm. The authorities objecting to his social activities, he reverted to lay status, though always regarding himself as a priest. Torres joined an armed guerilla group and was killed by government forces. (*See also* CARDENAL; LIBERATION THEOLOGY.)

total abstinence

See TEMPERANCE.

total depravity

A Calvinistic term for the entire corruption of human nature. The WESTMINSTER CONFESSION said that at the FALL Adam and Eve became 'wholly defiled in all the faculties and parts of soul and body', and their descendants are 'utterly indisposed, disabled and made opposite to all good, and wholly inclined to all evil'. According to this dire doctrine there is no natural knowledge of God, as the scholastics held, and no difference between good and bad people, as the Gospel shows.

total immersion

See BAPTISM.

touching

See GESTURES; KING'S EVIL.

tracts

Pamphlets with a religious or moral purpose, used at least from the time of WYCLIFFE. A Religious Tract Society was founded in 1799 by Anglicans and Nonconformists, and published missionary propaganda in 200 languages. It was absorbed into the United Society for Christian Literature in 1935.

Tracts for the Times were published from 1833 by the Oxford or ANGLO-CATHOLIC movement, which came to be called Tractarianism. (*See also* MARPRELATE TRACTS; NEWMAN; PUSEY.

Traherne, Thomas (1636–74)

Anglican country rector and chaplain at Teddington near London, where he died. His remarkable poetry and prose remained unknown till discovered in notebooks in 1896. The *Poetical Works* were published in 1903, and *Centuries of Meditation* in 1908. Traherne's writings, now famous, express unusual joy in creation, pantheistic and optimistic, in 'Rapture' and 'Thanksgivings'.

transcendent

What is excellent, surpassing all other: used of God as existing apart from the material universe and not subject to its limitations.

Transcendentalism described 19th-century optimism, especially in America, which believed in an Over-soul, union with which brought transcending of the individual self.

Transcendental Meditation (TM) was propounded by a Spiritual Regeneration Movement in 1959, as a technique for developing latent potentialities.

transept

In a cross-shaped church this is the part that traverses the central space between nave and chancel, either arm being the north or south transept. Transepts provided space around tombs or for tables for gifts.

Transfiguration

Change of form or appearance, especially the Transfiguration of Christ to selected disciples (Mark 9:2ff and parallels). The vision gave testimony, of Moses for the law and Elijah for the prophets, to Christ and his future glory. Some have regarded the Transfiguration as a resurrection experience. The mountain has been identified with Hermon or Tabor. The commemoration is on 6 August. (*See also* THEOPHANY.)

transubstantiation

Often thought to mean that the bread and wine are changed into the material body and blood of Christ, at consecration in the Eucharist, the medieval doctrine taught that the 'substance' is changed but the 'accidents' or appearance of colour, shape and taste remain the same. This theory developed in the 12th century and was affirmed by the Council of TRENT in 1551. But Article 28 of the Book of Common Prayer declared that the change of substance 'cannot be proved by Holy Writ' and had given rise to 'many superstitions'. More positively, the Body of Christ is eaten 'in a heavenly and spiritual manner'. (*See also* CONSUBSTANTIATION.)

Trappists

A reform of CISTERCIANS of the Strict Observance, introduced at the abbey of La Trappe in Normandy in 1664. The expulsion of Trappist monks in the French Revolution took them to other parts of Europe, Asia and America. Trappists emphasize liturgical worship, long hours of absolute silence, and vegetarianism. (*See also* MERTON.)

Treacle Bible

Popular name for COVERDALE's Great Bible of 1539, which rendered Jeremiah 8:22: 'There is no more treacle in Gilead', translated by the Authorized Version as 'balm'. (*See also* GENEVA BIBLE.)

tremendum

See HOLY.

Trent, Council of (1545–63)

Called an Ecumenical Council, it was summoned by Pope Paul III to Trento in northern Italy, in response to the Protestant Reformation. There were 25 sessions of cardinals, bishops and generals of orders, held to clarify Catholic doctrine and effect reforms, but no concessions were made to Protestants or Eastern Orthodox and Trent helped to perpetuate divisions. (*See also* COUNTER-REFORMATION; VERNACULAR.)

Tridentine

Of the Council of Trent.

Trinity

The word Trinity does not occur in the Bible and was first used by TERTULLIAN. But the concept is present in the three-fold baptismal formula (Matthew 28:19) and in the triple blessing (2 Cor. 13:14), and assumed in other verses. The doctrine developed out of belief in the divine sonship of Christ, with the Holy Spirit completing the triad. Trinitarian doctrine has been defined since the councils of Nicaea (325) and Constantinople (381), and has been accepted in East and West, and by the Reformed churches. Trinity Sunday is the Sunday after Pentecost. (*See also* CHRISTOLOGY; FILIOQUE; HOMOOUSION; JOACHIM OF FIORE; MONOTHEISM; SWEDENBORG; TRITHEISM; UNITARIANISM.)

triptych

Greek, 'three folds': a picture or carving with three panels side by side, or three writing tablets tied together. (*See also* DIPTYCH.)

Trisagion

Greek, 'thrice holy', in Eastern and Western liturgies in the chant, 'Holy God, Holy and mighty, Holy and immortal'.

tritheism

Belief in three separate gods, or denying the unity of substance in the three persons of the Trinity. Christian theologians in modern discussions with Jews and Muslims insist that we all believe that 'the Lord our God, the Lord is one.' (*See also* TRINITY.)

Turin Shroud

See SHROUD, HOLY.

Tutu, Desmond Mpilo (b. 1931)

Born at Klerksdorp, Transvaal, he trained as a teacher and was ordained Anglican priest in 1961. He studied at King's College, London, returned to teaching in Botswana, and became first African Dean of Johannesburg, and Archbishop of Cape Town in 1986. Tutu was a leading spokesman for black South Africans, calling for common citizenship, an end to the racist pass laws, and the freeing of Nelson Mandela. He led church people in civil disobedience, but opposed violence, and received the Nobel Peace Prize in 1984.

Twelfth Night

The night before Epiphany, which is 6 January, 12 days after Christmas, when Christmas decorations are taken down. Formerly there was merry-making, 12 bonfires representing the apostles, and a Twelfth Cake containing a bean or coin which made the finder King or Queen of the night.

twelve apostles, teaching of the

See DIDACHÉ.

Tyndale, William (1494–1536)

Reformer, Bible translator and martyr. Born in Gloucestershire, he studied at Oxford and Cambridge. He planned to translate the Bible into English from the original languages of Hebrew and Greek (instead of from the Latin Vulgate like WYCLIFFE), but was refused support from the Bishop of London and went to Germany. His New Testament was printed in Worms in 1526 and a revised edition at Antwerp in 1534. Three thousand copies of the Worms edition were printed, many of them smuggled into England where they were seized and burned; in 1994 the British Museum bought the last remaining copy for

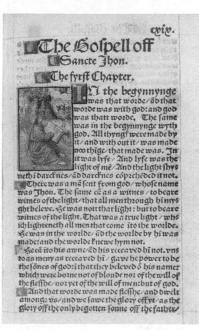

Tyndale's translation of St John's Gospel, 1526: Nearly 3000 copies of this New Testament were seized and burnt on the orders of Henry VIII. The only surviving complete copy was bought by the British Museum in 1994.

£1 million. Henry VIII tried to get hold of Tyndale, and he was seized by treachery, strangled and burned at Vilvorde near Brussels. Tyndale had translated the Pentateuch and some other parts of the Old Testament from the Hebrew. His translations into plain and vigorous English were the basis of the AUTHORIZED VERSION, and many of his words and phrases entered English language and literature; examples are 'let there be light', 'my brother's keeper', 'passover', 'scapegoat', 'signs of the times', 'salt of the earth', 'filthy lucre' and 'brotherly love', among many more. (*See also* AGAPÉ; PASSOVER.)

U

Uchimura, Kanzo (1861–1930)

Japanese Christian leader. He disagreed with American Calvinist teachers on evangelistic methods and with a government school when he was a pacifist in the Russo-Japanese war. Finding the churches too identified with Western values, Uchimura led the Mukyokai or No-church movement, abandoning church organization and making intense Bible study. The No-church is one of a number of independent Japanese Christian associations, which it is estimated will have about a million and a half members by the year 2000. (*See* HIDDEN CHRISTIANS; KAGAWA.)

Ultramontane

Medieval Latin, 'beyond the mountains', or south of the Alps: a name for emphasis in the Roman Catholic Church on the power of the VATICAN, as against national or diocesan church government. Stages of Ultramontanism may be seen in the JESUITS as a papal army, the declaration of papal INFALLIBILITY in 1870, and the appointment of conservative bishops by Pope JOHN PAUL II.

Umbanda

A new religion found throughout Brazil, combining native Brazilian, African and Christian traditions. Umbanda is led by priests and priestesses, under whom are mediums who are possessed and give messages. The most important rituals are dances, and shrines contain statues of Christian saints and African deities. (*See also* VOODOO.)

uncials

Capital letters used in Greek and Latin manuscripts from the fourth to eighth centuries, such as Sinaiticus and others. (*See also* CODEX.)

unction

Anointing the sick with oil is recommended in the Gospel (Mark 6:13) and the Epistle of James (5:14). Unction is also used at baptism and confirmation, as chrism, from Greek 'anointing'. The term is especially used of extreme unction, when a patient seems to be dying. In Britain the monarch is anointed with oil at the coronation. (*See also* HEALING.)

underground churches

See CRYPTO-CHRISTIAN; HIDDEN CHRISTIANS; UCHIMURA.

Uniate

From Latin via Russian for 'one': a church or member of Eastern Orthodoxy in communion with Rome but retaining traditional language and liturgy. There are Uniate churches throughout Eastern Europe and north Africa, the largest in the Ukraine. They are sometimes regarded as outposts of Roman Catholic imperialism, but the custom of allowing married clergy, as in Orthodoxy, has proved attractive. (*See also* MARONITES.)

Unification Church
See MOON.

Unitarianism
Churches that deny the Trinity and the divinity of Christ, and emphasize the unity of God. They reject the creeds, and are generally universalist, believing that all will be saved. Unitarians trace their origins to radical reformers, like SERVETUS and SOCINUS, continuing in Britain with Joseph PRIESTLEY, and in America with CONGREGATIONALISTS who became Unitarian in the 19th century. In 1961 a merger formed the Unitarian-Universalist Association with headquarters in Boston, Massachusetts. (*See also* RAM MOHUN ROY.)

Unitas Fratrum
See MORAVIANS.

United Methodists
A union of Methodist churches formed in 1907 by the Methodist New Connexion, BIBLE CHRISTIANS and Free Methodists. The union was itself absorbed into the uniting Methodist Church in Britain in 1932.

United Native African Church
See BLYDEN.

United Reformed Church
See CONGREGATIONALISM.

universalism
See UNITARIANISM.

Unknowing
See CLOUD OF UNKNOWING.

unleavened bread
See BREAD AND WINE.

Urbanist
See CLARE.

Urbi et orbi
Latin, 'to the city and for the world': a blessing given by the Pope from a balcony in St Peter's basilica, to the city of Rome and the world, now spoken in many languages.

Ursula
Legendary virgin and martyr, said to have been daughter of a British king who cruised around with her companions till they arrived at Cologne where they were killed, Ursula having refused to marry a pagan chief. The first trace of Ursula is a Latin inscription at Cologne in the fifth century, and by the tenth century her companions were said to be 11,000, perhaps from a misreading for eleven. Only two English churches were dedicated to Ursula, and she was more popular on the continent. In 1969 the reformed Roman calendar restricted Ursula's feast to local observance on 21 October.

Ursulines
A female teaching order founded in 1535 of virgins living in their own homes, though they were allowed to have convents from 1612. Ursulines spread widely, and in addition to three VOWS of religion they also vow dedication to education.

Ussher, James (1581–1656)
Anglican Archbishop of Armagh, noted for his calculation of the dates of the world wherein creation 'fell upon the entrance of the night preceding the twenty-third day of October' in 4004 BCE. This and dates following from it were inserted in the margins of the AUTHORIZED VERSION of the Bible.

usury

Charging interest on debts was forbidden in the Bible (Exod. 22:25), and this was continued in the Church, following ARISTOTLE's theory of money as solely a means of exchange. At the Reformation Luther and Zwingli forbade lending money for interest, but it was allowed by Calvin and became common with the rise of modern capitalism. Some Christian groups, and Muslims, still prohibit charging interest and have difficulty when banks award it.

Utopia

See MORE.

Utrecht, Declaration of

See OLD CATHOLICS.

V

Vahanian

See DEATH OF GOD.

Valdes

See WALDENSES.

Valentine

Two Valentines were in the list of martyrs for 14 February, a priest and a bishop, but neither had any connection with courting. The amorous link came perhaps from an old Roman festival of the god Pan in mid-February, or because birds are supposed to pair then, as Chaucer said, 'on Saint Valentine's day, when every fowl cometh there to choose his mate' (*The Parliament of Fowls*, l. 310).

Valentinians

GNOSTICS who followed a second-century teacher from Egypt, called Valentinus. Only fragments of his doctrine remain, but he contrasted the Creator God, the DEMIURGE, with Christ who brought redemption. The true knowledge (*gnosis*) was given only to 'pneumatics' (spirit-filled), contrasted with those who rely on good works. (*See also* MONTANISM.)

Vatican

Vatican City is an independent state within the city of Rome, ruled by the Pope and including St Peter's basilica, the Sistine Chapel and other buildings.

The smallest country in the world, of 108 acres and population about 1,000, it was established by pacts between the Holy See and the kingdom of Italy in 1929 and 1948.

The first Vatican Council, called by Pope Pius IX in 1869–70, criticized errors and modernism and asserted papal INFALLIBILITY. The Second Vatican Council, called by Pope John XXIII, met in 1962–5 and sought to bring the Church up to date (*aggiornamento*), with changes in language, liturgy, collegiality, ecumenism and religious liberty. (*See also* LATERAN.)

Vaudois

See WALDENSES.

vegetarianism

Abstaining from eating animal or fish products has been practised by many religious groups, among Christians by hermits and ascetics, some monastic orders, medieval CATHARI and modern ADVENTISTS. (*See also* ABSTINENCE; ANIMALS; ATHOS; TRAPPISTS.)

veil

'Taking the veil' is a popular expression for becoming a nun, joining a female religious order. The traditional veil, of various colours, covered head and shoulders but has often been limited or discarded nowadays. A white veil may be worn by females at confirmation.

Venerable

A title in the Roman Catholic Church for a person who has been 'beatified' and is allowed public veneration. In the Church of England it is the title of an archdeacon, or in popular regard a holy or noted person such as the Venerable BEDE.

Veneration of the Cross

A Roman Catholic ceremony for Good Friday, also called Creeping to the Cross, when a crucifix is kissed on the steps of the sanctuary.

Veni

'O come', the first word of several Latin hymns, to Immanuel or the Holy Spirit.

venial sin

See MORTAL SIN.

Venite

Psalm 95 as a CANTICLE, from its first words in Latin, *Venite exultemus*, 'O come, let us sing.'

Venn, Henry (1796–1873)

Anglican clergyman, clerical secretary of the CHURCH MISSIONARY SOCIETY. He said missionaries should create 'self-governing, self-supporting, self-propagating churches'. He secured 'native churches' in Sierra Leone and Lagos and advanced the African bishop Samuel CROWTHER. Some evangelical clergy opposed Venn but later ages approved his 'national' expressions of Christianity.

verger

An official who looks after the interior fabric of a Church, and shows people to their seats, or an officer who carries a staff before a bishop, from Latin *virga* for a rod or mace.

vernacular

The language of one's own country, from Latin for 'native'. Early church liturgies were in Greek, but by the fourth century Latin was the language of the Western Church. The Reformation demanded prayers 'understood of the people', as Prayer Book Article 24 put it, but the Council of TRENT decided the time was not expedient and so the Roman Church kept to Latin liturgy till the Second VATICAN Council when vernaculars were almost universally adopted.

Veronica

'A delightful legend without any solid historical basis' says an authority on saints about the story that Veronica was a woman who wiped the face of Jesus when he fell under the Cross, and he returned her cloth with the image of his face on it. The woman's name is suspiciously like *vera icon*, 'true image', and the supposed cloth has been preserved at St Peter's in Rome since the eighth century, the story no doubt being invented to explain the RELIC. (*See also* STATIONS OF THE CROSS.)

versicle

A short sentence said or sung in worship, answered by a 'response' from choir or congregation.

Vesper Chimes

See WAY INTERNATIONAL.

Vespers

Latin 'evening' prayers in the Western Church, sixth of the seven canonical hours in the BREVIARY. The Anglican service of EVENSONG is modelled on Vespers, with additions from COMPLINE.

vestments

Ritual dress of clergy when performing the liturgy. Vestments were derived from ordinary Roman clothing, such as the alb (a tunic) and the chasuble or cope (a cloak). Liturgical changes in modern times have produced many vestments in different churches. (*See also* CASSOCK; SURPLICE.)

vestry

A room attached to or in a church where vestments are kept and where the clergy vest. The word vestry is also used of the parishioners' or their representatives' meeting for business.

Via dolorosa

Latin for the 'sad road' in Jerusalem along which Jesus was taken from Pilate's judgement hall to Calvary. Processions still go along the traditional route every Friday bearing crosses. By extension, *via dolorosa* is used of any sad journey or experience.

via media

Latin, 'middle way': a term used by the Tractarians of the Church of England, midway between Roman Catholicism and Protestantism. (*See also* ANGLICANISM.)

Viaticum

Latin, 'provision for a journey': the Holy Communion given to a person in danger of death.

vicar

Latin, 'substitute': in the Church of England the priest of a parish whose tithes belong to a religious house or layman. Loosely, the title may be used of other clergy. From the eighth century the Popes have taken the title Vicar of Christ. (*See also* CURATE; RECTOR.)

vigil

From Latin, 'awake': a service of prayer at night, especially on the eve of a festival. There was a common belief that the Second Coming would take place at midnight (Mark 13:35) and believers should be watchful.

Vincent of Paul (1580–1660)

A priest from southern France, he was captured by pirates and was a slave for two years. He devoted his life to charity and the care of prisoners, founding the Lazarists from the priory of St Lazare in Paris, and Sisters of Charity who cared for the sick and poor.

Procession along the Via Dolorosa, Jerusalem: Every Friday pilgrims follow this traditional route taken by Jesus from Pilate's hall to Calvary.

Virgin Birth

Strictly speaking, the Virginal Conception, stated in Matthew 1:18ff. The Bible gives no suggestion that the actual birth of Jesus was other than normal, a notion that arose in apocryphal books from the second century. There is also no connection with the IMMACULATE CONCEPTION of Mary. That the conception of Jesus was normal, with Joseph as father, has been argued from the silence of most of the New Testament, and normal conception and birth would accord with the full humanity of Christ. Defence of traditional belief invokes the miraculous and the special nature of the Incarnation. (*See also* BROTHERS AND SISTERS OF JESUS; IMMANUEL; JOSEPH; PSEUDO-JAMES.)

Virgin Mary

See MARY.

Vitus

There were two saints of this name, in Italy and Sicily, the Italian being invoked by sufferers from epilepsy and St Vitus' Dance. By transference he was patron of dancers and actors. Churches were dedicated to him, such as the Cathedral in Prague. Feast day 15 June. (*See also* WENCESLAS.)

Vladimir (956–1015)

Apostle of the Russians, he imposed baptisms and built churches and monasteries. In 1988 1,000 years of Christianity in Russia were celebrated at Kiev in the Ukraine, commemorating Vladimir, with public liturgies. At the statue of Vladimir 5,000 Baptists gathered to witness 70 public baptisms in the river Dnieper.

vocation

Paul invited his readers to follow 'the vocation wherewith you are called' (Eph. 4:1), the Christian life and occupations being regarded as vocations. A vocation has also the special sense of a 'call' to the full-time ministry of the Church, or into a monastic order. (*See also* WORK.)

Voltaire

See THEODICY.

Voodoo

A mixture of African and Christian beliefs and rituals, practised in Haiti and other parts of the Caribbean and southern USA. The name comes from Dahomey (Benin) where *vodoun* or *vudu* is a spirit or god. American Voodoo devotees usually attend church, as well as temples where priests and priestesses sing, dance and are possessed by spirits. Images and songs mingle the names of African deities with their Christian counterparts. (*See also* MACUMBA; UMBANDA.)

votive

See VOW.

vow

A solemn promise to perform some religious duty, activity or way of life. Vows may be private or public, such as wedding vows. They may lead to the adoption of a way of life, with the three monastic vows of poverty, chastity and obedience. Votive masses are for personal or communal needs. (*See also* CANDLE; EX VOTO; URSULINES.)

Vulgate

The Latin version of the Bible in the vulgar, public or common tongue. It was the work of JEROME, translating from Hebrew and Greek, finishing the gospels in 384 CE and the whole Bible in 404 CE. The Vulgate became the official Bible version of the Western Church, and until 1943 all Roman Catholic translations were required to use it.

Waco

See BRANCH DAVIDIANS.

wake

A vigil before a church celebration and then merry-making on the feast or annual fair. Wake is used of holidays in the north of England, and in Ireland of watching by a corpse and feasting at a funeral.

Waite

See ROSICRUCIANS.

Waldenses

A community organized by Peter Waldo, or Valdes, of Lyons in France (d. 1217). He gave all his goods to the poor and with others began preaching, attacking the worldliness of the Church and being told in return that lay people could not preach the Gospel. Waldenses or Vaudois appointed their own ministers and became popular in France, Spain, Italy and Germany. Waldo died in Bohemia and his followers there joined the Hussites. A strong community in Italy was harshly persecuted and evoked Milton's sonnet 'On the Late Massacre in Piedmont'. Waldenses still exist in Italy, have a college in Rome, and have united with Italian Methodists. (*See also* HUSS.)

Walsingham

A pilgrimage centre in Norfolk, England, said to have been there since 1061 when a replica of the house of Jesus in Nazareth was built in wood. An Augustinian priory and a Franciscan friary were destroyed at the Reformation. The shrine church was rebuilt and opened in 1931 as an Anglo-Catholic centre, with a new Roman Catholic Church nearby. (*See also* LORETO.)

Wandering Jew

A medieval anti-Semitic legend of a Jew, sometimes called Ahasuerus, who was supposed to have mocked Jesus on the way to the Cross and was doomed to roam the earth until the Second Coming. Another version identified the Jew with JOSEPH OF ARIMATHEA.

war

See CRUSADES; JUST WAR; PACIFISM.

Watch-night

A British Methodist vigil dating from 1742, formerly held on New Year's Eve in place of public carousals, and now often combined on the first Sunday in the New Year with a COVENANT service.

Watts, Isaac (1674–1748)

Minister of the Independent congregation at Mark Lane in London, through ill health he retired to Stoke Newington. Watts fostered the growth of music and hymn-singing in Nonconformist churches. His hymns are generally more theistic, less Christological than those of Charles WESLEY, and many are still sung, among them 'O God Our Help in Ages Past' and 'When I Survey the Wondrous Cross'.

Way

See CHRISTIAN.

Way International

A biblical and household fellowship founded by Victor Weirville of the Evangelical Reformed Church in the USA. At first it was Vesper Chimes; a radio station of The Way Inc. was begun in 1955. Way theology rejects the Trinity, regarding Jesus as Son of God but not God the Son. In 1970 The Way Corps for leadership was started. It has been criticized for a weapons training programme and for anti-Semitism.

Wee Frees

Popular name for a minority of the Free Church of Scotland which refused to enter a union with the United Presbyterian Church in 1900. In 1988 the Lord Chancellor of Britain, Lord Mackay of Clashfern, was suspended from the Wee Frees because he had attended Roman Catholic Masses for two of his deceased friends, and the tiny Church split as a result.

week

See HOLY WEEK; LORD'S DAY; SABBATH; SUNDAY.

Weil, Simone (1909–43)

French Jewish writer and mystic, she suffered ill health but worked in a factory and as a cook for the republican army in Spain. After visions of Christ she became a Christian but never joined

the Church because it accepted Old Testament tales of war and tribalism. She escaped to England in the Second World War, living on starvation rations to show solidarity with people on the continent, and died at Ashford of anorexia nervosa.

Wellhausen, Julius (1844–1918)

German biblical scholar, one of the most influential in critical method. He elaborated the sources of the Pentateuch as J, E, P, D (Jehovistic, Elohistic, Priestly and Deuteronomic), and in the gospels maintained the priority of Mark.

Wenceslas (907–29)

Not a king, but duke of Bohemia who tried to improve the religion of his people, and was killed in a pagan reaction led by his brother. His relics went to St Vitus' Cathedral in Prague, which became a place of pilgrimage. J. M. Neale's 19th-century carol 'Good King Wenceslas' is purely imaginary and not based on any known incident in the saint's life. Feast day 28 September. (See also VITUS.)

Wesley, Charles (1707–88)

The 18th child of SAMUEL and SUSANNA WESLEY, at Oxford he was one of the founders of the METHODISTS and the HOLY CLUB. Ordained into the Church of England, and influenced by the MORAVIANS, he joined his brother John in itinerant preaching, though his marriage in 1749 made him more settled and he had eight children. Charles became the great hymn-writer of Methodism, with some 6,000 hymns, many still sung, such as 'Hark the Herald Angels Sing' and 'Love Divine'.

Wesley, John (1703–91)

The 15th child of SAMUEL and SUSANNA WESLEY, he became fellow and tutor at Lincoln College, Oxford. After ordination he went as a missionary to Georgia but following disagreements returned home. He experienced conversion at Aldersgate Street in London on 24 May 1738, three days after his brother CHARLES. He followed WHITEFIELD's example of open-air preaching and at Bristol founded the first METHODIST chapel, the New Room. Wesley travelled 8,000 miles a year on horseback and recruited ministerial and LAY PREACHERS. In 1784 he ordained ministers, against the wishes of Charles, and sent ASBURY and COKE to America. A first conference of preachers in 1744 became an annual event and the nucleus of Methodist organization. He wished to remain in the Church of England, but his ordinations made a breach. At his death there were 294 preachers in Britain and over 70,000 Methodists. (*See also* BUNTING; PERRONET.)

Wesley, Samuel (1662–1735)

Father of Charles and John. Rector of Epworth in Lincolnshire from 1695, he had a chequered career, wrote verses and pamphlets, disagreed with his parishioners, was imprisoned for debt, and was disabled by being thrown from a wagon.

Wesley, Samuel Sebastian (1810–76)

Grandson of CHARLES WESLEY. Named after Sebastian Bach, he became organist at four cathedrals and conducted the Three Choirs' Festival five times. He composed anthems and hymn tunes which have remained in use.

Wesley, Susanna (1669–1742)

Youngest daughter of an eminent Nonconformist minister, Samuel Annesley, she married the Anglican SAMUEL WESLEY in 1690; they had 19 children. Susanna was methodical, taught all her children to read, and read prayers and a sermon on Sunday evenings at the rectory during her husband's many absences. She supported her sons' METHODIST movement and is commemorated by a marble monument at Wesley's Chapel, London.

Wesleyan Reform

Expelled from Wesleyan METHODISM in 1849 for rejecting centralized authority, preferring congregational autonomy, the Wesleyan Reform Union remains a small conservative evangelical society, working closely with the Countess of HUNTINGDON's Connexion, and with missionaries in six areas of the world. (*See also* CONGREGATIONALISM.)

Wesleyans

See METHODISM.

Westminster Abbey

Formerly a monastery west of London. The present ABBEY, dating from the 13th century, has been called 'the most French of all English Gothic churches' (Pevsner). The monastery was dissolved in 1540 and became a church under a dean, a 'royal peculiar', meaning not under the bishop of London. Since the Norman Conquest the Abbey has been the place for the coronation of the monarch.

On 9 July 1998, ten statues of modern Christian martyrs of various churches, placed on the west front of Westminster Abbey in niches vacant since the Reformation, were unveiled in the presence of the Queen, the Archbishop of Canterbury, Cardinal Hume, and many others including the ambassadors of the ten countries represented, with the exception of China. The figures, from left to right, represent: Maximilian Kolbe, a Franciscan monk in Poland killed by the Nazis in place of a fellow prisoner in Auschwitz in 1941; Anglican catechumen Manche Masemola of South Africa, killed by her pagan parents at the age of fourteen in

The west front of Westminster Abbey showing the statues of the ten contemporary martyrs unveiled on 9 July 1998

1928; Archbishop Janani LUWUM of Uganda; Russian Orthodox Grand Duchess Elizabeth, shot by the Bolsheviks in 1918; American Baptist Martin Luther KING; Archbishop Oscar ROMERO of El Salvador; German Lutheran Dietrich BONHOEFFER; Indian Presbyterian Esther John, killed by a fanatic in Pakistan in 1960; Lucian Tapiedi, an Anglican in Papua New Guinea, murdered in 1942; Wang Zhiming, an evangelical pastor in southern China, executed in 1973 but later rehabilitated.

Westminster Cathedral

Basilica of the Roman Catholic Archbishop of Westminster. A striking building in Byzantine style, largely in red brick, it was opened in 1903. The interior decoration in marble and mosaic is unfinished, but the STATIONS OF THE CROSS by Eric Gill are noteworthy.

Westminster Confession

Begun as a revision of the Anglican ARTICLES, this became a Presbyterian statement of faith, teaching PREDESTINATION. The Confession was adopted in Scotland in 1649, and approved for England but rejected when episcopacy was restored in 1660. The Confession became a model for Nonconformist churches. (*See also* PRESBYTERIANISM; TOTAL DEPRAVITY.)

Whitby Synod

See ANGLICANISM; CELTIC CHURCH; COLMAN; HILDA; WILFRID.

White Friars

See CARMELITES.

White, Ellen

See SEVENTH-DAY ADVENTISTS.

White, Gilbert (1720–93)

Anglican clergyman and naturalist. Born at Selborne in Hampshire, he refused other livings to remain curate at his beloved birthplace. He began to keep a 'Garden Kalendar' in 1751; his 'Naturalist's Journal' formed the basis of his *Natural History and Antiquities of Selborne* (1788), which became and remains a classic for naturalists and general readers. (*See also* MARTIN.)

Whitefield, George (1714–70)

He met the WESLEYS at Oxford and followed them to Georgia. Back in England he was ordained and began open-air preaching with great success. He was supported by the Countess of HUNTINGDON, who agreed with his Calvinism against the Wesleys. Whitefield raised large sums for an orphanage in America, visited it several times and died there at a relatively early age. Whitefield was the leader of

Calvinistic Methodism and the outstanding preacher of his age.

Whitsunday

English name for PENTECOST, so called because candidates for baptism on that day wore white garments.

Wicca

See WITCHCRAFT.

Wiclif

See WYCLIFFE.

widows

They were cared for in the early Church (Acts 6:1), their duties being detailed (1 Tim. 5:3ff).

Wilberforce, Samuel (1805–73)

Anglican bishop, third son of William Wilberforce. A controversial figure, suspected by both LOW and HIGH CHURCH and called 'Soapy Sam', he criticized liberal publications and disputed evolution with T. H. Huxley at Oxford in 1860. (See also DARWINISM.)

Wilberforce, William
(1759–1833)

Member of Parliament for Yorkshire, he became a member of the CLAPHAM SECT, took up social reform, and with Thomas CLARKSON worked for the abolition of SLAVERY, seeing Bills outlawing it approved in 1807 and 1833. He supported CATHOLIC EMANCIPATION, the Bible Society and the CHURCH MISSIONARY SOCIETY. (See also NEWTON.)

Wilfrid (634–709)

Supporter of the Roman way of monastic life, against the Celtic, he became bishop of Ripon and helped achieve the Roman victory at the Synod of Whitby. After many setbacks, Wilfrid spent his last years at Ripon still trying to bring England into closer touch with Rome. Feast day 12 October. (See also CELTIC CHURCH; HILDA.)

William of Ockham

See OCKHAM.

William of Norwich (1132–44)

A boy murdered on Good Friday. Jews were accused of his death but no evidence was produced or action taken. This was the first 'blood libel' in England, accusing Jews of ritual murder at Passover/Easter. In 1997 a chapel of Holy Innocents was set aside at William's tomb in Norwich Cathedral for reconciliation between Christians and Jews. (See also ANTI-SEMITISM; HUGH.)

Williams, John (1796–1839)

Congregationalist missionary to the Pacific Islands. He sailed with his wife to Tahiti in 1816, won the confidence of the king and helped to draw up a code of laws. He went to other islands, teaching arts and sciences and translating parts of the Bible. Visiting Erromanga, he was killed by islanders in retaliation for cruelties they had received from an English crew.

Williams, Roger (1604–83)

Founder of the American colony of Rhode Island. An Anglican clergyman, he set up his own church. Told to leave Boston, he took refuge with Indians, learned their language and built a settlement called Providence with a Baptist Church. Back in England, he published *The Bloudy Tenent of Persecution* (1644). He gave Quakers a place in his settlement, though he disliked their views. He died in Providence, leaving six children.

wine

See BREAD AND WINE.

Winifred/Winefride (d. 650)

Patron saint of north Wales, about whose life little is known but who had an ancient cult. She is said to have been a virgin who refused a princely seduction and was beheaded. She lived at Holywell where there was an ancient miraculous spring; it is still a place of pilgrimage, though the water was diverted in mining operations. Feast day 3 November.

Winstanley

See LEVELLERS.

wisdom

In the Bible, wisdom was said to have been with God at creation (Prov. 8–9), and Paul spoke of Christ as the Wisdom of God (1 Cor. 1:24). In Christian thought wisdom was identified with Christ, as the LOGOS, and it was also a gift of the Holy Spirit. (*See also* BULGAKOV; HAGIA SOPHIA; SEVEN GIFTS.)

Wise men

See MAGI.

witchcraft

There were medieval fears of witches, mostly women, who were thought to fly through the air, meet in covens and eat human flesh – mostly unbaptized babies. There is no evidence for such fantasies, which no doubt originated in deaths from plagues and high infant mortality. Modern claims for witchcraft (WICCA) testify to the romancing fancies of devotees. (*See also* BLACK MASS; INQUISITION; MALLEUS MALEFICARUM; SATANISM.)

Wittenberg

East German town with a university where Luther lectured. On the door of the Schlosskirche he nailed his 95 theses in 1517, so that the town is regarded as the cradle of the Reformation. A Concord of Wittenberg on the Eucharist was agreed in 1536 by Lutherans but later rejected by Swiss Zwinglians.

Wolsey, Thomas (1474–1530)

Son of a butcher in Ipswich, he was ordained and quickly rose to power through the patronage of Henry VIII, becoming Lord Chancellor, Archbishop of York and a cardinal. Wolsey became powerful and rich, but opposed the royal divorce. Impeached by the House of Lords, he was taken to London on a charge of high treason but died on the way. His biographer wrote that Wolsey said, 'Had I but served God as diligently as I have served the King, he would not have given me over in my gray hairs' (G. Cavendish, *Negotiations of Thomas Wolsey*, 1641).

women, status of

According to records there were no women among the 12 apostles, but Jesus had women companions (Luke 8:2ff) and women were the first witnesses of the Resurrection, led by Mary Magdalene. Mary the mother of Jesus was present at Pentecost, with others (Acts 1:14). A woman apostle Junia is named in Romans 16:7. Paul wrote of the husband as head of the wife, but also said that in Christ there is neither male nor female (Eph. 5:23; Gal. 3:28). Restrictions on the role of women depended on social conditions, as changes in their status affect the Church today. (*See also* FEMALE ORDINATION; FEMINIST THEOLOGY; SERVER.)

Woodbine Willie

See STUDDERT-KENNEDY.

Woolman, John (1720–72)

American Quaker preacher, born at Northampton, New Jersey. He wrote and spoke against slavery, urging

Quakers to support negro rights. He died at York on a visit to England. Woolman's *Journal*, 1774 and often reprinted, gives a homely account of his 'Life, Gospel-labours, and Christian Experience'.

Word of God

See LOGOS.

work

The Bible stresses the need to work, and not be idle (Exod. 20:9; Gal. 6:9). At the Reformation the 'work ethic' developed by Puritans was almost sacramental; many toiled hard and became rich. The Christian doctrine of work is vocational; we are called to it by God. (*See also* GAMBLING.)

worker priests

Some French and Belgian priests after the Second World War noted the alienation of workers from the Church, took jobs in industry and joined trade unions. There was limited success, but the Vatican intervened to stop clergy becoming labourers in 1953. (*See also* JOCISTS.)

world

The Bible regarded the world as the creation of God, to be enjoyed by human beings (Gen. 1:28). But for ascetic movements, in both Catholicism and Protestantism, 'the world, the flesh and the devil' were lumped together as almost equally evil. Understanding of the Kingdom of God on earth as in heaven, and interest in social justice, provided more positive attitudes. (*See also* ECOLOGY; SEXUALITY.)

World Council of Churches

See ECUMENISM.

Worldwide Church of God

An ADVENTIST movement founded in the USA in 1933 by Herbert W. Armstrong. With a 'Radio Church of God' it held meetings to baptize members of the radio audience. Television and periodicals, such as *The Plain Truth*, spread the message. This church also teaches the descent of British and Americans from the lost tribes of Israel. (*See also* BRITISH ISRAELITES; TELEVANGELISM.)

Worms

A town in the Rhineland where LUTHER defended his doctrines at a diet before the Emperor Charles V in 1521. His teachings were formally condemned in an Edict of Worms, but Luther declared: 'Here I stand. I can no other. God help me. Amen.' (*See also* WITTENBERG.)

worship

There is no systematic description of early Christian worship, but much of it was modelled on that of the Jewish synagogue: psalms, prayers, Scripture reading and a sermon or homily. Distinctive of Christian worship was the EUCHARIST, either in the course of a communal meal, or at a separate gathering of church members from which catechumens were excluded. There are many varieties of worship, from Quaker silence to HIGH MASS. (*See also* HYMNS; LITURGY.)

Wounds, Five

The gospels indicate the piercing of the Lord's side on the Cross, and the risen Christ showed the print of the nails (John 19:34, 20:27). The Five Wounds became subjects of devotion in the middle ages, under the influence of BERNARD and FRANCIS. The wounds also figure in Protestant devotion, Watts writing in a hymn 'See from his head, his hands, his feet', and Wesley writing of being 'concealed in the cleft of thy side.' (*See also* SACRED HEART; STIGMATA.)

Wren, Christopher (1632–1723)

Architect of the baroque St Paul's Cathedral in London, after the Gothic building had been burnt down in the great fire of 1666. A Latin inscription in St Paul's, said to be by his son, reads: *Si monumentum requiris, circumspice* ('If you seek for a monument, gaze around'). (*See also* DUNSTAN.)

Wycliffe, John (1329–84)

Called the 'morning star of the Reformation'. Born in Yorkshire, he became rector of Lutterworth in Leicestershire and a popular preacher and teacher. As the scandal of a divided papacy arose, with the election of an antipope in 1378, Wycliffe attacked the Pope as Antichrist and said the Church would be better without one. He wrote first in Latin, then appealed to the people in English and became a leading English prose writer. He criticized monks with 'fat cheeks and great bellies', and attacked the worship of saints, pilgrimages and transubstantiation. He began to translate the Bible into English, from the Latin Vulgate, a work completed by his disciples. Wycliffe had many followers, LOLLARDS in England and HUSSITES in Bohemia, and there was persecution. Although he died in peace, his bones were later dug up and burned. (*See also* ROLLE; SCHISM; TYNDALE.)

X

Xavier, Francis (1506–52)

Spanish Jesuit, who vowed with IGNATIUS LOYOLA and five others to follow Christ in poverty and preach salvation. In 1541 Xavier sailed from Portugal to Goa in India and worked there and in Sri Lanka. In 1549 he went on to Japan, studying the language and making many converts, in a mission which later endured great persecutions. After three years he went back to Goa, then set off for China but died on the way. His body is still venerated in a magnificent shrine in the Church of Bom Jesu at Goa. Xavier is credited with baptizing till his arms were weary, and is regarded as Apostle of the Indies and Japan, and Patron of Foreign Missions. Feast day 3 December. (*See also* HIDDEN CHRISTIANS.)

Yahweh

See ADONAI.

year

See CALENDAR.

YMCA

Young Men's Christian Association, founded in London in 1844 by George Williams to win young men to Christian life by prayer, Bible reading, clubs and holiday centres. A parallel YWCA (Young Women's Christian Association) sprang out of two organizations founded in 1855 and united in 1877.

yoga

A Sanskrit word meaning 'union', or discipline, related to the English word 'yoke'. There are forms of Christian yoga, emphasizing self-control, meditation and union with God.

York

See PRIMATE.

Young, Brigham

See MORMONS.

Yule

An old Nordic festival at the end of the year, lasting 12 days. The origin of the name is obscure, but it became identified with CHRISTMAS, in words such as yuletide and yule-song, now used only in the north of England.

Zaccheus

In a story told only in Luke (19:2ff), he was a rich publican or tax collector who climbed a tree to see Jesus. Jesus stayed at his house and Zaccheus promised to restore extortions and give half his goods to the poor.

Zachariah

Appears only in Luke (1:5ff), where he is named as a priest and father of JOHN THE BAPTIST. He saw the angel Gabriel who promised the birth of John, and on professing incredulity he became dumb till the child's birth, when he uttered a canticle of blessing. Feast day 5 November. (*See also* BENEDICTUS.)

Zarathustra

See ZOROASTER.

Zealots

One of the disciples of Jesus is named 'SIMON the Zealot' (Luke 6:15). According to Josephus, the Zealots inspired fierce resistance to Rome, which led to the fall of Jerusalem in 70.

Zen

A Japanese form of Buddhism, the name deriving indirectly from Sanskrit for 'meditation'. Zen has attracted attention in the West, and its techniques of meditation and mind-control have been studied by religious orders and praised by the TRAPPIST monk Thomas MERTON.

Zinzendorf, Nikolaus Ludwig Graf von (1700–60)

Born in Dresden, he travelled widely and organized meetings with the BOHEMIAN BRETHREN and MORAVIANS, founding a Brotherhood of Herrnhut, 'the Lord's keeping'. He became a Moravian bishop, visited England and America, and conversed with John WESLEY in Latin. Zinzendorf emphasized feeling in religion, opposing both the rationalism and the dry orthodoxy of his day with a 'religion of the heart'. (*See also* PIETISM; SCHLEIERMACHER.)

Zionist African churches

Independent churches in southern AFRICA, of Pentecostal type, distinguished from Ethiopian African churches. They have charismatic leaders, stress divine revelations through angels, but reject African traditional religions. Some Zionists were influenced by an American Evangelical Christian Catholic Church, founded in Zion City, Illinois, by John Dowie in 1896.

Zoroaster

Western form of the name of Iranian prophet Zarathushtra or Zardusht. His dates are disputed; he may have lived about 1200 BCE. Legends are told of his miraculous birth and youth, miracles and imprisonment, long life and future birth as a world saviour. Zoroaster believed in one God, Ahura Mazda, 'the Wise Lord', who is just and good, and opposed by a hostile spirit, Angra Mainyu or Ahriman. He taught the good moral life, judgement, resurrection of the dead, and eternal bliss of the righteous. Through the Persian domination of much of western Asia, influencing Jews and Greeks, Zoroastrian thought affected Judaism and early Christianity, enlarging beliefs in heaven and hell, ANGELS and DEMONS, resurrection and eternal life. (*See also* ESCHATOLOGY; PARADISE.)

Zwingli, Ulrich (1484–1531)

Leading Swiss reformer. He was chaplain to soldiers in papal service and became minister at Zurich. Zwingli studied the New Testament in Greek and lectured on it, attacking the authority of the Pope, pilgrimages, purgatory, invocation of saints, the sacrifice of the Mass, and clerical celibacy, himself being publicly married in Zurich Cathedral. In a Colloquy of Marburg in 1529 he disputed with LUTHER on the presence of Christ in the Eucharist, which according to Zwingli was purely symbolic, and they parted without agreement. War broke out between Swiss cantons supporting Zwingli and others that did not; as chaplain he carried his forces' banner and was killed in a battle at Cappel. Zwingli inspired the REFORMED CHURCHES, and disputed with both Lutherans and ANABAPTISTS. His symbolical interpretation of the Eucharist was widely influential. (*See also* WITTENBERG.)

Chronology

BCE	4	Birth of Jesus
CE	29	Crucifixion, Resurrection, Pentecost
	34	Martyrdom of Stephen
		Conversion of Paul
		c. 40–64 Paul's epistles
	49	Council of Jerusalem
	64	Martyrdom of Peter and Paul in Rome
	70	Fall of Jerusalem to Romans
		Gospel of Mark
	85	Gospels of Matthew and Luke
	94	Josephus' *Antiquities*
	95	Persecution by Domitian
		Revelation–Apocalypse
		Gospel of John
	140	Hermas
	155	Martyrdom of Polycarp
	197	Tertullian writes of martyrs
	205	Clement of Alexandria
	230	Origen succeeds him
	250	Persecution by Decius
	285	Monastic movements
	303	Persecution by Diocletian
		Alban martyred in England
	313	Constantine issues tolerant edict
	323	Eusebius' *Ecclesiastical History*
	325	Council of Nicaea
	363	Julian Apostate
	374	Ambrose bishop of Milan
	380	Church as imperial religion
	382	Canon of Old and New Testaments
	404	Jerome's Vulgate Bible
	410	Fall of Rome to Visigoths
	426	Augustine's *City of God*

431	Patrick in Ireland
451	Council of Chalcedon
	Nestorian missions to Asia
525	Benedict founds monastery and rule
563	Columba in Iona and Scotland
597	Augustine in Canterbury
622	Rise of Islam
635	Aidan at Lindisfarne
638	Jerusalem and Egypt fall to Arabs
664	Synod of Whitby
711	Arabs enter Spain
719	Boniface in Germany
731	Bede's *Ecclesiastical History*
732	Arabs defeated in France
800	Charlemagne Holy Roman Emperor
	Nestorians in China
871	Alfred the Great
988	Vladimir in Russia
1054	Schism between East and West
1077	Henry IV at Canossa
1084	Carthusians founded
1095	Urban II launches Crusades
1099	Jerusalem sacked, Latins rule
1166	Waldensian reform
1170	Death of Becket
1187	Saladin retakes Jerusalem
1204	Fourth Crusade sacks Constantinople
1209	Francis of Assisi founds friars
1215	Dominic founds preachers
1232	Inquisition founded
1274	Aquinas' *Summa theologica*
1309–77	Popes at Avignon
1321	Dante's *Divine Comedy*
1373	Lady Julian's *Revelations*
1388	Wycliffe's English Bible
1390	Chaucer's *Canterbury Tales*
1401	*On Burning Heretics*
1415	Council of Constance
	John Huss martyred
1418	Kempis' *Imitation of Christ*
1431	Joan of Arc burnt
1453	Fall of Constantinople to Turks
1492	Columbus discovers America
	Muslims and Jews expelled from Spain
1494	Hilton's *Scale of Perfection*
1498	Savonarola hanged
1516	Erasmus prints Greek New Testament
1517	Luther issues 95 Theses

1529	Luther–Zwingli Colloquy
1530	Augsburg Confession
1534	Tyndale's English New Testament
1536	Dissolution of English monasteries
	Henry VIII's Supremacy over Church
	Calvin in Geneva
1540	Jesuits founded
1545	Council of Trent
1549	Xavier in Japan
	First Prayer Book of Edward VI
1555–6	Martyrdoms of Latimer, Ridley and Cranmer
1562	Teresa's Carmelite reforms
1563	Thirty-nine Articles
	Foxe's *Book of Martyrs*
1572	Massacre of St Bartholomew
1597	26 Japanese martyrs
1598	Tolerant Edict of Nantes
1605	Gunpowder Plot
1611	Authorized (King James) Bible
1614–39	Final persecutions in Japan
1620	Pilgrim Fathers go to America
1625	Little Gidding community
1656	Pascal's *Provincial Letters*
1662	Ejection of Dissenters
1667	Milton's *Paradise Lost*
1668	Fox founds Friends
1678	Bunyan's *Pilgrim's Progress*
1682	Penn founds Pennsylvania
1685	Revocation of Edict of Nantes
1689	Toleration Act in England
1698	SPCK founded
1701	SPG founded
1722	Zinzendorf founds Herrnhut
1725–60	Great Awakening in America
1738	Whitefield and Wesleys begin Methodism
1759–73	Jesuits suppressed in Europe
1780	Raikes founds Sunday Schools
1789	French revolutionary secularism
1799	CMS founded
1804	BFBS founded
1811	Primitive Methodism begun
1829	Catholic Emancipation
1830	Mormons founded
1833	Slavery abolished in British empire
	Tracts for the Times
1836	Strauss' *Life of Jesus*
1845	Newman moves to Rome
1854	Immaculate Conception dogma

1857	Livingstone's *Missionary Travels*
1858	Bernadette's visions at Lourdes
1859	Darwin's *Origin of Species*
	Hidden Christians emerge in Japan
1863	Colenso rejects deposition in Natal
1864	Crowther Anglican African bishop
1865	Booth founds Salvation Army
1867	First Anglican Lambeth Conference
1870	Vatican Council declares papal infallibility
	Old Catholics secede
1879	Christian Science founded in Boston
1881–5	Revised Version of Bible
1893	Chicago World Parliament of Religions
1895	Massacres of Armenian Christians
1910	World Missionary Conference, Edinburgh
1913	Prophet Harris in Ivory Coast
1917	Russian Communism persecutes Church
1921	Kimbangu imprisoned in Congo
1928	Opus Dei society founded
1929	Vatican State established
	Oxford Group founded
1932	British Methodist union
1934	Barmen Declaration of Confessors
1939–45	Holocaust
1945	Bonhoeffer executed
1947	United Church of South India
	Dead Sea Scrolls discovered
1948	World Council of Churches founded
1949	German Kirchentag
1952	Revised Standard Version
1959	Teilhard's *Phenomenon of Man*
1960	Charismatic movements
1962	Second Vatican Council
1968	Martin Luther King assassinated
1972	United Reformed Church
1973	Gutiérrez' *Theology of Liberation*
1977	Uganda: Archbishop Luwum shot
1978	Pope John Paul II elected
1980	El Salvador: Archbishop Romero shot.
1981	Visions at Medjugorge
1992	English Anglican female ordinations
1993	Papal encyclicals against birth control
1997	Mother Teresa dies

Thematic Bibliography

General

Barrett, D.B., ed., *World Christian Encyclopedia*. Nairobi, Oxford University Press, 1982. Country-by-country study, with masses of details and statistics.

Bettenson, H., ed., *Documents of the Christian Church*. Oxford, Oxford University Press, 1977. Primary texts from the first days to the present.

Bowker, J., ed., *The Oxford Dictionary of World Religions*. Oxford, Oxford University Press, 1997. On all religions, with over eighty contributors.

Brown, A., ed., *Festivals in World Religions*. London, Longman, 1986. On the major religions and with useful calendars.

Cross, F.L. and Livingstone, E.A. eds, *The Oxford Dictionary of the Christian Church*. Oxford, Oxford University Press, 3rd rev. edn, 1997. The standard dictionary, with great detail and valuable bibliographies.

Davies, J.G., ed., *A Dictionary of Liturgy and Worship*. London, SCM Press, 1979. Valuable on churches, rituals and devotions.

Hinnells, J.E., ed., *A New Dictionary of Religions*. Oxford, Blackwell, 1995. A popular world study updated.

Hinnells, J.E., ed., *Who's Who of World Religions*. London, Macmillan, 1991. Short accounts of religious leaders past and present.

Macquarrie, J. ed., *A Dictionary of Christian Ethics*. London, SCM Press, 1967. Histories and discussions of life and practice.

McManners, J., ed., *The Oxford Illustrated History of Christianity*. Oxford, Oxford University Press, 1990.

Smith, J.Z., ed., *The HarperCollins Dictionary of Religion*. San Francisco, Harper Collins, 1996. All religions, with details of American varieties.

Wakefield, G., ed., *A Dictionary of Christian Spirituality*. London, SCM Press, 1983.

Biblical

Brown, R.E., *The Birth of the Messiah*. New York, Doubleday, 1979. Standard and detailed work by a critical Roman Catholic scholar.

Brown, R.E., *The Death of the Messiah*. New York, Doubleday, 1994. Also standard, considers many of the problems with care and detail.

Bruce, F.F., *New Testament History*. New York, Doubleday, 1971. Conservative scholarship.

Cohn-Sherbok, D., ed., *Using the Bible Today*. London, Bellew, 1991. Contemporary interpretations of Scripture and guides to use in schools.

Kümmel, W.G., *Introduction to the New Testament*. London, SCM Press, 1977.

Pagels, E., *The Gnostic Gospels*. New York, Viking Penguin, 1979.

Parrinder, G., *Son of Joseph*. Edinburgh, T. & T. Clark, 1992. The parentage of Jesus.

Rivkin, E., *What Crucified Jesus?* Nashville, Abingdon Press, 1984. Not just who was responsible but what brought it about.

Sanders, E.P., *Jesus and Judaism*. London, SCM Press, 1985.

Sanders, E.P., *Paul and Palestinian Judaism*. London, SCM Press, 1977.

Sanders, E.P., *The Historical Figure of Jesus*. London, SCM Press, 1993.

Vermes, G., *Jesus the Jew*. London, SCM Press, 1973.

Vermes, G., *The Religion of Jesus the Jew*. London, SCM Press, 1993.

History and Churches

Atiya, A.S., *A History of Eastern Christianity*. London, Methuen, 1968.

Barraclough, G., *The Medieval Papacy*. London, Thames & Hudson, 1968.

Brooke, C.N.L., *The Monastic World*. London, Elek, 1974.

Davies, J.G., *The Early Christian Church*. London, Weidenfeld & Nicolson, 1965.

Farmer, D.H., *The Oxford Dictionary of Saints*. Oxford, Clarendon Press, 1978.

Fox, R.L., *Pagans and Christians*. Harmondsworth, Penguin, 1986.

Frend, W.H.C., *Martyrdom and Persecution in the Early Church*. Oxford, Blackwell, 1965.

Goulder, M., *A Tale of Two Missions*. London, SCM Press, 1994.

Hilton, M., *The Christian Effect on Jewish Life*. London, SCM Press, 1994.

Houlden, L., *Judaism and Christianity*. Part of *The World's Religions*. London, Routledge, 1988.

McKenzie, J.L., *The Roman Catholic Church*. London, Weidenfeld & Nicolson, 1969.

Marty, M.E., *Protestantism*. London, Weidenfeld & Nicolson, 1972.

Moore, R.I., *The Origins of European Dissent*. London, Allen Lane, 1977.

Moule, C.F.D., *The Origin of Christology*. Cambridge, Cambridge University Press, 1977.

Pritz, R.A., *Nazarene Jewish Christianity*. Leiden, E.J. Brill, 1988.

Ranke-Heinemann, U., *Eunuchs for the Kingdom of Heaven: The Catholic Church and Sexuality*. Harmondsworth, Penguin, 1990.

Riley Smith, J., *What were the Crusades?* London, Macmillan, 1977.

Rowe, M., *Russian Resurrection*. London, Marshall Pickering, 1994. A history of Russian Evangelical churches.

Underhill, E., *Mysticism*. Oxford, Oneworld Publications, 1997. Standard and often reprinted.

Wand, J.W.C., *Anglicanism in History and Today*. London, Weidenfeld & Nicolson, 1961.

Warner, M., *Alone of All Her Sex*. London, Pan Books, 1985. The myth and cult of the Virgin Mary.

Zernov, N., *Eastern Christendom*. London, Weidenfeld & Nicolson, 1961.

Modern Movements and Views

Baker, J.A., *The Faith of a Christian*. London, SCM Press, 1996.

Barker, E., ed., *New Religious Movements*. New York, Edwin Mellen Press, 1982.

Bruce, S., *Religion in the Modern World: From Cathedrals to Cults*. Oxford, Oxford University Press, 1997.

Cone, J.H., *God of the Oppressed*. New York, Seabury, 1975.

Dunn, J.D.G., *Christology in the Making*. London, SCM Press, 1980.

Gibellini, R., ed., *Frontiers of Latin American Theology*. New York, Orbis, 1979.

Gibellini, R., ed., *Paths of African Theology*. New York, Orbis, 1994.

Heine, S., *Women and Early Christianity*. London, SCM Press, 1987.

Hick, J., *God and the Universe of Faiths*. London, Oneworld Publications, 1993.

Hick, J. ed., *Truth and Dialogue*. London, Sheldon Press, 1974.

Hinnells, J.R., ed., *Comparative Religion in Education*. London, Oriel Press, 1970

Hollenweger, W.J., *The Pentecostals: The Charismatic Movement in the Churches*. Minneapolis, Augsburg Publishing, 1972.

King, U., *Towards a New Mysticism*. London, Collins, 1980.

King, U., ed., *Turning Points in Religious Studies*. Edinburgh, T. & T. Clark, 1990.

Klostermaier, K., *Hindu and Christian in Vrindaban*. London, SCM Press, 1969.

Küng, H., *On Being a Christian*. Harmondsworth, Penguin, 1976.

Linzey, A., *Animal Theology*. London, SCM Press, 1994.

Loades, A., ed., *Feminist Theology*. London, SCM Press, 1990.

Macquarrie, J., *Jesus Christ in Modern Thought*. London, SCM Press, 1990.

Macquarrie, J., *The Mediators*. London, SCM Press, 1995.

Neill, S.A., *A History of Christian Missions*. Harmondsworth, Penguin, 1964.

Panikkar, R., *The Unknown Christ of Hinduism*. London, Darton, Longman & Todd, 1964.

Parrinder, G., *Jesus in the Qur'ān*. Oxford, Oneworld Publications, 1995.

Parrinder, G., *Avatar and Incarnation*. Oxford, Oneworld Publications, 1997.

Race, A., *Christians and Religious Pluralism*. London, SCM Press, 1983.

Reuther, R., *Womanguides: Readings toward a Feminist Theology*. New York, Beacon Press, 1985.

Robinson, J., *Honest to God*. London, SCM Press, 1963.

Saliba, J.A., *Perspectives on New Religious Movements*. London, Chapman, 1995.

Sutherland, S., *God, Jesus and Belief*. Oxford, Blackwell, 1984.

Wiles, M., *Faith and the Mystery of God*. London, SCM Press, 1982.

Wiles, M., *Christian Theology and Inter-Religious Dialogue*. London, SCM Press, 1992.

Witvliet, T., *The Way of the Black Messiah*. London, SCM Press, 1986.

Thematic Index

Churches and Societies

Africa
Aladura
Albigenses
Amish
Anabaptists
Anglicanism
Anglo-Catholicism
Assemblies of God
Assyrians
autocephalous
Baptists
base communities
Béguines
Bereans
Bible Christians
Bogomiles
Bohemian Brethren
Brahmo Samaj
Branch Davidians
Brethren of the Common Life
Brethren of the Free Spirit
British Israelites
Buddhism
Camisards
Cao Dai
Carmelites
Carthusians
Catholic Apostolic
Chaldeans
Cherubim and Seraphim
Ch'ondogyo
Christ Apostolic Church

Christ Army Church
Christadelphians
Christian Science
Christian Socialism
Church Army
Church Missionary Society
Church of Scotland
Church of South India
Cistercians
Clapham Sect
Communism
Confessing Church
Congregationalism
Coptic
crypto-Christian
Dominicans
Doukhobors
Ebionites
Essenes
Focolare
Free Churches
Freemasonry
Friends, Society
German Christians
Hallelujah Movement
Hidden Christians
house churches
Huguenots
Hutterites
Illuminati
Independents
Islam
Jacobites
Jamaa

Doctrines

dogma
dualism
ecumenism
encyclical
eschatology
evangelical
expiation
exposition
faith
feminist theology
fideism
filioque
fundamentalism
Gnosticism
God
goddess
grace
hades
heaven
hell
heresy
Hesychasm
Holy Ghost, Spirit
homoousion
hope
hyperdulia
hypostasis
immaculate conception
immanence
immortality
impassibility
imputation
incarnation
inerrancy
infallibility
interim ethic
just war
kenosis
kerygma
koinonia
Latitudinarian
liberation theology
limbo
Messiah
miracle
Monophysitism
monotheism
Monothelitism

Montanism
mortal sin
mystery
mysticism
myth
natural law
Neo-Platonism
Nicene Creed
odium theologicum
original sin
orthodoxy
paradise
patripassianism
perfection
Pietism
Platonism
pneuma
Polytheism
post-modernism
predestination
prevenient grace
probabilism
providence
purgatory
Quicunque vult
quietism
real presence
redeemer, redemption
repentance
resurrection of Christ
resurrection of the dead
revelation
Sabbatarianism
Sabellianism
salvation
sanctification
satisfaction
schism
scholasticism
sin
Son of God
Son of Man
soteriology
soul
suffering servant
Sunday
supererogation
Syllabus of Errors

teleology
theism
theocracy
theodicy
theological virtues
theology
theophany
theosophy
Theotokos
Thirty-Nine Articles
Thomism
total depravity
transubstantiation
Tridentine
Trinity
tritheism
Ultramontane
Westminster Confession

Themes and Concepts

abortion
adultery
agnostic
allegory
anathema
animals
anthroposophy
anti-clericalism
anti-semitism
apartheid
architecture
art
artificial insemination
blasphemy
blood
body
born again
celibacy
charismatic
chastity
children
circumcision
communes
concordance
concupiscence
conscience
contraception

cosmogony
criticism
cult
diaspora
divorce
ecology
election
euthanasia
existentialism
experience
free will
gambling
Golden Rule
grail
guardian angel
hagiography
Holocaust
homosexuality
humanism
humour
inner light
ladder
Mammon
millennium
modernism
numinous
opium of people
pacifism
pantheism
persecution
polygamy
race relations
reincarnation
religious education
revivalism
sacred
sacrilege
Satanism
scruples
sect
secular
sexuality
slavery
sobornost
sola scriptura
solifidianism
spiritualism
state and religion

suicide
summum bonum
swastika
vegetarianism
via media
voodoo
wisdom
witchcraft
women, status
work
world

Rituals and Practices

ablution
agapé
All Saints
All Souls
alms
anaphora
Angelus
anniversary
anthem
apologetics
apostasy
asceticism
banns
baptism
bells
benediction
bidding
blessing
bread and wine
burial
camp meeting
candle
canticle
carnival
carol
cassock
censer
chasuble
christen
Christian Year
Christmas
class meeting
cloister
collect

colours
commandments
commination
compline
concelebration
conciliarism
confession
confirmation
consecration
contemplation
continence
contrition
conversion
covenant
crib
Cross
crucifix
dance
dead, prayers for
detachment
devotion
direction, spiritual
dirge
discernment
dismissal
doxology
drama
Easter
eastward
elevation
Ember Days
enthusiasm
epiclesis
Eucharist
evangelization
evensong
excommunication
exegesis
exorcism
extempore prayer
extreme unction
ex voto
fasting
feasts
female ordination
flagellants
font
foot-washing

pyx
quire
relics
renunciation
reordination
requiem
reservation
retreat
rings
rite, ritual
Rogation Days
rood
rosary
rostrum
rubric
sacrament
sacrifice
sanctuary
Sanctus
scapular
screen
secret
see
sermon
server
sext
Shema
shrine
Sign of Cross
silence
Spiritual Exercises
spirituality
spirituals
Stations of the Cross
stigmata
stylite
suffrages
synod
tabernacle
televangelism
temperance
Tenebrae
testimony
tithe
tonsure
tracts
transept
triptych

Trisagion
unction
usury
veil
versicle
vespers
vestments
vestry
vigil
vow
watch-night
widows
worship
wounds, five
yule

People

angel
Angelic Doctor
Anti-pope
apostle
archangel
archbishop
archdeacon
archimandrite
beadle
bishop
Black Virgin
Blessed Virgin
boy bishop
brothers and sisters of Jesus
cardinal
celebrant
clergy
curate
curia
deacon
dean
devil's advocate
disciple
elder
father
godparents
hermit
Holy Father
Holy Innocents
Holy Office

Index of Proper Names

This index shows where individuals not listed by name in the encyclopedia can be found.